C4 496470 0

D1577108

WELLINGTON

WELLINGTON

A Journey Through My Family

JANE WELLESLEY

Weidenfeld & Nicolson

LONDON

First published in Great Britain in 2008
by Weidenfeld & Nicolson

1 3 5 7 9 10 8 6 4 2

© Jane Wellesley 2008

All rights reserved. No part of this publication may be
reproduced, stored in a retrieval system, or transmitted,
in any form or by any means, electronic, mechanical,
photocopying, recording or otherwise, without the prior
permission of both the copyright owner and the above publisher.

The right of Jane Wellesley to be identified as the author
of this work has been asserted in accordance with the
Copyright, Designs and Patents Act 1988.

A CIP catalogue record for this book
is available from the British Library.

ISBN: 978 0 297 85231 5

Typeset by Input Data Services Ltd, Bridgwater, Somerset

Printed and bound in the UK by
CPI William Clowes Ltd, Beccles, NR34 7TL

The Orion Publishing Group's policy is to use papers that
are natural, renewable and recyclable products and made
from wood grown in sustainable forests. The logging and
manufacturing processes are expected to conform to
environmental regulations of the country of origin.

Weidenfeld & Nicolson

The Orion Publishing Group Ltd
Orion House
5 Upper Saint Martin's Lane
London, WC2H 9EA
An Hachette Livre UK Company

www.orionbooks.co.uk

For
my nieces and nephews

Natasha · Davina
Arthur · Honor · Gerald · Sofia
Charlotte · Mary · Frederick
Eleanor · Oliver
and
Skye

NEWCASTLE UPON TYNE CITY LIBRARIES	
C4 496470 00 39	
Askews	May-2009
	£20.00

CONTENTS

ILLUSTRATIONS   ix

FAMILY TREE   xii

Prologue   1

1   Born to Serve   13

2   The Cut of a Soldier   38

3   Gallantries of Dreams   59

4   Beyond the Still Valley   87

5   A Soldier's Wife   105

6   Return to Palena   135

7   Heirs and Graces   154

8   Alone and Sad   176

9   Prince of Waterloo   198

10 'That Damned Infernal Family'   225

11 No. 1 London   245

12 Thistles and Thistledown   272

13 Arthurolatry   311

    Epilogue   334

ACKNOWLEDGEMENTS   336

NOTES   339

SELECT BIBLIOGRAPHY   353

INDEX   356

ILLUSTRATIONS

Unless otherwise credited all pictures belong to the author, or other members of her family.

SECTION ONE

Garret, 1st Earl of Mornington, English school (© Trustees of Stratfield Saye Preservation Trust)

Dangan Castle, County Meath, from 'Old England's Worthies', Lord Brougham and others, published London c.1880s (Bridgeman Art Library)

Arthur Wellesley, c.1778 (© Trustees of Stratfield Saye Preservation Trust)

Richard Wellesley aged 15, by Daniel Gardner, 1776 (© Somerset Trust)

Hyacinthe Gabrielle Roland, later Marchioness Wellesley, by Elizabeth Vigée Le Brun, Rome, 1791 (Fine Arts Museums of San Francisco)

Lady Anne Wellesley, watercolour, c.1789 (© Somerset Trust)

Henry Wellesley (later Lord Cowley), by John Hoppner (© Trustees of Stratfield Saye Preservation Trust)

Richard, Marquess of Wellesley, 1805, by Robert Home (Bridgeman Art Library)

Marianne Paterson, Marchioness Wellesley, by Andrew Robertson (© Trustees of Stratfield Saye Preservation Trust)

The First Duke, by John Hoppner, (© Trustees of Stratfield Saye Preservation Trust)

The Storming of Seringapatam, 4 May 1799, engraved by Thomas Sutherland, after William Heath (Bridgeman Art Library)

Kitty, 1st Duchess, after a portrait by Thomas Lawrence (Mary Evans Picture Library)

Study for equestrian portrait of the First Duke, Francisco Jose de Goya y Lucientes, c.1812, British Museum, London (Bridgeman Art Library)

The Eton Boys, Arthur, Charles and Gerald Wellesley (nephew of First Duke) in the grounds of Stratfield Saye, by Richard Barrett Davis, c.1820 (© Trustees of Stratfield Saye Preservation Trust)

Kitty seated at her easel, by John Hayter, 1828 (© Trustees of Stratfield Saye Preservation Trust)

Anne, Countess of Mornington, after painting by Priscilla Burghersh (National Portrait Gallery)

Gerald Valerian Wellesley, Prebend of Durham (Dean and Chapter Library,
    Durham Cathedral)
William Wellesley-Pole, later Lord Maryborough (National Portrait Gallery)
Meissen plate decorated with a scene of Apsley House, c.1818 (Bridgeman Art
    Library)
Pot lid showing Walmer Castle
First Duke, by Thomas Lawrence (Royal Collection © 2008 Her Majesty
    Queen Elizabeth II)
First Duke and his grandchildren seated in the Library at Stratfield Saye House
    by Robert Thorburn, 1853 (© Trustees of Stratfield Saye Preservation Trust)
First Duke's funeral (Bridgeman Art Library)

SECTION TWO
Arthur, 2nd Duke and his brother Lord Charles Wellesley (Courtauld Institute
    © Trustees of Stratfield Saye Preservation Trust)
Elizabeth Hay, Lady Douro, later 2nd Duchess, by James Swinton, c.1834
    (© Trustees of Stratfield Saye Preservation Trust)
Sophia Pierrepont, Lady Charles Wellesley (National Portrait Gallery)
Angela Burdett-Coutts, by unknown artist, c.1840 (National Portrait Gallery)
Evelyn, 3rd Duchess
Henry, 3rd Duke, by Carlo Pellegrini, published in *Vanity Fair*, 3 January 1885
    (National Portrait Gallery)
Ball at Apsley House, June 1908 (Courtauld)
'Maudie', 5th Duchess, and her daughter Lady Anne Wellesley (National
    Portrait Gallery)
Kathleen, 4th Duchess, published in *Vogue*, 1917 (© Vogue)
The Wellington family, watercolour Lady Eileen Wellesley, 1902
'A Very Interesting House Party', *Illustrated London News*, c.1910
Dorothy Ashton, Lady Gerald Wellesley, later 7th Duchess, diptych, 1914 and
    1923
Gerald, later 7th Duke, as a young man
'Mitey', Lady Serena Lumley (later James)
'Cissie' Dunn Gardner, later Mrs Robert Ashton and Countess of Scarbrough,
    as a child
Robert Ashton
'Scamp' Ashton, c.1911
Dorothy Ashton as a child
Valerian Wellesley, later 8th Duke, with his mother, Dorothy, 1915
Valerian with his father, Gerald, later 7th Duke, 1916
Valerian in bath, 1916
Valerian in sunhat with flowers, 1917
Valerian at Eton, 1929 (photo © David Parsons)
Valerian and his sister Elizabeth on the island at Sherfield Court
Valerian, Elizabeth, Mary Coke and David Parsons dressed as pirates at Penns
Lady in a Red Hat (Vita Sackville-West) by William Strang, Kellingrove Art
    Gallery and Museum, Glasgow (Bridgeman Art Library)

Dorothy with W. B. Yeats, Penns-in-the-Rocks
Penns-in-the-Rocks, by Rex Whistler, 1932 (© Trustees of Stratfield Saye
    Preservation Trust)

SECTION THREE
The Bullingdon Club, Oxford, June 1936
Valerian on beach with Dorothy Hyson and others, c.1931
Lady Rose Paget, 1938
Elizabeth Wellesley at races, 16 February 1938
'Morny', 6th Duke, in uniform of The Dukes, c.1940
Elizabeth marries Thomas Clyde, November 1939
Valerian and Gerald at a fancy dress ball at the Austrian Embassy, 1935
Valerian and Gerald in uniform, 1942
Valerian, by now Marquess of Douro, in garden in Jerusalem, 1944
Diana McConnel in Palestine
Valerian and Diana's wedding, Jerusalem, 1944
Valerian and Diana, 1944
James McConnel
Margaret McConnel (née Houldsworth)
Sedgwick cotton mill, Manchester, watercolour, c.1820
McConnel trademark
William McConnel c.1890
Framed photograph of Douglas and Malcolm McConnel with their first
    salmon, Knockdolian, 2 September 1903
McConnel family, 1901
Douglas in trenches, 1915
Ruth with her mother Daisy
Ruth, aged eighteen
Douglas with Matchless motorcycle, 1921
Douglas and Ruth's wedding, 1920
Diana McConnel as a baby, 1922
Douglas, Ruth and Diana outside Knockdolian
Valerian and Diana with children, Cyprus, 1956
Gerald, 7th Duke and grandchildren
Gerald, 7th Duke, Apsley House
Valerian and Diana, by now 8th Duke and Duchess with all their children
8th Duke at Stratfield Saye; with 8th Duchess; presenting rental flag to Her
    Majesty the Queen, 2005; and with grandson Gerald, Sandhurst, 2007
The author with her parents

While every effort has been made to trace copyright holders, if any have been
inadvertently overlooked the publishers will be happy to acknowledge them in
future editions.

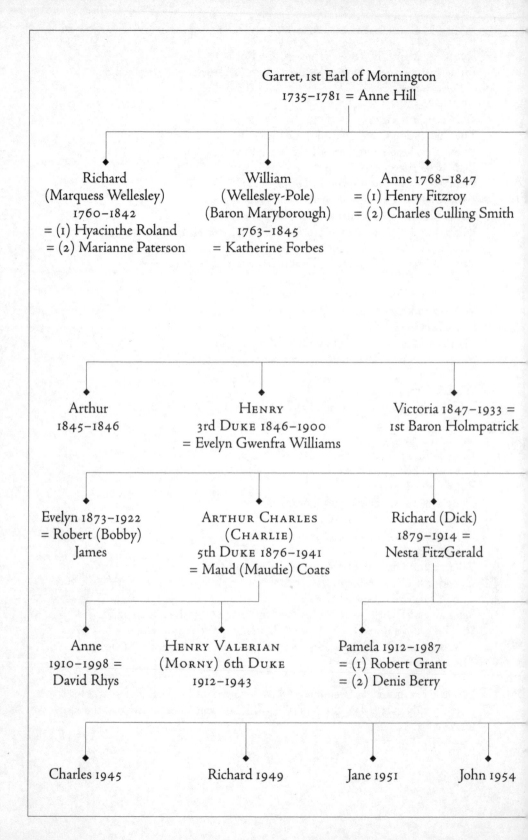

Garret, 1st Earl of Mornington
1735–1781 = Anne Hill

Richard
(Marquess Wellesley)
1760–1842
= (1) Hyacinthe Roland
= (2) Marianne Paterson

William
(Wellesley-Pole)
(Baron Maryborough)
1763–1845
= Katherine Forbes

Anne 1768–1847
= (1) Henry Fitzroy
= (2) Charles Culling Smith

Arthur
1845–1846

HENRY
3rd DUKE 1846–1900
= Evelyn Gwenfra Williams

Victoria 1847–1933 =
1st Baron Holmpatrick

Evelyn 1873–1922
= Robert (Bobby)
James

ARTHUR CHARLES
(CHARLIE)
5th DUKE 1876–1941
= Maud (Maudie) Coats

Richard (Dick)
1879–1914 =
Nesta FitzGerald

Anne
1910–1998 =
David Rhys

HENRY VALERIAN
(MORNY) 6th DUKE
1912–1943

Pamela 1912–1987
= (1) Robert Grant
= (2) Denis Berry

Charles 1945

Richard 1949

Jane 1951

John 1954

The
WELLESLEY FAMILY

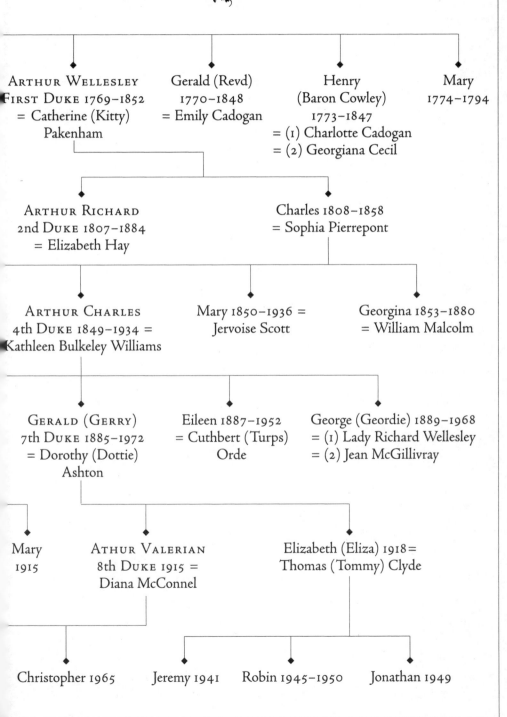

ARTHUR WELLESLEY
FIRST DUKE 1769–1852
= Catherine (Kitty)
Pakenham

Gerald (Revd)
1770–1848
= Emily Cadogan

Henry
(Baron Cowley)
1773–1847
= (1) Charlotte Cadogan
= (2) Georgiana Cecil

Mary
1774–1794

ARTHUR RICHARD
2nd DUKE 1807–1884
= Elizabeth Hay

Charles 1808–1858
= Sophia Pierrepont

ARTHUR CHARLES
4th DUKE 1849–1934 =
Kathleen Bulkeley Williams

Mary 1850–1936 =
Jervoise Scott

Georgina 1853–1880
= William Malcolm

GERALD (GERRY)
7th DUKE 1885–1972
= Dorothy (Dottie)
Ashton

Eileen 1887–1952
= Cuthbert (Turps)
Orde

George (Geordie) 1889–1968
= (1) Lady Richard Wellesley
= (2) Jean McGillivray

Mary
1915

ATHUR VALERIAN
8th DUKE 1915 =
Diana McConnel

Elizabeth (Eliza) 1918 =
Thomas (Tommy) Clyde

Christopher 1965

Jeremy 1941   Robin 1945–1950   Jonathan 1949

Prologue

Dawn has not yet broken, but Arthur Wellesley, the First Duke of Wellington, is at his desk writing letters. It is Sunday, 18 June 1815; the place is Waterloo, a hamlet in Belgium, twelve miles south of Brussels. He is forty-six years old and five feet nine inches in height; his hair is still dark; his aquiline features are dominated by his piercing blue eyes. For the third night running, Wellington has managed only a couple of hours' sleep, but he is a lean, fit man, and ready for the demanding day ahead. For the last twenty-one years, his military career has been building up to this point. By nine o'clock in the evening, Wellington will have changed the course of European history. But the victory will be at a great cost: over 70,000 men will die at the battle of Waterloo.

Three days earlier, Wellington had been one of the guests of honour at the Duchess of Richmond's ball, a party, given in a huge coach warehouse in Brussels, that would earn its own place in history. The Duchess had checked some weeks before with Wellington: 'May I give my ball?' 'Duchess,' replied the Duke, 'you may give your ball with the greatest safety, without fear of interruption.'[1] His firm reply owed more to tactics than to the truth. It was essential that the Emperor's spies observed the unconcerned revelries of the English community. Ever since Napoleon had returned to French soil on 1 March, the Allies had been mustering their armies. Tsar Alexander had voiced the views of many when he told Wellington at the Congress of Vienna, 'It is for you to save the world again.'[2]

On the day of the ball – Thursday, 15 June – word reached Wellington that Bonaparte had crossed the border into Belgium. The Duke issued orders that the army should be ready to march at a moment's notice, but for the benefit of the 'numerous friends of Napoleon who are here', he declared, 'let us therefore go all the same to the Duchess of Richmond's ball'.[3] Wellington arrived late, but rumours were already flying around the room. Georgie Lennox, one of the Richmonds' daughters, who had known Arthur since she was a small girl, rushed up to ask him if they were true. 'Yes, they are true, we are off tomorrow,' replied the Duke. One observant guest at the ball noted, 'Although the Duke affected great gaiety and cheerfulness, it struck me that I had never seen him have such an expression of care and anxiety on his countenance.'[4] Others were taken in by the appearance of serenity that 'beamed' over his face.[5] As the latest news of enemy movements arrived, a council of war was held in the Duke of Richmond's study, a map of the area spread out in front of them. It was later said that Wellington identified the village of Waterloo – 'we shall not stop him there [Quatre Bras], and if so, I must fight him *here*'.[6] The ground was not unknown to him: the year before he had reconnoitred it on his way to take up his post as Ambassador to France.

Some of the officers at the ball bade farewell to their friends, and hurried off to join their units; others, preferring to stretch out the minutes they had left before going to an uncertain fate, went to the front still dressed in their evening clothes. Tokens were thrust into hands and pockets by young girls fearful for the safety of a sweetheart. One keepsake, a purple velvet handkerchief sachet given to Henry Percy by one of his dance partners, would play an important part in the drama of the next few days.

Shortly after seven the next morning, the Duke left Brussels. 'There he goes, God bless him, and he will not come back until he is King of France,' said a maid to her mistress. A few hours later, near Ligny, Wellington met up with Marshal Blücher, who as commander of the Prussian army would play a crucial role in the campaign. As they discussed their strategy, they climbed a windmill to scan the enemy troops massing in front of them. Among the 80,000-strong army, their telescopes fell on the figure of one man: the Emperor himself. In fact, in the many years that Wellington had been engaged in fighting against Napoleon and his forces, this was the first time he had his adversary in his sights. He may have formed the same opinion as his niece Emily and her husband Fitzroy Somerset – 'short and fat'.[7] However, like many others, he had great respect for the generalship of his opponent.

Shortly after the meeting of the two Allied Generals the Prussians were, as predicted by the Duke, 'mauled' by the right flank of the French army at the battle of Ligny. Three miles away, at Quatre Bras, Wellington's Allied army narrowly managed to maintain its position against a determined onslaught from the French. Blücher, faced with no alternative, retreated; Wellington, to prevent Napoleon from driving a wedge through the two armies, was forced to follow suit. 'I suppose in England they will say we have been licked. I can't help it: as they [the Prussians] have gone back we must go too.'⁸ But the French were following hard on British heels: Lord Uxbridge is said to have urged his cavalry, 'Make haste! For God's sake gallop, or you will be taken!' As the army re-formed, Wellington maintained his customary sangfroid: some of his men observed him sitting on the grass enjoying the gossip in the London papers; others saw him sleeping in his cloak, with a copy of the *Sun* shading his face. But the weather had broken, and a violent storm crashed onto the landscape. It was a good omen. The veterans of the Peninsular War knew that Wellington's victories were often preceded by a deluge. It was Saturday, 17 June – the eve of the battle of Waterloo.

As Wellington wrote his letters in the early hours of Sunday morning his troops, in the countryside around Waterloo, were having a wretched night. It was still raining, but every man was trying to get some rest and shelter. Sodden blankets provided makeshift tents, lumpy haversacks pillows for weary heads. Some cavalrymen slept on their horses. Most went hungry – the supply wagons were still forcing their way along the muddy road from Brussels, through the forest of Soignes. One popular Sergeant had acquired quantities of gin the day before from a fleeing Belgian. The veterans of the Peninsula did what they could to stiffen the resolve of the new boys. Nervous dread hung in the air. A seasoned Private in the 28th Regiment of Foot reminded his comrade 'that it was far better to die on the field of glory than from fear', but he later confessed that, when the man turned away from him and, with a burst of tears, cried out, 'My mother!', 'The familiar sound of this precious name, and the sight of his sorrow, completely overcame my attempts at concealment, and we wept together.'⁹

Wellington's own tears were to flow after the battle, but in the early hours of Sunday morning there would have been few thoughts of home: the woman on his mind was Lady Frances Wedderburn-Webster, with whom he had dallied since arriving in Brussels in early April. He wrote warning her to be ready to leave the capital 'at a moment's notice', but he went on, 'I will give you the earliest information of any danger that may come to my knowledge; at present I know of none.'¹⁰ In London Kitty, Wellington's wife, avidly scoured the press for information, but the news would not yet have reached England that the campaign had commenced. However, *The Times* of Saturday, 17 June had confirmed the 'intelligence' that 'Buonaparte' had arrived at Maubeuge, the 'Head-quarters of the rebel army'. The leader column went on to cite 'highly important events being about to take place. Something in the nature of a Declaration of War against this black and atrocious rebellion.'[11] Arthur was always in Kitty's prayers, and this Sunday, when she went to church, would be no different. She would worry, but her anxiety was tempered by confidence in her husband's ability to defeat the great enemy. 'Ah! wait a little, *he* is in his element now; depend upon him',[12] she had told friends.

At the inn in the village of Waterloo Wellington shaved and, with the help of his valet, donned his customary white buckskin breeches, white stock and dark blue frock coat[13] worn over the gold knotted sash of a Spanish field marshal. His boots – hessian with tassels – were likely to have been one of two new pairs from Hoby in St James's Street; 'the last', he had written in April, 'were still too small in the calf of the leg & about an inch & half too short in the leg'.[14] He breakfasted on tea and toast, and may have tucked a crust of bread and a hard-boiled egg into his pocket to stave off any later hunger.[15] Soon after 7 a.m. Wellington rode out of the village astride his favourite horse, the chestnut stallion Copenhagen. His low cocked hat carried no ornamentation apart from the large black cockade of Britain, and three smaller ones for Spain, Portugal and the Netherlands. The Duke would spend the day putting off and on his dark blue cape – 'I never get wet when I can help it'. He carried a sword, but his most important 'weapon' was his telescope. He was attended by his retinue of ADCs and other staff. 'They all seemed as gay and unconcerned as if they were riding to meet the hounds in some quiet English county,'[16] wrote one observer.

His arrival on the battlefield heartened his bedraggled troops, who were doing their best to get dry and make sure their muskets were in order. 'The morning of the 18th June broke upon us and found us drenched with rain, benumbed and shaking with cold,' wrote one of his soldiers; but as Wellington passed along the lines of his army, he was roundly cheered. The Duke's chosen command post was under a lone elm tree, standing on the ridge of Mont-Saint-Jean which straddled the road from Brussels. From this vantage-point he could see the French army stretched out in front of him, and to his right the château and outbuildings of Hougoumont, and in the centre, the farm of La Haye Sainte. To both farmhouses he had sent some of his best troops.

Meanwhile Napoleon, having decided to delay the battle in the hope that the ground might dry off, was riled by one of his marshals praising the effectiveness of the British infantry. He retorted, 'Because you have been beaten by Wellington you consider him a great general. And now I will tell you that he is a bad general, that the English troops are bad troops, and that this affair is nothing more serious than eating one's breakfast.'[7] His mood may have been affected by an uncomfortable condition: the night after Ligny, Napoleon was in pain from haemorrhoids. Nevertheless, by nine o'clock he was on his saddle and inspecting his troops, and the sound of 'Vive l'Empereur' drifted over to the Allied ranks.

'There', the Duke had said, pointing at a British Private, 'it all depends on that article, whether we do the business or not.'[18] The 'business' was now before him, and his army numbered a little over 73,000 men, supported by 157 guns; the French force was 77,500 men and 246 guns; critically, Blücher's Prussians numbered 49,000, with 134 guns. Much of the battlefield, three miles wide and one and a half deep, was already covered in mud; the corn, which had been shoulder-high in places, had been flattened by the rain. But, for Wellington, the ground had one feature unique to his battle strategy: the reverse slope, where he had placed the greater part of his infantry.

Just before 11.30 in the morning, the roar of the French guns signalled the start of the battle. Wellington had instinctively placed himself near Hougoumont, which took the force of the first attack, and for part of the time he himself gave the orders. This small bastion, defended by 2,600 men, would see some of the fiercest fighting during the day, as more and more French troops were sent to take it. Many years later, when Wellington was asked to nominate the 'bravest soldier in the British army at Waterloo', he claimed that the success of the battle 'turned upon the closing of the gates of Hougoumont'.[19] At one point, the defences there were broken by a huge Frenchman nicknamed, 'L'Enforceur' who, armed with an axe, stormed the château with thirty other French troops. All were massacred except a fourteen-year-old drummer-boy, whose life was spared by the British.

Two hours after the start of the battle Napoleon committed a quarter of his entire army when he launched a massive infantry attack headed by Marshal d'Erlon. This phase of the battle involved the British heavy cavalry, including the Scots Greys, who galloped at the French guns with the cry of 'Scotland forever'. As the huge grey horses thundered past the Gordon Highlanders, some of the Scotsmen grabbed their countrymen's stirrups, and were carried into swirling smoke and musket fire. As British swords struck French breastplates, one soldier was reminded of the sound of 'a thousand coppersmiths'[20] at work. Two of France's prized eagle standards were captured,[21] but at great cost; by the end of the British cavalry charge, many lay dead on the field, including Major-General Sir William Ponsonby, who had led the Scots Greys. When found, the collar of the jacket on his bloodied body lay open, revealing a locket with a picture of his wife, Georgiana.

Amid the chaos and carnage, Wellington was ever visible. As one of his ADCs noted, 'It is hardly possible to describe the calm manner in which the hero of that day gave his orders, and watched the movements and attacks of the enemy. In the midst of danger, bullets whistling close about him, round shot ploughing up the ground he occupied, and men and horses falling on every side, Wellington sat upon his favourite charger, Copenhagen, as collectedly as if he had been merely reviewing the household troops in Hyde Park.'[22]

As rumour circulated in Brussels that a victory dinner was being prepared for the Emperor, the third phase of the battle began. At 3.30 p.m. Marshal Ney ('the bravest of the brave') placed himself at the head of the French Light Cavalry as they charged, between the two vantage-points of Hougoumont and La Haye Sainte, towards the Anglo-Allied infantry. By the time Ney reached the infantry it had lined up into squares. As the earth shook under the enormous mass of men and horses, the command 'Prepare to receive cavalry' rang out, just before the French force attacked, shouting 'Vive l'Empereur!'. One Ensign serving with the 1st Foot Guards was in the same square as Wellington; 'every man in the front ranks knelt', he wrote, 'and a wall bristling with steel, held together by steady hands, presented itself to the infuriated cuirassiers ... Our Commander-in-chief, as far as I could judge, appeared perfectly composed; but looked very thoughtful and pale.'[23] Soon after, the inside of the square had become like a hospital, full of 'dead, dying, and mutilated soldiers'.

While the French cavalry continued their attacks on the squares, Wellington, spotting weak points with the help of his telescope, rode the battlefield, giving orders and encouraging and exhorting his men to hold fast, his visibility a critical battle strategy. 'We had a notion, that while he was there nothing could go wrong,' said one of his officers later. As he arrived at a unit the cry would go up, 'Silence – stand to your front – here's the Duke.' In some places the air was like a furnace; men's faces were as black as sweeps'. At 4.30 Wellington heard cannon fire from the Prussians, but they were still some way away to the east.

At six in the evening, Napoleon issued the order that La Haye Sainte must be taken. There, throughout the day, a force that numbered only

376 men of the King's German Legion had withstood numerous attacks, but now they were running out of ammunition. Ney, frustrated by earlier battle failures, threw substantial men and armoury into taking the farmhouse. By 6.30, with the building on fire and the defenders suffering an unyielding barrage of shots, the few survivors were forced to abandon their position. This was the most dangerous point in the entire battle, as it opened up the centre of Wellington's line; Ney took every advantage of this, pounding the line at close range.

Some of Wellington's troops, witnessing the carnage around them, judged that the end would be apocalyptic. 'I had never yet heard of a battle in which every body was killed; but this seemed likely to be an exception, as all were going by turns,'[24] thought one. Another possible outcome presented itself to an artillery officer, when he picked out the figure of the Emperor surrounded by his staff. 'There's Bonaparte, Sir,' he said to the Duke, 'I think I can reach him, may I fire?' 'No! No!' replied Wellington. 'It is not the business of commanders to be firing upon each other.'[25]

When the line threatened to break, Wellington wrote an order to one of his officers, Shaw Kennedy, to get troops and 'all the guns you can find' to the spot. Kennedy reported later that Wellington then 'put himself at their head ... in no other part of the action was the Duke of Wellington exposed to so much personal risk'.[26] But though his troops were clamouring to charge the enemy, he cautioned them, 'Wait a little longer, my lads, you shall have at them presently.' The Duke was waiting for the Prussians, and fortune favoured him when Ney was refused reinforcements by Napoleon. The Emperor, in the last hours of his reign, was reserving the Imperial Guard, his best troops, for what he expected would be the final rout.

The sun was beginning to sink when Napoleon, who for much of the day had been stationary at his command post at La Belle Alliance, rode to within 600 yards of Wellington's front line to launch the final attack. As the famous Imperial Guard – Les Invincibles, as they were called – marched into battle, they were saluted by their Emperor. On their backs they carried ceremonial dress for the victory parade into Brussels. The advance would prove to be the last French attack of the Napoleonic Wars. Even to the Allies they were an impressive sight – 'the heroes of many memorable victories',[27] as one British officer called them. But when the first column approached the top of the hill, their enemy, unknown to them, was waiting on the reverse slope. Wellington could not resist giving the order himself, 'Up Guards! Make ready! Fire!' As 1,500 men stood up, the advancing French, now at close quarters, were caught in a hail of bullets.

But the day was not yet won, and Wellington knew it. He was spotted nervously sliding the tube of his telescope in and out of its socket. At last the moment came: at 7.30 p.m. the cry rang out – 'The Prussians have arrived!' Snapping his telescope shut, Wellington rode to his command post at the top of the ridge. A ray of light from the fading sun lit up the 'Great Chief' as, standing up in his stirrups, he raised his hat and waved it towards the enemy. His troops needed no further encouragement. 'No cheering, my lads, but forward, and complete your victory.'[28]

One of his officers later described the scene:

> I have seen nothing like that moment, the sky literally darkened with smoke, the sun just going down, and which till then had not for some hours broken through the gloom of a full day, the indescribable shouts of thousands, where it was impossible to distinguish between friend and foe. Every man's arm seemed to be raised against that of every other. Suddenly, after the mingled mass had ebbed and flowed, the enemy began to yield; and cheerings and English huzzas announced that the day must be ours.[29]

When one of Wellington's ADCs urged him to take care – 'your life is too valuable to be thrown away' – the Duke replied, 'Never mind. Let them fire away. The battle's gained: My life's of no consequence now.'[30] In the French ranks, among the Imperial Guard a cry was heard which, in its eleven-year history, had never been heard before. 'La Garde recule!', rapidly followed by 'Sauve qui peut!'

The battle was over by nine o'clock. Most of Wellington's staff were dead or wounded. Fitzroy Somerset had lost his arm; Lord Uxbridge, more famously, his leg: 'By God! I've lost my leg!' 'Have you, by God?' The surgeons' instruments had been blunted by use.[31] One man welcomed deafness because it blotted out the cries of the wounded. In the 27th Foot Regiment's square, every man lay dead.[32] The eight and a half hours of brutal fighting had none the less contained instants of compassion and humanity. A French officer gave one of the wounded British officers[33] a draught of brandy from his flask, and directed that he should be wrapped in a cloak and a knapsack placed under his head.[34] The Allies at Hougoumont had spared the life of the drummer-boy. The sight of the corpse of a tortoiseshell kitten in the mud reminded one man of home. Over the three days of the campaign, 120,000 men had died, over half of them at Waterloo. At Hougoumont, where the bodies lay among the disfigured apple trees, the perfume of the jasmine and honeysuckle was soured by the smell of death.

When Wellington met Blücher at 'La Belle Alliance' inn, which throughout the battle had been behind enemy lines, the two men shook hands. The seventy-five-year-old Prussian General commented, in the language common to both men, 'Quelle affaire.' Afterwards, in the moonlight, Wellington rode slowly back to the inn at Waterloo. He spoke to no one. One who witnessed the scene thought it resembled more the 'aspect of a little funeral train than that of victors in one of the most important battles ever fought'.[35] When Wellington reached the inn one of the first things he did was to order the doctors to move his most trusted ADC, the gravely wounded Alexander Gordon, to his own bed. He then sat down to eat supper. Every time the door opened he looked up hoping to see a familiar face, but most of the places at the table remained empty. He drank a single glass of wine, with which he toasted 'the memory of the Peninsular War'. Shortly after, exhausted, he fell asleep on a pallet on the floor, only to be woken by Dr Hume, his Surgeon General.

> As I entered the room he sat up on his bed, his face covered with the dust and sweat of the previous day, and extended his hand to me, which I took and held in mine, whilst I told him of Gordon's death, and related such of the casualties as had come to my knowledge. He was much affected. I felt his tears dropping fast upon my hands, and looking towards him, saw them chasing one another in furrows over his dusty cheeks.
>
> He brushed them suddenly away with his left hand, and said to me, in a voice tremulous with emotion, 'Well! thank God! I don't know what it is to lose a battle, but certainly nothing can be more painful than to gain one with the loss of so many of one's friends.'[36]

The following morning the battlefield was a scene of total destruction. 'The whole field was strewed with the melancholy vestiges of devastation', ran one account:

> Soldiers' caps, pierced with many a ball, – eagles that had ornamented them, – badges of the legion of honor, – cuirasses' fragments, – broken arms, belts, and scabbards, shreds of tattered cloth, shoes, cartridge-boxes, gloves, Highland bonnets, feathers steeped in mud and gore, – French novels and German testaments, – scattered music belonging to the bands, – packs of cards, and innumerable papers of every description, thrown out of the pockets of the dead, by those who had pillaged them, – love-letters,

and letters from mothers to sons, and from children to parents; – all, all these, and a thousandfold more, that cannot be named, were scattered about in every direction.[37]

Wellington began writing his Despatch at the inn and finished it after his return to Brussels on Monday morning. Four in every ten of his officers who had attended the Duchess of Richmond's ball had been killed in the battle. Young Henry Percy, one of the survivors, was selected to carry to London the captured French eagles and the Waterloo Despatch. He remembered the velvet handkerchief case which still lay in his pocket and discovered that the Despatch fitted neatly inside it. It was thus that the dramatic news of the victory was borne over the Channel, and raced through English lanes to be delivered to the Minister of War. Then Percy, still in his bloodied scarlet tunic, dashed into the house where the Prince Regent was attending a ball and, on bended knee, laid the captured French eagles at his feet. 'Victory, Victory, Sire.'[38]

Back in Belgium, Wellington wrote to a friend, 'My heart is broken by the terrible loss I have sustained of my old friends and companions and my poor soldiers. I shall not be satisfied with the battle, however glorious, if it does not of itself put an end to Buonaparte.'[39] To another he commented, 'I hope to God I have fought my last battle.'[40] Both wishes were to be granted. But if Wellington was a hero even before the battle, now some would give him a place among the gods. Handel's 'See the Conquering Hero Comes' would greet him wherever he went; cities, streets and squares would be named after him; 'Duke of Wellington' public houses would spring up around England as his old soldiers celebrated their 'Great Chief'; statues would be raised to proclaim the man and the battle.

Kitty's heart swelled to bursting when she heard the news of the great victory. At seven and eight years old, her boys Charles and Arthur would be just mature enough to grasp the importance of the event, but they would be the first of Wellington's descendants to live in the fierce light of their father's fame. A hundred years later, when Wellington's great-great-grandson Valerian, my father, was born, the light was more benign. Now, as the world approaches the bicentenary of the battle, his descendants can luxuriate in the warm glow cast by their great ancestor. Maybe they can even reclaim him into the family. 'I am but a man', the First Duke would insist when pressed to reveal a pride in his deeds. For me, he is but a great-great-great-grandfather.

*

When, in 2004, I stood with my father, the 8th Duke, on the battlefield of Waterloo, I realised how little I knew about our famous ancestor. My father talked about the army, his own experiences of war, and the pride of association with one whom some would call the greatest British General. All my life the public figure of the First Duke has eclipsed the private: his victory over Napoleon at the battle of Waterloo was an iconic moment in history which defines his legacy. When I was a small child, my first awareness of him was the statue that stands guard, imposingly, at the main gate of Stratfield Saye. This child's-eye view of the great man still holds: his heroic deeds and extraordinary life tower over all his descendants.

Millions of words have been written about the First Duke of Wellington, many of them in his lifetime, and some of them far from complimentary. Every step he took, every battle he fought, every word he uttered, every letter he wrote; all have been pored over and analysed by historians. But now I wanted to know about him as a husband and father, brother and uncle, and several grades of grandfather. And how hard was it to follow in his shoes – to be 'the Duke of Wellington'?

For my father, born in 1915, the year of the centenary of the battle, his great-great-grandfather was, when he decided to pursue a career in the army, both supreme role model and inspiration. But he never expected to inherit the title, since he was the son of a younger son. As with his illustrious forebear, fighting for King and Country, with the sacrifice and devotion to duty that went with it, was a natural instinct for my father. In fact war has not only shaped the destiny of the Wellesley family, but also played a significant part in my father's life. Born during the First World War, he met and married my mother (herself the only child of a distinguished soldier) in Jerusalem during the Second World War.

And what of the women, who so often become footnotes in a family's history: Kitty Pakenham, who, even among the family, is a rather shadowy, tragic figure, and the other Duchesses who followed in her footsteps as consorts to successive Dukes and, sometimes, mothers of their heirs? And, of course, my mother, Diana McConnel, the 8th Duchess, whose Scottish blood runs through my generation.

Although my father is the 8th Duke, the First is only four generations behind him. The line of descent has zig-zagged its way through the last two centuries – sometimes passing sideways and, in the Second World War, backwards. The family still lives in Stratfield Saye, Hampshire, and Apsley House, London, the two houses that were the First Duke's homes.

All eight Dukes, with different measures of commitment, served in the British Army; for my father, it has been one of the passions of his life. But the military tradition is coming to an end: I have four brothers, but none of us chose a military career. When my father's tenure of the title is over, that baton will have been dropped.

An era is closing, and not only of the military tradition. My father is the last Duke who can claim to have met people who knew the First Duke of Wellington. He can say, 'My grandfather was the First Duke's grandson.' That simple statement has an irresistible resonance for me. A little over sixty years separates my father's birth and the death of the First Duke, when the country went into mourning and Queen Victoria called him 'the greatest man England has known'. When my parents' generation has taken its last bow, with it will go a set of values and experiences which are very different from those of mine.

My journey begins, and will conclude, with the First Duke. But it is through my parents that I reach back to earlier generations, and now, with their diamond wedding anniversary already in the past, I savour the privilege (in my middle years) of exploring some of their memories, and of discovering more about my grandparents. By the end of my quest, I hope to be able to relate to the First Duke of Wellington not merely as a public figure who belonged to the nation in life, and in death was still claimed by it. Perhaps, despite his fame and glory, I will be able to wrest him from his lonely column and reclaim him back into the family.

ONE

Born to Serve

When he was a child growing up in Ireland in the 1770s, the future Duke of Wellington's only apparent ability was a flair for playing the violin. His father, Garret, whose life was steeped in music, will have smiled with pleasure to see the small hands drawing the bow across the strings of his instrument. But Arthur's mother Anne, far from being the proud parent, may even have winced as she heard the strains of the music. She saw little advantage in men having musical gifts: her husband's considerable reputation as a composer had helped him earn an Irish earldom, but it had made no contribution to the family purse. Anne was strong and immensely practical, but she was not a warm mother. This tough, sharp, ambitious woman's indifference to her third surviving son – 'he's food for powder and nothing else' – would be one of the spurs that drove Arthur upwards. His father's artistic disposition lived on in his son, but when the moment came that Arthur believed it was holding him back, he covered it with layers of determination and discipline and pushed it to the inner recesses of his being.

Garret's own childhood was idyllic. An only son, he was born on 9 July 1735, when his parents had become reconciled to the idea that two daughters would be their only children. He grew up with little memory of his mother Elizabeth, who died when he was only three years old, leaving him to the doting care of his sisters. His father Richard had been born a Colley, another of the small band of Anglo-Irish families who had been intermarrying for centuries; Richard adopted the name of Wesley when his uncle through marriage, Garret Wesley, died childless and left him a fortune and estates, including Dangan Castle in County Meath. Richard seems to have had an amiable disposition: his good friend Mary Granville (later Mrs Delany) described him as valuing 'his riches only as they are the means of making all about him happy; he has no ostentation, no taste merely for grandeur and magnificence. He improves his estate and all the country round him as much as if he had a son to enjoy it (which there is no great probability of his having)." When the unexpected son and heir arrived, Mrs Delany stood as his godmother.

Richard was a keen amateur violinist, playing, it was said, 'well for a gentleman'. His little son would listen happily to the sound of his father's fiddle, beating time with his hands. Once, when a visitor to the house tried to remove the violin from his father's hands, Garret objected, but when the child heard him play, he was entranced. The guest was the noted violinist and composer Matthew Dubourg, who since 1728 had been Master of the Dublin Castle Band. From that moment, the toddler would sit at Dubourg's feet whenever he played at Dangan.² It soon became clear that Garret was a musical prodigy: according to a contemporary, he was able to play the organ, violin and harpsichord, 'almost by instinct', before he was five. He wrote pieces which he called 'serenatas'.

The great musical event of Dublin in the 1740s was a visit from Handel, whose flagging popularity at the court of George II prompted his friend Dubourg to encourage him to make the trip. He arrived in November 1741, having just completed a new oratorio called *Messiah*. Before his arrival he had been in touch with several of the charities in Dublin, including Mercer's Hospital, of which Richard Wesley was a governor. Handel finally agreed to the first performance of the oratorio being in aid of three charities, including Mercer's, and *Messiah* was first performed on 13 April 1742 to an audience of 700.

Might a small boy of seven have sneaked into the back of the hall to listen to the heavenly music? If not, Garret certainly heard Handel perform when he visited Dangan and delighted all Richard's neighbours, who gathered to hear the maestro play the organ in the great hall of the castle.³ If, in later life, Garret told his own children about the concert, at least one of his offspring would have relished the account; when Arthur, as a grand old man, served as a director of the 'Ancient Concerts', he selected several pieces by Handel. It is said that when Handel left Ireland in August 1742, he presented Richard Wesley with one of the organs he had brought with him from England.

The Wellesleys of the eighteenth century may have had music in their veins; but the strongest family tradition, going back seven centuries, was one of service to the Crown. The 'Welles-leighs' were originally from 'Somersetshire', having been rewarded with lands there for their passive acceptance of the Norman Conquest. An early member of the family arrived in Ireland in 1171, as official standard bearer to the invading

King Henry II. Over the following centuries the Wellesleys established themselves in the country, as, with a mixture of luck, opportunism, manipulation of conflicting loyalties and strong marriages, they dug their roots into the Irish turf. And it was often the women who brought riches into the family – including the estates in County Meath. But whenever the status of Wellesley property or possessions was questioned by the representatives of the Crown, 'Bearing the Standard of the Lord the King in his Wars to Ireland' was always invoked to ratify ownership.

Of the many Wellesleys whose names spring off the pages of the chroniclers of these times, I am drawn to a namesake of my father's, one young 'Valerian Wellesley', who, left a ward at the age of ten in 1603, was contracted in a marriage to which, when fourteen, he objected forcefully, 'being fully resolved in my owne mynde to keepe my selfe at libertye until God shall graunt me best judgement to make choice for myself'.[4] Clearly his strong will persisted: later in life his estates were confiscated for his shift towards Roman Catholicism. His son Garret changed his name to Wesley and recovered the family footing, and the estates, by claiming he was an 'innocent Protestant' and managed to pass this considerable inheritance on to the next generation, another Garret. It was this Garret Wesley who, failing to produce an heir, procured one in the shape of his cousin Richard Colley, grandfather to Arthur, who would in his own unique way become the consummate standard bearer to the Crown.

Richard spent a considerable part of his inheritance on his estates, and his status in society was enhanced when, in 1746, in recognition of his charitable ventures and patronage, he was made a baron, choosing the title of Mornington. There is no record of why he picked the name but it may have been because a fifteenth-century Richard Wellesley had, through a successful marriage, acquired large estates including the manor of Mornington (originally Marinerstown), not that far from Dangan.[5] When Richard died in 1758, his son Garret inherited a large fortune which gave him an income of £8,000 a year (over a million pounds in today's value). Having completed his education at Trinity College, Dublin, in 1757, he immediately set about finding himself a bride. It looked briefly as if he might marry a duke's daughter when he set his cap at Lady Louisa Lennox, daughter of the Lord Lieutenant, the Duke of Richmond, but, Lord Mornington was informed, she had developed an 'insurmountable dislike to him'. In the end it was a Miss Anne Hill, just sixteen years old and the daughter of a banker, who became Lady Mornington.

The fair Anne must have had attributes that appealed to Garret, for she had no fortune; he may even have loved her. They married on 6 February 1759. Garret's godmother, Mrs Delany, had the newly-weds to dinner and reported back to her sister about their demeanour: 'Lord Mornington seems *very happy* as well as his Lady, a pair of good-humoured young things, but I think her education not finished enough for her to make any considerable figure, nor her judgment sufficient to get the better of some disadvantages *he* has had in his education.'[6] This perceived lack of judgement was compounded by Anne's strong temper, inherited from her father Arthur, who was described by a contemporary as having a '*little pepper* in his composition'.[7]

Just before her eighteenth birthday, on 20 June 1760, Anne gave birth to their first son, Richard. By this time, Garret had established a Musical Academy and become the first Professor of Music at Trinity College. Three months later at the age of twenty-five he was created an Irish earl, and the following year the new Earl and Countess were bidden to George III's coronation. Arthur, born in 1769, was their sixth child. Such was the inconsequence of his birth that confusion has always surrounded both its date and place. Claims include 6 March, and 3, 29 and 30 April – at Dangan, on the road between Dangan and Dublin, and at sea. But in 1815, when her son's fame was at its zenith, Anne Mornington insisted she remembered the details: 1 May 1769 at 6 Merrion Street, Dublin – an elegant new townhouse round the corner from St Stephen's Green, the largest public square in Europe. Arthur's arrival in the family was preceded by Richard, another Arthur (who died of smallpox when very young), William, a short-lived Francis, and Anne, named after her mother. The choice of Christian name was to honour his maternal grandfather, Arthur Hill, of the peppery constitution.

The world that Arthur was born into was in a state of impending change and upheaval. Six years before his birth, Britain had emerged from the Seven Years' War as the most powerful colonial power in the world, having vanquished for now her principal enemy, France. In the year of his birth, patents were registered for Richard Arkwright's spinning machine and James Watt's steam engine. Both these inventions would help to drive the Industrial Revolution forward. In the year before Arthur's birth, Samuel Adams in Massachusetts had written a circular letter objecting to taxation without representation and calling on colonists to unite in their actions against the British government, thereby sowing seeds for the American struggle for independence. Closer to home, George III had been on the throne for nearly a decade but there was great dissatisfaction amongst some of his subjects. In 1769 John Wilkes, the journalist and outlawed radical politician, founded the Bill of Rights Society, which ultimately led to the Parliamentary Reform Act, to which the future Duke of Wellington would be so implacably opposed. As Britain reached out to find new parts of the world to conquer or colonise, the explorer James Cook landed on Tahiti. However, for Arthur Wesley, by far the most significant event of 1769 would turn out to be the birth in Corsica on 15 August of Napoleon Bonaparte.

Three more children, Gerald in 1770, Henry in 1773, and Mary in 1774, completed the Mornington family. Later in life Richard, the first-born, would dismiss his parents as being 'alas! frivolous and careless personages like most of the Irish nobility of that time'; this displays an element of ingratitude given that it was Richard on whom were showered all the advantages the Morningtons could provide. When Arthur was still a toddler Richard was sent briefly to Harrow and then Eton, where he became a hugely successful scholar. Meanwhile Arthur's childhood was unremarkable and largely unrecorded.

Arthur's first taste of education was at a small diocesan school in the town of Trim, a few miles from the rolling parklands that his grandfather had created at Dangan. The stone building which housed the schoolroom was known as Talbot's Castle – named after the fifteenth-century warrior dubbed in Shakespeare's *Henry VI Part 1* 'the scourge of France'. Maybe the young Arthur was inspired by accounts of Talbot's exploits, but the only anecdote that has survived from those early years presents an insecure, lonely child who craved attention. One day, Arthur's cousin and fellow schoolmate, Richard Crosbie (later to attain notoriety for his ballooning), climbed the 'Yellow Steeple' – the tower of the abbey which lay beside the school. When Crosbie's 'last will and testament' floated down from the top the steeple, Arthur was distraught to see that his friend had not left him anything and he burst into tears. This sensitivity cannot have endeared him to his stern-willed mother, who was already convinced that Arthur was the dunce of the family, and was said to treat him if not harshly, with marked neglect.[8]

By the late 1770s Garret's purse was depleted by bringing up seven children, and with his Irish estates already mortgaged, he decided to move the family to London. Possibly he imagined that his catches and glees, for which he now had a loyal following, would have the chance of a wider audience. A society which promoted music of that kind had been established in the city a few years earlier and it was becoming quite fashionable. The Morningtons also believed that their children would benefit from getting away from Ireland, and the danger of 'a singularity of pronunciation that hereafter might be a disadvantage ... in society'.[9]

Today Dangan Castle is a dark ruin: sheep graze in the great hall where Handel once played and rooks nest in the thick grey stone walls. On the land round the house there is nothing to suggest the grandeur and elegance of the park that Arthur's grandfather created, which was described by Mrs Delany as 'magnificent', with its wide gravel walk to a large lake scattered with small islands. The house in Merrion Street is part of a smart hotel, happy to proclaim its association with the First Duke, and an area of the hotel grounds is called 'Lady Mornington's garden'. Would Richard's generous benefactor, Garret, have been dismayed that the family on whom he had bestowed his name and worldly wealth were so eager to escape their birthplace in search of richer pastures? Arthur returned as a young soldier to the court of the Viceroy, and his elder brother, Richard, would serve two terms as Lord Lieutenant of Ireland; but none of their generation of Wellesleys, or any subsequent members of the family, re-established roots on the island. Famously, in a moment of pique, Wellington was said to have uttered the words, 'Because a man is born in a stable that does not make him a horse.'[10] But, in speeches during his time as Prime Minister when he was pleading for Catholic Emancipation, his concern for his country of birth was evident. When I went to see the high monument that commemorates Wellington in Dublin's Phoenix Park, I asked the taxi driver why the statue had never been blown up by the Republicans. 'Because,' he replied, 'he was an Irishman.'

When the Morningtons arrived in London, Garret took rooms for his family in Kingston House, Knightsbridge.[11] The house had been built in 1757 for the Duke of Kingston, whose wife, after his death, was tried and convicted of bigamy by the House of Lords. Fortunately for the Morningtons, she was forced to leave the country and part of the house was let. Arthur's new school in London was Brown's Seminary in the King's Road, where his lacklustre educational programme continued. Later in life Arthur confessed to his friend and biographer, George Robert Gleig, that at this time he was 'a dreamy, idle and shy lad'. One of the highlights of his time there was when his brother Richard, by now a student at Christ Church, Oxford, gave him a tip of a shilling.

Despite his continuing output of fashionable compositions, with such titles as 'Gently hear me, charming maid',[12] Garret's finances did not improve in London. He even wrote to his agent in Ireland with a scheme to raise money through a kind of lottery: 'If you will send me ten numbers I shall take two and give each of my Children and my Lady one, but don't let these numbers run all in order, but different thousands if possible.'[13] But his music continued to be the focus of his life and each week he would breakfast with his namesake, Charles Wesley, to make music with the Wesley children. Such was his dedication to his profession that the 1944 *Oxford Companion to Music* cites him as having been 'a man of cool courage, for he is reputed to have been the first member of the British aristocracy who dared to walk through the streets of London openly and unashamedly carrying a violin case'.

On 22 May 1781 Garret Mornington, who had been born with such wealth of talent and possessions, died leaving considerable debts for his son and heir, Richard. Before Anne had reached forty, she was left a widow with seven children. Richard took care of the arrangements for his father's funeral and, in spite of the family's situation, spent £80 to ensure he was buried with due pomp and ceremony. An account of the expenses lists all the items, including cloaks and crape hatbands for the whole family, a huge canopy with sable plumes, two coaches for the mourners and even a pair of black gloves for the Morningtons' house-keeper. As the small cortège wound its way up Knightsbridge and through the toll-gate at the top, they would have passed close to a new red-brick building a few hundred yards from the church in South Audley Street where the 1st Earl of Mornington was to be laid to rest. Named after its original owner, this was Apsley House, which in future years would be Wellington's London residence.

Garret was only forty-six when he died: the age at which his unprom-ising son, Arthur, would score his name into history by winning a battle near the Belgian hamlet of Waterloo. On the day of the funeral, Arthur must have felt intensely the loss of his father's sympathy. He was left with a mother who was soon to dismiss him with the heartless words, 'I vow to God I don't know what I shall do with my awkward son Arthur.'[14] For Arthur, a twelve-year-old middle son, the future must have seemed bleak.

*

My own father was the treasured first-born when he entered the world in Rome on Friday, 2 July 1915. He was born in a great hall, frescoed with busts of Roman emperors, one of whom was Valerian. His parents, Gerald and Dorothy, designed and commissioned a tiny little font made of the semi-precious stone verde antico, and christened their son in the small chapel attached to the house. They called him Arthur Valerian. His mother immediately began an album of photographs – carefully writing 'Valerian's book' on the cover. A simple grey-bound volume with black leaves, its first few pages show a young mother lying in a huge baroque carved bed cradling her baby in her arms; others, in profile, reveal Dorothy smiling tenderly at the tiny infant. Over ninety years on, some of the photographs have faded, but as I look at these touching images I feel immensely sad. Seven and a half years after Valerian's birth, Gerald and Dorothy's marriage fell apart.

When Lord Gerald Wellesley married Dorothy Ashton on 30 April 1914, two families smiled approvingly. Gerald, born in 1885, the third son of the 4th Duke of Wellington, was a clever, artistic, gifted linguist who had entered the Diplomatic Service in 1908, serving three years as a Secretary at the British Embassy in St Petersburg, where he had learnt to speak Russian. 'One's friends, the Grand Dukes and so forth, invariably spoke French but I always made a point of talking Russian to my coachman',[15] he later recalled. Since 1912 he had been attached as Second Secretary to the Embassy in Constantinople. As a younger son, he had grown up knowing he would inherit very little money and must earn his living. He had wanted to be an architect, but his parents 'mistrusted a career which they considered hazardous and uncertain', and he was 'guided into the safer paths of the Foreign Office and diplomacy, where a modest competence and an eventual pension were assured'.[16] The year before his wedding, on leave from Constantinople, he had been briefly engaged to Violet Keppel (the daughter of Edward VII's mistress Alice), but the arrangement had been broken off. He was now nearly thirty. His diplomatic career would be more agreeable with a wife by his side.

Dorothy's prosperous industrialist father had died when she was only nine, and her mother, left a wealthy widow, had married the Earl of Scarbrough. Dorothy herself had inherited a fortune and an estate in Cheshire when her only sibling, christened Robert but known as 'Scamp', succumbed to tuberculosis in 1912. 'I became, to my misery, an "heiress",' she wrote many years later. But while burying her sorrow in a frantic round of hunting and socialising, she also pursued literary aspirations; by the time she became engaged to Gerald, she was a published poet. Her *Early Poems* had appeared under the pseudonym of 'M.A.' (Miss Ashton). In her memoir, *Far Have I Travelled*, she explained how her engagement came about: 'From time to time I became engaged to this young man or another, but they always jibbed at the last moment or else I did. I think young men and women were in some sense afraid of me. For after years of solitude I became somewhat mordant in my judgement of humanity. Yet when my mother asked G.W. to Sandbeck I began to feel differently, and later when he asked me to marry him I said "Yes".[17]

The marriage took place on Thursday, 30 April at the Priory Church of St Bartholomew the Great in Smithfield. The choice of one of London's oldest churches – it was built in 1123 in the reign of Henry I – rather than a more fashionable venue, reflected their shared love of historically interesting buildings. Dorothy wore a 'gown of white and gold brocade, with a train of the same material slung from the shoulders'.[18] She had a wreath of bay leaves, covered by a tulle veil held on either side by a bunch of orange blossom. Her bridesmaids wore primrose satin frocks and mobcaps. Dorothy was given away by her stepfather, 'Dandy' Scarbrough, of whom she was very fond. But as she walked down the aisle she can only have mourned the absence of her brother Scamp. The couple, as was the custom of the day, were showered with lavish gifts, including a diamond and sapphire pin for Gerald from the Queen of Spain. When they set off for their honeymoon the bride was wearing 'a dress of dove-coloured charmeuse, with a large black hat with blue feathers, and a gendarme cloak of dove colour and blue'.[19]

The Gerald Wellesleys returned to Constantinople via Florence and Venice, the serenity of their honeymoon slightly marred by the presence of Dorothy's new mother-in-law in the former and an aunt in the latter. It rained all the time, but as they left Venice for their new home, 'the Salute appeared to me like a dome of many-coloured glass, staining the white radiance of eternity'. My grandmother wrote these words, with their quotation from Shelley, many years later in her memoir. 'Few will deny', she went on, 'that the voyage from Venice to the Golden Horn is one of the most beautiful journeys in the world; the islands, light gold at dawn, deep gold at dusk, lavender coloured by day; night descending with its great stars and greater moon. As the sunny days glided by life seemed enchanted.'[20] The enchantment carried her through to their arrival in Constantinople and a move into a large wooden house, cooled by the breezes of the Bosphorus.

When the house was ready, Gerry and Dottie threw a party to celebrate. 'The Gerrys last night gave a very notable *festa* in their wonderful garden,' wrote one of their guests. 'We went up through a beautifully lit tunnel on to a terrace high up, and sat on carpets under pine trees by the light of Japanese lanterns and listened to wonderful Greek singers.'[21] While Gerald went to work in the Embassy, Dorothy roamed in the hills. She lay in the sunshine relishing the heat and the smell of the wild rosemary, lavender and thyme. In the evening they ate outside and watched the fireflies dancing. Gerald bought a white mare and stallion, called 'Snow' and 'Dapple' respectively, and they would ride through Constantinople's Belgrade Forest. One evening, as they passed through a dusty village, they came across a tiny kitten with blazing sapphire-blue eyes. For Dorothy it was love at first sight and Gerald tucked the small creature into his pocket.

But the enchantment was soon to end. On 28 June 1914, a mere two months after their wedding, an assassin's bullet killed Archduke Franz Ferdinand, heir to the Austro-Hungarian Empire. On 4 August Britain declared war on Germany and two German warships slipped through the Dardanelles and dropped anchor opposite the Wellesley house. Their guns, Dottie wrote to her half-sister Serena (known as Mitey, but whom she called Mite), 'seeming to be pointing in our direction'. The Ambassador ordered all the women and children to leave. Dorothy initially refused, but in the end decamped to Sofia with her frightened maid, leaving Gerald behind. She wrote again to Mitey on 17 October: 'For three weeks we refused to go but at last we had to as he said he would telegraph the Foreign Office in London if we didn't. So then I was afraid it might do Gerry harm so I went – We all think it's absurd & everyone is furious. I am going back soon anyway as I must go back to Gerry & it is *deadly* here.'

Dorothy may have been bored in Sofia, but when news arrived of the Russians shelling a village on the Black Sea, it was a little too close for comfort. In any case, she had concerns other than for her own safety: she was pregnant, and convinced the baby would be a boy. When Turkey lined up alongside Germany in early November, Gerald and the last remaining Embassy staff had to flee Constantinople, ending up in Salonica, where the Wellesleys were reunited. Gerald had to break the news to his wife that they had lost everything from their house on the banks of the Bosphorus. However, there was a small consolation for Dorothy when she saw, staring out from a white bundle in their chauffeur's pocket, a pair of sapphire-blue eyes.

In Salonica the couple boarded a destroyer which carried them to Gerald's next posting in Italy. The sea journey was not without incident. One night they were held up by a German submarine and the heavily leaded Foreign Office bag was thrown over the side into the deep waters of the Adriatic. When they finally reached Rome, Dorothy was exhausted and worried about the health of her unborn child. But soon she was revived when Gerald returned from an outing in high spirits: '"I have found the perfect house." We went to see it and perfect indeed it was. It had a great marble salon below for summer days, and above was a lovely sitting room with little balconies facing south. There were also two dining-rooms, one for summer, the other for winter. We transformed the garden into a charming Baroque affair, and I made a little spring garden for myself among the ilex trees I had planted.'[22] Their Italian neighbours soon called Gerry and Dottie's house 'Casa Vellesli'.

It was here in the great hall of Casa Vellesli that my father took his first breath. I suspect that the date of Valerian's birth – a hundred years and two weeks after the battle of Waterloo – gave some pleasure to his father, already a keen devotee of his great ancestor. Since the world was at war, the mood for the Waterloo centenary was sombre. 'Echoes from the Field of Battle', ran a headline in *The Times*. 'A hundred years ago today the fate of the world was decided upon the field of Waterloo. To-day, after the lapse of a hundred years, the Low Countries are the scene of a mightier struggle, and once more the fate of the world hangs upon the issue; but the foes of a hundred years ago are brothers-in-arms against a common enemy.' In Paris the oldest British residents placed a wreath in the cemetery at Neuilly-sur-Seine, where lay many French and British soldiers who had died at the battle of the Marne; in London a wreath of ivy in the form of a heart garlanded with red, white and blue ribbon was put at the foot of the equestrian statue of the Duke of Wellington; at Wellington College (founded in memory of the First Duke) Gerald's father, the 4th Duke, planted in the grounds an acorn from the Stratfield Saye oak by the grave of Copenhagen, the horse that carried Wellington for fourteen hours at the battle. As the Wellington school corps paraded across the playing field, there were many among the spectators who reflected that some of these young boys would soon be called to sacrifice their lives for their country.[23]

In May 1915, to the relief of the British, Italy had formally entered the war on the side of the Allies. The Ambassador, Sir Rennell Rodd, recounted later how 'the wives of two of my secretaries, Lady Gerald Wellesley and Mrs Parr, ransacked their jewel boxes and brought all they could spare to be sold for the cause'.[24] In spite of the constant anxiety about friends and family on the front, Rome was truly the perfect posting for a couple who derived so much inspiration from classical art, history and poetry. When diplomatic and charitable duties permitted, the Wellesleys would go on expeditions to the countryside to search for the stones they loved: porphyry, verde antico, giallo antico. In an uncultivated field they discovered a site where there must once have stood a grand Roman villa; they filled 'sacks' full of their treasures. Closer to home, in the Borghese Gardens, they found another prize: 'an adorable little Greek piece, a Grecian girl figure, probably once part of a vase'. The prim English nanny was shocked when the soil-clad articles were dumped in Valerian's pram to be taken home, where they were washed carefully and added to the growing collection.

Gerald and Dorothy would scour antique and junk shops looking for curiosities. One of their best finds was a picture by Longhi of an eighteenth-century rhinoceros called Clara, who for seventeen years did her own Grand Tour of Europe, at a time when the sight of the huge, strange creature enthralled her audiences. When, in 1758, Clara died in London at the age of twenty, she was the most famous animal in the world. My father has known the picture all his life: my grandfather gave it to him when he got married, and it has hung in every house he has lived in.

But the real pleasure for both of them was their son. Dorothy proudly sent her half-sister a picture of him: 'Darling Mite, Here is a naked photograph of Valerian looking like a tadpole, all head! I will try and do some better ones later; also a delightful one of Gerry, I think, in his bathing dress, don't you love it?' My father has some hazy memories of those early years of his life. He remembers macaws flying round the great hall in front of the frescoes of Roman emperors. There were trips to the Tuscan countryside, where Valerian's treat would be to ride on a donkey. Once, he remembers, he was extremely upset when 'one of the donkeys had been badly beaten by its owner and had awful raw marks all over its body'. There was always talk of war, and somehow this penetrated the consciousness of the child. 'I remember once, when I was riding on a donkey, we were on a hill, and when I looked down into the valley I saw what looked like a lot of smoke, and I asked if that was the war.'

As war progressed, food became scarce. Dorothy recalled in her memoir that 'there was no fish, no meat, no milk for the child, nothing but endless heaps of pasta to be consumed as best one could in small quantities'. By the spring of 1918 the effects of an inadequate diet were taking their toll on Valerian, and now Dorothy was expecting another baby. The Wellesleys set off to a villa in the Alban Hills, but the heat became more and more oppressive. One evening, when Dorothy found Valerian sitting in his bath sucking at the sponge, she dragged the tub outside and let him run naked round the terrace. An aunt of Dorothy's came to stay, and her cousin Robin Hollway too. After her brother

Scamp, Robin was the relative Dottie loved the most. They would lie together under lime trees as she read poetry to him. He had been badly wounded on the Western Front, and later suffered dreadfully from shellshock. On a night-time recce, a sniper's bullet got him; he had hung on to some barbed wire for hours, and then managed to crawl back to his trench. He was eventually evacuated on a hospital ship, which was the scene of another kind of hell. 'Why did they lay the wounded and dead on pallets of straw side by side?' he sobbed to Dorothy. To the little Valerian, Robin appeared like a rather romantic figure from *Peter Pan*.

By the time the summer's heat began to subside, the war was drawing to a close. In October 1918 the Wellesleys packed up and returned to Britain. They docked at Southampton on a bright day and their first stop was with Gerald's parents, the 4th Duke and Duchess, in Hampshire. Dorothy's health and spirits were revived by long walks in the countryside – 'over hedges and across ditches, which delighted my father-in-law.' By Christmas the family had moved into a house in Ebury Street, London, which they had borrowed from their friends Harold and Vita Nicolson. It was meant to be haunted by the ghost of a lady who had been the mistress of a king, and 'a cat which was said to walk through the air towards one with a malign expression on its face'. It was here, on Boxing Day 1918, that Gerald and Dorothy's daughter was born; with the special permission of the King, they christened her in the Chapel Royal, St James's Palace, and named her Elizabeth. My father, not yet four years old, remembers his little sister bawling her head off throughout the short service. Robin Hollway was one of the godparents, Mitey another.

By now the country was in the throes of the terrible 'Spanish' influenza that would kill more Britons than had died in the entire war, and up to 59 million people worldwide. It was common to see soldiers carrying coffins out of houses on the streets of London. The Wellesleys, with Dorothy's fortune, were able to buy both 43 Portland Place – 'an Adam house with the original colours and medallions by Angelica Kaufmann' – and Sherfield Court in Hampshire – 'a charming little Queen Anne manor' on the border of the Wellingtons' Stratfield Saye estate. My father remembers the nursery quarters high up in the London house: 'There was a top passage with a rail with banisters and one day I stuck my head through as far as I could to see down below, where there was a ball which was attended by the Prince of Wales, who was a glamorous figure in those days – very dashing and good looking.'

In the morning, Valerian would often go down to Gerald's room and watch his father shaving. 'I was fascinated by the old-fashioned cut-throat razors which he used to sharpen on a strap, and then the routine of foaming the soap in a wooden bowl with a badger's-hair shaving brush, which no one does now.' London could be exciting – my father recalls watching, as a seven-year-old, from the nursery window as a statue was unveiled in Portland Place to commemorate Field Marshal Sir George Stuart White, a hero of the Boer War, with a band playing and great crowds. But Sherfield Court was the home my father loved best as a child. 'It had this magical island. You went out of the house onto a terrace, which was a nice place to sit, and then there was the moat, with a bridge across it to the island. To the child's eye it seemed quite large, though it was probably not more than an acre and a half. It was the fact that it was an island which appealed to me – it was our own little world. We played all sorts of games, but our favourite was pirates.' For Dorothy, this little bit of land held another kind of magic. In the reign of Elizabeth I the scholar George Puttenham lived in a house there and wrote *The Arte of English Poesie* which, when it was published in 1589, was one of the first books of poetry criticism. Before that the island had a less romantic association: in the Middle Ages prostitutes were tried there, and it was called the Court of the Harlots. When Dorothy wandered around the moat in the twilight hours she wished 'that the old house would rise like Camelot from the waters'.

The island was full of old gnarled apple and plum trees; there was a nuttery and one damson tree. Dorothy covered the moat in waterlilies by tying bricks to their roots and throwing them in. Valerian and Elizabeth thought they looked like green paving stones and called them 'link-pads'. It was at Sherfield that Dorothy was able to indulge her passion for gardening. She believed that 'the single flower holds within itself the purest of all beauty; for the best flowers can contain the whole of existence within an eighth of an inch'.[25] She used part of a long-neglected farmyard and a high brick wall to protect her plants from the cold winter winds. To the delight of the children, she also built a swimming-pool and turned the piggery beside it into a pool house where, on hot summer nights, she would sleep on a camp-bed so that in the morning she could dive straight into the pool.

As soon as they returned to England Gerald had left the Diplomatic Corps and articled himself to H.S. Goodhart-Rendel, to pursue his goal of becoming an architect. When he married Dorothy she had made it clear that she did not want to be a diplomat's wife for the rest of her life, and in any case with the financial security that she brought to the marriage he could 'now please himself'. By 1921 Gerald had qualified as a FRIBA and set up his own partnership with Trenwith Wills; their offices were in Bedford Row, a brisk stroll from Portland Place. The Wellesleys divided their time between their two houses, and for Valerian and Eliza, life assumed an harmonious routine. Dorothy's second book of poetry appeared – this time under her married name of Lady Gerald Wellesley.

The first seven years of my father's life were spent bathed in a warm glow of family fun and affection. He had a doting mother and father, two sets of attentive grandparents, a younger sister to tease, homes in the tranquillity of Hampshire and the bustling West End of London and the comfort of being part of a small family of four. Then, early in 1923, his parents separated and his world collapsed.

A poignant picture is drawn in a letter written by Harold Nicolson, who was staying at Portland Place at the time. Valerian was then with his father, who decided one day to go to Sherfield. 'They started off after breakfast and walked to the bus', wrote Nicolson to his wife Vita,

> Gerry straight-backed and defiant carrying a grip with their mutual night clothes in it, & Valerian struggling under a large parcel of brocade. So large was the parcel that it protruded beyond Valerian, & its sharp brown paper corner came up against and even *scratched* the shiny blue door which so diversifies the otherwise symmetrical alignment of No. 43. There was a long and rather petulant pause while the handkerchief was got out and the door dabbed to see if it was really serious – & then they started off again to walk to the bus together.[26]

For a while Valerian went to a day school in London, and he and his sister lived at Apsley House with their grandparents. A year after the separation, on 1 May 1924, he was sent to a prep school. Ludgrove had been established in 1892 for the single purpose of preparing boys for Eton, so there could be no other choice of school for him. I suspect that it was one of the few uncontentious decisions his parents made about arrangements for their children. In those days the school was in Barnet, with large grounds and lawns on two levels leading down to a pond. The boys slept five or six to a dormitory and there was as much emphasis on winning at games as there was on learning. The headmaster, Frank Henley, was a distinguished sportsman who had played cricket for Oxford. 'I remember my father drove me there in his Morris Minor and we were both in floods of tears.' His father wrote to him the following day from his offices in Bedford Row; the letter was typed so it would be easier for the little boy to read.

My darling Valerian, I was thinking of you all last night and wondering how you were getting on. I am sure you will like school and being with boys of your own age. When you begin to play cricket you are sure to find that there are other boys who know just as little about it as you do and the same is true of work and everything else. When you find that you do a thing about as well as the other boys of your own age you must then begin to try and do it better. I am sure you will find it all great fun and I am only frightened that you will forget about your Daddy and Mummy who love [you] more than anyone else does. I will come and see you in about a month or six weeks. Your loving Daddy

Valerian's mother, who was staying with the Nicolsons in Sussex, wrote to her son on Vita's monogrammed paper: 'My darling I am writing to you from Long Barn. I have left Nigel [her son] at Sherfield to play with Elizabeth, & am on my way to London to finish the flat . . . I do so much want to get a letter from you, so I hope you wrote yesterday . . . Are you beginning to enjoy yourself darling? Write and say if you are happy. Yr own loving Mummy.' My father probably did send letters to his mother (boarding schools usually ensure that their charges keep in touch with their parents), but if Valerian wrote to say he was happy, that was far from the truth: he was miserable. The school was comparatively small, with fewer than seventy boys, and whereas before at his day school no one had known of his parents' separation, now it was common knowledge. 'I was very much aware of the split-up of my parents, and unhappy and ashamed of the fact that they didn't live together. Ashamed that when other boys' parents came down to take them out, they were always a pair.'

When I talked to my father about this distressing time, I was shocked to learn of the open censure from the parents of his friends, including the mother of his best friend. 'I didn't get invited to stay with my friend in the holidays – I think she disapproved very strongly of the fact that my parents weren't living together . . . In those days you stuck together, even if you may have had other people in your lives, but if you did it all went on very discreetly.' I sense the hurt even now. 'I don't think I talked about my parents much, I suspect that I avoided it because it would immediately get me into a conversation where I had to explain so many things.' However, though Ludgrove holds few happy memories, Henley was a caring headmaster, writing a long, chatty letter to Valerian in October 1924, when he was recuperating from an appendix operation.

'We miss you in Vth Division very much. Goodbye now, & don't sneeze – it hurts!!'

Later letters to Valerian at Ludgrove contain melancholy appeals to a lost innocence. A fortnight after Valerian's tenth birthday in July 1925, Gerald wrote to his son: 'It is less than a fortnight now before you come home which is very exciting ... Terence the tortoise has escaped through the little hole out of the five-ten court. I have got another tortoise too big to get through the hole. I have given his shell a rub with oil which makes him look very smart.' Gerald ended the letter 'Love and xxxxxxxxxxxxxxxxxxxxxxxxxxxx from Daddy'. In May 1926 Valerian's grandmother said she hoped he would come and stay in the holidays and 'see my birds – but I cannot take any of their (birds) eggs – I want to breed Blue birds they are very very precious.' She ended the letter, 'Ever darling Valerian your loving Granny Kathleen Wellington'. A few months later the headmaster's wife took Valerian onto the terrace of the school and gently told him that Granny had died.

Perhaps my grandparents tried to keep the bitterness of their separation away from their children: if so, it did not work for my father. When the time came for him to move on from his prep school to Eton, the change came as a welcome relief. He could leave behind the prying disapproval of his friends' parents and swim in a bigger pond where boys were encouraged to think for themselves and stretch out towards being independent adults. Eton was where Valerian began to remove himself from his parental orbit – creating a personal life that would be filled with his own interests, ones that did not necessarily chime with those of his mother and father.

*

For Arthur Wesley Eton was not a fulfilling experience. He had failed to excel in any way either at his school in Meath or Browns Seminary in Chelsea. Now, under the patronage of his eldest brother Richard, the new Lord Mornington, he arrived at Eton in the autumn of 1781 seemingly ill-equipped to deal with an establishment that numbered at the time 300 pupils, all of whom were challenged to achieve great heights in sporting and scholarly ambition. In lessons he was slow and near the bottom of his class, his name appearing at number fifty-four out of seventy-nine.[27] In any case, Richard had set a high bar for all his younger siblings. He was one of the most celebrated classical scholars of his day, admired for his Latin and Greek verses.

In contrast, one of the younger brother's most distinguishing characteristics was his shyness. Later in life Arthur admitted to George

Robert Gleig that he 'contracted few special intimacies among his contemporaries'. 'His was indeed a solitary life', Gleig continues, 'a life of
solitude in a crowd; for he walked generally alone; often bathed alone;
and seldom took part in either the cricket matches or boat-races which
were then, as they are now, in great vogue among Etonians.' However,
something must have happened to give Arthur confidence; one of the
few stories about his Etonian days concerns a fight with a fellow pupil,
'Bobus' Smith, brother to Sydney, later Canon of St Paul's. Bobus, who,
strangely, later became famous for his ugliness, was swimming in the
Thames when Arthur started throwing stones at him from the bank.
This unprovoked attack led to a fight and according to Smith, 'he beat
me soundly'. There may well be an apocryphal element to this anecdote,
since it can only have benefited the teller to be able to boast that 'I was
the Duke of Wellington's first victory', and Arthur himself did not recall
the incident.

However he did remember Raganeaus, the 'house' where he boarded,
presided over by an Eton 'Dame' (part matron, part mother), and when
he visited his sons there nearly thirty-five years after he had left the
school he went out into the garden to see the 'broad black ditch over
which he used so often to leap'. He apparently remarked, 'I really believe
I owe my spirit of enterprise to the tricks I used to play in the garden.'
On one of these visits he was meant to have run along the top of the
Long Wall with 'unexampled gaiety'.[28] He also recollected that in his day
they called the room next to the kitchen where the maids slept 'Virgins'
Bower', and he seemed to know that there was a way through it. Apparently there was a tree near the house which he liked to climb and which
was later known as Duke's Tree. Arthur's solitary inclinations are reflected
in another story about his days at Eton. No doubt embellished by several
generations of star-struck young Etonians, it was recounted by a later
occupant of the room Arthur had slept in:

> ... when all the good burgomasters and thrifty tradesmen of Windsor and
> Eton had retired to rest, young Wellesley [Wesley at the time] on the
> commencement of a cold winter's night would be proceeding up old icy
> Father Thames, in a lonely skiff, to the vicinity of Maidenhead Bridge, and
> there, wrapt in single blanket, and watching with a single gun, he would be
> ready by daybreak to get a shot at the wild ducks, or other wild fowl,
> which were accustomed to congregate under shelter of the eyots, and other
> harbours of refuge on the Thames.[29]

*

My father was charmed by this Eton tale. Of the thousands of anecdotes about his ancestor, it is one with which he can dare to identify. It is not merely the allure of the lone adventure – squeezing through a small window; scrambling across roofs; clandestinely obtaining the gun, the skiff and the ammunition; finally, returning to a room unobserved and with an explanation for the booty. It was at Eton that my father's enthusiasm for shooting developed. As a pastime in the holidays, it was his way of escaping to a solitary world in the woods where he could immerse himself in the sounds of nature, train his eye on his prey and forget the upsetting consequences of his parents' separation.

*

For Arthur, the best times of his schoolboy years were those he spent with his eccentric maternal grandmother, Lady Dungannon, at her house in Brynkinalt, North Wales. There he found himself in another fight, this time with a young local blacksmith, with whom he was playing a game of marbles. On this occasion Arthur was roundly beaten and his opponent, remembering the incident many years later, boasted he had 'beaten the man who beat Napoleon' and that 'Master Wesley bore him not a pin's worth of ill-will'.[30] Without his illustrious military career, it is likely that the only impression Arthur would have left on Eton was his name, stealthily carved by him on the kitchen door of his boarding-house. His younger brother Gerald easily overtook him scholastically and Henry, the next one, was following close behind. Maybe it came as a relief to Arthur when in 1784 his mother and brother decided that he no longer merited the cost of Eton and packed him off to a tutor in Brighton.

After Brighton, Arthur's mother took him with her to live in Brussels; they were accompanied there by the son of a rich Yorkshire baronet who had been a close friend of Lord Mornington. John Armytage was roughly the same age as Arthur and the arrangement was mutually beneficial: Arthur and his mother shared John's lodgings and in return Armytage enjoyed Lady Mornington's protection. Given Anne's attitude towards her son, the atmosphere in the house must have been less than congenial, but the landlord, a Belgian lawyer called M. Louis Goubert, clearly made a favourable impression on Arthur. Years later he would recall: 'As I rode into Brussels the day after the battle of Waterloo, I passed the old house, and recognized it, and pulling up, ascertained that the old man was still alive. I sent for him, and recalling myself to his recollection, shook hands with him, and assured him that for old acquaintance' sake he should be protected from all molestation.'[31]

John and Arthur behaved like typical sixteen-year-olds. They 'pursued their studies in a desultory way', but put as much energy into enjoying themselves. John's memory of his teenage friend was that he was 'extremely fond of music, and played well upon the fiddle, but he never gave indication of any other species of talent ... there was no intention then of sending him into the army; his own wishes, if he had any, were in favour of a civilian's life'.[32] As it happened, after a year in Brussels, Lady Mornington could stand it no longer; she returned home and packed Arthur off to the Royal Academy of Equitation in Angers, France. He entered the Academy in January 1786 – one of 334 students for that year, a third of whom were English – and was registered as 'Mr Wesley, gentilhomme Irlandais, fils de Mylaidi Mornington'.

The academy, with its classical façade, two vast courtyards, stables and surrounding pavilions, had a grand air about it. The regime, little changed over two centuries, was designed to train and civilise the young sons of nobility from all over Europe. Arthur learnt the arts of horsemanship and sword display; he studied mathematics and the humanities; above all, perhaps, he encountered a motherly woman with a compassionate nature, the Duchesse de Séran. Many years later, just after Waterloo, when the Duchess was an old lady, he bumped into her at a reception in Paris and introduced her as the person 'in whose society he had passed the happiest part of his life, and to whose matronly kindness he owed more gratitude than he could ever repay'.[33]

Arthur fell in with the sons of a couple of other Irish peers. In the evenings they would sometimes go into town, dressed in their scarlet jackets adorned with yellow buttons and sky-blue facings, and have a night out at one of the many inns. Though he went on to enjoy a strong constitution, Arthur's health at the time was not good and this provided an excuse for him to lie on his sofa playing with his white terrier, Vick, or, less benignly, sit at his window with his friends dropping change onto the heads of passers-by. Sometimes the students were allowed to play games of chance – but under strict supervision and the rigid constraint that if the stakes became too high, the winnings would be confiscated and put in the 'poor box'. According to the records of the academy, Arthur showed an early display of charitable instinct by one day persuading his fellow gamblers to play for gold.

By the time Arthur returned to England late in 1786, the clumsy, shy boy had become a confident young gentleman who could speak good French, ride well and was beginning to form his own ideas about life. He may not, however, have forgotten his mother's harsh opinion of him, since it was reported that her first sighting of the transformation was at the Haymarket Theatre, when she exclaimed incredulously, 'I do believe there is my ugly boy Arthur!'[34] Initially she had not recognised the tall young man with a healthy complexion and powdered hair. But her persistent dismissal of her third son's attributes and abilities was no longer echoed by others. When asked if he had any English boys with potential, the director of the Academy of Equitation had cited – 'One Irish lad of great promise, of the name of Wesley.'[35]

Many of Valerian Wellesley's burdens lifted off his shoulders when he arrived at Eton in January 1929. Being descended from the school's most famous old boy may even have garnered him a little glory. 'I had a wonderful feeling of liberty and it was great to have my own room – my own kingdom. I could even choose what to hang on my walls.' His father, Gerald, gave him the watercolours that had decorated his own room when he had been at Eton. But Valerian's years at the college did more to form him than the influence of his parents, whose dissenting views of life were the cause, for him, of so much upset.

Eton in 1929 numbered over eight hundred students, but in other respects it had changed little since the First Duke's time. Its intake was still dominated by the sons of wealthy landowning families and the aristocracy. The boys were all divided between houses where the quality and compassion of the housemasters and dames played a crucial role in the successful development of the pupils under their charge. Valerian's housemaster was 'Tuppy' Headlam, who was known to be witty but rather idle – a combination which endeared him to the boys. 'I remember him with great affection – he was quite a character, often making jokes in obscure Latin.' On one occasion, when Valerian got into trouble with the French master – a mildly sadistic character who liked to twist the ears of his victims – Tuppy confessed to Valerian that he 'could not stand the fellow'. The enlightened attitude towards discipline made for a happy house and Valerian found this restorative. However, it did not save him from punishment when Headlam discovered a huge batch of cigarette butts in the candle-holder on his windowsill. 'The penalty was ghastly, 500 lines a day for a fortnight, Ovid and Horace, I still remember it – "Eheu fugaces, Postume, Postume ..." I could quote a lot of Ovid once.'

Unusually for a housemaster, Headlam was unmarried, but had a host of glamorous friends who would often visit him. One of his girlfriends was Anna May Wong – at the time a famous Chinese-American actress who made her debut as an extra in *The Red Lantern* (1919) and had her first starring role in 1922 in Hollywood's first colour movie, *The Toll of the Sea*. 'She was tremendously attractive and all the boys got very excited when she accompanied Tuppy on his evening rounds of the boys' rooms.' Anna May went on to make a huge number of films, but her involvement in Headlam's lively social life may have contributed to the fact that she died in 1961, aged only fifty-six, of cirrhosis of the liver.

A crucial decision that all Etonians have to make is whether to be a 'wet bob' – a rower – or 'dry bob' – a cricketer. In Valerian's case, the decision was made for him. He came down with a bad attack of measles in the first summer he was at the school and spent most of the 'half' (Eton's word for term) in the sick wing, the 'San'; when he eventually recovered he had missed too much cricket to qualify for a team so he started rowing. This left him with enough time to pursue another sport and he took up shooting, which became one of the enduring pleasures of his life.

When Valerian won his colours in the Eton shooting eight, his grandfather, the 4th Duke, was delighted; himself a keen sportsman, he too had been in Eton's shooting team. Part of the attraction of the sport was that every school weekend the team would travel round the country, playing against their long-standing rivals, including Harrow and Winchester. 'It was great fun,' remembers my father gleefully. 'We weren't much supervised and would often manage to sneak into the local pub for a quick smoke and a glass of beer.'

To Valerian's huge regret, in the year he went to Eton his mother decided to sell Sherfield. For Dorothy the property was uncomfortably close to the Wellington estate and her estranged in-laws. For Valerian the last traces of the halcyon days before his parents' separation disappeared as the house, its moat and the magic island went under the hammer. To this day my father regrets the end of that chapter of his life. Dorothy had, with Vita's help, found a house in Sussex called Penns-in-the-Rocks. On seeing it for the first time Dorothy felt that 'Penns had waited for me all my life'. When Valerian and his sister Elizabeth first visited Penns, their mother made them get out of the car halfway down the drive. 'We ran through a little wood about fifty yards from the drive and there was this great cliff of rocks, and that was exciting.' The rocks would become the setting for endless adventures and escapades, but they could never replace Sherfield and the island.

There was a compensation for the young Valerian. 'I wanted a dog so badly. My mother kept it a secret but one day when I went down for tea in the library at Penns, she said "I have a little present for you". She lifted a cloth off a chair and underneath it was a small Labrador puppy.' The dog was given the name Bess, after the Great Queen, and became the first in a succession of much-loved Labradors. By the time my father entered his tenth decade he had owned ten dogs, the most recent being a golden Labrador named Yasmin. The first of the band of faithful companions was captured in 'Black Bess', a little sketch by Dorothy:

> I am very black and shiny,
> My eyes are like the pebbles of a stream,
> When I was tiny,
> I was very lean.
> But now, I'm very fat.

Bess's image was reproduced on a black and turquoise ashtray made by Elizabeth for her cigarette-smoking brother. When, in 1932, Rex Whistler, a close friend of Dorothy, painted the two Wellesley children on the 'Rocks' with Brutus, their mother's Great Dane, Bess, and Eliza's dog, Dan, can be seen in the background sprinting across the lawn in front of the house.

An important strand of Valerian's life began when, aged fifteen, he joined the Eton corps. Soon after, the cadets had to parade in Windsor Castle in front of the King George V. My father was feeling unwell, and to his huge embarrassment he fainted and had to be carried off. When the ceremony was over Queen Mary asked Valerian what was wrong. 'Well I think I've got measles, Ma'am', he replied. 'Oh poor boy,' said the Queen, and the King added, 'And high time too!' (meaning these childhood diseases must be got rid of). 'It was awful meeting the King and Queen in those circumstances. I remember trying to get to my feet and bow, but I couldn't remain standing because I was feeling so terrible.'

Valerian's father was delighted when he reported that he had joined the Political Society, and full of advice and comment about various aspects of the curriculum. 'I was so glad to get your happy letter and to hear that you have a chance of playing in the school side for soccer,' wrote Gerry to his son early in 1933. 'Why not dissect a comparatively fresh dog-fish, they are often caught I believe and are not very expensive, or get a cod's or salmon's head from a fishmonger.' He would regularly go to the school to see his son, often with Elizabeth. Valerian's mother never visited him at Ludgrove or Eton. 'I think', my father told me, 'it was because she didn't want to embarrass me.' By the time he was a teenager, it became clear to Valerian that his mother's drinking was a problem.

When Valerian entered the final straight of his time at Eton he had grown to be six feet tall and his blond good looks were beginning to attract the attention of girls. His sister Eliza remembers him coming home, 'blowing into the house like a whirlwind' and then off out for furtive trysts with girlfriends, many of whom were older than her. Some of them would turn up at Eton and take him out for tea – preferably in a private house, where innocent kisses would be snatched in the privacy of deep, soft sofas. The most glamorous of these girls were the Paget sisters, daughters of the Earl of Anglesey.

Liz was the first one to turn his head; another was going out with Rex Whistler; later, Rose would become a serious girlfriend. Plas Newydd, the Anglesey home in North Wales, an eighteenth-century house with spectacular views over the Menai Strait and Snowdonia, was the setting for many high-spirited weekends, when the carpet would be rolled up, records would be put on the gramophone and everyone would waltz round the large drawing room. Valerian discovered another lasting pleasure. He loved to dance.

Valerian left Eton in July 1934, just after his nineteenth birthday. 'I wanted to have a career in the army whether there was a war or not. The First Duke was a great hero to me at school, and maybe that was an influence.' If Valerian had got his way he would have gone straight to Sandhurst, but both his father and his tutor at Eton put pressure on him to attend university first. It was advice of which his ancestor would have approved. He had admonished a nephew:

If you are worth your salt you will learn soldiering when you get your commission, and at Cambridge you will get that education both of learning and of habit, which you can never get again. Besides you will have the advantage which a man must always lose who is brought up with a view to a particular profession, the advantage of a free standing-point untrammelled by the ingrained prejudices that take root in the finest minds which are kept in one circle. You can afford the money and the time for two educations, avail yourself of these advantages, be educated first, as if for the pulpit or the bar, and then you will have a double chance of making a first-rate soldier.

The Duke added, 'I would give more than I can mention that I had had a university education.'[36] In the autumn of 1934, with Europe once more threatened by the rise of a dictator, Wellington's great-great-grandson, Valerian, went up to New College, Oxford.

TWO

The Cut of a Soldier

Arthur Wesley joined the army on 7 March 1787 – not long before his eighteenth birthday. 'Arthur has put on his red coat for the first time today ... Anyone can see he has not the cut of a soldier!'[1] wrote his unyielding mother to a friend. Richard had secured the commission for him through patronage and payment, but there was little evidence of familial affection there either; describing Arthur's situation to a possible sponsor as 'perfectly idle', he conceded that 'it is a matter of indifference to me what commission he gets, provided he gets it soon'. The first rung of Arthur's military ladder was as an Ensign in the 73rd (Highland) Regiment of Foot. Apparently, one of the first things the young Ensign did was to weigh a Private, with and without his equipment. 'I was not so young as not to know that since I had undertaken a profession I had better try to understand it,'[2] he told a friend in later life. The 'idle' boy had found his footing.

By the end of the year, Lady Mornington was in a more positive – almost motherly – frame of mind. 'There are so many little things to settle for Arthur who is just got into the army and is to go to Ireland in the capacity of Aid De Camp to Lord Buckingham, and must be set out a little for that, in short I must do everything for him and when you see him you will think him worthy of it,' she wrote breathlessly to her old friends Lady Eleanor Butler and Miss Sarah Ponsonby, who were known as the Ladies of Llangollen. She went on, 'He really is a very charming young man, never did I see such a change for the better in anybody.'[3]

Arthur's ADC's pay would reduce his toll on the family expenses (which no doubt contributed to Lady Mornington's enthusiasm about her son's prospects), but his career was not quite launched. He had transferred into the 76th (Hindoostan) Regiment of Foot to become a Lieutenant but, since they were destined for the East Indies, in January 1788, with the permission of the King, he acquired an exchange to the

41st. On the way to take up his post in Ireland, Arthur passed through Wales and stayed with his maternal grandmother, Lady Dungannon. Together they went to visit the 'Ladies', who agreed with his mother's verdict, pronouncing him 'handsome, fashioned tall and elegant'.[4] This was the young Arthur Wesley who stepped off the packet boat from Holyhead. Eight years before he had left the island as a shy, small boy unable to excel at anything other than playing his fiddle. Now he still carried his violin case, but he had the stride of a confident young man.

Arthur's lodgings in Dublin were at Lower Ormond Quay on the banks of the Liffey, a short ride from the Castle and his duties as one of the ADCs, whom the Vicereine dubbed her 'awkward squad'. These duties revolved round the ceremonial and social life at court. Since 1782 Ireland had hosted its own independent Parliament, but it was still yoked to the British Crown – and most of the guests at the Castle were there by dint of their dependent status, through their titles, pensions or civil posts. Dublin aspired to be one of the most elegant cities in the world, where the arts flourished and an explosion of new buildings offered a view of wide streets and leafy squares surrounded by graceful homes. Arthur threw himself into the rounds of socialising of which the vice-regal court was the centre. Opinions differed about his social skills; a young woman who was lent Dangan as a honeymoon venue described him as 'extremely good humoured and the object of much attention from the female part of what was called "a very gay society"'. Others found him rather 'mischievous' and one fashionable Dublin hostess gave him a lift to a picnic outside Dublin but refused to offer him a ride home: 'He was so dull that I threw him over and and brought back *le beau* Cradock.' Unperturbed, Arthur, who had in any case loitered near the band for part of the evening, got a lift back with the musicians. He had his revenge on his rival when, twenty years later, he replaced Cradock as Commander-in-Chief in Portugal.

When Arthur arrived back in Ireland he was expected to fill the family's Irish parliamentary seat of Trim, left vacant by his elder brother William who had gone to join Richard as an MP at the Palace of Westminster. His election was a foregone conclusion but he had at least to show his face in the borough. There was a hint of his down-to-earth approach to life when he opposed the conferment by Trim of the Freedom of the Corporation on the famous Irish nationalist Henry Grattan by suggesting that mere 'respectability' was no qualifying attribute, since on that basis 'the whole community would belong to the corporation'. He won the day and went on to get elected in spring 1790; but for the next two years the grandeur of Dublin's Parliament House stilled his tongue. Along with all the other silent, undemocratically elected Irish MPs, the twenty-one-year-old with his boyish figure, high colour and red coat crowned with large epaulettes was dismissed by another Irish nationalist, Wolfe Tone, as one of 'the common prostitutes of the Treasury Bench'.

Arthur's youthful enthusiasms embraced all the traditional pursuits of young men with too much time on their hands. He would bet on almost anything, including the time it might take him to walk from Cornelscourt outside Dublin to Leeson Street. *The Times* of 25 September 1789 reported that 'The Hon. Captain Wesley won a bet of one hundred and fifty guineas last week of Mr Whaley by walking five miles in fifty-five minutes.' A less heroic story appeared in the same paper two years later. It concerned a brawl in the house of 'Ann Maria Swettenham' which resulted in Arthur and two fellow ADCs being indicted on three counts, of 'making a great affray', 'riotously and forcibly' entering her house and 'violently assaulting herself, her child, and her servant maid'. Arthur was found guilty and made to pay a fine of £10.[5]

These kinds of court appearances were quite commonplace in the Dublin of the day and likely did not incur the wrath of his family; nor did the imposition of another fine, this time, in an act of pre-cognitive bravado, for beating a Frenchman and seizing his stick in a Dublin bawdy house. But while he was happy to have a good time with his friends, he was also intent on improving his mind – perhaps discreetly, so as not to spoil his racy reputation. When a visitor picked up the book Arthur had been reading in a room at Dangan, they discovered it to be Locke's *Essay Concerning Human Understanding*. The central tenet of Locke's philosophy was that all knowledge derived from experience. Arthur's efforts at self-education had begun.

Arthur's new-found interest in books may have helped to nurture a relationship that would eventually prove to be the most significant of his life. Kitty – (the Hon. Catherine Dorothea Sarah) – Pakenham was a favourite at the court of the Viceroy. Her gaiety, delicate beauty and perfect figure made her stand out from the crowd of young women who danced their way around the ballroom at the Castle. Like Arthur, her background was Anglo-Irish – she was the third daughter of Lord Longford. Her parents' house, Pakenham Hall, was about thirty miles from Dangan and, more pertinently, her maternal grandparents owned a property called Summerhill which was next-door to the Wesleys'.

No one can be sure exactly when Arthur first caught sight of Kitty, but many years later, her niece, Kate Foster, who after being orphaned became like a daughter to Kitty, wrote a brief account of her aunt's relationship with Arthur. 'Often has the Duchess [as Kitty was to become] in speaking of past days described young Arthur Wellesley and his brothers, when visiting at the Castle of Summer Hill, where she, as the gayest of the gay, was then residing. It was there … that she first received the homage of the youthful and ardent heart.' Kitty herself claimed that she was fifteen at the time and that she loved him from the moment she first saw him. Kitty was three years younger than Arthur, so this 'homage' must have been paid soon after he arrived in Ireland. But 'Lady Longford's Lily', as she was known for her fair complexion, was not yet launched in society so he bided his time until, according to Kate Foster, Kitty was 'plunged in the world and sought after by grave and gay admirers'.[6]

Kitty's upbringing had been very different to Arthur's; she came from a warm, supportive family and was close both to her six siblings and to her parents. She had grown up knowing she was loved and appreciated. Like many young women from her background, she could paint, play music, dance and write soulful verse. Her love of books had been nurtured from an early age by her paternal grandmother, Elizabeth, Countess of Longford, a cultivated woman who boasted a large and fine library. Kitty grew up under her mother's regime, in which high fashion was spurned and a strong religious ethic was instilled in the girls. Kitty had many admirers among the young men who did the rounds of the balls, concerts, picnics and other events of the Dublin social calendar, but she would not have had her head turned by the mere cut of an officer's uniform, or his skill on the dance floor. She would, however, have relished a philosophical discussion and have been charmed by a young man's fondness for playing the violin.

By 1792 the flirtation had blossomed into a full romance. When not seeking each other's attention at the social gatherings in Dublin or the surrounding countryside, they spent time at Pakenham Hall or at Coolure, a wild, romantic spot on the shores of Lough Derravaragh, where Kitty's uncle Thomas Pakenham lived. Here the lovers could walk beside the lake in the evening and watch the wild-fowl landing in formation on the small islands scattered around the water. As they embraced in the shelter of twilight, did they talk of a future together? Kitty's enlightened grandmother Elizabeth was all in favour of the relationship, but her parents, though happy to condone a friendship between the couple, could not countenance a marriage. In June 1792 Lord Longford died, but if anything his eldest son, Thomas, who inherited the title, was even more implacably opposed to the union.

Some time in 1792, Arthur made an approach to the new Lord Longford to ask for the hand of his sister. Not only was the proposal summarily dismissed, but Arthur was given a lecture on how he might improve his character and career prospects. He was reminded (as if he needed to be) that he was merely a younger son with no inheritance coming his way, whose energies, according to the account Kitty gave to Kate, 'had seldom been displayed, except in gaiety, which was his delight, and music which was his favourite occupation'. Thomas saw no reason to throw his sought-after sister away on a penniless young cavalryman whose family had all but abandoned Ireland in favour of their British rulers.

This was a pivotal moment in my great-great-great-grandfather's life. Having overcome the effects of a lonely, introspective childhood, surrounded by siblings who were more successful and self-possessed, there still lurked within him the memory of his father's sweet melodies on the violin, and the satisfaction of discovering his own modest talent with the instrument. Though this sensitive, artistic side to his nature may have helped him fall in love, ultimately it had won him no favours in his advance through life. He realised that he had to sacrifice his violin. Elizabeth Longford, for me the pre-eminent Wellington biographer, describes his dramatic action: 'He burnt it in the summer of 1793 with his own hands: burnt the hours strolling beside the little waves at Coolure, the bouquet of wine at Angers, the dozing in Brussels, the mooning by the Thames at Eton and the lingering on the ancient bridge over the Boyne at Trim; burnt all the dreams and poetry going back to his childhood when he had listened enraptured to his father's playing.'[7]

In future years observant eyes would note his slender fingers, but though music would be one of the pleasures of his life, Arthur never played the violin again.

*

In the autumn of 1934, when my father went up to Oxford, Europe was already shaping up for war. Hitler had become Chancellor of Germany the year before, and Mussolini was poised to invade Abyssinia. But as Valerian settled into his digs, he could not have known that it would be only five years before the world was once more gripped by conflict and he would be called to serve his country. For now, though, he was determined to have fun, and his most useful assets were his dashing good looks and his highly polished evening shoes.

My father has always loved dancing – a pleasure that survives into his nineties – and when he was a young man he spent many evenings gliding round grand ballrooms or smooching in subterranean nightclubs. His father had insisted that his son went to New College – known for educating hardworking Wykehamists – rather than Christ Church, the more traditional option for an old Etonian. However, New College was a creditable alternative for a future soldier: in the First World War, it was second only to Christ Church in the number of its members killed in action. But if my grandfather hoped the choice of college would restrain Valerian's extra-curricular activities, he was to be disappointed. Valerian spent much of his free time at Christ Church, where most of his friends were undergraduates, and often he headed up to London.

'This Young Man Will Cause a Flutter', was the headline in one society column. It went on:

> Mr Wellesley . . . is going to cause plenty of interest among the susceptible young women (if there are any nowadays, when it is more fashionable to be impressive than impressionable) who will be debutantes this year.
>
> He is very fair, very good-looking, and has the kind of polished elegance you would expect from his father's son.
>
> Lord Gerald Wellesley's exceedingly alert and well-informed brain seems to have been shared by this young man, too.
>
> When the time for Commem. balls comes round again, there will be some memorable Oxford parties circling round this particular under-graduate.

My father laughed when I read him this cutting from a scrapbook. 'I think I would take issue with several of those statements – not least of which "alert and well-informed brain!"' He read History and Languages, but his memories of studies are overtaken by those of his social life. He admits (rather ruefully) that it took him four years to get his degree; he was rusticated for a year after failing a French exam. Soon after going to Oxford he was invited to become a member of the exclusive Bullingdon Club, famously satirised as the 'Bollinger Club' in Evelyn Waugh's *Decline and Fall*. There was a club dinner at least once a week, and an annual dinner where the members all donned their distinctive dress – Oxford blue tailcoats, with ivory silk lapel facings and brass monogrammed buttons, and mustard waistcoats. 'I can still get into mine' claims my father, though recently he gave it to a grandson.

Oxford was regarded by the society pages as being a suburb of London's West End,[8] where in the mid-1930s the nightlife was pulsating. Britain was emerging from the Depression, which had seen unemployment reach 3 million in 1932. The season was packed with grand parties and there was a tantalising array of clubs, from the smartest – the Four Hundred or the Café de Paris, where white tie was mandatory – to livelier venues like the Nest and the Bag of Nails which boasted hot jazz and welcoming girls.

One evening my father and I sat at Apsley House, sipping sherry while he reminisced about those days. 'The dances were things like the Charleston, foxtrot and waltzes – slow which I hated, and Viennese which I loved.' My father learnt to dance after spending a couple of holidays in Munich. One of the young men who went with him was Tommy Clyde, whose father was American but who had grown up in England with his mother, first met Valerian at Eton and become a close friend at Oxford. One view of the upper echelons of London society was that it 'consisted of six hundred people who all knew each other and much of what was going on between each other but who successfully kept this knowledge from the outside world'.[9] The season dominated the social calendar; from the start of spring, every Monday *The Times* published a list of the events and parties over the coming months.

All the hostesses had lists of approved young men – and a few die-hard older ones. White tie – tail-coat and stiff collar – was obligatory for dances or balls and the evening had an established routine. The hostess of the ball would give her own dinner party for the most favoured guests, and there would be other satellite dinners. 'When you arrived at the ball, everyone was given a dance card and you would rush around making sure you "booked" all your favourite girls.' Rendezvous would be agreed – under 'that chandelier' or near the 'champagne bar' – and the chaperones would sit near the dance floor, the more elderly ones occasionally raising their lorgnettes to check that their charges were behaving in a decorous fashion.

There was no shortage of men but not all of them were deemed desirable – a classification that required a young man to be good-looking, a good dancer and good company, and (an essential factor for the mothers) from a 'good' family. One girl described how, when she looked at her mother, she could 'always tell what sort of chap I was dancing with by her expression – smiles for rich young lordlings, down to positive frowns for penniless subalterns!'[10] Valerian got enough 'ticks' to ensure that he was on most of the guest lists. 'You were always meant to ask the girls that had been sitting on either side of you at the dinner to dance and you'd get a black mark if you didn't.' When the party was drawing to an end, some of the more chaperoned girls would have been taken home by their mothers but some were allowed more latitude. 'You had to go and ask permission to take their daughter off to a club. You'd have to say which one you were going to and you would be given strict instructions as to when they had to be back home.'

Valerian would go off in a group, often sharing a taxi with another couple. When they got to the Four Hundred, the newly opened club that became the smartest and most fashionable in London, the doorman would recognise 'Mr Wellesley' and, after signing the book, they would be ushered into the club. If my father had been unusually efficient, or had a thought-through plan to impress a particular girl, he would have booked a table. The head waiter, who was called Mario, ran a system where all the members had their own bottles of whisky. 'When I returned home after four years away at war, Mario gave me a big hug and I said to him, "I know it's a long time ago but I don't suppose I have got any booze left?" He went and had a look and came back with half a bottle of whisky with a line drawn where the level had been on the bottle and the date I had last been there.' My father was always itching to get on the dance floor. 'I loved the smoochy dances, like a foxtrot. My favourite tune was "Night and Day".' At this point my father broke into song, and had we been able to put a Cole Porter record on a gramophone, I think we would have found ourselves dancing round the library at Apsley House – as we have done, many a time, at family parties.

The year after my father went up to Oxford the country marked George V's Silver Jubilee – a chance, amongst other things, to celebrate the end of the Depression. Fashion embraced the occasion: there were Jubilee dresses, hats, and even fingernails – painted red, white and blue and emblazoned with a small gold crown.[11] But on 20 January 1936 the King died, and the exuberance of the previous year yielded to black armbands and the sombre colours of mourning. Many thought it a bad omen when, on the way to Westminster Hall for the lying-in-state, the Maltese Cross which adorned the Imperial State Crown, sitting on the coffin, fell to the ground to be retrieved by a Sergeant-Major from the Grenadiers.[12] The new King, who was following the bier, was heard to exclaim, 'Christ! What will happen next?'[13] As the popular Prince of Wales ascending the throne, he was the first bachelor King since George III and the object of many a young woman's fantasy. Gradually, however, over the following months speculation and rumour mounted as King Edward VIII's romance with Mrs Simpson became known.

My aunt remembers that Wallis Simpson rented a house in Regent's

Park, near their father's home in Chester Terrace. 'We weren't supposed to know, but the King would be nipping in and out to see her. I met Wallis once when I went to the ballet with my father. I remember she was beautifully made up and very gracious.' My father recollects that his parents' generation were very shocked by the way the King flaunted the relationship when, during the summer, the couple went on a yacht, cruising round the Aegean. However, he and his friends were not that distracted by it, being too caught up in their own adventures.

That summer, by now sharing digs above a barber's shop with, amongst others, Jack Profumo, Valerian celebrated his coming-of-age. His mother complained triumphantly to her friend W.B. Yeats that she had been unable to copy out a poem due to the 'arrival of that whirlwind my boy for his 21st birthday'. A few weeks before, in June, an informal Bullingdon Club photograph had been taken. Jack, who remained a close friend of my father's, is not among the group – he may have been sitting his finals on that day. However, Neville (later Lord) Wigram, a fellow Old Bullingdonian, nonagenarian and MC-decorated officer, brings a copy to a reunion lunch of the two old soldiers. All the young men in the black-and-white photograph are wearing different garb – some in tails, others in tweed jackets and baggy caps. Of course my eye is instantly drawn to my father, not only because he is standing in the centre of the group, but also because of his dapper appearance. 'It was a grey flannel, pin-stripe, double-breasted suit', he instantly remembers when I show it to him. Sporting a long-collared shirt, Bullingdon tie and a silk hand-kerchief in his right-hand pocket, he strikes a nonchalant pose. His hair looks as if it has been 'coifed' with some oil – 'I had a natural wave and a lot more hair then,' he says a touch defensively, for which there is no need. In today's parlance, he looks extremely 'cool'.

Neville and he reminisce about those days. Both of them joined the Oxford University Training Corps (OUTC), but there were other students who vocally opposed the idea of war; in early June there had been a debate at the Oxford Union 'That Peace and Freedom are not safe in the hands of the Conservative Party'. One of the speakers was Harry Pollitt, Secretary of the Communist Party of Great Britain; while the meeting was going on, the audience could hear fireworks being let off and the sound of a hunting horn. In the end the motion was carried by 234 votes to 122, prompting the Secretary of State for War, Duff Cooper, to dismiss the resolution as 'a foolish action by a lot of silly boys'.[14] Neville, who was at Magdalen, remembers Cooper coming down to the university to address the OUTC. 'He reminded us that Germany was rapidly rearming and that we would all be called upon.'

My father, while not immune to the political debates of the time (he canvassed briefly for the Conservative Party in his mother's constituency), never questioned his role in the event of a war: fighting for his country was part of his 'raison d'être'. The League of Nations had censured Mussolini's invasion of Abyssinia in October 1935, though in effect Britain and France stood limply on the side-lines. But the British public's opinions of events in Europe were beginning to polarise and the Spanish Civil War, which began in July 1936, reinforced this tendency. Many saw the choices as stark ones – anarchy against order, fascism against communism. 'I remember that some of my mother's friends went off to fight against Franco.' On the Wellesley side of the family, Valerian's grandfather, who had died in 1934, was succeeded by his 'Uncle Charlie', who actively supported the Franco cause.

As a harbinger of ill-tidings, on 30 November 1936 Londoners' gazes were caught in horrified wonder by the sight of the Crystal Palace on fire; the glow from the flames could be seen over the whole city. Eleven days later, King Edward VIII's abdication speech was broadcast to the nation. A rumour briefly circulated that the Duke of York would refuse the throne, and instead it would pass to Princess Elizabeth, with Queen Mary as Regent. 'I was staying in a house party, and like everyone else that was there, I felt very sad. He was much older than me, but I knew him slightly, and at one moment he had had a romance with my first cousin, Anne Wellesley, Morny [the 6th Duke]'s sister.' Valerian's sister Eliza was in Paris at a finishing school. 'All the girls were all in tears', she told me. 'We all thought he was a very glamorous figure – wildly good-looking and attractive. And it was all so romantic – the handsome prince giving up his throne for love.' It was a dramatic ending to the year. As the *Daily Telegraph* commented, 'Serious alarms at home, graver alarms abroad, a deepening sense of gathering storms, feverish military, naval and aerial preparations, revolution and civil war have kept Europe continually on tenterhooks ... Within a single twelvemonth three Kings have reigned over us.'[15]

A week before the coronation of George VI, 'Miss Elizabeth Wellesley – Coronation Debutante' was featured in *The Bystander*.

Miss Elizabeth Wellesley is the only daughter of Lord and Lady Gerald Wellesley; her mother will present her at one of the Courts and is giving a dance for her on June 29th. She was a maid of honour at Queen Charlotte's

Ball last week; is eighteen this year. Lord Gerald Wellesley is a brother of the Duke of Wellington, he was appointed Surveyor of His Majesty's Works of Art last year. Lady Gerald Wellesley, who was Miss Dorothy Ashton, of Croughton, Cheshire, has won a considerable reputation with her poems, and has written a life of Sir George Goldie, founder of Nigeria. She and her husband have a London house in Regent's Park, and an attractive place, Penns Rocks, at Withyham, in Sussex. They have one son, Arthur Valerian, aged 12.[16]

The caption accompanied a full-page black-and-white portrait of my aunt Eliza. Apart from the misprint of my father's age, it highlights the awkwardness of the Gerald Wellesleys' arrangements when it came to the coming-out of their daughter; appearances had to be kept up. 'The prospect of going about London with ―― [Gerry] to bring Elizabeth out (who is anyway already out) is enough to destroy me',[17] Dorothy had written earlier in the year, but knew she had to do her duty. On 2 March Eliza's mother took her to her first dance – and had to recuperate immediately with three weeks' holiday in France, in time for the 'next misery'.[18] 'The whole thing was hell for my mother, and I'm impressed that she managed to get through any of it. She hated parties', Eliza told me.

The coronation of King George VI outdid even the Jubilee and became the last great British celebration of Empire. Department stores vied with each other to achieve the most patriotic display of royal and imperial symbols and images: one Indian Rajah was so impressed with Selfridges' efforts – 'The Empire's Homage to the Throne' – that he bought the display and shipped it back to India to re-erect in his palace.[19] Dorothy described the coronation season as a 'mixture of dignity and vulgarity', but she steeled herself to do what was expected of her. She was present at the first court of the new King and Queen, dressed by Rosemary of Brook Street in a 'Gown of gold and pink lamé. A gold trim lined with pink.'

My grandmother was not the only one who regarded the whole ritual with some dread. 'I didn't enjoy the season,' says my aunt. 'There were these ghastly lunches – I couldn't understand why I had to go and have lunch with a load of giggling schoolgirls. And then you'd get back and maybe there would be a cocktail party, then a dinner, and then a dance – sometimes more than one a night. The worst of it was that my father insisted that I was down to breakfast at 8.30 the following morning!' She admits, however, that her father was very long-suffering when, due to her mother's increasing absence, he had to assume the role of chaperone. 'I don't remember my mother coming to many of the dances but my father was wonderful. He would patiently sit with all the other chaperones but his eyes would light up when I said I wanted to go home.'

As the season progressed, the rules were slackened: Eliza simply did not come down for breakfast and she learnt to how to finesse the overwhelming array of functions. Her mother gave 'a small dance' (as it was described in the 'Season's Lists' in *The Times*) for her on Wednesday, 29 June, borrowing 21 Park Lane, her Scarbrough stepfather's house. 'The truth is that I don't remember very much about it,' says my aunt. When we look at the list of guests, she comments, 'They're mainly all my father's friends. My mother must have loathed it.' The group invited for dinner included Gerry and Valerian, Mitey (now married to Robert – 'Bobbie' – James), Rex Whistler and a gang of friends of Valerian's – Nick Villiers, 'G' Gerard Leigh, George Brodrick and Eric Penn. Jack Harris's band played and the house was filled with the scent of sweetpeas.

Two days later, my aunt was presented at court. 'It was terrifying – walking across a crowded room and then giving a perfect curtsey. Even though I had met the King and Queen, I was so nervous – worried that I would trip or something.' Eliza was also anxious lest something would happen with her mother, who presented her. 'But she did look marvellous,' she remembers wistfully, 'she had wonderful pale skin like Valerian. She could be very elegant.'

Away from grand parties, for Eliza and her fellow debutantes some of the raunchier nightclubs were daring, dangerous places precisely because they were decreed by the chaperones to be out-of-bounds. 'I was determined to go to the Bag of Nails, and persuaded a great friend of my brother and me [Rupert Gerard] to take me. Valerian was quite protective of me and was furious with both of us, but probably more with his friend.' Millie Hoey, who ran the club, was a well-known figure in London nightlife of the 1930s, and she became a friend to many of the young men, and some of the girls. She was invited to all the weddings, including my aunt Eliza's, and when my father was away in the war he, like many of his fellow officers, would get cards from 'Millie and all the girls'.

My father would never talk openly to me about his sexual conquests, but the nature of relationships formed with girls he met in the Bag of Nails was very different from those with the debutantes or other girls who had done the season. But 'gels' from upper-class families could get reputations for being 'fast' and young men from similar backgrounds would be viewed as 'bounders' if they treated women badly. Flirtations in the smoke-filled clubs, with sultry jazz playing in the background, were exciting but mostly innocent. Even if the fumbling continued in the back of the cab, a young man, when he delivered a girl back to her anxious parent, would never be invited into the house. The gossip columns of the day were mild concoctions of social commentaries about parties and their hostesses, and what everyone was wearing; rarely did they stray into speculation about affairs, whether inside or outside a marriage. 'Nothing ever got into the papers,' says my father. 'There were "social columns" in magazines like the *Tatler* and *Bystander*, where they just used to talk of who they had seen at Lady So-and-So's ball or an Ascot race meeting, but never any serious sort of gossip. Except, occasionally, if there was a notorious adultery going on and then only in very guarded language.'

Perhaps not surprisingly, in the spring of 1938 my father failed his finals and was sent down to equip himself for the next attempt. 'I went to a crammer in London. I stayed in some lodgings in Oakley Street. I was out every night, so it was even worse than being at Oxford. I also did a stint in France to polish up my French.' His recently widowed landlady, an attractive forty-year-old, ensured that when my father returned to Oxford he not only passed his finals, but also was less innocent in other respects. When Valerian left Oxford with his degree, he did not regard the academic qualification as essential for his chosen career. 'I think from quite a young age I wanted to be a soldier. I couldn't imagine leading a life which involved sitting in an office. I hated the idea of going into business or the Stock Exchange or anything like that. I wanted an outdoor life. And I wanted to see the world, get around a bit, not be too static, not get too stuck in one place.'

In September 1938, as the Munich Crisis loomed, many were convinced that war was not only inevitable, but imminent. So desperate was my father to enlist that he flew down from the West Coast of Scotland where he was fishing and stalking and reported to the Grenadiers' headquarters. 'They took one look at me and said, "When we want you we'll let you know." I remember feeling very humiliated.' The Grenadiers were the family regiment and, as far as Valerian's father was concerned, there was never any question of his son joining another. But my father ended up in The Blues – the Royal Horse Guards. To this day, he is rather sheepish about what went wrong. 'They wouldn't have me!' he protests. When I press him for the reason behind this rejection, he concedes that it might have had something to do with his failure to answer letters. One of his old friends from that time, Colonel David Smiley, recalls there were always 'loads of brown envelopes lying around for Valerian. I seem to remember that he didn't turn up for an interview.' 'My father was furious that I didn't go into the Grenadiers. He never quite forgave me.'

But my grandfather's fury at his son's defection was more than matched by my grandmother's delight: Scamp, her beloved brother who had died in 1912, had been in The Blues, and when Valerian donned his uniform the sight of the young, fair officer would have conjured up memories of him. There were other serendipitous aspects: Valerian owed his commission to two senior officers of the regiment, 'Reggie' (Earl of) Pembroke and 'Charlie' Anglesey. Both men had been close friends of Scamp, and Valerian had often stayed with the Angleseys at Plas Newydd. Anglesey, a descendant of Wellington's brave second-in-command at Waterloo, was also the father of Lady Rose Paget, whom, in 1938, my father had begun to court.

Both of Rose's parents were unconventional: her father, though Lord Chamberlain to Queen Mary, was a keen home-movie maker, notably of 'Pink Shirts', which sought to parody Mosley's British Union of Fascists; her mother was both artistic and bohemian. Rose inherited these unconventional streaks and became a ballet dancer at Sadler's Wells. 'To my Darling Valerian with love from Rose', she wrote on a black-and-white photograph she gave to my father in 1938. Many years later, after her death, one of her obituaries told the story: 'Her most prominent and persistent suitor was the handsome Valerian Wellesley ... although Rose Paget twice allowed herself to become engaged to Wellesley, twice she broke it off.'[20] I have never quite pinpointed what went wrong; my father is hazy about the details but they did spend his last holiday before the war together, when they went to Klosters to ski with a group of other young people including my aunt Eliza and Tommy Clyde. Six months after the war began Rose married a young Squadron Leader, John McLaren. He died a tragically early death in 1953. As Rose McClaren, she remained one of my father's most treasured friends until the day she died.

It was soon after the skiing holiday, in April 1939, that my father enlisted in The Blues. There followed six weeks of intensive training at Stoney Castle Camp, Pirbright, but it seems not to have dented Valerian's ability to have fun. Often accompanied by fellow cadet and close friend Tommy Clyde, he would find himself driving back to camp from London in his old 'banger' in time to be on parade at 6.30 a.m. 'I would then have to put on uniform and supervise the recruits doing PT or something. I sat one morning on a horse in the gym and I remember Tommy coming up to me and saying "For God's sake wake up, you're fast asleep and get that lipstick off your face", after having got in at five, and this was about half past six. We had great stamina but how we didn't kill ourselves I don't know. I suppose there was very little traffic and it took about half an hour down the Great West Road.'

After Pirbright my father, now officially a junior officer – Cornet Wellesley – was based at Windsor, where his induction as a cavalryman continued.

> We used to start the day by going to riding school at some ungodly hour, with the riding instructor who was called the Rough Riding Corporal-Major. One would go round and round, either bare-back or with your stirrups crossed over so that you were just riding on the saddle without stirrups, which was very uncomfortable. If he was in a really bad temper, it was 'off, dismount, three horses up, move' and you used to run forward and jump onto another horse three ahead, which was effectively a punishment for being lazy. We did exactly the same drill as the troopers, except when we were parading on the square, when the officers had to take command at the head of their troops. Then there were things like sword, lance and revolver drill. You had to jump fences and put your sword through a dummy and then you had to return your sword, which was very difficult, then pick up a tent peg off the ground with your lance, then pull out your pistol and jump another fence and shoot another dummy. All these were old Cavalry exercises and were part of the normal training for a young officer.

All ranks, officers included, were drilled in every aspect of how to look after their horses. 'I used to be able to cold-shoe a horse,' says my father. 'I couldn't make the actual shoe but did all the rest, including nailing the shoe to the horse's hoof – which obviously required total precision. I really enjoyed working with the farriers.'

As the pace of events in Europe quickened – in the middle of March Hitler had marched into Prague, by the end of that month Franco's Nationalists had won the Spanish Civil War – conscription was introduced. By the summer trenches had been dug in Kensington Gardens, barrage balloons hung over London, and at the seaside holidaymakers were helping to stuff sandbags. Everywhere there were posters giving advice about how to deal with a gas attack – *Vogue* even featured a handbag specially made to disguise gas-masks – but the King and Queen maintained normality by going ahead with their tour of Canada. Contingency plans were put in place: France agreed, in the event of war, to provide British subjects with enough petrol to get them to a Channel port.

But the partying went on; if anything, there were even more balls than in a normal season. As the *Tatler* of 12 July insouciantly reported: 'Despite the none-too-good news from Europe the social racket still goes on and quite right too, for what is the use of squealing before you are hurt?'[21] One party in particular sticks in the memory of my father: held on 17 July, it was given for Barbara McNeill, a popular blue-eyed blonde. Her mother's house was conveniently close to Penns, and Valerian had met her earlier in the year. 'I adored Barbara', my father says, as he thinks back to that summer nearly seventy years later. 'She was a very sweet person and a wonderful dancer.' His romance with Rose Paget was over; it was to be the memory of Barbara's shy smile and infectious laugh which would accompany my father when he finally set off for war.

As August drew to a close, all the young men were called up to their regiments – sometimes through tannoy systems in public places. On 1 September Hitler's troops marched across the border into Poland, and the next day, as a mass evacuation of mothers and children from cities went on, the Cabinet finally agreed to send an ultimatum the following morning. When Chamberlain made his broadcast to the nation at 11.15 a.m. on 3 September, announcing, 'This country is at war with Germany', my father was on guard at Windsor, standing on the ramparts looking over the town. 'The prospect of war had been hanging over our heads for so long that in some ways it was a relief. But none of us underestimated the seriousness. We had grown up with our parents talking about the horrors of the First World War.'

The young men and women who had danced their way through the previous few years now exchanged letters, wishing each other 'luck'. My grandfather had joined the Grenadiers – relieved that at last he could serve his country; in the First World War he had been forced to remain in the Diplomatic Service. My grandmother – still mourning the loss of her great friend Yeats, who had died in January of that year – prepared Penns for evacuated children, as she and her friend Hilda Matheson supervised the digging of trenches in the garden.

Eliza was with her mother at Penns on the day war broke out. For some time she had been going out with her brother's friend, Tommy Clyde. After hearing the broadcast on the wireless she went into her bedroom and wept for fear of the unknown world, and the anguish that might lie ahead. Knowing that at any moment Tommy could be sent off with his regiment – the Second Household Cavalry – on 6 November the couple announced their engagement. Two weeks later they were married. Valerian was going to give his sister away, but at the last minute Gerry managed to get back from France where he was involved with a wartime Intelligence operation, and Eliza walked down the aisle on the arm of her father. The church – St Peter's, Vere Street – was chosen because, according to my aunt, 'it had the shortest aisle'. She admits that she would have preferred to 'go off and get married in a registry office' without any fuss. Her mother, insisting that in wartime it would be inappropriate, forbade her to wear white. Instead Eliza wore 'a wide-skirted dress of sapphire-blue velvet under a short, close-fitting jacket'. Her 'halo hat' was of similar velvet, and her bag, to match the outfit, concealed a gas-mask. Valerian was best man. Inevitably, the occasion carried the strain of Gerald and Dorothy appearing together in public; it was the first time they had seen each other for several years.

The highlight of the reception (at Gerald's house in Chester Terrace) was the wedding cake, designed by Rex Whistler and made by Fortnum & Mason. Rex was a familiar figure to both Valerian and Eliza when they were growing up. Eliza had had a big 'crush' on the artist, who would write exquisitely illustrated letters to her. For Eliza, one of the saddest days of the war was in July 1944, when she heard of Rex's death in France. One of the wax garlands of flowers which crowned the cake hangs today in a frame on the wall of my aunt's sitting room, a poignant token of love and loss.

Naturally my father is wistful about some aspects of his pre-war life. 'I had a wonderful, fun time with a mass of interesting friends – men and women. I admit that I didn't think much about the future and I can see that I led quite a narrow life, but we had a fairly fatalistic attitude. We knew war was coming and that some of us would not return, and we just wanted to have a good time while we could.' By the time the guns stopped firing across the world he was married, had a child and had become the heir to a dukedom. And the social order that had ruled his world had gone for ever.

*

After the Longfords' rejection of his proposal in 1792 Arthur may yet have felt the door to Kitty was still ajar, so he sought to prove himself in the eyes of her family. He finally opened his mouth in the Irish Parliament. He condemned the imprisonment of Louis XVI and France's invasion of the Netherlands and, closer to home and more controversially, he supported the government's move towards a more liberal attitude to Roman Catholics. 'I have no doubt of the loyalty of the Catholics of this country, and I trust that when the question shall be brought forward, we shall lay aside animosities, and act with moderation and dignity, and not with the fury and violence of partisans.'[22] Of course his words fell on deaf ears: a few days after his speech the French King's head was triumphantly held up to the crowds in the Place de la Révolution. And it would be another thirty-six years before Arthur's convictions on Catholic Emancipation were put to the test.

Arthur maintained his rapid progress up the military ladder as, in the course of the year, with money borrowed from his eldest brother, he acquired commissions – first as a Major and, soon after, a Lieutenant-Colonel – in the 33rd Regiment of Foot. This was the regiment that, many years later, would proudly carry his name. Buoyed up by his enhanced professional status, Arthur made a second proposal to Kitty, some time in 1794. But once again he was flatly rejected. Tantalisingly, only one letter from this whole episode survives; undated but headed 'Barracks, Tuesday', it is addressed to the 'Hon. C.D.S. Pakenham'.

> If this letter should reach you, I hope you will impute my troubling you this second time to the fear I have that my first letter may have offended. It never was intended to offend, and if any expression it contained could at all tend to give offence, I hope that the determination I have just received is, in your eyes, a sufficient punishment for a crime of much greater magnitude.
>
> As Lord Longford's determination is founded upon prudential motives and may be changed should my situation be altered before I return to Ireland, I hope you will believe that should anything occur which may induce you and him to change your minds, my mind will still remain the same. In the mean time with best wishes for your happiness believe me
>   Your most attached and obedient servant
>   A.Wesley[23]

'My mind will still remain the same': these seven words would help seal the fate of Arthur's personal life. Kitty was heartbroken. Her brother and her mother forbade her to have any contact with Arthur and she gave a solemn undertaking that she would uphold this ban.

Though contact was forbidden, Kitty would have followed Arthur's progress anxiously. As he kicked his heels waiting for his chance of going to war, he still had to make the occasional visit to Ireland, to seek favours from the Viceroy or on family business; Dangan had been sold by Richard. Did she ever torment herself by contriving to be in the same place as he – to catch a glimpse of his face? She was still a young and pretty girl whose popularity would have ensured that she was bidden to all the parties at the Castle and the assemblies in the Rotunda ballroom.

Forced to forswear his love, Arthur now focused on getting mud on his uniform. Fortunately for posterity, he failed to be chosen for an expeditionary force, most of the members of which were struck down by yellow fever and ended up in a graveyard in Martinique. Finally, in the middle of 1794, he got his wish when he sailed from Cork to Ostend and his first engagement with the enemy.

Since the beginning of 1793, England had been at war with revolutionary France. The British Army was ill-equipped and poorly trained; many new recruits had no uniforms or weapons and suffered both from lack of discipline and the leadership to impose it. Unlike the navy, there was no formal training for army officers, most of whom had, like Arthur, acquired their commissions through a combination of purchase and patronage. They were detached, both geographically and professionally, from their men; later in life Arthur recalled this: 'No one knew anything of the management of an army ... we had letters from England, and I declare that those letters told us more of what was passing at headquarters than we learned from the headquarters themselves'.[24]

Arthur had the misfortune of being part of the Duke of York's ill-fated expedition in the Netherlands. He acquitted himself well, however; he made his first independent strategic decision when he moved his troops by sea to be in a better defensive position, and when he was about to face enemy fire for the first time he calmly held his ground to the advancing French column until, at the last minute, he gave the order to his troops to fire a volley. The location was Boxtel in Holland; the date 15 September 1794. This modest engagement marked the start of a series of personal military victories which would culminate twenty-one years later at Waterloo – less than a hundred miles away.

Soon after, he was being treated for an 'aguish complaint', from fatigue and damp. He left a strong impression on one of the doctors he consulted. 'I have been attending a young man whose conversation is the most extraordinary I have ever listened to ... If he lives he must one day be Prime Minister.'[25] The following year Arthur was back in Dublin, acting once again as an ADC to the Viceroy – by now Lord Camden – and sitting in the Irish Parliament as the inconstant member for Trim. He was desperate to get a new job and even attempted to obtain a position as a civil servant working at the Irish Revenue or Treasury Boards, writing obsequious letters to that end: 'I assure you nothing but the circumstances under which I labour would induce me to trouble Your Excellency's Government.'[26]

Luckily the army beckoned once more; his regiment was destined for the West Indies. Arthur, still suffering from ill-health, was prescribed four different pills, one of which could be used with the 'best success for dogs and horses' and, if it did not work, should be strengthened with 'two tablespoons of melted grease or the fat of a freshly killed fowl'.[27] He survived the medical regime and set sail in November 1795, only to find himself at the mercy of a violent storm. Seven ships from his convoy were wrecked and the others, in a battered state, returned to Portsmouth. The second attempt was even more futile: after seven weeks of being tossed about on the waves by unforgiving winter weather his ship was blown back to England. As they sat out the rest of the winter in the calm retreat of Poole, events overtook the regiment and their destination was changed from the West to the East – India and its princely riches.

Providence had intervened. Arthur was spared a watery grave or a lonely tomb in a West Indian cemetery. He was now poised to enter the phase of his life which would shape and define his career. This time he knew that he would be away for a long period, and he methodically put everything in place for his departure. He briefed his successor to the parliamentary seat of Trim; his brother Richard had identified a cousin who could take over the responsibility. Richard was determined to remove all vestiges of the family from Ireland: 'If Arthur has good luck he will be called to act on a greater stage than dear Dublin.'[28]

Before he set sail, Arthur spent nearly £60 on books at 'Mr Faulder', a bookseller in Bond Street. He was minded to make good use of the long journey. Included in the list of purchases were works by Rousseau, Voltaire, Frederick the Great and Plutarch. Conscious of a wide gap in his education, he purchased *Caesaris Commentaria* – in Latin. Adam Smith's *Wealth of Nations* is listed, as are twenty-four volumes of Jonathan Swift. There were several books about India as well as dictionaries, grammars and maps. Almost all the books that he packed in a corded trunk bought for the purpose were intended to equip himself for the task that lay ahead, and to improve his knowledge of the world.

In June 1796, with the prospect of a six-month journey to a distant land, the twenty-seven-year-old Arthur Wesley finally set sail with a heavy trunk and a crushed heart. His future adversary was several steps ahead of him. Napoleon had already been appointed Commander-in-Chief of the Army of Italy and after several decisive victories had entered Milan; he had also become a husband – he married the widowed Josephine de Beauharnais, six years his junior, in March 1796. Napoleon's rise to the higher ranks of the French army had been prodigious. Arthur may have purchased his place in the British Army, but over the next nine years, doggedly and determinedly, he would learn his craft. By the time he returned, no one, least of all his family, would be able to say 'he has not the cut of a soldier'.

THREE

Gallantries of Dreams

In the summer of 1940 Valerian Wellesley was living in a tent which was pitched on the paddock of Aintree racecourse in Liverpool. He was sharing the billet with John Warrender. The two young men were among many waiting to embark with their regiments for the Middle East. John, an officer in the Scots Greys, had been sleeping in a box in the grandstand, but when he bumped into Valerian, a tent out in the open air seemed a more appealing prospect. The days were long and hot, ideal weather for carefree holidays, but with no organised routine the heat served only to increase the soldiers' frustration. Britain had just managed to evacuate half a million troops from Dunkirk and Churchill had delivered his iconic 'We'll fight them on the beaches' speech. The country was on standby for a German invasion. All the men camped at Aintree were desperate to play their part – to get on with the job of fighting a war.

The soldiers under Valerian's command saw a mild-looking officer who appeared younger than his twenty-four years. Driven by boredom and inactivity, they started to play up and provoke him, hoping to take advantage of his inexperience. Early one morning, on one of the hottest days of the year, Valerian ordered his men to form up on the racecourse in full kit. After parading, the men were issued with basic rations and, with Lieutenant Wellesley at the head of the column, taken on a twenty-mile march. With the briefest stop for food and water, the soldiers trod the lanes of Aintree until they could scarcely put one foot in front of the other. 'When Valerian returned his feet were so blistered he could hardly walk,' remembered John, 'but after that he never got another peep out of his men. Valerian was gentle-looking but extremely tough – and I admired him enormously.' Warrender, who succeeded to the title of Lord Bruntisfield, became a valued friend of my father's and I went to visit him in Edinburgh to get some insight into what were strange, unsettling days – waiting for their war to begin.

'When I first met Valerian I was still at Eton and he was this glamorous young man from Oxford who used to breeze in when I was having tea with Eliza, and Billy [Eliza's governess] would make a huge fuss of him. He seemed much older [six years] and I minded my "ps and qs" with him a bit but he had everything that I was longing to get, like a car.' When they met up again at Aintree, John was flattered that Valerian was so friendly to him – 'he treated me like a younger brother' – and they quickly fell in together. The decisive twelve-hour exercise for his troublesome troops sorted one of Valerian's problems, but it did not solve the challenge of how to spend the idle days waiting for news of embarkation. After Italy entered the war in mid-June Allied ships could not sail through the Mediterranean, and moving vast numbers of soldiers became a more complicated and lengthy exercise. Troop movements were kept from everyone until the last minute for fear that the information would fall into enemy hands. As the summer progressed, Paris fell to Hitler (conspicuously photographed visiting Napoleon's tomb) and a little bit of Britain was invaded as the Germans occupied the Channel Islands. To keep fit and pass the time, every morning Valerian and John would run round the racecourse, jumping some of the smaller fences. 'We ran out of steam pretty quickly, but if we'd had a competition, Valerian would have won hands down!'

The mess was in the Winner's Enclosure and the old tins from rations were all buried near the 'Chair' – 'I expect they're still there, just where the horses land'. When a group of French marines who had been evacuated from Dunkirk arrived, their billet was next door to the famous 'Canal' jump. Both John and Valerian volunteered to make contact with them and act as interpreters, Valerian finally putting to good use the months spent in France on leave from his elongated spell at Oxford. The 'Free French' who had recently been set up by de Gaulle were trying to recruit them, but the majority of them were very frightened and clearly anti-British. 'We had to ask them to surrender their arms, which they were very unhappy about, and it didn't help when they noticed that I was wearing a Napoleonic eagle [a regimental badge of honour from the Peninsular War]', remembers John with a chuckle. I suggest to him that perhaps they would have been even less friendly had they realised that one of the officers dealing with them was the great-great-grandson of their Emperor's vanquisher.

Finally news came through of their imminent departure on the *Empress of Britain*, a luxury liner which had been requisitioned as a troop carrier. There was just time for John and Valerian to make a trip to see their girlfriends, Maxine Birley and Barbara McNeill. My father talked to me nostalgically of the weekend when the two friends drove south from Liverpool, in his 'old banger' of a car. 'It was quite romantic really – it was beautiful weather and we went for long walks on the Downs.' Notwithstanding his reckless flirting, I knew that Barbara was a serious girlfriend of my father's, and had war not intervened their attachment might have progressed to something more permanent. My mother's acceptance of the importance of this relationship to my father was affirmed when, many years later, Barbara became one of my godmothers.

Farewells to family were less sentimental affairs. For their weekend with their girlfriends Valerian and John stayed at Penns-in-the-Rocks, Dorothy's magical house in Sussex. 'I know my mother was upset at me going off to war, but she didn't show it.' But Dorothy knew what was in her son's mind: a few years earlier she had written, 'He yearns for ... the gallantries of his dreams.' When I press my father to remember what he felt at the time, spontaneously he uses words that have been employed by thousands of other men of his generation: 'We didn't really think that we might never see each other again – that we might never come back. I suppose it was in the back of one's mind but one didn't dwell on it.' He adds, with unusual directness – 'those that did probably had nervous breakdowns.'

There was one more adventure for the two young men before they embarked on the huge liner. The food in the mess was pretty basic and sometimes if they had money in their pockets they would eat at the local pub, or one of the many cheap restaurants along the dockside. According to John, one evening they had eaten a good, cheap Chinese meal and 'were pretty drunk'. They were wandering rather aimlessly along the docks when they came across an Indian gentleman who was doing tattoos. My father admits he was to blame:

> I said to John 'Let's go and get one' and the man said 'What do you want', so I picked up my cigarette case which had my regimental badge on it, propped it up and he did it there and then. In those days it wasn't done electrically – it was just a needle and a bottle or two of ink, so it took much longer and was very painful. At the end the man took a piece of paper covered in Vaseline, slapped it on the tattoo, and said keep it on there for forty-eight hours!

It seems that John by this time was going green around the gills and was beginning to get cold feet. When I went to see him, I was curious to know what happened next. He took off his watch and underneath was a small, rather exotic beetle with outstretched wings. 'Unlike your father, I decided to try and conceal mine.' Years later, whenever the two old friends met up, before long they would be rolling up their sleeves and laughing at these mementoes of youthful exuberance.

When Lieutenant Valerian Wellesley finally climbed the gangway onto the deck of the majestic liner he was dressed in his full khaki kit, the left sleeve of his shirt firmly buttoned but rubbing rather painfully against a patch of tender skin. He was armed with his standard supply revolver; in his pocket he carried a cigarette case (a gift from Eliza and Tommy) filled with Trumpers filtered cigarettes, in his heart the hope that Barbara would be waiting for him when he got back. Among the items in his tin-lined wooden trunk were a number of red cotton spotted handkerchiefs, a blue Collins bird book, binoculars, a Swiss army knife, a fishing reel and a prayer book. With the strict secrecy of wartime movements, nobody came to wave the liner off. On 6 August it slipped quietly into the Mersey and out to the Irish Channel for what, unknown to all 3,000 of its uniformed passengers, would be its last journey from Britain.

Valerian and a troop of men under his command were put to work policing the ship, his task being made more complicated by the presence on board of fifty girls from the Queen Alexandra Nursing Service. 'They were frightfully smart – they wore grey uniforms with red facings', remembers my father. 'The girls were much "in demand" and I was meant to check that there was no improper behaviour on the deck – or in the lifeboats. It also meant that I couldn't get up to anything myself!' John Warrender had sailed with a broken heart but, appropriately for a young man who had not yet reached his twenty-first birthday, far out into the Atlantic his heart was mended.

Everyone on board the *Empress of Britain* realised their destination was the Middle East, but only the Captain could know the route they were following. After about a week land was spotted in the distance; it became clear that they had crossed the Atlantic and were sailing down the east coast of America, the blazing lights of the coastal towns at night a contrast to the strict blackout on the ship. When the *Empress* reached Mexico, she swung round and adopted a course due east, to strike the African coast at Freetown, where the ship moored about half a mile out to sea. No one was allowed ashore, but flotillas of little boats appeared alongside selling their wares. 'Come and see my sister – all pink and clean inside just like Lady Astor!' was one of the cries, John Bruntisfield told me gleefully.

Proprieties were observed, the *Empress* was refuelled and rationed, and a few days later it was the first British troop ship to round the Cape of Good Hope. When the liner tied up alongside the jetty in the harbour at Cape Town the whole dock area was teeming with local families. 'When we came ashore the people were absolutely wonderful', my father recalls. 'Every man was grabbed by a family and taken off to their homes, to be looked after and entertained.' Once again Valerian and John hovered in a world far removed from the realities of war: 'I went to a ball where we danced all night.' After four days all the troops had to report back on board and the ship's Commandant ordered Valerian to go with a couple of troopers and make sure no one was left behind.

When the ship set off again, up the east coast of Africa, the heat became unbearable. Conditions on board were luxurious for many of the officers but the living arrangements below deck, with blacked-out portholes and cramped bunks, were dreadful. Two men died of heatstroke. Finally the *Empress* and the rest of the convoy reached Port Said and everyone disembarked for their different destinations: Valerian to Tulkarm and John to Sarafand, in Palestine. They did not see each other for the rest of the war, though there were a couple of occasions when, as wireless operators, they found themselves hooked into the same connection. Personal dialogue was forbidden but I am sure they managed some subtle references to 'beetles' or Barbara.

Valerian reached the Tulkarm base of the First Household Cavalry Regiment (1HCR – the composite regiment of The Blues and The Life Guards) towards the end of September where he was reunited with other friends and fellow officers, including Lieutenants (later Colonels) 'G' Gerard Leigh, and David Smiley – both of whom, today, are among the small group of distinguished nonagenarian Household Cavalry officers. David remembers the night that Valerian and a couple of others from the First Reserve arrived in the camp. 'The Major of my squadron, Henry Abel Smith, had arranged a little surprise. Everyone was having dinner at a long table out in the open and suddenly there was a lot of firing and it seemed as if we were being ambushed.' In my father's account of the story, some of the 'new boys' dived under the table but he and fellow officer Max Gordon sat there unperturbed, though he admits that it was probably more from doziness than sangfroid. They got their own back on Abel Smith when they doped his drink with a toxic substance that turned his urine bright green; the camp doctor was in on the joke, which stretched it to its full worth.

When I hear such stories of schoolboy-style pranks from the lips of these old soldiers, my mind's eye plucks the images of their fresh-faced younger selves from a photograph of the officers of The Blues taken just after war was declared. My father stands in the back row, between two fellow officers long since gone. To my surprise, his upper lip is crowned with a thin moustache (to which he had never admitted before) – and to my civilian eye, his regimental cap is worn at a slightly provocative tilt. Youth and innocence stare out at me from many of the faces; their uniforms confer on them instant glamour and glory.

'There was nothing glamorous about war', John Bruntisfield reminded me firmly, but he also reflected rather wistfully on the essential role of trust and friendship. 'We didn't think about the sacrifices that might be required of us, though I suppose we were quite proud to be doing something for our country. And in good regiments, spirit and comradeship were everything.' I might dismiss the juvenile japes as trivial boys' games, but I can see that humour plays an important part when sanity and survival are indivisible.

Within days of arriving at Tulkarm, Valerian was on the move again. This march was to prove historic: it was the last to be undertaken by the complete First Household Cavalry Regiment with everyone mounted on horses. 'It's extraordinary to think', my father says, 'that in the early part of 1940 the country sent an entire cavalry division out to the Middle East, 15,000 men and about 8,000 horses.' David Smiley was one of only four officers who accompanied the horses when, early in February 1940, they set off from Newark to Dover on the first leg of their journey to Palestine. 'In the British standard railway cattle wagon the animals stood at right angles to the railway line, eight in a wagon. This, with those big black horses, was a tight fit; getting the last one squeezed into the wagon was physically demanding as well as a test of the farriers' patience.' The Mediterranean was still open, so they travelled from Marseilles on a cargo boat called the *Rhona*. The ventilation on the ship was poor and during the five-day journey to Haifa the horses were regularly given snorts of oxygen. 'I gave myself a dose now and then, and found it most stimulating,' wrote David Smiley later.

Valerian's first military duties involved patrolling on horseback: both Arab villages (with the local police, who were looking for arms) and the border with Syria, which was controlled by the Vichy French. Cavalry regiments had originally gone out to Palestine to counter the Arab Rebellion (1936–9), movement on horses being suited to the terrain. In the end the 1HCR horses saw few months of active service. Early in 1941 it became clear that it was impractical to maintain the regiment as a mounted unit. 'One of the saddest days I can ever remember was when, in February 1941, I had to take fourteen old black horses of my troop into the Judaean hills and shoot them,' reflects my father. 'Those fine old creatures who had taken part in all the great state occasions of the last ten years, including the 1936 coronation, ended their days on a desolate Palestinian hill, as fodder for vultures and jackals.' Even against the backdrop of a war where many men and women lost their lives, my father's emotional memory of the bleak death of these animals does not surprise me. Caring for and controlling their horses was not only an essential part of each man's training, but was integral to their effectiveness as soldiers. The bonds between cavalrymen and their horses were strong and humanising.

Training for their new life as a fully fledged twentieth-century regiment began with courses in Morse code, wireless operating and, most important of all, driving and maintenance. For men who had learnt their skills at riding school and had never been behind a wheel, this held its own challenges. Meanwhile, the deployment of the regiment hung in the balance, with the War Office convinced that they should be brought home to further months out of the action. They had a powerful ally in the Prime Minister, Churchill, but in the end events overtook everyone.

Iraq had always been strategically important for armies needing a corridor from Europe to South-East Asia, but its real value in the Second World War lay in its oil, the precious liquid that kept the wheels of war turning. When war broke out Iraq severed relations with Germany but did not come in on the side of the Allies, and when Italy and Vichy France joined the Axis powers their agents fed and fermented anti-British feeling across the entire Arab region. In the spring of 1941 this culminated in the deposition of the pro-British Regent of Iraq, who was replaced by a strongly pro-German regime. British women and children were evacuated from Baghdad to an RAF base at Habbaniya, which was promptly besieged by the Iraqi army, while the British Embassy in Baghdad was also surrounded. Finally the men of 1HCR had a military goal in their sights.

With a desperate shortage of vehicles, anything with four wheels was requisitioned, including, for the Commanding Officer, a Haifa taxi – a low-slung Plymouth saloon of a vivid green hue, there being no time to paint it with more conventional colours. Much of the military transport consisted of clapped-out vehicles that were intended for training purposes or in desperate need of servicing. Many of the drivers had less than twenty-four hours' experience. This was the column that set off for the 1941 invasion of Iraq.

The invasion involved a journey of 500 miles. It was the first time, since Alexander the Great in the 330s BC, that an army had swept through the desert from the shores of the Mediterranean to the banks of the River Euphrates. 'It has never been forgotten by those of us who were there. We were all in open trucks and the searing heat – sometimes over 120° in the shade – seemed to bounce off the black volcanic rock which covered much of the desert. There were permanent clouds of dust, a shortage of water and for me the final straw was when my dark glasses blew off in a sandstorm', remembers my father. The troop movement orders had been typed at the headquarters of the British Army, on the fourth floor of the King David Hotel in Jerusalem. The typist was one Miss Diana McConnel.

The column of men, called Habforce, moved along the Haifa line of oil pipes, taking advantage of the cool pumping stations that were dotted at intervals of eighty miles. Apart from these oases in the desert the ground was some of the bleakest on earth. In Jordan the force was joined by Colonel John Glubb – known as Glubb 'Pasha' – and his famous Arab Legion. These fierce warriors with long black ringlets and lean dark faces wore khaki drill robes, garlanded with belts of ammunition. Each carried a rifle, a pistol and a silver dagger and on their heads they wore red and white check kuffiahs. Fearless in action and indomitable in spirit, they were hugely respected by the Household Cavalry, who affectionately called them 'Glubb's girls'. Recruited from Bedouin tribes across the entire region, they had a detailed knowledge of the desert, which became a vital factor in the success of the campaign. Part of their job was to protect the column's long and open flanks from dissident bands of rebels and marauding tribesmen, one of whom became a notorious tormentor of the British forces and was hunted by them for the rest of their time in the Middle East.

The name of Fawzi (al-Kawukji) has been familiar to me for many years as the man who led my father, and many others, a merry dance. 'He really was a thorn in my flesh – and in those years I spent a lot of time trying to capture him.' When he talks of Fawzi, I can always detect a grudging hint of respect from one fighter to another. Fawzi had impressive credentials: an officer in the Turkish army in the First World War, the most prominent leader in the 1936–9 Arab Rebellion, and a Minister in the anti-British Iraqi regime. However, to debunk the myth of a romantic Nationalist leader – he loathed the British and the treatment of his prisoners could be barbaric: 'some had petrol poured over them' and were 'burnt alive', while others were 'stripped naked and turned loose in the desert to die',[2] wrote David Smiley.

Soon after crossing the border into Iraq, when the regiment were grabbing a few hours of rest, Valerian spotted a covey of sand grouse flighting into a water hole. One of the first things he had done when he arrived in Palestine was to buy a 16-bore gun, which he carried with him for the rest of the war. 'I managed to shoot a brace, which I carried back in triumph intending to have them for breakfast. Alas, such was the heat that by the morning they were putrid.' In any case, there was no time for breakfast that day: the column left in the early hours of 15 May and at 7.50 hours, just as the sun was beginning to resume its fierce heat, for the first time in the war the regiment came under fire.

'LONDON 3,827 miles BAGHDAD 55 miles.' This was the signpost that greeted Habforce when, after six days, it reached Habbaniya. By then a combination of the RAF's well-aimed bombing and news of the imminent arrival of the land forces had broken the siege. The regiment bivouacked on the shores of Lake Habbaniya, next to the Imperial Airways Rest House; finally Valerian and the rest of the regiment could cool down.

On 5 June Valerian wrote to his sister Eliza and her husband Tommy:

I've had no news from home for 3 or 4 months and am beginning to feel rather forgotten. I also sent two cables asking for news but heard nothing ... We are in action at last or rather have been, for an agreement has been signed and a troubled peace reigns. This probably gives you a line as to where we are. We have been bombed and machine-gunned from the air and fought a few minor battles with luckily few casualties, about two killed and a dozen or so wounded. We were fairly heavily shelled which was unpleasant at first, but one soon gets used to it and can tell by the sound whether it is worth diving into a trench. One day when I can say more, I will write and tell you both all about it. We had a most hellish journey here across hundreds of miles of desert and the heat is very trying, about 115 in the shade, and going up all the time. We were rationed for water on the way here, gallon a day per man, cooking, washing and shaving included. I didn't believe I could be so thirsty, our mouths were so dry, we couldn't talk, and you wouldn't believe how sore one's lips and face become from the heat and sand. Luckily I had the foresight to take some cold cream! You may remember I was never a great tea drinker; now I drink it all day long, hot strong and sweet with condensed milk out of a large tin mug, and live for the next cup. Sometimes one feels it has saved one's life. There is nothing like it for thirst quenching. Bully and biscuits are the staple diet and very tired one gets of them, but luckily since we have reached our destination, by efficient looting and scrounging, our diet has become almost civilised occasionally but still nearly all out of the tin, unless we happen to find a chicken or a sheep left about unattended.

At present we are bivouacked by a large lake on the edge of the desert. When we arrived we went quite mad at seeing so much water and rushed straight at it head first and had a good wash. I have never been so dirty – quite unbelievable!

Good bye both of you, and many congratulations on a fine piece of cooperation [the birth of their first child Jeremy], the results of which I long to see.

The two days at Habbaniya were welcome respite, but Baghdad called: the Embassy was still surrounded by Iraqi insurgents and Valerian's 'A' Squadron, with most of the rest of the regiment, moved to about five miles east of the city. They encamped on the reverse slope of a ridge which straddled the road into Baghdad, with a clear view of the irrigated land planted with date palms and in the distance the mosque and minarets of the city. As the fighting on the outskirts intensified, soon the road was filled with refugees. To the south of the regiment's position was Khadimain, its mosque glinting in the sun. During a reconnaissance towards the village, G's squadron came under heavy fire and were forced to leave the body of one of their number – a Corporal Shone. The following day Valerian and his troop went back to try to reclaim him.

When they found Shone's body, it was lying on a patch of open ground and impossible to recover without further endangering life, but Valerian moved his troop further forward to try to pinpoint the enemy's position:

I lay for a long time looking at the village through my binoculars. I could see no sign of life whatsoever but from time to time I could hear in the distance the bark of a dog or the cry of a child. The colour of the houses blended perfectly with the desert. The sun was getting up and blurring the edges and the line between buildings and sand quivered and danced in the heat. If the MGs were there, they were either well dug in on the forward edge of the village or in the houses themselves.

Valerian placed some of his troops on each flank in supporting positions, leaving himself with his Corporal-of-Horse Maxted, his soldier servant

Trooper Pearson and two others to move forward in arrow-head formation.

As I walked I kept my eyes glued on the ridge ahead of us hoping I would get some warning if the enemy were still in position. It was very still and hot and the sun shimmered on the golden dome of the Mosque. I could now hear no sounds from the village and that I found a little disturbing. Twenty-five yards, fifty yards, seventy-five yards and we continued to walk steadily ahead. When we had gone nearly a hundred yards I was beginning to think we had got away with it and was wondering how we were going to get Shone's body back. Like most pre-war troopers he was a big man and we had come unencumbered with a stretcher. It therefore came almost as a surprise when a veritable storm of MG fire suddenly descended on us. We tried to wriggle our puny bodies into the hard unyielding sand and just waited for this terrible cacophony of sound to stop. After what seemed an age but was probably not much more than a minute the fire seemed to slacken and I raised my head slightly to see if I could see anything.

Judging from the rate of fire, Valerian reckoned that they were up against two pairs of Vickers machine-guns which, ironically, were British-made weapons supplied to the Iraqi army by British Army training teams. Having precisely pinpointed the position of the enemy it was clear that they could advance no further, and, more crucially, they were unable to recover the body of their fallen comrade. My father told me what happened next.

I gave the order to fall back one by one and I told Maxted to go first and try and get more covering fire going to help us get out. When there was a pause I gave Maxted the signal to move. I then witnessed something, which I shall always regard as one of the most courageous acts I have ever seen. Most men under the circumstances would have run back to the ridge doubled up and as fast as their legs would carry them. Laden with rifle, fifty rounds of ammunition and equipment they would have arrived puffing and panting and in no fit state to take command of a situation, let alone aim a rifle in the right direction. Not Maxted – he stood up all six feet three inches, brushed himself off like a good soldier and marched erect and straight with his rifle at the short trail across that hundred yards of desert as if he was on the parade ground at Windsor. It was a magnificently defiant gesture. He was the old soldier amongst us all, and he knew that behind him on the ground lay some very frightened young men.

Whatever his own feelings were (and he must have been as afraid as we were), he wasn't going to show it. The movement had triggered off more firing and I watched him go back to the ridge as the bullets flicked up the sand all round him with a full heart and a prayer on my lips. Once he was back I sent the others back one by one. They kept well over to the left as I looked back and soon Maxted had the rifles of the section on the ridge firing away at the enemy positions in the village. It was now my turn and I stood up feeling rather lonely and with an uncomfortable sensation in my back as I tried rather unsuccessfully to emulate my Corporal-of-Horse. However, all went well and I arrived back to find Maxted as cool as a cucumber giving fire orders.

Corporal-of-Horse Maxted was one of the most important people in my father's life: 'In a way he was the person who trained me and taught me more than anyone else.' Not only was he the man who steered my father through his training at Pirbright, but Maxted's courage and fortitude were an inspiration to him throughout the war. 'He was a very impressive man – very smart and very charming – and one of the senior staff officers would have spotted his potential.' He was from a very different background to my father and the social constraints and conventions of their generation confined their friendship to the battlefield or the bar-racks. 'If it was a special occasion, say after we'd been providing a Royal Escort, Maxted would say to me "Sir, come and have a drink with us before lunch." Then we might talk about the war, we would talk about our shared experiences – from the trivial "Do you remember that rice pudding we had in Syria, sir?" to the triumphant, "That walk near Khadimain was pretty hairy!"'

Maxted and Trooper Pearson were part of his 'team' during the war and when they were on the move, rank and class became irrelevant. 'We took it in turns to do the cooking, we all ate the same food, we all slept alongside our vehicles.' Clearly, the bonds my father formed with these men were both liberating and life-enhancing. 'If it had not been for the war, I would never have got to know people like Maxted and Pearson. They talked about their families, their wives, their problems. I was a bit of an "agony uncle" as well as being their Commanding Officer. I do regard them as friends – albeit friendship forged in very different cir-cumstances to the others in my life.'

After the war Maxted stayed on in The Blues. When he left the army, my father helped him get a job at the House of Lords working for Black Rod. His magnificent frame, clad now in the red and gold uniform of the Men of Arms, would greet the Peers as they arrived at the door to the Lords. 'He was a great soldier and a great friend.'

Back on the outskirts of Baghdad in the summer of 1941, one section of Valerian's troop remained in position near the enemy and the only way of getting them back was to send a runner or go himself. He opted for the latter.

> The ridge soon disappeared and I had a twenty-yard gap before I could reach the next dune. I reckoned I had little to fear from the MGs. The Vickers is difficult to traverse quickly and can't engage opportunity targets at short notice. I had not reckoned, however, with enemy riflemen. Hitherto, apparently all the fire directed at us had been from MGs. As I crossed the first gap I became acutely aware that I was now the target of enemy rifles. In Wild West films, as the hero dodges from rock to rock, with outlaws, Red Indians or whatever firing at him, the bullets make a rather satisfactory whine as they go off into space. The reality was very different, as I remembered from my days in the butts at Bisley and Pirbright. A bullet passing fairly close makes a most unpleasant crack as it breaks the sound barrier, particularly if it's just over one's head! The same fusillade of shots followed me each time I dodged from dune to dune. I felt like an Aunt Sally at a fair-ground shooting range, but at the same time there was within me a little pang of exhilaration, rather like jumping several big fences out hunting. In any case I reckoned that if a man could successfully engage a brief running target at 500 yards, he was rather a better shot than I believed him to be.

Valerian was disheartened not to have recovered the body of their dead comrade, but relieved when he got his entire troop back to camp without suffering any further casualties. When he had made his report and his duties were over, a fellow officer ventured, 'You look done in – have a whisky.' Spirits were rationed to one bottle a month per officer, so this represented a generous gesture. 'I didn't really like whisky at the time and used to take my ration in gin, but I accepted it gratefully and, not having eaten since first light, it took effect quickly. I suddenly felt far better and I have been a great believer in the medicinal qualities of whisky ever since!' Valerian rejoined his troop, who had just cooked up a 'splendid' stew of bully beef and onions. He made sure both that their rum ration was a generous one and that they all knew how well they had performed. For some it had been their first time under fire. 'That night we all slept soundly beside our trucks with the contentment of happy men.'

Valerian and his troop were part of the northern column which was disadvantaged for being 'an armoured car regiment without armour' and in the end, on 31 May, being unable to break through the enemy fire that protected the mosque of Khadimain and the westerly approach to the city, to their great disappointment they did not enter Baghdad and enjoy the fruits of victory. An armistice came into force at 4 a.m. and the southern column crossed the River Tigris into the city which the men had called 'Catch Father'. Baghdad was liberated and the pro-German regime removed.

Over sixty years later, when an invasion of Iraq was once again on the horizon, my father's memories of his experiences in 1940 came flooding back. Interviewed by the *Sunday Times* early in 2003 he declared, 'The forced march across the desert has never been forgotten by any of us who were there ... There was a lot of bluff and bombastic talk coming out of Baghdad then, but when we bombarded them on the outskirts of the city, they just had enough.'[3] These words may read like a call to arms, but the old soldier in him recognised that the duty of today's army to serve its nation was being stretched to breaking-point. He also wrote a letter on 24 January to the *Daily Telegraph* which included the following passages:

> Mr Blair tells us we may be about to invade Iraq. If that is to be the case, the armed forces of this Country should be told what are the aims and objectives of such an expedition. British servicemen and women are not automatons. They should be made aware in specific terms exactly what these are. I am not sure and nor I suspect are the majority of people in this Country.
>
> Perhaps the real truth is that Mr Blair at all costs wishes to remain in step with President Bush. I suggest that instead of invading Iraq, the United States of America should use its considerable influence in sorting out the problems of Palestine. That would make a real contribution to peace in the Middle East.
>
> If we are to invade Iraq then it must be in support of a clear United Nations Mandate.

The letter was never published. When the 2003 invasion of Iraq was successful he watched the aftermath in dismay, as it became clear that his fears, like those of many other old soldiers, had been realised.

*

In 1941 Baghdad had fallen, but no one could rest on their laurels while Fawzi was still out there and Valerian's squadron became part of a contingent whose task was to hunt down and capture the Arab guerrilla. Their first engagement with Fawzi's men, near a city called Abu Kemal, nearly turned into a disaster when they were lured into an ambush, bordered by the River Euphrates on one side and a high ridge on the other. 'Had we moved just a bit further up the road, the net would have closed.' As it was, the squadron was forced to turn tail and run. 'We held off the enemy for as long as we could and then ran like hell for the trucks and leapt aboard, driving off at great speed under heavy fire from all sides.' By this time Fawzi was in league with another faction of the enemy – the Vichy French in Syria. After the successful invasion of Iraq, Syria was the next target since German aeroplanes were now using it as a base from which to threaten the Allied supply lines. Valerian's troop was ordered to reconnoitre an area which might be part of the approach route. This operation turned out to be 'one of the most chillingly frightening of the entire war, although I was not within a half-mile of the enemy and not a single shot was fired'.

In the British Army of the 1940s, wireless technology was fairly primitive and communication relied primarily on key and Morse code, with a range of up to fifteen miles. It was an essential part of any operation that there was a prearranged drill for a unit to keep in touch with headquarters and Valerian agreed to give his position every half-hour, whether in range or not. By the time the troop had gone about forty miles there was silence on the airwaves and the desert stretched all around them, with no signs of life. On the dot of 11.30, as agreed, the signal to HQ was tapped out; to their great surprise there was a faint reply asking for their position. 'Had the squadron set up a relay station or were the signals bouncing off some kind of feature in the atmosphere? It was mysterious and I could not help feeling faintly uncomfortable.' Bang on 12 noon the process was repeated and this time the reply was quite clear. Valerian's uneasiness turned to alarm when a few minutes later through his binoculars he could just about make out a faint cloud of dust. Could it be Fawzi? There was no time to deliberate; capture by the guerrilla leader was not an option. Without taking his eye off the horizon, Valerian gave Maxted the order to move immediately. The troop grumbled – they had a 'brew' on the go. The midday sun was beating down, distorting and elongating any distant object, but as the image in the lens began to clear, Valerian could just about make out a dozen trucks. 'There was something on the leading vehicle which made it appear much higher than the others. Suddenly the penny dropped. It was an armoured car with a turret. It could only be one of ours that Fawzi had captured at Habbaniya. The column was now barely 1,000 yards away and closing fast. I raced to my vehicle and jumped in.' The chase was on.

As Valerian stood in the back of his armoured car, never taking his eye off the enemy, he worked out the mystery of the signals. Obviously Fawzi had a base camp somewhere in the desert and since the captured armoured car wireless set was tuned in to one of their frequencies, he had been able to pinpoint their position. 'To begin with they were gaining on us but then the going got better and we started to level-peg on parallel courses with Fawzi slightly to the south of us.' As the trucks continued their breakneck speed over the bumpy terrain, the wireless operator managed to get a jerky message to HQ and finally Valerian was able to make out another troop from his squadron coming to their rescue. The quarry had slipped from Fawzi's grasp, but once again it had been a 'near-run thing'.

Valerian's next operation against the enemy struck a small historic note: apart from the odd skirmish in Africa, it was the first time since 1815 that British soldiers had been lined up against a force of Frenchmen – with a Wellesley on the front line. On this occasion it was the Vichy French rather than the Emperor's men, the battle was in the air as well as on the ground, and de Gaulle's Free French were fighting alongside the Allies. 1HCR was following another oil pipeline. The initial advance began well but quite soon, when the French realised that the force had no air support, they began to bomb them mercilessly. At one point Valerian's troop was acting as escort to the guns, desperately trying to protect them from attack by Fawzi and his men. It was an impossible task and all the vehicles were damaged but they kept going – 'two punctured radiators were plugged with chewing gum!' When they were forced to stop, everyone grabbed a spade to dig slit trenches which were then used by those following on behind. At one point David Smiley was sharing a slit trench with G. 'The bomb we were both watching seemed to come straight at us,' remembers G. 'I was convinced it would hit us; I think I said "This is it" and shut my eyes. In fact it burst about twenty yards away, riddling my truck with splinters.'

Progress was hard but orderly and as they were getting closer to the outskirts of Palmyra their passage across the desert was watched by the rest of the brigade, who were cheered by the sight of this column's disciplined advance, regardless of bombs falling all around.[4] It was to prove a big boost for morale and the official regimental history of the war dwells on the moment:

> The driver and commander of each truck had their eyes fixed on the desert in front; the passengers all had their eyes fixed on the planes overhead. They could see the bombs leave the bomb-racks, and give advice to the driver how best to take evasive action. They could see the rest of the Brigade watching them, and no doubt all instinctively felt, 'Now we will show them what we can do.' The seed of the regimental spirit which had germinated in the Iraq fighting had now grown into a very healthy plant.[5]

When the column reached the outskirts of Palmyra on 22 June it found the fort and airfield heavily defended by the French. Cover was sought in the low-lying hills around the area. Valerian managed to find for his troop a small re-entrant with a cave at the far end, which provided respite from the shelling. Tragically it did not save one of his men. There was one French fighter aircraft which was constantly strafing the area and finally, as dusk was falling, Corporal Reeve from a neighbouring troop tired of the bombardment and, jumping out of his slit trench, started firing his heavy Hotchkiss machine-gun at the aircraft. One of the rounds punctured its target and, as the plane crashed, exploding only yards away from where Valerian's troop was encamped, fragments of the aircraft hit and killed Corporal Fowler. That night Valerian and his men buried the body in a deep hole in the desert, placing old tin petrol cans filled with sand over it to ward off marauding jackals. Valerian used his prayer book to say a few words and they erected a cairn of stones, crowned with a crude wooden cross, and carefully noted the position of the grave. Nearby David Smiley was enacting a similar but more detached ritual with the remains of the French pilot. Together the two graves flanked the deathly pile of wreckage. Reeve was awarded an MM (Military Medal) for his act – the first decoration won by the regiment in the Second World War.

*

Valerian wrote to Eliza and Tommy in early June 1941:

> Since I last wrote we have been having a very hectic time in action on and off all the time. Very uncomfortable, very tiring, and exciting or extremely frightening at odd intervals. The heat is terrific and very trying, and yet at night it is so cold you can hardly sleep. Our water is down to half a gallon a day for the moment, and the old bully and biscuits are still our everyday food. We are now in a different theatre of war not far removed from the other. Any way we have advanced about 150 miles in the right direction,

and I hear, were mentioned on the wireless the other day, 'a famous cavalry regiment is advancing etc.' Since last Sunday we have [had] a most unpleasant time. Bombed and machine-gunned fairly continuously. The gunners who were in France say that Sunday and Monday were as bad as any day at Dunkirk. I am at the moment in a large cave in a hill, so quite happy. Great excitement! Seven RAF fighters have come over (first time) and shot down 3 out of 4 bombers who were bombing us.

For the next few days the bombs continued to drop – mostly 250-pounders, but with the occasional 500-pound monster. The regiment was dispersed over quite a large area and Fawzi continued to make his presence felt by his disruption of supply lines. The temperatures went up to 120° in the shade and the men were running short of food and water. But for the time being the orders were to harass the enemy with gunfire and use patrols to identify their positions. Just to the east of the town stood the ancient ruins of Palmyra, which in the third century AD had been ruled by the formidable Queen Zenobia. The huge columns and fallen pillars provided the French with imposing natural fortifications. G, David and Valerian were all sent on separate patrols to crawl through the ruins and locate enemy positions. The day before Valerian went, he climbed to the top of the nearest hill to study the area through the lenses of his binoculars. 'I could see a jumbled-up mass of standing and fallen columns and ruins of all shapes and sizes – not the easiest ground to search at night.' Soon after midnight he set off with his troop of twenty men. Just before they reached the ruins, the moonlight revealed an abandoned vehicle on their path, the heavy scarlet cloak in the back indicating that it belonged to an officer of the French Camel Corps. At the ruins the troop divided into two to cover more ground, with Maxted in charge of the second group. They moved slowly forward, 'supporting each other and remaining in constant visual contact'. When they reached the other side one of Valerian's fittest troopers shinned up the telephone pole and cut the wires, which they placed across the road as a trap.

As dawn was breaking, Valerian led his men out of the ruins and past the car abandoned by the French officer, grabbing as he went a souvenir of the patrol – the scarlet cape. (For many years it lay on my father's bed, until it lost its battle with the moths and my mother insisted that it be thrown away.) Although his mind was on other things, he knew he would always remember the eerie beauty of the ruins in the moonlight. 'As I looked back at them, now catching the first rays of dawn, I swore to return one day.'

*

My father did just that when, in the early 1990s, he went on a trip to Syria with my mother. Part of the tour took them round the ruins of Palmyra. My father asked the guide if there was anyone he knew who remembered the war of 1941. 'All dead,' he replied rather gloomily, adding – to my father's slight discomfort – that he considered Fawzi Kawukji to be 'a great patriot'. But he agreed to go with my father to try to locate some of the landmarks from the map of his memories. 'I found the track to the Ottoman fort where we had bumped into the French staff car.' He eventually discovered the little valley where his troop had briefly taken refuge and he climbed to the top of the hill whence he could see the valley through which the regiment had advanced towards Palmyra. 'Then it was all noise and dust, the crash of the bombs, the rattle of machine-guns, engines revving, and men shouting as they made for cover. Now it was absolutely still with not even a wind to stir the dust.' In the visitors' book at the hotel where they were staying he was asked to write something. 'I said that I had particularly enjoyed being in the ruins again, which I had last visited at about 3 a.m. on the night of 27 June 1941. Afterwards I thought – what on earth will future generations think I was up to? – an assignation with a beautiful woman perhaps, or communing with the ghost of Queen Zenobia. I rather enjoyed the thought that I had left a conundrum behind me.'

In the summer of 1941, after the night patrols in the ruins of Palmyra, for a few days there was no air activity and supplies were restored. An operational stalemate set in, with the French maintaining control over the area through their positions on the high ground and the palm groves outside the town. On Sunday, 13 July Valerian attended an outdoor service at Regimental Headquarters:

> In the middle of the service a French vehicle approached flying a white flag. Col. Eric [Gooch, the Commanding Officer] turned to me and said 'You speak French, go and see what those fellows want'. Those fellows turned out to be two Vichy French officers with a case of champagne and news of a ceasefire. Our meeting was formal and courteous with lots of saluting and they insisted that we drank a glass of champagne with them. Any awkwardness that might have existed soon disappeared and we all agreed that a war such as we had campaigned against each other must never happen again.

The following day, back in Palestine in the historic seaport of Acre, the Vichy French sat down one side of an arrangement of tables in the shape of an H; the British and their allies were opposite, with the interpreters in between, to negotiate the terms of the peace. The conference was in the Sidney Smith Barracks, a long, low wooden building about fifty yards from the sea. The summer sun was blazing down on the tin roof and iced lemonade was served to the delegates. By the evening all the conditions had been agreed and, appropriately for the Free French, it was Bastille Day, 14 July. One of the witnesses on behalf of the British and Allied forces was Douglas McConnel, Chief of Staff at the British Headquarters in Jerusalem.

After the signing of the armistice, the next stop for the regiment was Persia. Valerian missed this, the regiment's third successful campaign in the Middle East, as a sinus condition required a minor operation. After convalescence he was reunited with 1HCR in the Allenby Barracks in Jerusalem. Their principal duties at this time were to guard Government House and the residence of the GOC – the McConnel house. For Valerian and his fellow soldiers it was a frustrating period, feeling cut off from the real action in the war. But, characteristically, Valerian shifted his energy into a fierce round of socialising, spending quite a bit of time in Cairo.

'See you at Shepheard's' was as familiar a refrain in the Middle East during the Second World War as it had been in the First. Soldiers on their way to and from the fighting in the desert would decamp into Cairo and gather at the famous Long Bar which was presided over by Joe. The barman, who knew everyone by name and the exact location of their units, was always immaculately dressed in white jacket and bow tie. He spoke several languages fluently, including English, French, German and Russian. 'He was totally charming', remembers my father, 'and knew everything, but we were all told to be very careful what we said in the Long Bar – there was a suspicion that Joe quietly traded information between his clientele.' Shepheard's was like an oasis: clean, cool, elegant and sociable. The garden was full of sweet-smelling flowers, the beds were made up with freshly laundered white linen and there was always a friendly face at the bar. Taxis would disgorge dusty, tired officers who would be rapidly transformed into smart-looking young men with money in their pockets and a determination to have fun.

Lots of the soldiers left luggage in the hotel when they went back to the desert – the basement assumed the appearance of an exotic jumble sale with big-game trophies, tennis rackets, swords, books of poetry, cricket bats, bicycles, skis, brown paper parcels and battered old luggage that looked as if it was last used in the First World War, and probably was. Messages were left with the hall porter or on a board, which would be covered in cables, letters and notes. A ticker-tape machine issued a constant stream of news – often bad. Just after Pearl Harbor on 7 December 1941, Valerian was standing beside the machine when he read of the sinking by the Japanese of two British battleships, the *Prince of Wales* and the *Repulse*, in which 840 men died. Often messages were not picked up for months, sometimes never. The young men who laughed and drank at the Long Bar or dined with their female companions at tables laid out in the garden among the bougainvillaeas, followed the maxim 'Eat, drink and be merry, for tomorrow we may die'.

One of my father's amorous adventures involved an exotic Druze princess who came from a mountain tribe in Syria. Amal al-Atrash was a well-known singer and actress with jet-black hair, blue eyes, a colourful reputation and the added allure that she was rumoured to be spying for the Allies. For a period in the winter of 1941 she was based at the King David Hotel, and had hooked up with an officer in the Wiltshire Yeomanry. Valerian met her at a party:

> We danced quite a bit but she got frightfully bored with this party, so I took her back to her room at the King David. We were sitting there and we had a bottle of champagne and things were going well and suddenly there was the most appalling banging on the door and this furious voice (which I recognised) was shouting, 'Have you got him in there, are you with him?'. She said, 'Oh my God, quickly come on', so she opened the door out of the sitting room into a bedroom. It was quite dark and I collapsed onto the bed, only to find that it was occupied by a large woman! You can imagine what fun my brother officers had about that part of the story. So, having pushed me into the bedroom and locked me in, she opened the door to her suite, and I heard a great argument, 'You've got him, what have you done with him', but she refused to open the door into the bedroom. And I suddenly remembered I had left my Sam Browne belt over a chair but thank God he didn't see it and finally she kicked him out. He must have realised I was there. The story got around – needless to say my own brother officers wheedled it out of me.

By Christmas, Amal was out of the picture and the partying was beginning to pall. 'Hope you had a lovely Christmas. Mine was foul,' Valerian wrote to his sister. 'Very wet and very cold. Six of us, all men, celebrated by dining rather gloomily at the King David Hotel ... No women here, very dull! Real snow fell for New Year's day, an occurrence of once in 20 years. Tommy will no doubt remember Maxted who has got an MM. He was my Cpl of H through the campaign and as a third of my troop have since been made up I am rather proud.' Soon after writing this, Valerian heard that he had been awarded an MC for gallantry during the Iraq and Syria campaigns. When I asked him about the award, his response was reticent. 'It's difficult to talk about these things. I suppose I did a lot of reconnaissance patrols and gathered quite a bit of useful information. I was sitting having dinner when I heard that I had been awarded it and I was delighted. It was a great honour and my father was thrilled and wrote me a very nice letter.'

Valerian's mother, living in lonely isolation in her house in Sussex, wrote of her feelings in strange confessional letters (later published under the title *Beyond the Grave*) to the ghost of her friend and mentor W.B. Yeats:

> My son out there in the Middle East forces me to keep a hard grip on myself. He is gallant, and has, as you foretold, found himself in action, and for courage and the inborn law of leadership, won his M.C. during his first six weeks, on his first night patrol among the ruins of Palmyra. I pray to the Ancient Gods that he is living in some heroic ecstasy. That state of mind alone could carry him, who hates machines, through such a war. His letters show that he is living in that state of mind, but I never needed confirmation of my faith in that boy. He only needed something to fight against; his inner solitude will serve him well.[6]

At the start of 1942 Valerian was sent to Cairo to do a wireless course. Gerry had arrived in the city some months before. 'We are writing this at the best cabaret here. Fancy finding us at such a place!' were the opening words of a joint letter that Valerian and Gerry wrote to Eliza. 'V is very well & I have been very much interested in hearing all his activities.' In England Eliza and her husband Tommy were based in a small house on Salisbury Plain, near his regiment (2 HCR), who were living under canvas. The Clydes' 'facilities' were put to use when the regiment received a royal visit. 'The sound of Queen Mary pulling the plug was heartily cheered by the villagers, I hear,' wrote Valerian. 'How very tactless of you to have such a loud one. I am here on a short course and it is lovely seeing Daddy after nearly two years.' Gerry then took up the tale. 'We are watching a girl dance a "danse du vente". She has nothing on but a heart made of silver sequins! We think that, whatever people may say, she has her heart in the right place. But the trouble is

she reeks of garlic! It seems V knows her <u>intimately</u>!' Rebutted immediately: 'Not at all, just a dance or two, that's all. There's a girl singing
"my heart belongs to Daddy" now. We are so backward here, but it's a
raging new success.'

In March 1942 this period of training continued when the regiment
was sent to Cyprus. The move came as a great disappointment to those
who had hoped that they would be deployed in the Western Desert, but
it was part of a bigger plan which anticipated that Cyprus might be used
by the enemy as a staging-post for an attack.

To begin with, Valerian was bored and depressed by their operational
inactivity, but things perked up when he was put in charge of the catering,
writing to Eliza and Tommy,

> ... it's rather fun going round the villages on recces buying excellent local
> produce. I am also running a farm for the mess, pigs and hens. My first hen
> was presented to me this morning by my Greek interpreter. I personally
> think it must be a bribe, and that he must have done something for which
> he thinks he is going to get a raspberry. I also went and bought some fish
> and asparagus in the market after an I [Intelligence] conference at HQ.
> I've just bought another chicken, (live) for 1s 6d, not bad! So I am now the
> complete housewife.

In a later letter he describes other elements of the animal menagerie: 'I
bought five young rabbits some time ago to eat later, but we are now so
fond of them we can't do it. One has produced ten babies which is not
bad going even for a rabbit.'

But by the end of June the novelty had worn off and once more
Valerian was chafing at the bit. 'It is very boring here and horribly hot.
About 110° in the shade in the daytime and doesn't drop much below 90°
at night.' Evidently his superiors acknowledged his frustration when, at
his request, he was seconded for a period to the 12th Lancers, who were
training in the Western Desert. 'They were a splendid regiment,' says my
father, 'extremely professional but with a nice light touch and bags of
cavalry spirit and dash. They had an excellent war record and I learnt a
lot from them.' The Commanding Officer was Colonel George Kidston,
who liked to go off 'trailing one's coat', as he called it. His presence in a
lone jeep would provoke a few shots and help to reveal the artillery
positions of the enemy. On one occasion Valerian accompanied him. 'I
was in the back of the jeep and at one particular stop I glanced down and
saw a mine about 18ins from our offside rear wheel. I immediately tried
to draw his attention to it: "Colonel" and again, "Colonel". "What is it?",

he replied, "I am watching something interesting." "I think we are in the middle of a minefield." At this point he put down his binoculars, looked over the edge of the jeep and exclaimed, "By God so we are!"' In the end Valerian guided the driver back along the exact tracks, giving precise and rapid instructions, 'Straight, right hand down, slightly left etc.'

Valerian's stint with the Lancers stood him in good stead when, in late summer 1942, his regiment was finally moved west to take part in the desert war. At 21.40 hours on 23 October the battle of El Alamein commenced. Eight hundred Allied artillery guns positioned along the Alamein line started pummelling Rommel's lines; twenty minutes later the advance of the infantry and the sappers started. Valerian was watching from a lookout point behind the lines. 'The noise was deafening and I even felt quite sorry for those chaps I had been watching for the last three weeks.' The following morning he saw for the first time German Stuka bombers making repeated attacks on the infantry, who were pinned down just short of their objective. 'It was an awesome sight and sound – the planes made a terrifying screaming noise as they dived to low levels to drop their bombs.' Valerian was sent by RHQ to tell the infantry that the regiment was in a defensive position to their south and would give immediate support if an attack should develop from that direction.

It was quite hard to 'map read' in the desert: there were no features on the ground other than infrequent mounds of stones, numbered and map-referenced. Valerian had stopped briefly to get his bearings using his compass when 'a stentorian bellow demanded to know "what the f—— hell do you think you are doing" and "get that f—— vehicle out of it!"'. After a 'pretty dodgy' passage he eventually found the Commanding Officer, who was crouched in an extremely shallow slit trench with his battalion spread in similar positions over a small forward slope. They were being mortared regularly and accurately every few minutes and had already suffered a number of casualties. 'Not surprisingly, he did not show any great signs of enthusiasm when I delivered my message from RHQ and he advised me to get back to my unit as soon as possible.'

In early November the Allies finally broke through the enemy defences and the regiment got the chance it had been waiting for – to take up the pursuit. 'I shall never forget my feelings of elation as my squadron got through the last gap in the minefields and fanned out with miles of open desert and good going ahead of us.' Soon they were meeting hundreds of prisoners, mainly Italian; these were immediately disarmed, but feeding and watering them was a more complicated business since rations were already running very low. One Italian who spoke good English vol-

BELOW: Arthur's father Garret, the 1st Earl of Mornington, a successful composer, who earned himself the accolade of being the first member of the aristocracy to walk through the streets of London carrying a violin case.

ABOVE: Dangan Castle, in County Meath, the childhood home of Arthur and his siblings. Handel played the organ in its great hall; nowadays sheep graze in the ruins.

BELOW: Silhouette of Arthur as a young boy – the only surviving image from his childhood. A lonely, overlooked child, he spent his early life in Ireland, before the family left the country for good to settle in England.

LEFT: Richard, Arthur's eldest brother, at the age of fifteen. There was a strong likeness between the five Wellesley brothers, and Arthur at the same age would have looked very similar.

The French actress Hyacinthe Roland, painted in 1791 when she was Richard Wellesley's mistress. She married him after the birth of their fifth child; none of the Wellesley family, particularly the women, approved of the union.

Arthur's eldest sister Anne (above left) and his youngest brother Henry (above right), who were captured and held prisoner by the Revolutionary French in 1794. An intelligent woman, Anne was resentful of the wealth and success of her brothers. Henry later became a successful diplomat and was created Lord Cowley.

Richard Wellesley (above), Arthur's eldest brother, who, as Governor General of India, was given the Irish title of Marquess Wellesley. 'History is spacious enough for the fame of both brothers', he wrote. But this was not to be. His marriage to Marianne (right) in 1825, was the second for both of them. The First Duke fell heavily for her charms; he was furious when his brother married her.

This magnificent Hoppner of
the First Duke, when still
Arthur Wellesley, with his grey
charger Diomed, was painted
after his triumphant return from
India, where he learnt his
'soldiering'. The painting
dominates the dining room at
Stratfield Saye.

The storming of Seringapatam
in India in 1799.

Kitty Pakenham claimed that she loved Arthur from the moment she saw him. She became his wife fourteen years after he first proposed to her. Apart from their two sons, 'Douro' and Charley, the marriage was a disaster.

Goya's chalk drawing depicts Wellington soon after Salamanca. Perhaps the most honest of all the images of the First Duke, the stress of the battlefield is evident on his face.

BELOW: *The Eton Boys*: Stratfield Saye House can be seen in the background, and the three Etonians in the foreground are Kitty's beloved boys, and her nephew Gerald (son of Arthur's brother Henry) whom she brought up.

ABOVE: Kitty at her easel. No doubt she whiled away many an hour like this when her husband was engaged elsewhere.

BELOW: Gerald Wellesley, by all accounts the most amiable of the brothers. He became Prebend of Durham, and but for a flighty wife would have been made a bishop.

ABOVE: Arthur's stern mother, Anne Mornington, in old age surrounded by images and memorabilia from the lives of her sons, from a painting by Priscilla Burghersh, Wellington's favourite niece.

William, the second brother, was created Lord Maryborough, in 1821. The least popular of all the Wellesley brothers, his obituary notice in 1845 described him as 'an undignified, ineffective speaker, an indiscreet politician'.

BELOW: A pot lid showing Walmer Castle, the seaside retreat which (as Warden of the Cinque Ports) Wellington loved, and where he died.

ABOVE:
A porcelain plate depicting Apsley House, Wellington's London residence. The house is still lived in by the family, though it was given to the nation by my grandfather in 1947 and now houses the Wellington Museum.

Lawrence's painting shows a triumphant Wellington in front of St Paul's, where in November 1852 he would be laid to rest in the crypt near Nelson.

My father's favourite picture, showing the First Duke in the library at Stratfield Saye House, with four of his grandchildren, two of whom, the little boys in brown and blue, respectively became the 3rd and 4th Duke. My father can say, 'My grandfather was the First Duke's grandson'.

Wellington's funeral cortège as it passed Apsley House. One and a half million people were on the streets of London to watch the procession.

unteered enterprisingly, but unsuccessfully, to become an officers' mess waiter; a well-known German officer who was taken prisoner turned out to be a terrible snob and worked hard to ingratiate himself with his captors: 'I have never seen armoured cars work like that before. You have learnt all we can teach and now we must learn from you.' By the end of one day the floor of Valerian's armoured car was covered in captured pistols.

The euphoria of the chase was short-lived. On 13 November the regiment was ordered to withdraw. To this day my father remembers his feeling of great disappointment and even bitterness, which he shared with the rest of the men. 'We had done all and more than had been asked of us. We had captured virtually the entire Folgore Division, about 10,000 men and a large quantity of guns and equipment. We had advanced about sixty miles and neutralised any threat from the south.' Unfortunately they were also running out of provisions as the main supply route was being switched well to the north of them.

I confess that when I first started talking to my father about his wartime experiences, I was always interested in what he had to say, but often found it hard to relate to the subject. The language could be quite detached – the accounts necessarily unemotional and circumscribed by military manoeuvring rather than dramatic incident. These impressions were compounded by reading the dour, astonishingly detailed official history of the 1HCR's experience in the Second World War. I knew that I could never really imagine what it was like to be facing an enemy with the idea of 'kill or be killed', but I wanted to find a way of making some connection to this hugely important part of my father's life. As time progressed and my ignorance and lack of understanding of war was replaced by a few scraps of knowledge, gradually my wariness of the whole subject disappeared. I found that my way in was to focus on the details – to zoom in on a tiny square which was about Valerian's, or David's, or G's, or John's very personal experience of what was going on immediately around them; the more of these squares I could see, the better my understanding.

As the regiment was withdrawing from the desert, en route to the Turkish border with Syria, Valerian agreed to let his troop stop for a quick 'brew'. 'What you did was quite dangerous. You took an old tin, punched holes in it, filled it full of sand, poured petrol in, set it alight and then put an old kettle over it.' Valerian knew they did not have much time and was

walking over to ask them to get a move on when the whole thing
exploded. He and Trooper Pearson, who was walking beside him, were
covered in flames and rolled themselves in the sand to extinguish them.
Years later, when Valerian met Pearson's widow, she thought that he had
saved her husband's life. 'My recollection is that it was the other way
round', Valerian told her. He passed out in the ambulance which evacuated him to Alexandria and when he woke up he was in a tiny white
room barely big enough to hold a bed. 'I thought My God, I'm in heaven
or something. I didn't know where the hell I was!' He lay swathed in
bandages until he was moved to a hospital ship which went to Haifa by
the direct route through the Mediterranean, taking advantage of the
convention of war that the enemy would not sink a ship that sailed under
the flag of the Red Cross. When he reached the military hospital he was
in a ward of twenty-four other badly wounded officers. Considering that
he had been engulfed in flames, he was lucky to emerge from the incident
with only minor scars.

   While Valerian was recovering from his burns, he had plenty of time
to reflect on his life. October 23 1942 had marked the start of the battle
of Alamein – the turning-point of the war. It was also the day that
Valerian received a letter from his girlfriend Barbara McNeill telling him
that she was going to marry Michael Astor. A few months earlier, in a
letter to Eliza, he had written that 'I am surprised that Barbara hasn't
had any letters from me for a month. I have been writing very regularly.
I haven't heard from her for five weeks. I am sore too but I continue to
write. She doesn't bother.' He realised that he had not been as assiduous
as he might have in writing to her and news may well have reached her
of his various indiscretions, but 'I was extremely upset though I realised
she couldn't wait indefinitely for my return'. Michael, who was an old
friend of Valerian's, later wrote, 'we both found ourselves isolated by the
war from the company of the people we each wanted to see'.[7] Michael
and Barbara's engagement was announced in *The Times* on 27 October
and they were married five weeks later.

When Valerian left hospital in early 1943 life could provide no consolation
in the regiment's new encampment: a 'godforsaken place' called Raqqa
on the Turkish border with Syria. Apart from a 'Beau Geste'-style fort
which had been a base for the French Foreign Legion before the armistice,
there were no signs of human life for miles around. It rained constantly
and the camp was bogged down in water. There was brief respite for
some training, near Aleppo, but it was not until June that the regiment

escaped to higher ground when they moved to Slenffe, a 6,000-foot-high mountain near the coast. It seemed unsuitable terrain for an armoured car regiment but it was to prove invaluable experience for the mountain warfare that they would face the following year.

In the middle of September 1943, soon after Italy had surrendered to the Allies, Valerian got some news which would alter, irretrievably, the pattern of his future life. His first cousin Morny, the 6th Duke, who had joined the crack troops of the Commandos, had been killed at the Salerno landings. He had held the dukedom for a brief two years, since the death of his father in December 1941. Morny's death meant that the title passed back a generation to Lord Gerald Wellesley, and Valerian, as his son, immediately assumed the courtesy title of Marquess of Douro. There was little time to consider the consequences of this tragedy but Gerry sent a telegram to his son suggesting that they meet in Cairo to discuss some immediate practicalities. Not able to give his full name – forbidden during the period of the war – Gerry signed himself 'Daddy Wellington'. Naturally they met at Shepheard's. The main topic of conversation was the problem of Apsley House. With the prospect of large death duties, the option of maintaining both Stratfield Saye and Apsley House as private homes seemed out of the question. The seed was sown for a plan which would see my grandfather giving Apsley House and a collection of works of art to the nation.

By November 1943 the course of the war was beginning to turn. During this month the RAF continued their heavy bombing of Berlin. Germany had occupied Rome but the Allies had entered Naples, and the new Italian government formally declared war on Germany. British scientists joined the team of Americans who were working feverishly on splitting the atom. In Britain the Allied Expeditionary Force was forming in early preparation for the invasion of Europe. The Russians had taken back Kiev and Hitler had made what would prove to be his last speech to the Nazi Party. In Ireland, the Prime Minister Eamon de Valera had finally agreed to confiscate the German Embassy's radio transmitter. By the end of the month Roosevelt, Churchill and the Chairman of the People's Republic of China, Chiang Kai-shek, met in Cairo at the Mina House Hotel to discuss their strategy in the war against Japan. The conference was followed immediately by one in Tehran which involved the Russians rather than the Chinese. During these few weeks many of the Chiefs of Staff attending the conferences took a few days off and stayed in the King David Hotel in Jerusalem. 1HCR was assigned the responsibility of providing round-the-clock protection for the VIPs and Valerian found himself on duty in the hotel. This routine task gave him the opportunity to re-establish contact with a girl who worked in the building and whom he had met several times at different social functions when he was stationed at the Allenby Barracks in Jerusalem. She was Diana McConnel, the twenty-one-year-old daughter of the GOC.

FOUR

Beyond the Still Valley

S ome years ago my mother gave me a picture which had been gathering dust in an attic. It is a watercolour painted in soft autumnal colours, showing a brick-built mill beside a canal, smoke billowing from the chimneys, and a barge in the foreground being steered by a man standing in its bow with a pole. Two men at the stern are talking to each other as they go about delivering their cargo. On the other side of the canal a barge approaches from the distance. The picture evokes industry and enterprise: the function of the buildings, and the water beside them, is the focus for the artist. There is no signature on the front of the picture and no title on the back, merely a label which indicates that it was framed in Manchester.

My mother's maiden name is McConnel. Throughout my life I have been proud of my Scottish blood; perhaps as her only daughter I have felt a need to affirm it for fear of its being lost in the Wellesley strain. I was aware that cotton had been the McConnel trade and I had seen some of my mother's family portraits and silhouettes from the nineteenth century, showing characters with firm gazes and strong profiles. But I was woefully ignorant of the details of my Scottish roots, and the 'mill' picture hanging on my wall was a nagging reminder of that. The Wellington myths live and breathe, but who are the McConnels?

James McConnel, my great-great-great-grandfather, was born in 1762, seven years before Arthur Wesley. They may have belonged to the same generation but they were from totally different backgrounds: Arthur's elegant Dublin townhouse was a stark contrast to James's birthplace, a simple thatched cottage on a farm in the wilds of south-west Scotland. The farm was called Hannastoun and when I look at the Ordnance Survey map, to my great pleasure I discover that it still exists. So, one warm spring day I set off to find it.

Thanks to a nineteenth-century family account I know exactly what I am looking for:

It was pleasantly situated on the north-east side of a farm road, leading from the Garroch burn to the present homestead, about two-thirds of the way up the hill, and commanded a beautiful view of the richly wooded Garroch valley immediately below, bounded on the east by the hills through which the river Ken finds its way, and on the west by the fine mountains of the Kells range, conspicuous among which is the bold summit of the Millyea, about two thousand six hundred feet above the level of the sea.[1]

Little has changed in the Glenkens (as this part of the world is known), which is still a ravishingly beautiful landscape dotted with small farms and villages. After passing the Garroch burn, the track off the road takes me through a wood, crossing a carpet of bluebells, and I emerge the other side to glimpse the fields that would have been familiar to James.

The McConnels are part of the Macdonald clan: in Gaelic they are Mac-Dhomhnuill – 'son of Brown-eye'. Depending on which roots you dig up, the McConnel family tree boasts saints and sinners, rulers and runaways. By the time James McConnel was born there was a rich mix of adventure and enterprise in his blood. His forebears had fought for kings and been martyred for their religion; in trade as blacksmiths, they had honed the scythes and hooks which were grasped as weapons by the rebelling Presbyterian Covenanters, and then turned tail and shod the horses of the dragoons who were hunting down the rebels. By the year of James's birth the unrest of the previous century was over and his father (also James) and grandfather, Samuel, had settled down to till the land, renting the farm of Hannastoun near the town of Dalry. James's mother, Mary Cannan, was herself from strong Covenanter stock, and her family could be traced back to AD 171, when 'Canan, a captain of Galloway was created governor for Scotland'.[2] But the vigour of her roots did not sustain her constitution: she married at eighteen, gave birth to James two years later, had two more children who lived only for a few weeks, and died in childbirth when James was five years old. In later life he wistfully remembered his fragile young mother and the way his father's hands could encircle her slender waist.

James's father married again and had four more children. The McConnels' life was one of 'hardy simplicity': no shoes or stockings were worn except on Sundays, and their diet consisted mainly of oatmeal – for breakfast and supper. James later recounted an incident when, in the absence of his father, his stepmother 'stealthily indulged herself in a cup of tea'. James received an education at the parish school, but the teachers were often students or probationers for the Kirk and he would only have acquired the bare rudiments of reading, writing and arithmetic from them. As I look around from the point where the cottage would have stood, it is easy to imagine the bleak winters: the hills covered in snow, the ground rigid with frost. Life would have revolved round a small radius, with church and school about five miles away in New Galloway. Strangers would rarely be seen in the valley but occasionally a pedlar would appear with his exotic wares. His close neighbour and future business partner, John Kennedy, gives a taste of the excitement of such an event. 'I can recollect the greatest delight I ever had was when the pedlar, with his box of Birmingham wares, came round, and he opened his pack and displayed his beautiful stores for sale, and drew out, by pressing on a secret spring, the private drawers which contained his best knives, buckles, watch-chains, and seals.'

As I arrive, a stranger, at the new Hannastoun farmhouse, built in the 1830s, the present occupants are tending to their cattle and sheep. It seems that I am not the first descendant of James McConnel to turn up on their doorstep – visitors from the Australian branch of the family had been there a few years earlier. The spring sunshine has now given way to rain and the Millyea Mountain is shrouded in cloud. The farm looks prosperous, as it was when James's grandfather Samuel was the tenant; in his will he left over £300 to his heirs. But this commercial acumen bypassed a generation, and as James grew into manhood it becomes clear that the farm was slipping from his father's grasp. James's life was narrow and austere, his relationship with his stepmother was bad and, perhaps most of all, he wanted to know what was on the other side of the hill. John Kennedy, who left three years later, suffered the same feelings.

I remember how I used to long to know and see places beyond the still valley and the blue mountains that surrounded the place of my birth, and had remained stationary ever since the creation, and were unable to utter a simple sentence or account for themselves. These natural objects used to produce in me sometimes the deepest melancholy; and a singularly lonely feeling would be excited by the external silence all around us, only broken by the bleating of a solitary sheep, or the crowing of a neighbour's cock at a distance, or the thrashing flail at work in the open air, beating out the scanty grain of the black oats, which was spread on a skin, or the noise of the wintry flood over rocky precipices, or on Sunday, by the church bell; the sound came up the vallies from miles distant, and on other days when it called to sacrament. All this produced in my mind the deepest melancholy and made me think 'what can I do to see and know something besides this?'[3]

Three of James's Cannan uncles had 'escaped' and discovered what lay beyond the hills; one, a planter in Jamaica, had written to suggest he become a carpenter; another had a successful machine-making business in Chowbent, Lancashire. James knew that if he was to advance in life he needed to learn a trade, and Chowbent was his destination when one cold February morning he set off on foot, carrying in his pocket a 'passport' from his local minister. It was 1781, the year that the twelve-year-old Arthur Wesley walked in procession with his siblings and mother to bury his father in the Grosvenor Chapel in London. The steps of the nineteen-year-old James were towards the Industrial Revolution and the promise of a new life.

His journey took him through the town of New Galloway, past the familiar church and school, but once he was a few miles beyond he was in unknown territory, where the landscape was even bleaker and wilder than Hannastoun's. As I drive along the road that crosses the rocky moorland I think about James starting out on his great adventure. What did he expect to find in the outside world? No doubt he had heard tales of America's adopted son Paul Jones ravaging the coast of his native Galloway, and the minister would have recounted stories of London's anti-Catholic Gordon Riots. But when he reached Dumfries, only thirty miles from home, he would have been astonished to see the lamps in the streets and wagons pulled by four horses; in his remote valley, even carts were unknown.

When he finally arrived in Chowbent he was on safe territory with family and he received a welcome reserved for a special nephew. His aunt had a reputation for looking after the young men in her care – many of them Scotsmen – and James experienced the warmth and affection that had been lacking at home. For the next seven years he was housed, clothed and fed, as he trained to be a machine maker. Brought up in the Church of Scotland, James's religious allegiance shifted here and he became a Unitarian. It was David Cannan, another of his uncles, who introduced him to this Christian faith, which held that reason and belief were complementary and that religion and science could co-exist. The Unitarian chapel, built in 1752, dominated Chowbent, but many of Cannan's neighbours and fellow townsmen were wary of these modern beliefs and abused him for promoting them.

Not long into his apprenticeship James was given the task of delivering a clock to a customer seven miles away. Try as he might, he could not make it comfortable to carry, and his shoulders hurt so badly that he was 'sorely tempted to throw his burden on the ground, and to run away then and there for ever from clock, clock-making, and machine making', as one of his sons later recounted. 'But he withstood the temptation.' Maybe it was in this moment of truth that James determined to complete his apprenticeship and pursue his dream.

It was not all work at the Cannans': on the Sunday that John Kennedy joined the group, there was a celebration going on to mark the wedding of a former apprentice. 'After dinner, all the Scotchmen of the establishment assembled at the Bear's Paw, to hear the news from the native country,' Kennedy later remembered. 'But such a Sunday I never saw before! For everybody in the place seemed to come to the alehouse as soon as dinner was over; and such carousing and drinking was quite unknown in our native glen.' James survived the carousing and completed his apprenticeship. At twenty-six, he was now a fully qualified machine maker and Manchester, the home of the Industrial Revolution, was but ten miles away. It was there he headed next.

James's first sight of the city was from the top of the hill in Pendleton. He would have looked down green slopes and grassy fields to Salford; beyond he would have seen the outlines of the huge red-brick palaces that were springing up by the new canals, creating the teeming hive of industry and enterprise that made Manchester the second most important town in the kingdom. Now, as James arrived there, it was 1788, the eve of a bloody revolution in France, and both Arthur Wesley and Napoleon Bonaparte had stepped onto the first rung of their military ladders. The young Scotsman's sights were set on a less perilous path to advancement, but one which was no less bold.

Soon James went into business with John Kennedy. The beginnings of their enterprise are the stuff of local legend, recorded many years later by the *Manchester Evening Chronicle* in a story headlined 'Business Founded on Two Derelict Mules, Huge Concern Started by a Stroke of Bad Luck'. A customer who had ordered two spinning-mules from James defaulted; although James 'might have been excused for considering it a knock-down blow ... he turned the caprice of fate to his own advantage ... and laid the foundation of the firm which to-day owns 500,000 spindles'. In 1795 James's contribution to that 'foundation' consisted of one carding-engine, value £6, the two mules (£70) and about £92 in hard-earned money and other assets. Two years later James and John Kennedy were listing their firm in the Directory of 1797 as 'twist manufacturers and machine makers'[4] and they were now prosperous enough to buy a plot of land and build their first mill. When James had sat outside the cottage in Hannastoun, his gaze fixed on the horizon, could he have imagined that he would one day own a cotton mill?

When I start to explore the McConnel story, the beginnings of the trail are lit up for me by the discovery of two rare, privately published books which record much of the early family history: *Facts and Traditions* (1861) and *A Century of Fine Cotton Spinning* (1913). The latter is a slim volume with an elegant art deco cover. The first time I open it I get a wonderful surprise: there, as the frontispiece, is my watercolour. I learn that the mill was called the Sedgwick and was built in 1820; perhaps the picture hung on the wall of my great-great-great-grandfather's office. Suddenly my small painting is part of the family record, but do any of the McConnel mills still exist?

When James McConnel arrived in 1788, Manchester had a population of about 43,000. The streets were narrow and badly paved, but even then the town had many modern amenities: Strangeways was a park with mazes, lakes and woods; the Infirmary, erected in 1752, provided baths for the use both of patients and the public; there were regular 'Gentlemen's Concerts' and the Assembly Rooms, built soon after James arrived, hosted balls, tea parties and card-playing. The great actors of the day rehearsed their repertoire here before moving to London; the city boasted two travelling libraries and intellectual aspirations were soon to be fed by the Literary and Philosophical Society founded in 1791. Merchants met at the Exchange and on the pavements outside. When, in the mid-1790s, the new Chamber of Commerce passed a resolution positing the view that 'the exportation of cotton twist was detrimental to the manufactures of this country', James and John were not the only members of Manchester's rapidly expanding population who disagreed.

In the John Rylands Library in the University of Manchester I find a book which suggests that some of the McConnel/Kennedy mills might still be standing. Most of the mills were built in an area called Ancoats, alongside the Rochdale Canal, which was finished in 1794 and became the main artery for the industrial heart of Manchester. After the cotton mills fell silent in the 1950s the area became a ghost town, but crossing the canal now I can see a number of these giant structures, some clad in scaffolding with huge banners advertising new flats. I am clutching a photocopy of my painting, and by counting floors and windows I can identify the Sedgwick mill. It is still standing. When I go into the building I am met by another surprise: down one wall of the development company's huge open-plan office is a large chart of the history of the McConnels and the cotton industry – complete with illustrations, including a portrait of James McConnel and my own mill picture. The chart displays the McConnel trademark – a stag's head with a bale of cotton carried on the antlers – which was used right up until 1960, nearly two centuries after James's birth. I am beginning to appreciate what an extraordinary legacy my mother's forefather left behind.

To begin with, James and John Kennedy had operated out of their workshop, sometimes sleeping on shavings on the floor to save the cost of lodgings[5] so that they could put everything they earned back into their business. It was in 1797 that they took the big step of buying land to build their own mills (the first one was finished in 1805) and as their enterprise grew, so did their confidence and they acquired a house to live in near the mills. In May 1799, just in time for the dawn of the new century, James married a 'tall, graceful and good-looking' girl, twenty-one-year-old Margaret Houldsworth.

The Houldsworths were another 'cotton' family. James met Margaret through her brother Thomas, who became a prosperous MP and pillar of the Establishment. James was well into his thirties when he started courting; with his business well-established he now wanted some home comforts – a family who could appreciate the fruits of his endeavours and sons who would eventually inherit the firm. James was a shy man, not incapable of romantic gestures but brusque as well; and business was still the higher priority. Just before their marriage he wrote to his bride, advising her that urgent business might detain him and cause the ceremony to be postponed. In the event the wedding went ahead as planned. One of Margaret's bridesmaids was a young heiress called Mary Chaworth who later became romantically involved with the young Lord Byron. 'Had I married Miss Chaworth perhaps the whole tenor of my life would have been different', Byron later wrote. The two girls knew each other well when they were growing up in Nottinghamshire and would visit each other's houses.

Married life suited James. He was fond of music and Peggy (as Margaret was known) had, according to one of her sons, 'a good ear, and natural taste for music, and sang very nicely'; 'My boy, Tammie' was her favourite air. Every day James came back from the mill for a meal at lunchtime. On one occasion he was horrified to find that his new wife had used an important legal document to cover pots of jam that she was making. He stormed back to the mill but, just before he got to his office, realised that he had been too hard on Peggy. He went home to reassure her that she was forgiven, and from then on there were apparently few harsh words in their marriage.

In 1802 Peggy gave birth to their first child, Henry. Soon after, in 1804, James bought a plot of land in the Polygon, Ardwick, and built a house with stables and garden for about £7,000. A daughter-in-law later described it as 'an excellent substantial house, everything about it good and handsome, solid mahogany doors and satin damask curtains and furniture in the principal rooms, yet nothing showy or staring'.[6] By the time the house was finished in 1806 and the McConnels were able to move in, they had three more sons to fill it up. They were no longer living 'above the shop' or just round the corner. The McConnels were going up in the world.

The business continued to thrive. By 1802 McConnel and Kennedy were employing 312 people. They bought most of their raw American cotton through dealers in Liverpool, but eventually the firm used an American broker. The spun cotton was at first sold to domestic outlets, and as they became more successful they spread their net wider to the Continent. Much of James's and John's success lay in their ability to build and maintain their own machines, but they were also canny businessmen, dealing only with reliable clients who were unlikely to run up big debts. Their profits soared and they had a good reputation as employers: their skilled spinners earned decent wages, they paid for medical treatment and some housing was provided. In 1809 they were amongst the first employers to light their works by gas. In 1818 a factory inspector's report commended the firm: 'The neat conditions of the rooms, and the attention to cleanliness and ventilation gave us much satisfaction.' It concluded that 'the persons who work in the mills of Messrs. McConnel & Kennedy enjoy for the most part a good state of health'.

To mark their new social standing, in 1811 the McConnels threw a large ball, inviting all the respectable families in Manchester. 'Country dances were the principal amusement of the evening,' remembered their then eight-year-old son James:

> A thick cord divided the dancing-room, which measured about thirty feet long and eighteen wide, into two parts lengthways, and on either side two long files of ladies and gentlemen carried on briskly these then favourite and fashionable dances. The cord was removed to give space for the more measured and dignified movements of the minuet, and to permit my eldest brother, Henry, then ten years old, to exhibit his

'College Hornpipe', in which he acquitted himself to the admiration of the assembled guests.[7]

At this point the Napoleonic Wars were at their height, and much of the wealth generated by McConnel and Kennedy could be directly attributed to the conflict: the shortage of cotton on the Continent meant they could sell to Europe for twice the amount they were paid in their home market. Also, even more crucially, exporting was a hazardous business under conditions of war, risking confiscation by enemy authorities, but the rewards were high if their bales got through.[8] I find it gratifying that the military exploits and triumphs of one of my great-great-great-grandfathers indirectly helped the commercial enterprise and success of another. In June 1815, when Wellington had left the bloody battlefield of Waterloo and was writing his Despatch, James McConnel was more concerned with sorting out some credit they were owed. James's dogged persistence in all monetary matters certainly paid off: a year later the firm had 1,000 people working for it, and was the fourth biggest employer in Manchester.

As his business empire burgeoned, so did his family. James and Peggy had nine surviving children – seven sons and two daughters. James's sense of the deficiencies of his own schooling meant that his offspring received a decent education. He was keen to open their eyes to the outside world: 'We were permitted to see everything in the shape of conjurors, lecturers, panoramas, &c that came to the town,' wrote one of their sons. The McConnels were very hospitable and, without notice, James frequently brought home, 'for pot-luck', some stranger or bachelor. 'Regular dinner parties assembled at four, and broke up at ten; and my father, being of temperate habits, was obliged to protect himself from too much wine, in that wine-drinking period, by the use of very thick glasses, which held less than the others distributed round the table.'[9]

'My father was, in business matters, pains-taking and persevering, rather than acute,' wrote one of his sons. 'He possessed common sense, rather than talent; was thoughtful, prudent, and even somewhat timid, rather than impulsive or rash ... He was perhaps a little too sensitive as to the good opinion of others; but, when amongst friends, the expression of his native kindliness of disposition was unrestrained, and he was warm-hearted and genial in manner, and fond of innocent mirth.' James's hair went grey when he was quite young, which he always attributed to having used hair powder in his youth. He was conservative in his dress, always wearing a white cambric neck-cloth and never adopting the more fashionable collar, but he made one gesture towards the sartorial practices of the day. 'At one time he wore his boots over his trousers; then came the great change ... of wearing them under the trousers ... the old style of boots was called "Hessian", as the new is called "Wellington",' records *Facts and Traditions*. James ends the reminiscences of his father, 'He was a devout man. I remember, as one instance, how constantly, in watching the progress of events which led to the downfall of Napoleon I, he attributed those events to a superintending Providence.'[10] (Though Wellington might have found this judgement ungenerous, even he claimed that on the day of the battle of Waterloo 'the finger of Providence was upon me'.)

After Waterloo the firm continued to trade with Europe, but gradually the competition increased and after 1820 they once again concentrated on the domestic market. In 1826 John Kennedy retired from the business and James's two eldest sons, Henry and James, joined him and the firm became known as McConnel & Co. James never moved from Manchester, but in 1821 he re-established his roots in Scotland by buying two farms in Wigtownshire, about twenty miles from where he was born. A Whig by instinct and conviction, despite his prominent position in the commercial life of Manchester and unlike his partner John Kennedy, James never took much part in public life, though he did serve as a Commissioner of the Highways. John was closely involved with the Literary and Philosophical Society of Manchester, and was a founding director of the Liverpool and Manchester Railway.

If my two great-great-great-grandfathers could ever have met, it would have been at the opening of the railway on 15 September 1830, when the Duke of Wellington, as Prime Minister, was the guest of honour. The Duke travelled in a carriage especially decorated for the occasion. 'A canopy twenty-four feet long was placed upon gilded pillars, and so contrived as to be lowered when passing the tunnel. The drapery was of rich crimson cloth, and the whole surmounted by a ducal coronet.'[11] The engine pulling their train stopped at one point to take on a supply of water and some of the passengers alighted to stretch their legs, including the popular MP for Liverpool, William Huskisson, and Wellington. The two men were in conversation when Stephenson's 'Rocket' approached at speed from the opposite direction. Huskisson failed to get out of the way in time and was fatally injured. Wellington had no desire to continue the journey, but he was persuaded, and the huge crowds gathered along the line had no idea about the accident.

A number of the people who turned out to watch the trains were openly hostile: they saw the development of the steam engine as a direct threat to their livelihoods, and the Duke was not a popular figure in Manchester. James McConnel, by this time not in the best of health, would not have sympathised with the Duke's politics but he had his own experience of mob rule. The previous year he had written an account for the firm's records of the trouble that broke out during a spinners' strike. 'During the day a large body of weavers from the country have entered several power loom factories and thrown out or demolished every thing that came within their reach. One mill they have burnt to the ground.'

If James was on the platform to witness the arrival of the Duke, he would have applauded the first inter-city railway, seeing the opportunities afforded by mass travel on a network; the Duke on the other hand was highly suspicious of the whole venture and for the rest of his life advised people against travelling by train, particularly if they were women. Less than a year after this historic opening James was dead. He died at his home in the Polygon on 3 September 1831, six months short of his seventieth birthday. He was buried alongside those four of his children who had died in infancy, and when Peggy died fifteen years later all the McConnel remains were reinterred alongside hers in a church in Upper Brook Street.

When I visit Manchester, I know the church is still standing but I have no idea whether it is in use, or what state it is in. Upper Brook Street is close to Manchester University so I walk round the corner to find it. As I approach I can see the outline of its roof and spire but it soon becomes clear that it is propped up by scaffolding and stands, a stubborn remnant of the nineteenth century, in a sea of car salerooms and warehouse stores. I am reassured that the church survives, but when I peer through the railings I am shocked by the state of the graveyard, which is strewn with rubbish, with no sign of any gravestones.

I discover that it has not been a place of Christian worship for many years and that the Sunday School building attached to the church is now used as a centre for Islamic studies. I am welcomed into the centre and when I explain the reasons for my interest, am told that there is a dispute with the council about plans for restoring the church and that for the last ten years access to it has been barred on the grounds of health and safety. I am able to have a furtive look round the old graveyard, and this closer inspection reveals an even more depressing picture. The grass is covered in a layer of filth and invasive undergrowth, and littered with broken glass from the windows of the church. Originally there was a large, flat stone covering the family vault, engraved with the names of James and Margaret and their four infant children, William, Mary Cannan, May Anne and Margaret. It is impossible to work out whether the stone is still there.

I feel a responsibility to my ancestor to try and uncover the vault, and when I return to London I write to Manchester City Council, alerting them to the fact that in this dilapidated graveyard lie the remains of someone who played an important part in the industrial history of the city. The council is well aware of the state of the building and has for some time been considering what to do about it. Over the course of the next few months renovation starts, but it quickly establishes that the structure is in an even more perilous state than was originally thought and access to the graveyard is barred. However, one morning I receive an email from a contact in the Preservation Department, with an attachment. When I open it, I find myself looking at a photograph of a very old engraved stone. I can easily read the first words: 'In Memory of James McConnel'. I allow myself the credit for having at least saved the stone, if not the graveyard itself.

The spirit of adventure that propelled James to leave his desolately beautiful homeland lived on in his children. Three of his seven surviving sons emigrated to Australia and ensured that the McConnel flag was raised on the other side of the world: Mount McConnel in Queensland was named after the youngest son.

William, the sixth son and my great-great-grandfather, was on the surface less adventurous than some of his brothers. He was born in 1809 when his parents were already living in their smart house in the Polygon. As a boy he was a great athlete – a runner and jumper – and he was known to have walked an extraordinary fifty miles one day and twenty-three the next. He worked his way up in the mills, starting off as a spinner, and when his father died in 1831 his brothers Henry and James made him a partner. At this point McConnels, with 1,500 employees, was the biggest firm in the business but difficult times lay ahead. The three brothers worked frantically hard to keep the enterprise going and by the mid-1840s they had weathered the storm. Not unlike his father, William's main focus in life was the family business but on 29 July 1852, aged fifty, he married Margaret Bradshaw, twenty-eight years his junior. William made up for his late start: the couple had eight children.

By 1861 William was in sole charge of the family firm. 'Capable, clear-headed and energetic', he had the foresight to lay in a huge stock of cotton before the outbreak of the Civil War in America; once again the McConnels bucked the trend and survived the crisis. As he entered old age, William began to feel the pull of his homeland, and he rented different places in western Scotland. Finally, in 1872, he put down permanent roots by acquiring Knockdolian, an estate in the region of Carrick (now South Ayrshire). The house, a Scottish baronial mansion built in 1840 above the banks of the River Stinchar, commands glorious views up the valley. With the purchase of the property, his home for the rest of his life, my great-great-grandfather became the latest McConnel to defy King Charles I's challenge in a letter of 1636, referring to the 'enormous numbers of mountain savages called McConnell ... who were never to hold land in their native country again'.[12]

William loved his new property and developed a strong interest in farming, fishing and country life. Fitness, hard work and a late marriage proved a successful formula for longevity. But sadly he was deprived of companionship in old age when his much younger wife predeceased him, just before his eightieth birthday. By then he had handed over the formal running of the cotton mills to his eldest son John, but he continued to take a strong interest in the business.

I am impressed to discover that in his eighties he started to play golf and he continued to fish and shoot. I know that he was a keen reader: I have a fine old photograph of him in his later life which shows him surrounded by books. I also own many of the books he bought for the house, showing his reading habits to be quite eclectic. The collection ranges from a complete set of the novels of the Irish writer Maria Edgeworth, who was a close friend of Kitty, the first Duchess of Wellington, to a set of political biographies, including a volume (with uncut pages) on Marquess Wellesley, the First Duke's eldest brother. William survived to see the dawn of the twentieth century and died in 1902, aged ninety-three.

Knockdolian was inherited by William's son John, who was also running the family business. He has an unusual claim to fame in the McConnel family history: he was a passenger on the *Lusitania* when it was torpedoed in 1915 by a German U-boat. When rescued from the sea he was, in his own words, 'as black as a collier', and his head was plastered with mud; the theory was that he had been sucked down by one of the funnels, and then blown out again.

John and his wife Edie had no children but his brothers and sisters and their families would stay regularly at Knockdolian, including his brother William Houldsworth McConnel and his five children. William

Houldsworth, my great-grandfather, inherited much of his father's and grandfather's practical skills and thinking. He became a civil engineer, settled in Hampshire and in 1884 married Florence Banister, the daughter of a Surgeon General. Their eldest child, Merrick, born later that year, was followed by two daughters, Muriel and Eryl, and lastly Malcolm and Douglas, identical twins born at Knockdolian on 9 June 1893. On the staircase at Knockdolian there is a huge portrait of the two boys, innocent, fresh-faced twelve-year-olds, who stare out from the canvas, one seated on a bench, the other leaning against it, their arms resting alongside each other. The painting dominates the house. Like most twins they did everything together – they were inseparable and many idyllic summers were spent there with their uncle John.

One late-April day in 1908 both boys were with their father, who was showing them a new electricity generator at their house, Heath End in Hampshire. It had been raining heavily and the fourteen-year-old twins were wearing mackintoshes with long, loose sleeves. No one knows precisely how it happened but it is likely that Malcolm's curiosity took him too close to the machine. The death certificate states: 'Accidentally killed through his clothing being caught in the rapidly revolving spindle of an engine & his body being consequently dashed with great force against objects close to the said spindle.' Douglas never spoke about the accident. He was already a gifted sportsman and successful scholar of Winchester; he would become an outstanding soldier, but he never got over the loss of his identical twin.

In 1912, shortly after leaving Winchester College, Douglas became a 'gunner' when he joined the 113th Battery of the Royal Field Artillery at Deepcut. Two years later, as railway stations and ports the land over echoed to the sound of marching boots, he set off for the Western Front. Like most of his fellow soldiers, I am sure he believed that the war would soon be won. But for the next four years being at the front became his 'job' – a grim, harrowing, depressing occupation with short spells of leave. He was one of the lucky ones – he survived. After it was all over, he wrote a list of the battles in which he took part – Mons, Marne, Aisne, Ypres, La Bassée, Neuve Chapelle, Festubert, Loos, Somme, Vimy, Messines, Passchendaele, Cambrai, Lys, Arras. A heavily used *The Western Front at a Glance*, a battered 'Field message and sketch book' and a 'Field Artillery Training' guide, still splattered with Flanders mud, are testament to the months and years of Douglas's youth which were swallowed up by the Great War.

Douglas kept diaries, and every few days he wrote home to his parents, often on gossamer-thin sheets torn from his field book. His spare language and understated style reveal a stoical optimism. His parents kept everything he sent them, including the standard grey 'Field Service' postcards which allowed the sender to give basic information – 'I am quite well'; 'I have been admitted into hospital' and so on. Some of the letters still carry the now rusty wartime pins which the McConnels used carefully to keep the sheets together; occasionally his father added a note – 'See the *Times* map' – or corrected a date at the top of the letter where Douglas's tired mind had put the wrong one.

In one of the letters to his father Douglas explained the routine of the battery. 'We have an observation station somewhere near the enemy & we three subalterns take it in turns to spend 24 hours there. The Major never goes near the place, so all the commanding of the shooting of the battery falls on us, and as the other two have only just joined, I do a good deal of it myself.' A telephone wire ran from the observation post to where the guns were placed and the gunners fired their shells according to very precise instructions from the man in the observation post. There were others who were curious about life on the front-line. 'I had a visitor yesterday in my observation station. I shook hands with him & he was very ready to chat. What he was doing there I can't imagine. He goes by the name of Winston Churchill! He gave away no political secrets!'

'The Huns rather blew a trench in on the top of me on Sunday (dirty dogs),' Douglas wrote in May 1915, when he was fighting in the battle of Festubert in the Ypres Salient. 'They did no damage bar smashing my wrist watch and taking a few bits of skin off the back of my hand; they report every case that has drawn blood so don't be either surprised or alarmed if my name shd appear in the casualty list!' In his diary, after an even more sanguine account of the incident, he adds, 'It knocked me over and when I got up I found there was no breastwork left between me and the Germans. I moved up the parapet a few yards. My telephone connection was then broken again. There was no possibility whatever of mending the wire so after waiting about $\frac{3}{4}$ hour I made my way back to the observation station where I got some oxo, most excellent and refreshing.' A few days later, the bombardment was even fiercer.

The Germans started deliberately to shell all the houses in the RUE DU BOIS in which our Obs. Stn. was. It was most unpleasant and our house was shelled more heavily than any other. They kept it up solidly till 7 pm the next evening, hitting the house itself on an average of once a minute the whole time. We did not give much for our chances! We were saved by sandbags, in fact we had over 5 blind shells into the sandbags where we were. At about 7 pm Spittal managed to arrive & relieved me. I went down to the battery – a most lively walk.

It is not clear whether Douglas's letter reached his parents in time: a War Office telegram is included in the papers reporting him wounded. No doubt aware of the alarm the incident may have caused at home, soon after he added a postscript to a letter: 'This is a nice soft position.' 'The men have started gardens on the top of their dugouts!' reported Douglas. 'We have built ourselves a summerhouse & to give protection against any bit of shell that might arrive it has a sandbag wall. Outside the wall we have made a rock garden of vast boulders. We are a little short of rock plants, but what we have planted are at present growing finely. This gardening is our chief occupation, we water the gardens every morning and evening.' Ten days later: 'Our rock garden is getting on very well. Nearly everything we have planted is now growing nicely ... I thought the periwinkles were dead but they have suddenly taken on a new lease of life.'

Two years on, after several similar battles, the longest and most dev-astating of which was the Somme, things were little changed on the Western Front. In May 1917 Douglas's Commanding Officer wrote, 'I would like to bring to your notice the highly satisfactory manner in which Major D.F. McC performed the duties of liaison officer ... during the attack on V[imy] on April 9 ... his tact and judgement won the complete confidence of the G.O.C.' Douglas attributed the commendation to 'my presenting them with two bottles of whisky and one of port!'. But shortly after, his bravery was officially recognised when he was awarded a DSO. 'It was a pleasant surprise ... I did not expect it in the least,' he wrote to his parents. 'Well the battle was a success as it was bound to be with all this artillery. The infantry these days have only to walk quietly along behind the barrage and take any Huns prisoner that are left. I believe old women with knitting needles could have taken the ridge [Vimy] but holding it is a different matter altogether.'

Four months later the McConnels were faced with the news that every family dreaded. Their eldest son, Merrick, also a gunner fighting on the Western Front, was mortally wounded during a preliminary action in the drawn-out battle of Passchendaele. 'It is a great pity he could not just have got his leave,' wrote Douglas. 'He had a happy life and the finest possible death. It is up to us who are left behind to finish off this war for good and all.' The nurse who looked after Merrick later recalled the way he 'never complained and smiled every time she looked at him'. Shortly before he died, Merrick asked the nurse whether she thought his wounds were serious enough to get him back to England. He died at 12.45 p.m. on 14 September, the day that he was due to go home on leave to see Helen, his three-year-old daughter, and his wife May.

Four months earlier Merrick had written to Helen: 'Do you know that Daddy lives in a little room half in the ground, & one day early in the morning, two little swallows came in looking for a place to build their nest. They were not a bit frightened of Daddy, for they looked about for a long time & then flew away. Have you any making their nests outside your nursery window? ... Daddy is a tired man, & must go to sleep, but he sends you a kiss and one for Mummy which you must give to her, please. Goodnight little sweetheart.'

'So the war is over,' wrote Douglas in November 1918. 'It was a very tame ending as far as we were concerned as we were out of action at the time and we only knew about it by rumour ... anyhow as the show is over & the boche is Na Poo [finished], nothing else much matters.' The war may have been over but Douglas, along with many of the other soldiers who had survived, stayed out in Flanders for another five months: demobilisation was a complicated business for the army, with its huge baggage of equipment, arsenal and horses. Jerry, Douglas's favourite horse who had been with him for the entire course of the war, had an ignominious end: afflicted with a contagious eye infection, he could not be repatriated and, as recounted by Douglas, was sold 'to the local butcher for meat for 200 francs. What an end for the poor old beast. I shall collect the hoofs and tail and get them cured & mounted.' In one of his last letters from Flanders, Douglas requested: 'I want to ask you one thing mother & that is will you do all you can to make it easy for me to see as much of Ruth as I can when I get my leave? I am quite serious & mean every word and in consequence, except for Father, please don't let any single soul ... know I have asked you this.' He ends the letter, 'I can't write quite an ordinary letter tonight, so will stop.'

'Arrived Southampton this morning going to Deepcut, Douglas', read my grandfather's telegram, sent on 8 April 1919. He was home at last, complete with three Mentions in Despatches and his DSO. Six weeks later *The Times* announced the engagement between 'Captain Douglas F. McConnel, D.S.O., R.F.A., son of W.H. McConnel, of Heath End, Basingstoke, and Ruth, daughter of Major W.D. Garnett-Botfield, late

R.A. of Beamish, Albrighton.' Florence, Douglas's mother, must have been as good as her word.

Ruth's mother Susan, known as Daisy, was born a McConnel, so Douglas and Ruth were distant cousins and had known each other since they were children, having both spent holidays at Knockdolian. There was opposition to the union, principally because of the blood ties. 'If you think that I have not thought out every possible point of view *including* relationship you are just miles out', Douglas had written to his mother. Perhaps the uneasiness caused a delay in the wedding: it was announced, and invitations printed, for 4 March 1920, but did not take place until 20 April.

The wedding was at St Mary's Church, Albrighton, near Ruth's parents' house. Ruth was dressed in 'white charmeuse, slightly draped with orange blossom, train of the same material lined with white chiffon, wreath of myrtle and orange blossoms, with tulle veil'. The bride's gift to her groom was a Kodak camera, his to her was an elegant 'skunk stole', which Ruth wore as part of her 'going away' outfit. They spent their honeymoon in fashionable Biarritz.

When they returned to England Douglas took up a teaching job at the Woolwich Military Academy, and the family lived near 'The Shop' (as it was called) on Woodville Road. Douglas used his Matchless motorbike to get to work, and occasionally persuaded Ruth to venture forth in the sidecar attached to it. But soon it became increasingly uncomfortable. On 14 January 1922 Ruth gave birth to a baby girl, whom they christened Diana Ruth. Two years later John was born, but tragically Ruth suffered from a blood condition which meant he lived for a few hours only. Today a simple transfusion would have saved his life. Diana was to be their only child.

FIVE

A Soldier's Wife

One wintry day in Jerusalem, late January 1944, Diana McConnel was sitting at her desk on the fourth floor of the King David Hotel, the regional Headquarters of the British Army. Her job, with a civilian rank equivalent to a Captain, was in the Military Intelligence unit and her office was next door to that of her father, Major-General Douglas McConnel, the General Officer Commanding Palestine and Trans-Jordan. Most of the papers passing across her desk were routine, but one report caught her eye. It concerned a bomb plot by the Stern Gang, a Jewish terrorist group fighting to remove the British from Palestine. The plot was devastatingly ambitious: the targets were all the high-ranking British officials in Jerusalem – the High Commissioner, the Chief Justice, the Chief of Police, the Chief Judge, the Head of the Arab Legion and her father. The site was St George's Cathedral; the occasion, her own wedding the following Friday, 28 January, to Captain the Marquess of Douro. This intelligence document was the first Diana knew of the plot.

The bomb was found lodged in the arch that led to the courtyard outside the cathedral and was removed under cover of darkness. The wedding went ahead as planned; the security forces hoped that those responsible would turn up to witness the carnage.

I grew up with the extraordinary account of the bomb threat that hung over my parents' wedding. To me, one of the most remarkable aspects of the story is that my mother did not confide in my father. Her job gave her access to all the sensitive intelligence about the region so she had signed the Official Secrets Act, and that meant she could not discuss her work with anyone, even with her future husband, and even when it concerned a plot to murder them both. All these years later my father is still impressed by her coolness and discretion: 'When we left the church we were accompanied by a small army of outriders and police escorts but I thought that it was merely because I was marrying the General's daughter!'

Diana's father had trained her well. She had gone straight from the protective world of a girls' boarding school into the strange, schizophrenic environment of Jerusalem, dominated and controlled by men, and laced with high-octane socialising and the constant threat of terrorist attacks. She rapidly took on a level of responsibility that she would never have had in England. She arrived a shy young girl; when she left four years later she was a married woman who had lived through the twilight days of the British Mandate in Palestine. When I think about that time in my mother's life it strikes me that these were her most independent years – afterwards she would be surrounded by the responsibilities of being a wife, a mother and a consort. I suspect that the sense of freedom and excitement that is integral to the life of a single girl contributes to her lasting attachment to the region; she has since visited Jordan and other Arab countries regularly, but apart from a brief foray of twenty-four hours when my parents celebrated their fiftieth wedding anniversary, she has not returned to Jerusalem. I put a plan to her: that we leave my father at home by a warm Hampshire fire, and go on a trip to Israel. For her, it will be an opportunity to reminisce; for me it will give an insight into what she was like as a young woman. For both of us it will be a chance to spend some time together, talking about her memories of her early life.

'When I was growing up I vowed I would never marry a soldier.' As the only child of a soldier, the young Diana suffered the disruption and dislocation that different military postings wreak on the lives of wives and children. She was born on a cold mid-January Saturday, just as the snowdrops – in later life they would become her favourite flowers – were starting to push their way through the frozen ground. Diana's first home was in Woolwich, where her father Douglas was serving as an instructor at the Military Academy. In Diana's infant years two more English postings followed; but in 1927 Major McConnel was sent to the Quetta Military Academy in India to serve as a Brigade Major. Ruth accompanied him but Diana was left at home: the journey to the subcontinent was considered hazardous and the Indian climate too intemperate for a young child. She was entrusted to the care of her maternal grandparents, Susan (Daisy) and Walter Garnett-Botfield.

Daisy had been a talented painter, but when Ruth was three years old and she was trying to paint her portrait, she became frustrated by her restless sitter. 'If I can't paint my daughter, I'll give it up.' She threw down her brushes and took up the trowel; she became an ardent gardener and recruited Walter, at the time a retired army officer, to her new-found vocation. Together they scoured the world looking for rare species to bring home to Beamish, the house they built in the Midlands in 1908. One of the attractions when they bought the land had been a large grass field, which they turned into a garden. 'It seemed rather uphill work at first,' Daisy later wrote, 'as there was not a single tree or shrub of any kind.' But she had a limitless amount of energy for gardening and a benign attitude to things that grow in the ground: 'In our garden the plants are left at home where they choose to sow themselves. They are not raised by us but they just take their own line and sow themselves. We look after them and encourage them with top dressings and love.'¹ She had a stricter approach to grandchildren; at the age of five Diana was sent to a boarding school.

'It was hell – I hated it.' My mother remembers the misery of being sent away at such a tender age. 'Even though it was run by a woman who was a distant relative, they were very strict and I was lonely.' Holidays with Granny were more forgiving but there was still a firm regime – Daisy had strong religious beliefs and insisted that Sunday was devoted to church and bible reading, with no games, even ones for the benefit of children. But it is to her grandmother that Diana owes one of the greatest pleasures in her life: her interest in plants. 'I used to follow Granny round the garden and she would set me to work on weeding.' Daisy was a much-respected plantswoman, fêted by gardening luminaries of the time like E.A. Bowles and Reginald Farrer, and the Beamish garden was constantly being visited by other gardeners, who would be startled to see such a young child toiling away. 'How could you put your granddaughter to work?' they asked. 'Because she knows what are weeds and what aren't', Daisy would answer.

I like the picture in my mind of my mother as a little girl playing and working in this beautiful garden, but it is uncomfortable to think of her in a house filled with old people, who would sometimes fail to appreciate the needs and feelings of a young child. Many years later, after Diana was married and Ruth was living with Daisy in England, she wrote some confessional words to her daughter: 'I now know what it is like to be left stranded at Beamish! Like I left you as a child. I realise only too well some of what you had to put up with; I am so sorry that you may have had horrible times as I know now how very unkind both Aunt Eva and Granny can be if you don't go their way. I don't think that Granny means it, but if I'd anywhere of my own to go to now I'd go!' 'Aunt' Eva was Daisy's companion, a 'big, bossy' woman with a controlling presence in the house. While Diana's grandfather was alive his study was, for Eva, out of bounds. 'He couldn't stand her!' says my mother.

Eventually Ruth returned from India to rescue her daughter, and with a governess in tow they set off to rejoin Douglas. Diana was thrilled to be reunited with the father she adored; he came to meet them when their ship docked at Bombay. 'We travelled to Quetta on a rather magical train where you had separate sleeping and dining quarters and your own cook.' The family lived at 38 Survey Road, just outside Quetta, and life for Diana assumed a new and more tranquil routine. Unfortunately the governess was not a success: all three McConnels disliked her for being narrow-minded, humourless and racist. But lessons for Diana ended at lunchtime and the afternoons were for treats: riding her pony Jack Horner on expeditions with her parents, and the occasional children's party to which pets were bidden too; first among the guests were Diana's tortoise and her angora rabbits.

Diana's two years in India were happy ones, but Major McConnel's job changed again and Ruth and Diana headed back to England. On the boat home Diana developed an illness which was never diagnosed. In fact Diana's young years were dogged by ill-health, including two bouts of scarlet fever. 'The first time, when I was very small, they shaved my head – doctors believed you lost strength through your hair – and I was surrounded by a wall of white sheets dipped in some strong-smelling disinfectant.' Diana developed an understandable antipathy towards doctors that survives to this day; her robust constitution suggests, however, that some of the remedies worked.

Back in Britain, the unpleasant and ineffectual governess could be released from her duties and a more normal education took her place. One school Diana could bicycle to; another introduced the novelty of boys. 'Given that I didn't have any brothers it was quite nice to go to a mixed school.' But there was an even greater treat in being home. When I asked my mother what the happiest times of her childhood were, in spite of the governess, I expected her to say India, but there was a one-word answer – 'Knockdolian'.

Diana's first visit to the house in South Ayrshire was when she was four years old, and from the moment she stepped over the threshold one bitterly cold winter, she loved it. 'I remember running out of the back door and standing by the bank looking down to the bridge over the dark Stinchar river. I ran down the path towards it and on the way I found a dead bluetit. I gave it a full burial – in amongst the carpet of snowdrops.' At her tender age Diana could not have understood that eventually she would inherit Knockdolian; but ever since that day, it has been the most important place in the world to her – a refuge in her imagination and a home she never tires of visiting.

At fourteen, Diana was once again sent off to boarding school – to Benenden; but this time she was content to be away, knowing that for the holidays she would be reunited with both her parents. She discovered she had inherited some of Daisy's talent for painting, and the McConnel love of music came through in her modest skill at the piano. She was good at maths and unenthusiastic about French; she played lacrosse and tennis, and devoured novels about adventures in far-flung places. In the holidays she often saw her best friend and cousin, Cecilia Banister.

By the summer of 1938 Douglas knew that a posting abroad was imminent, and the days they spent that summer at Knockdolian were more precious than usual. While Douglas and Ruth cast their flies over the salmon lying in Blackstone, the deep, dark pool below the house, Diana and Cecilia teamed up for tennis matches on the grass court, or bicycled to 'Cowrie Cove' – named by the family after the tiny pink shells to be found there. Shells were an essential part of McConnel holidays: sweet souvenirs of treasure-seeking walks along rock-strewn beaches. There were picnics on the moor and the perennial challenge of walking to the top of Knockdolian Hill, the 900-foot-high local landmark which dominates the valley and from whose top, on a clear day, there is a glorious panoramic view for miles around. When Ruth and Diana set off for the south and the start of the new term, Douglas was left on his own. He wrote wistfully to his daughter the day after: 'The house seems very silent & full of ghosts, particularly the sort that say "nighty, nighty, sleepy tightly"!' He ended with the fisherman's eternal optimism: 'Perhaps I shall catch a fish tomorrow!' and then signed off as he always did, 'Best love Tuppenny [his nickname for his daughter] Daddy'. It would be another seven years before the McConnels were back at Knockdolian.

In the spring of 1938 Hitler had walked into Austria to claim it for the new German empire, and by the autumn he was threatening to invade Czechoslovakia. Britain was on stand-by and the older generation had a terrible feeling of déjà vu. 'What size gas-mask do you take?!' wrote Ruth to her daughter at Benenden. At the end of September Chamberlain returned from Munich waving his 'peace in our time' paper and, with the Allies' blessing, Germany annexed the Sudetenland. Two weeks later Diana got news from her father of his posting. 'It's a very good job, in fact I could hardly have got a better one,' he wrote, 'but the fly in the ointment is that the 8th Division is forming in Palestine and I have to take ship and sail for there in about 10 days!' There was just enough time for Diana to have special leave from school to see her father before he sailed on the SS *Strathnaver*. It was the height of the Arab Rebellion in Palestine and the country was too dangerous for wives or daughters. In those uncertain times, no one knew how long he would be away.

By March 1939 the rebellion was beginning to calm down and Ruth joined Douglas. She soon established her own routine: 'Each morning I go out rambling about looking for plants, seeds, bulbs etc.' She reported to Diana that Douglas was 'looking very well' and they had managed some fishing trips. 'I caught a queer little fish rather a round shape [she draws it] that went straight into a hole in the rocks! Daddy came to my rescue and pulled it out.' In May Douglas took up a new senior staff job in Jerusalem, and for the time being the King David Hotel became the McConnel home. Ruth wrote every few days to her daughter on the hotel's pale blue paper, with purple-lined envelopes. Her chatty letters darted between news of their social life – 'Daddy and I have been taught by Col. Ritchie how to do the Palais Glide! So tonight we want to try and do it!!' – to more serious incidents: a fellow plantswoman was in an 'upset, as she was in a house with some friends the other night when the man was shot by some arab & a bomb thrown inside the house, but it didn't do much damage & I think the man is getting better, but it is rather a shock & takes a little getting over'. The Arab Rebellion was formally at an end, but the McConnels were still living in a war zone.

By July Diana's long summer holidays were looming, and Ruth decided to go home rather than leave her teenage daughter to the 'boredom' of Beamish. She rented a house by the sea in Selsey, Sussex. Cecilia was among a group of friends who came to stay. In the day the girls lay in the sun on the beach or went shrimping or beachcombing; in the evening they would play cards or listen to the wireless. Their chatter was more about boys than bombs; their preoccupations the exams that lay ahead of them. Those few weeks were the last days of innocence for Diana and Cecilia. On 3 September, a few days before the start of the school term, war was declared.

For Douglas, on his own again in Jerusalem, the prospect of Christmas 1939 was a bleak one: 'Christmas will be a bit dull I expect . . . I cheer my self by the thought that we shall, someday, have a happy Xmas, all three of us together again.' When Diana returned to school in January 1940 for her last term, she was head of her house and, much to her father's delight, had passed her Matriculation: 'It's splendid. I always felt you could do it if you had the fortune to put things down in the way the examiner likes ... & I am delighted that you like the idea of coming out here even if it means leaving school earlier. I have made one or two enquiries about getting you a job after you arrive. The head of the police said he could find you one in the C.I.D. at about £2 a week ... I shan't let you take it unless it's a nice one.'

Soon after her eighteenth birthday, Diana kicked the dust of Benenden off her shoes and, armed with her 'matric' and a diploma in typing, set off with her mother for a reunion with her father. When they arrived in Damascus they found Douglas McConnel waiting for them with his staff car. Father and daughter had not seen each other for eighteen months; he had written to her only weeks before, 'I can't quite imagine you with curly hair but I expect it's nice. It will be good to see you again. Don't get grown up too quickly!' To Douglas it must have seemed as if the shy young girl with a mass of dark unruly hair standing on the quayside had done exactly that.

Before my mother and I left for Israel, I went to visit someone who had met her for the first time in Jerusalem all those years ago. Araminta (Minta to her friends) was the eldest daughter of the British High Commissioner, Sir Harold MacMichael, and was living in Jerusalem at Government House with her parents. 'I remember when Diana first appeared she had a huge man's wrist-watch and was wearing rather old-fashioned clothes.' Now the widowed Lady Aldington, she is two years older than my mother, which at the time made her the ideal person to take Diana under her wing. 'I was so pleased to have a potential new friend but it took me about four months to prise her away from her father, and get her out on the town.' The two girls rapidly became friends and would talk incessantly on the phone, with a secret code – 'cabbages!' – if they realised that the strict Lady MacMichael was listening on another receiver.

Diana may have been shy and uneasy about social life, but she quickly found employment. The first independent decision of her life had been to ignore her mother's advice to do a cooking course in her last term at school, opting instead to master the keyboard of a typewriter. The move stood her in good stead: she immediately secured a job in the typing pool at British Military Headquarters. It meant, too, that after such a long time apart father and daughter would be working under the same roof.

When my mother and I arrive in Jerusalem, our first port of call is the famous King David Hotel. For the British during the Mandate, it was the hub of all social, political and military activity. My mother worked on the fourth floor, and in the evening would often drink or dance in the basement in the fashionable nightclub, La Régence. The hotel paid the price for its strategic importance when, in 1946, a huge bomb planted by Jewish terrorists ripped its side off. By then Douglas, Ruth and Diana were safely back in England.

The strains of the dance band have long since died away, and the basement is now used for less glamorous activities like conferences and seminars. I detect a slightly wistful expression on my mother's face as she looks around, remembering. Perhaps she is thinking of her first visit there, almost certainly with Minta, wearing her favourite dress of black slinky velvet – probably one of the few English purchases in Diana's wardrobe that won Minta's approval. When I talked to Lady Aldington, she reckoned there were 'only about eight of us' – referring to the number of young single women in Jerusalem at the time. There were always swarms of youthful officers around, keen to escape the monotony of the barracks or the horrors of the battlefield. One of the regiments was the Black Watch, who marched under the Scottish flag – an added attraction for Diana.

'It was a heightened reality – almost surreal,' remembered Lady Aldington. 'We were floating on a magic carpet, but a lot of the time it was awful.' This strange, disjointed life was a typical pattern for most young people caught up in the war, whether behind the firing line or on it. But in that region, the war was being fought on several fronts. Though the Arab Rebellion had ended in 1939, there was still unrest in the countryside; Jewish terrorist groups were operating across the entire area; and, further afield, the British were fighting to prevent the Germans and their allies from controlling the oil pipelines and the Suez Canal. Like their contemporaries back home, Diana and Minta knew that friendships and flirtations could, abruptly and tragically, end. Understandably, my mother is protective about the details and identities of her admirers from those years; but I know that both she and Minta had close friends in the Black Watch who never returned for the second waltz.

Nowadays the King David is taller by two floors, but my mother's keen memory is able to work out exactly where her father's office would have been and to identify the room that housed the typing pool where she started her first job. The manager of the hotel, who shows us around, is amazed to think that my mother knew the hotel from all those years ago. He shows us the wonderful view towards the Mount of Olives and the huge golden dome of the Al-Aqsa mosque. At the time of her marriage her office was on this side of the building, and, more pertinently, it was this view that greeted my mother on the morning after the wedding. The hotel manager asks her whether she notices anything different in the grounds. Without a pause for reflection she replies: 'The palm trees have been moved!' He looks incredulous. 'Yes – I'm really impressed!' And so was I.

Life in Jerusalem had its own rituals and rhythms, some of them imported from home. There were fishing expeditions when Douglas could get away; beachcombing and walking in the hills, with the McConnels' beloved Ayrshire always the measure for achievement – 'Mount Carmel is even higher than Knockdolian Hill'. Above all, for Ruth there was the search for rare and interesting plants to send home to her mother or her gardener friends. Sometimes Diana was enlisted to draw the finds and she would meticulously record the crocuses, anemones and cyclamen that grow wild in the Palestinian countryside. One day, after Douglas had become a General and was commanding the whole area, a telegram arrived for him at HQ: 'Please look for crocus hyemalis with yellow antlers.' When the young communications officer on duty took down the words he assumed the worst; the message was in code and the General was involved in a spying plot. The matter was cleared up and Ruth was ticked off by her husband. 'Don't encourage this sort of thing. We do happen to be in the middle of a major war!'

Soon after Diana's arrival in Jerusalem the McConnels moved from their flat in the centre of the city to a house in the Talpiot area, then a leafy suburb right next door to a golf course, where Douglas could play the occasional round and Ruth could forage in the undergrowth for plants. Sometimes, when work permitted, Diana and her father would go riding, though always with an escort. And for Diana the house had another advantage – Government House, and Minta, were a few minutes away, on the other side of the course.

When the British Mandate came to an end in May 1948, Government House briefly accommodated the Red Cross. It then became the United Nations Headquarters, which it still is today. Unwisely, I have not arranged any formal access to the zone, hoping that we can just turn up. Alternating lines of UN-blue oil drums flank the main entrance to the compound and though the occupants of our vehicle may not look suspicious, we are certainly an unlikely foursome: our flamboyant Israeli guide Aviram (a gay, decorated ex-army officer), swathed in a turquoise pashmina; Mustapha, our charming Palestinian driver; my mother, immaculately dressed in tweed jacket, yellow cashmere jersey and brown wool trousers, and armed with a green stick that converts into a seat; and me, more conventionally dressed in jeans and trainers.

Aviram alights from the vehicle and with a slight flourish announces to the bemused security official that he has the Duchess of Wellington in the car; he is more than capable of looking after himself, but I join him to fill in details. By now the head of security is on the end of a phone listening rather warily to my story about a woman who was last here sixty-one years ago. Our timing is bad; it is nearly noon on a Friday in Ramadan, but he promises to see what he can do. While we await the verdict, we set off to try and find the house in Talpiot where the McConnels lived. The golf course has given way to a new development, so it is hard for my mother to get her bearings. One street looks very familiar and she has a vague memory of a nightclub nearby, but in the end none of the houses appears quite right. Memory Lane can be a frustrating place, so we are all relieved when, somewhat to my surprise, we get the call from the UN granting us permission to enter the zone.

'Dinners at Government House were always very formal – quite frightening,' says my mother as we walk up the drive, having been required to leave our two companions outside the heavily fortified compound. The two-storey Jerusalem stone building is little changed from the outside, other than the blue flag fluttering above it. 'That was Minta's room,' remarks my mother, pointing towards a window to the left of the front door. 'She had her own sitting room and we used to spend hours gossiping and exchanging stories. Sir Harold was a kind man, but he was very grand, and as the Queen's representative would always lead his guests into dinner and would then be served first.' The huge cavernous hall that was the dining room is now used for high-security international meetings, but next door is the drawing room leading on to the terraced gardens.

In the MacMichaels' time the grounds of Government House were home to a whole retinue of pets, including a donkey, a dog, rabbits, a pig, two peacocks called Pontius Pilate and Mrs Simpson, and tortoises; according to Lady Aldington, at night 'the noise of the tortoises mating in the sunk garden outside the front door was deafening as their shells crashed'. Nowadays the wildlife is restricted to the odd prowling cat. My mother remembers that originally the garden had lavender hedges and lawns bordered with beds of delphiniums and poppies and other herbaceous flowers. On this bright November day there is little evidence of the lushness of those times, but the UN has attempted to retain some of the British spirit of the place: rose bushes cover the incline that slopes down from the terrace. When the house was built in 1931 its location was chosen because of the 'noble view over the city of Jerusalem'; less auspiciously, the site was called the 'Hill of Evil Counsel'. My mother spontaneously invokes a McConnel tradition: I am directed onto a wall to grasp some seed pods off the branch of a Judas tree. They will be wrapped in cotton wool and carefully brought back to England and a pot in my parents' Hampshire garden.

Diana rapidly rose through the ranks and was soon out of the typing pool and into her own office. With responsibility came some tough assignments. Her father learnt of the death of a young officer and knew that the widow had to be told immediately; she was a friend of Diana's and General McConnel felt the terrible news would 'be better coming from you'. She was handling highly sensitive documents and orders, and in the spring of 1941 she typed the top-secret instructions for the invasion of Iraq. She was aware that the First Household Cavalry Regiment was part of the operation but she could not have known that one of their number, Lieutenant A.V. Wellesley, was destined to change her life.

Back in England, Cecilia's routine was very different to Diana's – less freedom and glamour, more rules and regulations. However on Saturday, 9 March 1941 she was to have her first grown-up night out. Her mother had bought her a luscious blue velvet dress for the occasion and a group that included her eldest brother and sister were going to one of the most fashionable restaurants in London, the Café de Paris. Cecilia, her sister Jean and their escorts arrived early and found their table under the balcony opposite the main staircase. The bandleader, 'Snake Hips' Johnson, was playing 'Oh Johnny' and Cecilia was itching to dance but they decided to wait for the rest of their party. Moments later there was a huge explosion and all the lights went out. A bomb had landed squarely on the dance floor. 'We were covered in soot and debris but apart from that were unhurt. My sister's date for the evening was a doctor and he went round helping all the wounded. My brother was frantic because he arrived in the area to find it cordoned off by the police. He started going to all the hospitals and it wasn't until much later that he discovered we were unhurt. Thank God he got to the restaurant late, otherwise we would have all been dancing.' Thirty people were killed in the explosion and many more wounded.

Though the British were on constant guard against acts of terrorism, there were no air raids in Jerusalem and on the surface the city was as colourful as ever:

To drive along the streets of Jerusalem is never boring – one sees Jewish men in flat, fur-edged hats with their uncut hair falling over their shoulders; Arab women in tall, almost medieval headdresses; Greek priests with buns and stove-pipe hats; officers of the Transjordan Frontier Force with high black fur headgear slashed with scarlet to match their belts; Arab Legion, Abyssinian clergy, Palestine Police, Americans, Bedouin, and British uniforms – it is quite a fashion show.[2]

These words, written in her diary in 1941, recorded the observations of the Countess of Ranfurly (Hermione) who was to play a crucial role in my parents' romance; her description of the Jerusalem of those days chimes perfectly with my mother's memories. She also writes of the more complicated aspects of the city. 'Wherever you go, for work or fun, there is an unspoken mental undertow of suspicion. No one asks, but everyone wants to find out, which side you are on – Arab or Jew.'

For Diana, escape from the city without her parents was rare, but in 1943, just before Minta got married, the two young women went for a few days to Haifa, a bustling seaside port on the northern coast of Israel. When my mother talks of her life in Palestine the story of this outing always resonates with me: the image of the 'girls' holiday' a shared reference point between us. We decide to drive to Haifa taking in, for my benefit, some of the countryside north of Jerusalem. We pass Nazareth and Bethlehem, dip a toe in the Dead Sea and drive down through the West Bank by the border with Jordan. My mother remembers that she and Minta borrowed her father's private car. Their journey took much longer than ours today: the two young women were constantly stopping to meet up with various officers whose regiments were operating in the area. To me what seems more surprising is that the daughters of the GOC and the High Commissioner were allowed on such an adventure without an armed escort.

'We stayed in a hotel up on Mount Carmel – quite small with wonderful views over the sea.' One highlight was being invited to lunch by an Arab Sheikh – it is not clear where they had met him – seated on silk cushions in a billowing tent carpeted with colourful rugs. 'We wondered quite how it was all going to end and were relieved when our host presented us with a very special gift – of two baby goats!' The goats were a compliment that they could not refuse and were taken back to the hotel where, much to the consternation of the owners, they lived in the girls' room.

The proudest and most fulfilled time of Diana's career in Jerusalem was when she acted as ADC to her father; it was a huge tribute to her that Douglas wanted his daughter as his right-hand 'man'. He rated her intelligence, discretion, efficiency and ability to deal with anything that came her way. Not only was she his confidante in all matters relating to his work, but she also accompanied him whenever he had to attend any ceremony, conference or occasion outside their offices in the King David. 'It meant that I got to read everything that came into my father's office and I sat in on all his meetings with people like Ben-Gurion.' Given the amount of time that father and daughter were separated when Diana was growing up, the years together in Jerusalem are another reason why that period of her life remains so special.

In the autumn of 1943 Diana received a letter from her McConnel grandfather – 'W H', as he always signed himself: 'There is a great deal of talk going on about how to run the life of the world when peace comes, a big subject which you and those of your age have to solve; when one looks back on our carelessness and indifference during the years between the wars, I for one am heartily ashamed, how we could have been so futile I can't think.' Ruth had been feeling unwell and she went home, hoping to benefit from a change of climate. W H, who had been devoted to Ruth since she was a child, was thrilled. He lived just long enough to see her; he died on 14 October. Diana was sad to know she would never see her favourite grandfather again – their last meeting had been when he waved her off for her journey to Palestine. It also meant that he missed the pleasure of an important new development in her life.

Towards the end of November, the King David Hotel played host to a number of VIPs who were visiting Jerusalem between two important Allied conferences – one in Tehran, the other in Cairo. The First Household Cavalry Regiment, who in 1941 had been stationed in the Allenby Barracks in Jerusalem, and were engaged subsequently in fighting in Iraq, Syria and Persia, were sent to guard the hotel. Valerian Wellesley, now the Marquess of Douro, found himself on duty in the hotel. He had met Diana before – the Jerusalem/Cairo social circuit was a pretty small one – he had even been to dinner at her parents' house. But this time it was different: both of them were free agents. Valerian's girlfriend back home had married someone else, and though Diana was never short of admirers, she was not 'attached'. Minta had got married in June that year and Diana's cousin Cecilia was about to get married to Nigel Irvine. Romance was in the air.

By early December Diana knew it was serious, and managed to get some time off to go to Cairo. Hermione Ranfurly, who was some years older and knew the McConnels well, was living in Cairo, working for General 'Jumbo' Wilson, Commander-in-Chief, Middle East. She was delighted to be co-opted as chaperone. On 6 December she wrote to Diana: 'If you can get leave – then let me know at once & I will reserve you a room in the Continental, & please tell your kind Papa that I will take my chaperonage seriously.' Five days later Hermione was greeting Diana in a note that might not have been so reassuring to Douglas: 'Welcome to the fleshpots ! . . . Valerian rang me this morning for news of you and is somewhere in the hotel.'

When I ask my parents about 'the proposal' they have very different recollections as to exactly where they were at the time. 'I think we were in the zoo,' says my mother to laughter from my father, who rebuts it with 'Weren't we sitting on a hill overlooking the golf course' – this suggestion is summarily rejected. 'I suppose the romantic thing would have been the pyramids at night,' he says rather ruefully, 'which it definitely wasn't', she quickly interjects. On this they agree. It falls to me to help bring back their memories. While foraging for clues to my parents' courtship I had uncovered some sentimental records from that time, which my mother had stashed away in a small brown case. The stash included the note from Hermione, photographs of Minta and the goats, family letters and, perhaps most touching of all, two hotel bills, carefully folded, the sheets kept together by a rusty pin.

In the 1940s the Continental Savoy Hotel, Cairo, presented their bills weekly on long sheets of elegantly monogrammed paper. For the week beginning 11 December 1943, Miss D. R. McConnel was in Room No. 125, Cpt Marquess of Douro was a chaste distance away in Room No. 17. The extras on Valerian's bill show that on the first Saturday he took Diana to the famous restaurant on the roof of the hotel where, after a romantic candlelit dinner, you could watch the cabaret with its belly-dancers, acrobats and the slightly lack-lustre card trick player, Mr Cardyman.[3] Five days later, Valerian splashed out again on the roof garden restaurant and cabaret. At the end of their leave – the following Monday Valerian had to be back in barracks – they each settled their own bills. I cannot resist the conclusion that it was on the second of their two extravagant evenings that Valerian and Diana had something to celebrate, and when I put this suggestion to my parents they seemed happy to accept it. The precise timing and circumstances remain a private moment to which offspring are not admitted.

When Diana returned to Jerusalem she was wearing, discreetly, a ring on her engagement finger; conveniently, there had been a jewellery shop opposite the hotel. It was a huge cabochon emerald, set in diamonds; when she showed it to Billy Bond, her father's driver, he thought it looked 'just like a lemon squeezer, Miss!'. For Valerian there was the daunting task of asking the General for his daughter's hand in marriage. 'Are you a salmon fisherman?' Douglas asked his future son-in-law, only half in jest. Valerian, hands behind his back with fingers crossed, replied immediately, 'Certainly, General'. Approval from Ruth was a more complicated business. Diana had rung her at Beamish to tell her the news. Daisy wrote at once to her granddaughter to offer congratulations. 'We are all thrilled to hear that you are engaged to be married ... we don't know much or in fact anything about him so tell us what he is in and what he looks like ... when Cecilia got married we thought it might be infectious ... It is sad for your mother that she is not with you.'

Whether or not she knew it, Daisy was expressing only a small part of the truth; Ruth was frantic, believing that it was not a suitable match. My mother had told me about Ruth's disapproval and I knew that cables were sent to and from Jerusalem and Beamish but it was not until I read my grandmother's letters from that time that I became aware of the strength of her objection. I can observe those events now from the secure position of knowing that Diana and Valerian have been married, and rarely apart, for over sixty years.

In December 1944 Arthur Valerian Douro was a handsome twenty-eight-year-old who had overcome a difficult childhood to emerge as a self-confident young man who wanted to enjoy life to the full. Eton had given him freedom from the complications of home life; Oxford, an education; the army, security and lasting friendships; and war had challenged him with responsibility and commitments. He was upper-class, but with a twist of Bohemia through the intellectual, artistic and separated lives of his parents. He was glamorous and eligible, and had a string of girlfriends behind him, some, like the Druze Princess Amal al-Atrash, with colourful reputations. Finally, through a tragic act of war, he had become the heir to a famous dukedom. He was not a straightforward catch.

At twenty-one Diana Ruth McConnel was a lustrous beauty, five foot six, with a mass of dark hair, huge green eyes, a fantastic figure and a warm, dimply smile. Her Scottish background celebrated industry, enterprise and an adherence to strict religious morality. She was a precious only child – all the more so because her birth sealed the impossibility of her parents having any more children. In their eyes she was probably destined for a solid marriage to a man who would prefer north to south, and the hearth and heather to polo and partying. Over the last four years she had grown up very quickly; she had been courted by many eligible young men and she had danced her way around the nightclubs and hotspots of Jerusalem, Cairo and Haifa; but she had also lived under the watchful eye of her doting soldier father and her concerned gardener mother. She had taken on responsibilities beyond her years but beneath the competent exterior lay a trusting vulnerability. The McConnels were very different stock to the Wellesleys.

Ruth was far away from her only child – unwell, depressed, self-absorbed and living in an atmosphere fraught with the uncertainties of a conflict-torn world and the preoccupations of the older generation. Valerian's father, Gerry, had been in touch with her, making it clear that he believed his son was not ready for marriage. Ruth was aware of the short passage of the courtship and the heady, transient passions that can be whipped up by war. She applied all the long-distance persuasion that she could muster but on 14 January 1944 Diana celebrated her twenty-second birthday in a unique, life-changing way. *The Times* of that day announced: 'A Marriage has been arranged [the idiom of the day] between the Marquess Douro, M.C., Royal Horse Guards, only son of the Duke and Duchess of Wellington, and Diana, only daughter of Major-General D.F. McConnel, C.B., C.B.E., D.S.O., and Mrs McConnel, of Knockdolian, Colmonell, Ayrshire'.

Diana and Valerian made their engagement public after deciding that they wanted to get married as soon as possible. It had not been an easy decision; apart from the cold wind of parental disapproval, they knew that the First Household Cavalry Regiment could be sent back to Europe at any moment. 'I worried about marrying Diana and then having to go off – possibly even making her a widow.' In deciding to seize the day they were like many other couples who got together during the war. The announcement brought one more attempt from Ruth to delay the union: 'If you persist in this marriage then it is for you to bear the consequences – I only hope you have got my letter suggesting you wait for a year.' She went on to say, 'I am afraid when you get this letter you will be either very miserable & not married or else married & at the moment happy – your future is yours.' She ended her letter: 'I am so distressed that I can't write any more.' The letter was written on 17 January and it would have reached my mother less than a week before her big day; it may even have coincided with the news about the bomb plot. In any case, the invitations had been sent out; the wedding was not going to be stopped by any kind of threats – whether from terrorists or troubled parents.

Friday, 28 January 1944 dawned a beautiful, clear, sunny day. Miraculously, in the two weeks since the announcement of their engagement, Diana had managed to organise everything. The last detail was in place when early that morning she had gone out to gather flowers for her bridesmaids' bouquets. She had planned to have orange blossom in her hair, but none could be found. Instead, the Chief of Police, a good friend of her father's, had sent one of his officers to pick lemon blossom which was growing near Beersheba. Ruth at the eleventh hour had written with conciliatory words: 'I know you will make a lovely bride & I think Valerian is terribly lucky'. Her peace offering was the tiara which her parents-in-law, William and Florence, had given her as a wedding present, but it was locked in a bank vault somewhere in the Midlands, thousands of miles from Jerusalem. The lemon blossom took its place.

Nearly sixty-two years later, as I stand with my mother under the arch at the entrance to St George's, it is the bomb plot that is uppermost in my mind. 'What did you feel when you read those top secret papers?' I ask, hoping, I must confess, for an emotional account of terror and panic that such a report would have struck in anyone of my generation. But my mother reminds me firmly that in those times she and her friends lived their lives in a very different way to ours. 'Every day we had to deal with what came our way, and we didn't stop to dwell on our problems. You were never sure what would happen the next day, which of your friends would be gone, for ever. It was all part of the job.'

The official car carrying Douglas and his daughter swept through the arch to arrive at the heavily guarded entrance to the church. Diana wore a dress of heavy white silk and carried white orchids, tied with an olive-green ribbon; her train was borrowed from Minta. 'O Perfect Love' was sung with everyone kneeling, as if for a prayer, and the hymn for absent friends had a special resonance. As the last words of 'I vow to thee my country' echoed through the cathedral the couple walked out into the last rays of winter sunshine, saluted by an arch of raised swords belonging to the Mounted Police – all ex-soldiers from The Blues.

The honeymoon in Beirut was cut short when Valerian was put on stand-by for imminent departure to Italy and the couple moved to Shepheard's Hotel in Cairo, where every evening they had to run the gauntlet of a bar filled with friends. Hot chocolate at Gropis was a more calming ritual. Valerian's call had still not come, but Diana's leave had run out, and she returned to her desk at the King David to resume her old routine. Valerian grabbed any chance he could to see her; once he hitched an illegal ride from an old friend in the air force, travelling, like an awkward piece of contraband, with his feet hanging out of the bomb chute.

The adrenalin that had carried Diana through the past months was gone, and now she had the worry of knowing that at any minute Valerian could be sent back to Europe. She faced the daunting task of building bridges with her new in-laws – strangers who played no part in her wedding – and the challenge of mending her relationship with her mother. With admirable dedication, she used the last day of her honeymoon leave to write to her father-in-law, acutely aware that he too had been against the wedding. Unfortunately the letter took three weeks to reach Stratfield Saye and she had to wait over a month for his reply. Finally it arrived. 'Dearest Diana I have just got your letter of Feb. 13 today. It gave me very great pleasure to hear from you as you are now one of the most important, if not the most important person in my life, and I do long to know you better.'

My mother's letters from this time have not survived, so I realise that I am putting my own interpretation on her experiences, some lit up by intense happiness, others fraught with uncertainties. Afterwards, her life gathered its own momentum and relationships moved on as events intervened to fortify or derail them; it is impossible for her to cast her mind back. I am sure, however, that when my grandfather's letter arrived it must have been a great relief. Diana had also written to her sister-in-law Eliza, whose comforting words provide an insight into some of the anxieties troubling my mother: 'Before I was married four and a half years ago I too was unbearably shy with an appalling inferiority complex. I loathed meeting people and went through agonies making polite conversation. I still get bouts of shyness when I shiver with fright, but I am a completely changed person now and Valerian won't know me when he gets home … being married gives one something and makes one feel important.'

Ruth, in the meantime, was suffering the chill of being sidestepped by her daughter. On 18 March she wrote: 'A red letter day yesterday as we got an airgraph from you to Granny, the first news from you to anyone here since you were married.' She had the added humiliation that friends of hers had seen a photograph of the wedding in the *Tatler* – 'we didn't think a bit good enough of you but nice of everyone else. It was a sideway view & made Daddy look tiny at the end of the row!' She ended the letter: 'Even if you are still annoyed with me I think you might write just an airgraph to say how you are, you may feel hurt but so do I!' Hurt that for both of them never really went away.

On 30 March the First Household Cavalry Regiment got its marching orders. On 5 April Valerian embarked at Port Said, destination Naples. By coincidence the ship was the SS *Strathnaver*, on which Douglas had sailed when he went to Palestine in 1938. In England Ruth had met Gerry. 'I am afraid your mother did not look well and seemed depressed at being sent back to bed by the doctor,' wrote Gerry to his daughter-in-law. 'Your grandmother had won a "highly recommended" for an alpine plant as minute as it is rare. Its name begins with Rhodo – but does not end with – dendron. Your relations say you know a lot about gardening & that you report that Valerian knows quite a lot. I therefore look forward to a lot of help for I know nothing.' Ruth's report of the get-together in London was less opaque:

> The Duke came to dinner with us at the Goring Hotel & was most nice & friendly – I don't think you need be worried about being frightened of him, he isn't at all frightening, I thought he was a little pathetic & he is having a hard time of it at Stratfield Saye trying to run things and get things straight. He says they only have lamps! and go about the passages with a torch! ... it sounds a most fearful place to run in wartime ... though I'm not sure he didn't say he had got an 'Aga' cooker.

When my mother and I fly home to my father, bearing gifts of stories of our adventures, I think about her life before, and after, Palestine. My mother is a strong woman but she often keeps her own counsel and I suspect that deep down there lurks some of the shyness of the young girl. Perhaps I can understand now where that comes from. My grandmother's reaction to the union was skewed by her distance from Jerusalem. Crucially, too, it must have been heartbreaking not to have seen her only child walk down the aisle. In one of her letters to her daughter Ruth said: 'You will both now prove to me that I was completely wrong – I hope – naturally.' They did; she was. But in 1944, as Valerian's regiment began to wind its way through Italy behind the retreating Germans, and Diana's two families tried to find their common ground, the new Marchioness of Douro was left in Jerusalem looking after her father and trying to concentrate on her job, while she worried about her husband's safety and the unknown territory of the life that stretched out before her. It was to be another six months before she was reunited with her new husband, made face-to-face peace with her mother and met her new in-laws.

*

'The Honourable Sir Arthur Wellesley KB' (the name had reverted in 1798) married 'the Honourable Catherine Dorothea Sarah Pakenham' on Thursday, 10 April 1806. Many years later Kitty would tell a friend, 'When I was a girl I made three resolutions. First, I determined that I would never marry a soldier [as did Diana]; secondly, that I would never marry an Irishman; and thirdly, that I would not be long engaged. And all those three resolutions I broke. I married the Duke of Wellington, a soldier and an Irishman, after an engagement of twelve years.'[4] The Kitty of their early courtship had been a gay, pretty, admired young girl, one of the glistening pearls of the Viceroy's court in Dublin; Arthur, in contrast, an overlooked, youthful soldier with mounting debts and gloomy prospects. Now Arthur, at thirty-seven, was a Major-General with an impressive record on the battlefield and a purse to prove it; his reputation was growing by the day, his star in the ascendancy. Kitty, on the other hand, at thirty-four had lost the confidence and innocence of youth. In the intervening years she had seen her beloved homeland first torn apart by unrest and rebellion, and then humiliated by the Act of Union. Her initial pining for Arthur had been quietened, briefly, by the attentions of an approved suitor but eventually she spurned him. The anxiety and ambivalence of her situation had taken its toll on her health and looks. As Arthur and Kitty stood side by side for the wedding ceremony in the Pakenhams' Dublin drawing room, the scene betrayed the awkward unfamiliarity of the couple. What had conspired to persuade both of them that they could rekindle a lost love?

In the summer of 1801 Arthur was in Mysore suffering the dual effects of a serious illness and the humiliation of being superseded in the command of an expedition. He had been in India for five years and the infrequency of his contact with home was compounded by the length of time it took for mail to reach the subcontinent – anything up to a year. When an old friend from Dublin, Colonel Marcus Beresford, wrote to him, he fell upon the contents of the letter – an irresistible mix of news and gossip. One passage in particular quickened his pulse:

> I know not if Miss Pakenham is an object to you or not – she looks as well as ever – no person whatsoever has paid her any particular attention – so much I say having heard her name and yours mentioned together – I hear her most highly spoken of by Mrs Sparrow. She lives so retired that nobody sees her – One night Tom Pakenham took me to sup at Lady Longford's –

I could not avoid looking with all my eyes at the lady and thinking of you and former times ... but I had not nerves to say anything about you – enclosed is a letter from Mrs Sparrow – she is a most charming woman, she talks so handsomely of you, that you ought to be flattered – I have seen much of her, and for her bear the greatest regard and highest opinion.[5]

Though the 'Sparrow' letter does not survive, Beresford's is one of the most significant documents of my family's personal history. The two letters led to a chain of responses and reactions that culminated in Arthur and Kitty's Dublin wedding and a bittersweet union of twenty-five years. The first of these responses – immediate and unequivocal – was a letter to Olivia Sparrow. 'Notwithstanding my good fortune, and the perpetual activity of the life which I have led, that disappointment, the object of it, and all the circumstances are as fresh upon my mind, as if they had passed only yesterday.'[6] The image of a young girl with grey eyes, soft brown curly hair and a flawless complexion had swum back into Arthur's sight. When he had written to Kitty saying that if ever her family changed their attitude, 'my mind will remain the same', he had meant it. However, Beresford was disingenuous in his depiction of the 'object': far from seeing 'nobody', Kitty had been pursued by the eligible, favoured Lowry Cole, a younger son of Lord Enniskillen.

Mrs Sparrow is the key figure in the drama. She was Olivia Acheson, one of Kitty's closest confidantes, and a friend of Arthur's. A few years earlier she had married Bernard Sparrow, a wealthy, older man. With time on her hands and an imagination fed by devouring romantic novels, Olivia Sparrow slipped easily into a role as matchmaker to her friends. No doubt at first she had encouraged Kitty to accept the attentions of Lowry Cole, but as word reached Ireland of Arthur Wellesley's military achievements on the subcontinent she may have wavered in her support. Additionally, Cole was a defender of the Act of Union, which by removing Ireland's Parliament from Dublin had blighted the city's social life, of which Olivia was a doyenne. There is a hint from Beresford that he was susceptible to Olivia's charms, so she would have found it easy to persuade him to write the letter, and to enclose hers. All she then had to do was await the vicarious pleasure of observing her plan unfold.

Whatever the precise chronology that led up to these letters, by 1801 Kitty had turned down Cole; later one of his brothers wrote, 'Lowry since that love affair with Kitty Pakenham seems like a burnt child to fear the fire.'[7] In the opinion of his family she had 'played fast and loose with his affections'. But for Olivia Sparrow the stakes were high. Kitty, a deeply religious, moral woman, would have suffered torment from the way she had treated Cole, and could never have taken the initiative herself to re-establish contact with Arthur; after all, she had promised her mother and brother not to have any communication with him. But surely she must have known of her friend's intervention and given her tacit approval?

Arthur's reply to Olivia mentions the 'disappointment' of all those years ago, and goes on to say, 'how much more would they [the disappointments] bear upon me, if I was to return to the inactivity of a home life'.[8] Arthur's years in India were tough, but any hardship he suffered was intermittently tempered by the company of women. Later a fellow officer observed, 'Colonel Wellesley had at that time a very susceptible heart, particularly towards, I am sorry to say, married ladies.'[9] The sense of domesticity may have been part of the appeal of these ladies, and served to remind Arthur, by 1801 into his thirties, of his single status. When he thought of going back to England, he dreaded returning to 'the inactivity of a home life', but in the same letter to Mrs Sparrow he was 'anxious to be home'. In response to her questions, his emotions were seesawing between wanting Kitty to know that he still felt the same, but not wanting to hope that these feelings could be reciprocated. In answering a question about his health: 'It is excellent ... if I could forget that which has borne so heavily upon me for the last eight years, I should have as little care as you appear to have.'[10]

Olivia Sparrow must have been pleased with this reaction. With a little encouragement, Arthur had revealed his hand: Kitty still occupied a special place in his heart. His letter had taken nine months to reach Ireland but Olivia would have wasted no time in passing on to Kitty the contents. 'My dearest Olivia,' wrote Kitty in May 1802, 'you know I can send no message; a kind word from me he might think binding to him and make him think himself obliged to renew a pursuit, which perhaps he might not then wish or my family (at least some of them) take kindly.' Whatever Olivia's attempts to persuade her to cast caution to the wind, Kitty was on an emotional knife-edge: 'My first wish, if I was not taking care not to wish about it, would be that he should return and feel himself perfectly free (I do not mean free from regard for those who sincerely regard him, but to act as he pleases) and then – I hardly know what to wish then, for fear of nursing a disappointment for him, for myself, or a vexation for my friends.'

Olivia's attempts to manipulate the situation are exposed: 'Perhaps you will be angry with me when I say I am by no means as certain as you seem to be as to what his present wish is. He now desires to be kindly remembered, but do not you think *he* seems to think the business *over?*' Also revealed is the existence of an earlier exchange of letters between Arthur and Olivia. 'In a former letter to you his words were, I believe, "You cannot say more to her than I feel."'[11] Quite how Olivia presented Kitty's confused sentiments to Arthur is not known, but once again there was a yawning abyss of time before word came back. Though Arthur may have eagerly awaited the latest instalment in the correspondence between Ireland and the subcontinent, he had other matters to occupy his mind. In 1802 he had been made a Major-General and by spring of the following year the outbreak of the Second Mahratta War was anticipated. In preparation, he was putting his military tactics and discipline into practice on a long march from Seringapatam to Poona on the other side of India; on one night alone his cavalry covered forty miles. He declared immediately at the top of his letter that if hers had arrived when it should have done, he would have been 'disengaged' and 'I should have been in England by this time'. Whatever Olivia had written, on the one hand he felt she had been 'too discreet', on the other that she had 'ended at last by a communication of your own observations on a subject in which you know me to be much interested'. He also admitted: 'I cannot trust myself to write any more about her.'[12]

In the year before these latest words reached Ireland, Kitty had gone through a further bout of introspection and depression, perhaps even convincing herself that her friend Olivia had made a terrible miscalculation in attempting to recapture Arthur's heart for her. She spent a lot of time brooding on her predicament and seeking guidance from God. Her thoughts surfaced in a poem she wrote while staying with her sister Helen Hamilton in Donegal in July 1802:

> Teach me, Oh God, to search and know my heart
> That there no cherished sin may claim a part.
> Let no fond error, loath to quit its place,
> Obstruct within my soul the work of grace.[13]

In the autumn of 1803, when it had been eighteen months since Olivia last wrote to India, Kitty, in an attempt to improve her mental and physical health, went to Cheltenham to take the waters. Her stay crossed with a visit to the spa by her rejected suitor, Lowry Cole. Was this a coincidence, or did she plan it? His family had their suspicions. 'I am beginning to think she wishes to bring on the subject again with Lowry, but he fights shy. She will deserve it as she treated him cruelly,'[14] wrote one of his brothers. If Kitty did make some attempt at reconciliation, her overtures were not accepted and she would have returned to Ireland in an even worse state than when she left. By the time her thirty-second birthday fell in January 1804, word had reached England and Ireland of Arthur's triumph at the battle of Assaye in September 1803. (In later life, when there were many more to compare it with, he described it as the 'greatest battle I ever fought'.) Kitty's heart would have swelled as the plaudits were heaped on her hero. Then, at last, Arthur's letter reached Olivia.

Aware of Kitty's mental state, Olivia wrote back immediately: 'Its chief subject has so entirely engaged my mind that I cannot delay my answer.' Olivia assured Arthur that she had not passed any of their correspondence to 'her' but she had noticed 'an evident increase in good opinion and interest in those friends who, I have heard, were formerly less favourably inclined towards you and whose heads and hearts can only be influenced by real worth and deserved fame': the Assaye factor at work. Whether through some late feelings of guilt about having misrepresented Kitty's 'disengaged state' in earlier correspondence, she now also conceded that her 'friend' must have a 'more than common reason for perseverance' in her state given that there had been 'frequent and otherwise unobjectionable opportunities for changing it'.[15]

When Arthur read it, both the prospect of going home, and Kitty, began to seem real. He was now worried that lurid tales of his exploits off the battlefield may have filtered through to Kitty's circle. One of his matronly admirers had warned him that the scandalmongers were attacking him. 'I only say', he wrote to Olivia, 'that it is impossible that any report of this kind respecting me for the last 20 months (since I received your letter in 1802) can be true; as I believe it will be admitted that while in the field with the Army I have done no mischief.'[16]

Eight months later, in March 1805, he set sail for England, confessing to a friend that 'I am anxious to a degree which I can't express, to see my friends again.' His reading material for his return journey reflected his preoccupations. On his outward voyage his library had included improving works; now his trunk was filled with novels boasting steamy titles like *Love at First Sight* (in five volumes), *Lessons for Lovers* (in two) and *Filial Indiscretion or the Female Chevalier*.[17]

I believe that at that time my great-great-great-grandfather wanted his romantic idyll to come true – a happy marriage to the woman he thought he loved. As far as his career was concerned, India had been the making of him: not only was he now a Major-General, but before he embarked for home, King George III had honoured him with the Order of the Bath. He was richer to the tune of £42,000 and his military credentials would ensure that he could never again be overlooked or considered mere 'food for powder'. The Pakenhams' resolute rejection of his suit had been a low and humiliating experience but it had spurred him on to make a success of his life. On the long journey home, as he paced the deck of HMS *Trident* or sat in his cabin reading his novels, he could reflect with satisfaction on his achievements.

Arthur broke his journey home at St Helena, a remote island in the middle of the South Atlantic that was a stopping-off point for ships crossing from one side of the world to the other. It was summer by now and the temperate climate seemed to Arthur 'to be the most healthy I ever lived in'. It provided welcome respite from the unbearable humidity of the subcontinent and the unpleasant effects of seasickness. He could not have imagined that ten years later the island would become an impregnable prison for his greatest enemy, Napoleon. For Arthur, his three-week stay there provided a very agreeable interlude.

The *Trident* dropped anchor off Dover on 10 September. If Kitty could have waved a magic wand, she would have wished herself into the crowd of people watching the passengers disembark. Soon she would have spotted a 'spare, well-knit, muscular man of medium height with long face and narrow jawbones, an aquiline patrician nose and firm chin, sunburnt complexion, close-cropped, light brown hair already faintly streaked with grey, and clear blue eyes of a strange intensity'.[18] But she would also have noted his impatience to organise his onward journey – to London, not Ireland. If thoughts of Kitty had occupied Arthur's mind as the ship cut through the ocean waves, now he was distracted by affairs of state. Not only was he intent on pleading the cause of his brother Richard, who had been recently dismissed from the Governor-Generalship of India, but also he was determined to be gainfully employed in Britain's war against the newly crowned French Emperor.

A chance encounter a few days after his return served to strengthen his political and military ambitions. Arthur was waiting in an anteroom at the Colonial Office to see Lord Castlereagh, the Secretary of State for War. Also in attendance on the Minister was a small man with one arm who was dressed in a naval uniform. Arthur instantly recognised him, but the compliment was not returned. Nelson proceeded to hold forth in a manner that Arthur later recalled was 'all about himself, and in, really, a style so vain and so silly as to surprise and almost disgust me'. Luckily for a serendipitous moment of history, Nelson then had the good sense to surmise that this was no ordinary soldier and when he found out his identity, there followed an exchange of which, in old age, Wellington claimed, 'I don't know that I ever had a conversation that interested me more.'[19] The two men never met again; less than six weeks later Nelson died a hero's death at Trafalgar.

Arthur may have been distracted from his single-minded pursuit of Kitty, but there was a spring in his step when, soon after arriving back, he went shopping in New Bond Street. He bought a whole repertoire of sheet music: romantic songs like 'Oh Lovely Lady' or 'Lady Beware', duets from popular light operas and sonatas by Mozart. He may have burnt his violin all those years ago, but music was still in his soul and he knew that Kitty was accomplished at the piano; perhaps he imagined musical evenings together when they could recapture the sweet sounds of their youth. Olivia would have approved of these purchases, but she was critical of Arthur's failure to make contact with Kitty. For four years Mrs Sparrow had been plotting to bring her two friends together again, and now that a small channel, rather than an ocean, separated them, Arthur was not playing his part properly. She wrote to him sternly and received an apologetic reply: 'All I can say is that if I could count myself capable of neglecting such a woman, I would endeavour to think of her no more.' He wanted to know Kitty's plans for the winter. 'Shall I go over to see her?' He shows willing but has a dilemma. 'I am very apprehensive that after having come from India for one purpose only I shall not accomplish it; & I think it not impossible that if the troops under orders for embarkation should be sent to the Continent, I shall be ordered to go with them, & possibly never see you or her again.'[20]

Arthur had no intention of missing out on the next major military expedition and hoped that Kitty could come over to London, but the Pakenhams were in mourning for a member of the family. Aware that at any moment Arthur could disappear over the horizon, once again Olivia stepped in as the go-between. She pressed him to renew his proposition and when he replied, she passed the letter straight on to Kitty, whose reaction was distraught: 'What can I say – I know nothing of his mind but what you have told me. You assure me he still regards me, he has authorised you to renew the proposition he made some years ago; but my Olivia, I have in vain sought in his letter for one word expressive of a wish that the proposition should be accepted of.'

Kitty's agitation when she read Arthur's letter is clear in the endless crossings-out and poor punctuation of her reply to Olivia. She detected, she thought, that 'he wishes to be sent abroad' and 'perhaps he is right, for I am very much changed, and you know it'. For this reason, she worried that she would not be able to 'contribute to the comfort or happiness of anybody who has not been in the habit of loving me for years – like my brother or you or my mother'. Kitty implored Olivia to read his letter again to find one expression that might suggest '"Yes" would gratify or that "No" would disappoint or occasion regret? Either would remove the uneasiness of uncertainty and I cannot perceive that he expresses any other.'

She had a perceptive view of marriage: 'I have been witness to all the happiness arising from affection where it was mutual and can feel what would have been the misery had that affection existed but on one side.'[21] Knowing how quickly my great-great-great-grandparents' relationship turned sour, to me this last sentence is the most poignant part of the letter. Kitty may have yearned for romantic love, but she knew how important it was to like and respect your spouse; there were several good examples of such solid marriages in her own family. She desperately needed reassurance that the course on which she was being steered by Olivia was not heading for a disastrous destination. She wanted Arthur to value and care about her for the person she had become, not the young girl he remembered. I wonder what Olivia now wrote to Arthur, and whether she revealed anything of this turmoil in Kitty's mind. Did it ever occur to her to listen to her friend and put the brakes on her match-making? It seems not, since Arthur's next move was to approach Lord Longford, requesting his permission to make a formal proposal to his sister. On receiving a positive response, he wrote immediately to Kitty asking for her hand in marriage. It was the first letter he had sent her for eleven years.

'To express what I feel at this moment would be quite impossible,' wrote a jubilant Kitty, but once again she showed her common sense:

> It is indeed my earnest wish to see you, besides the pleasure it must give me to meet again an early and truely valued friend, I do not think it fair to engage you before you are quite positively certain that I am indeed the very woman you could choose for a companion, a friend for life ... If when we have met you can tell me with the same sincerity which has ever distinguished you through life, that you do not repent having written the letter I am now answering I shall be most happy.[22]

Arthur, who received Kitty's reply on 4 November, ignored her concerns, declaring to Olivia that he was the 'happiest man in the world'.

*

As I make my way through the maze of my family's history, inevitably I reach moments when I wish I could go back through time and with a gift of divine intervention, plant myself in front of the characters in this drama – these relations for whom I am developing a strong affection. For how could my famous forebear – renowned for his clear thinking on the battlefield – have got it so wrong when it came to the most important decision of his personal life? 'Can't you see', I would shout at Arthur. 'Why are you behaving in such an ill-judged way? Listen to her! You must go and see her!' It seems so obvious that he should not have relied on the counsel of a scheming matchmaker or the fading sentiments of his youth. How much harder could Kitty have tried to force Arthur to confront reality? She was begging him to make the trip over to Ireland before their engagement was formalised and was – no doubt with a heavy heart – giving him every chance to pull back from the commitment. Whatever her romantic notions of love and marriage, she recognised that the most important aspiration for her union with Arthur was that she should be his 'friend for life'. The Pakenhams were a warm and loving family; the Wellesleys, taking the lead from the indomitable Lady Morn-ington, were, I fear, a rather cold one. This probably contributed to the keenness of Arthur's youthful courtship of Kitty, when he may have yearned to bask in that familial warmth. But in the autumn of 1805, what was really driving him forward? Despite her protestations to the contrary in later life, Olivia Sparrow must take her share of the blame; however, Arthur has to be answerable for his actions. What misplaced vanity made him think he need not find time to see Kitty – just once – before making his formal proposal? Historians have largely attributed his behaviour to being a man of honour who was sticking to his promise but I wonder whether, subconsciously (or worse still consciously), he wished to get his own back for the humiliation of having been turned down by the Pakenhams? Or perhaps he was just naïve.

But I cannot intervene, and the drama is moving inexorably towards the end of this act, against a background of major national events. As Arthur made his proposal, news reached England of the death of Nelson at Trafalgar, and emotions in the country swung between sorrow and cele-bration. Britain might now 'rule the waves', but on land she was struggling with her allies to contain the ambitions of the French Emperor. The departure of Arthur's regiment to the Continent seemed imminent, but in the end it was nearly Christmas before he embarked for northern Germany, and another opportunity had been missed for a quick trip over to Dublin. Instead Kitty was left still waiting and worrying, imagining that Arthur, the man she was now engaged to marry, might die on the stormy seas or lose his life in battle. In fact, six weeks later her intended was back in England, not having fired a single shot; the news of the battle of Austerlitz and Napoleon's crushing of the Austrian and Prussian armies in early December had arrived too late to stop the British expedition.

Now the country was in mourning again, this time for the Prime Minister, Pitt. His death would have been keenly felt by the Wellesleys, to whom he had been a good friend and patron, in particular by Richard, the eldest who, recently deposed as the Governor-General of India, was about to become the object of an anti-Wellesley campaign, whipped up by a retired Anglo-Indian merchant with a grudge against him. Arthur decided to stand as an MP for Westminster, so as to be in a better position to fight his brother's corner. In addition, while in Germany Arthur had been made Colonel of his regiment, the 33rd. This all meant more pressure and demands on his time, but there was a silver lining: the additional financial security focused Arthur's mind. Finally, as spring was nudging winter, his solicitors drew up a marriage settlement proposal, to be approved by Kitty's mother and brother. It involved the customary practice of setting up a trust which would provide for Kitty and her children if Arthur died; £6,000 came from the Pakenham side and Arthur put in £20,000, half of his 'prize' money from India.

Now all Arthur had to do was find time in his schedule for the ceremony. Given that April was sandwiched between his election at the beginning and Richard's possible impeachment at the end, that was not so easy. It must have seemed to Kitty as if everything else in Arthur's life took precedence over her. An aunt writing to a friend declared: 'It seems that it has been fixed these six months but kept a profound secret. She has suffered a great deal of anxiety since, as he was ordered abroad, was out in the hurricanes, then in Germany and since his return very ill. She bears the traces of all this, for she coughs sadly and looks but ill, which we all lament as Sir A. is expected in a very few days.'[23]

April 10 was finally chosen and Arthur arrived two days in advance with a clutch of brothers in attendance; he had less than a week to marry his bride and return to his post at Westminster. The unseemly haste was in stark contrast to the fourteen years of build-up – the years of courting, of rejection and silence, and the agonisingly slow prelude to their engagement. No one knows precisely when Arthur and Kitty caught sight of each other, but a story emerged many years later that he turned to his brother Gerald and whispered, 'She is grown damned ugly, by Jove!'.[24] I doubt the authenticity of this remark; but if my ancestor did indeed utter these words, I am shocked both by his lack of gallantry and by Gerald's decision to reveal the comment.

The wedding took place in the drawing room of the Longfords' house in Rutland Square, Dublin. One absent guest would have regretted not being able to attend the ceremony: Olivia Sparrow was in mourning after the recent death of her husband. However, Arthur wrote to her two days later expressing the 'sincerest sense I entertain of the obligation I owe to you for all the happiness I enjoy'.[25] But hardly had the ink dried on these words than he was back to his politicking at Westminster, leaving Gerald to accompany the new Lady Wellesley on her trip across the Irish Channel to London. She found her husband strangely unprepared for her. Arthur was still negotiating the deal for his marital home in Harley Street and continued to live in rooms in Clifford Street. Kitty was left to lodge in the house of a friend, probably the ubiquitous Olivia Sparrow. This unusual arrangement can only have added to the interest the couple attracted in London. When Kitty was first presented at court on 15 May 1806, Queen Charlotte told her she was happy to see her, 'so bright an example of constancy. If anybody in this world deserves to be happy, you do.' She then asked Kitty about the long period of silence and separation that had led up to the wedding. 'But did you really never write one letter to Sir Arthur Wellesley during his long absence?' 'No, never, Madam,' said Kitty, but the Queen pressed her, determined to get the full romantic picture: 'And did you never think of him?' 'Yes, Madam, very often.'[26] Little did Kitty know, but this answer foretold the tragic pattern of her future life.

SIX

Return to Palena

M y mother was a bride of only nine weeks when her husband sailed to Naples from Port Said in April 1944. Valerian was constantly in her mind but, despite her youth (she was still only twenty-two), she had already lived through four years of war and had learnt to adopt an outwardly stoical attitude. News was sparse; twentieth-century warfare demanded that as little information as possible passed over airwaves or through letters. Her work was demanding, and she continued to live with her father, whose calm counsel and experience of war provided a steadying influence. She gleaned what she could from the brief reports in the *Palestine Post*, and when a casualty list came through, like millions of other people round the world, she held her breath until she could be sure that Valerian's name was not on it. Letters, though censored and infrequent, were crucial staging-posts, as she waited to hear when she would be reunited with her husband. Meanwhile, for my father in Italy, there was now a real sense that he was taking part in a conflict that would eventually be won.

As with most of his generation who fought in the war, many of the images and events of those years remain vivid in his mind. Often, when we have talked about that time in his life, he would say 'I wish I could go back to Baghdad and see the area round the Khadimain Mosque', or 'I'd love to return to Palena' – the village in Italy where he spent several weeks in the summer of 1944. If we were to plan a trip, Iraq, once again war-torn, was out of the question; but an expedition to Italy could serve several purposes and, when I suggested it, my father's enthusiasm was instant and genuine. As a young man he had yearned for – in his mother's words – 'the gallantries of his dreams'; now he wanted to revisit the reality those dreams had become. My mother, too, would have a chance to see some of the places she had imagined as she plotted Valerian's progress through Italy; for me the trip would afford the simple pleasure of seeing my father enjoy the encounter with places from the life of his younger self.

*

We fly through the eye of a fierce storm to reach Naples, and somehow this unnerving start to our trip seems appropriate. My father's Italy is a land of haunting memories and unquiet ghosts. In 1944, as a young newly married Captain, he had the most frightening experience of his war – driving along a precipice-drop road in the middle of the night, being strafed by German fire. My mother remembers his recurring nightmare after the war, from which he would wake in the night, shaking and desperate to escape from a burning armoured car lying at the bottom of a ravine. And there is a sadder, more difficult connection to Italy: Morny's death. My father had never visited his cousin's grave; this poignant ritual would mark the start of our Italian pilgrimage.

Plot III, Row B, Grave 43, Salerno War Cemetery: Morny's final resting-place. The Italian gardener leads us to it, through rows of graves bordered by meticulously tended flower beds and carpets of neat, perfectly mown lawns. We have travelled from England with flowers from Strat-field Saye – Morny's home, my father's home. The day before my mother had gathered trophies of an English countryside: daffodils, narcissi, apple blossom. They have survived the journey with the promise of spring still on the petals. My father stands by the grave, bends and places the flowers carefully at the foot of the gravestone. He steps back and draws himself up to his full six foot – a slight stoop the only hint of his nine decades – and then bows his head, lost in his thoughts. I am moved by the silent salute from one soldier to another. There is so much their lives had in common: Morny was a mere three years older than my father; both their birthdays fell in July; both were great-grandsons of the First Duke; both went off to the same war to fight for their country. Morny's tragic death on the battlefield joins them for ever as bearers of the same title – Morny number 6 in the line, my father 8th.

From his birth in 1912, Morny had carried the courtesy title of the Earl of Mornington, hence his nickname. After leaving Stowe he gained himself a reputation as a 1930s playboy – a familiar and popular figure in the West End clubs. When he decided to join the army in 1935 it was expected that he would become a Grenadier Guard, but scandal hung over him: not only had he been found guilty of driving under the influence of drink, but news had leaked out of his intention to marry a dance hostess from the Bag of Nails. The Grenadiers would not accept him and their loss became the Duke of Wellington's Regiment's gain: in 1935 Morny was commissioned into The Dukes. He first saw active duty in 1940 when, attached to the King's African Rifles, he took part in the

Abyssinia campaign. His illness with malaria coincided with his father's sudden death in December 1941. At first he refused to take the title. 'I'm Mornington, as I always have been,' he protested. 'It's a far older title than the 'Duke of Wellington' ... and when I'm introduced fellows will laugh and probably say, "Is he the chap that owns all those pubs?"'[1] But he knew the responsibilities that went with the title: when he was sent home on compassionate and sick leave, he visited all his new tenants on the Stratfield Saye estate and made his maiden speech in the House of Lords – appropriately about the principles of soldiering. He then took the momentous decision not to return to his regiment. No doubt he had an understandable reticence about going back to a regiment that now carried his name; he chose instead to be seconded to the elite ranks of the Commandos.

The Commandos had been established in 1940. Trained as crack troops capable of surviving for days on their own initiative, they were named after the companies of fierce Boer horsemen who had made mincemeat of British units in South Africa at the turn of the century. Morny was recruited by Jack Churchill (no relation to Winston), an eccentric, swashbuckling figure who went to war equipped with a claymore, crossbow and arrows and bagpipes.[2] Churchill recognised in Morny an adventurous, courageous spirit and immediately put him in charge of his own troop. Morny's initial duties were to help build up the new force, with men who would, as Winston Churchill put it, 'develop a reign of terror', but it was not long before he was sent off into the heat of battle. For his mother Maud and his only sister Anne, so recently bereaved of husband and father, it must have been an agonising farewell.

It is 3.30 a.m. on Thursday, 9 September 1943. Captain the Duke of Wellington, leading his troop from No. 2 Commando, disembarks from the *Prince Albert* on a beach just north of Salerno. He is part of the vanguard for Operation Avalanche, as it was called – the biggest amphibious landing in history: 170,000 men. After the landing, for the next six days Morny, in the words of one of his comrades, fights 'like a lion'[3] as the battle to control the area seesaws backwards and forwards. The Germans' foothold on the hilly territory around Salerno has to be broken, control gained of the highway to Naples. At one point the huge viaduct that straddles a gorge above the town is in danger of being blown up and Morny hides in a cave overlooking it with his batman and two signallers, firing on the Germans to prevent them from laying the explosives. For two days they have no food and little water. When Morny finds a meagre ration pack in his kit he offers to share it, insisting that he is not hungry.

On Monday, five days after the landing, they get some rest and food, and Morny and the other troop Captains write up their notes. Using the only available paper, the back of a map, with candle grease spilling onto his words, he lists his recommendations for bravery: 'Sgt. 'Brien … DCM for complete disregard of his personal safety … Cpl. Webber for carrying out duties and attending to wounded constantly while under fire …Pte Peachey for continuing to fire his LMG after being particularly disabled by blast' and, crucially, 'Troop Sgt. Major Garland, wounded in the head, but continued his duties'.[4] Signed, 'Wellington, Capt'.

September 15 1943. Morny and 2 Commando are facing their biggest task yet: the Germans have taken three hills overlooking the area and are threatening the beachhead defences. Capturing a small hill – nicknamed the 'Pimple' – becomes Morny's objective. The hillside is rocky, the woodlands are dense, the steep terraces covered in vines and by now the light has gone. The first raid is highly successful, but just after midnight his unit is ordered back. The Germans are reassembling in force. Morny gathers his men together and once again they scale the hill, coming under constant enemy fire. There is a brief lull in the action when Morny is summoned back down to talk to Jack Churchill, his Commanding Officer, but, entirely at his own bidding – 'would you like us to go back to recapture the Pimple?'[5] – he returns to the fray with his men, including his troop Sergeant-Major, Lindsay Garland. This time the daring young Duke is met with a hail of machine-gun fire and grenades. After a valiant attempt to take the hill, Morny loses the fight and, in hand-to-hand combat with a German officer, his life. Garland dies alongside him. It is just before dawn on 16 September.

'I have the greatest admiration for Morny,' says my father as we stand looking up to the hills where his cousin met his death. 'We all went off to war without really thinking about the sacrifices that were demanded of us. We were doing our duty and it was not something we really analysed. But when friends and comrades were killed the enormity of it all came home to us. And Morny chose to fight in a unit that suffered far higher losses than any other part of the army. And he really did die a hero's death.' I had read an account by one of the fellow soldiers in his troop that 'it had never been his [Morny's] ambition to be a soldier, but because of his family history, he was expected to do his duty, become a soldier and earn a decoration'.[6] My father is not sure whether he believes this – he always saw his cousin as a naturally courageous, brave type – but I think that perhaps this is a pressure that he is unwilling to acknowledge; it has probably impinged on his life too, albeit without the tragic consequences. Though Morny carried the burden of this complicated legacy, he achieved the highest acknowledgement of his sacrifice: on the day of his death a citation for an immediate DSO for earlier bravery was already at Commando headquarters. In the event, since DSOs cannot be awarded posthumously, it became a Mention in Despatches.

Maud, the Dowager 5th Duchess and Morny's mother, received the news of her son's death in a letter from his Commanding Officer.

> He gave his life in the highest traditions of the British Army and of his illustrious name, leading his troops in a heroic attack against the German defences in the Mountains East of Salerno.
>
> His great gallantry and his personal charm had so endeared him to all of us that there is not an officer or soldier in No. 2 Commando, and indeed, in the Special Service Brigade, who does not grieve most deeply at this, his supreme sacrifice.
>
> May I, on behalf of all ranks, offer you our great sympathy in the hope that your suffering may seem perhaps a little easier to bear in your knowledge that your Son died – a shining example to us – and beloved by all who knew him.
>
> His death was instantaneous and in the hour of victory after a desperate action in which his personal bravery and powers of leadership won the admiration of those who fought with him.[7]

Over a century and a quarter earlier, in one of hundreds of letters of condolence that the First Duke wrote, he expressed the same sentiments: 'I hope you will derive some consolation from the reflection that he fell in the performance of his duty, at the head of your brave regiment, loved and respected by all who knew him, in an action in which, if possible, British troops surpassed every thing they had ever done before'.[8]

A soldier's loyalty and concern for his brothers-in-arms extend beyond death: Morny's Commanding Officer was no exception. When the fighting ceased to rage round Salerno and the autumn leaves had fallen, Jack Churchill returned to the 'Pimple'. The hill was scarred by the fierce heat of battle; the ground scorched and blackened. Churchill found several small mounds of earth where bodies had been buried, but he had other clues to search for: Morny smoked a pipe, carried his tobacco in a 'Compo' ration box, and had two metal stars of rank. Churchill was determined to find Garland's body as well. Eventually, on the top of the hill, under six inches of earth he found Morny and, lying close by, Garland. The bodies had been badly burnt, probably by Allied mortar bombs; but the clues were there and the distinctive Commando boots had survived the carnage. Churchill carried the remains of the two men to a temporary grave in a grass square near the town. Later, the Italian people gave the ground that is now Salerno Cemetery to the War Graves Commission – 'A perpetual resting place for the soldiers, sailors and airmen who are honoured here.' Morny's and Garland's are just two of the 1,847 graves of fallen servicemen and women.

The Salerno War Cemetery is only a few miles from where Morny died; in effect he lies 'where he fell', surrounded by comrades from all ranks and many regiments. His simple granite headstone is identical to the others but for the inscription '*Virtutis Fortuna Comes*' (the family motto, 'Fortune favours the brave') and 'To "Morny" the happy warrior, his sorrowing mother and sister'. Garland's grave is a few paces away: 'Treasured memories / of our darling Lindsay / Good night dear one / wife daughter mum and dad'.

I have never visited a war grave cemetery before and I am struck by the timelessness and calm serenity of this peaceful place, a pure contrast to the noise and violence of the battles that brought the men here. Every single grave signifies a life sacrificed, represents a family left irretrievably damaged and diminished. In Italy alone there are thirty-seven Commonwealth war cemeteries and the graves of 38,000 casualties of the Second World War. The War Graves Commission has 23,000 cemeteries, memorials and other locations round the world, commemorating the 1.7 million men and women of the Commonwealth forces who died during the two world wars. My mother's uncle Merrick died in September 1917, leaving Helen, his daughter, to grow up with only the slenderest memory of her father's voice reading her a bedtime story. My father's uncle, Captain Lord Richard Wellesley, was killed at Ypres on 29 October 1914, a few weeks after the start of the war. He had a two-year-old daughter, Pamela, and his wife Nesta was pregnant. Mary was born on 15 January 1915 and would never really overcome the pain of growing up fatherless. Now frail and infirm, she still has on her wall a photograph of her father, 'Dick', cradled in the arms of her grandfather, the 4th Duke. Both of my great-uncles are buried in war cemeteries in Belgium, at Lussenthoek and Hooge Crater. On several occasions my parents have laid flowers on the graves of their uncles, usually after visiting the battlefield of Waterloo.

All these far-flung outposts of Britain and the Commonwealth are, like the Salerno Cemetery, lovingly cared for by local gardener custodians. They are planted with trees and shrubs from their adoptive countries –

the entrance to Salerno is flanked by umbrella pines – but also adorned with some of the treasures and trademarks from British gardens, imports from 'home'. In the Salerno Cemetery, roses are growing along all the flower beds; it is too early in spring for them to be out, but by summer their sweet scent will fill the air and maybe a few late blooms will linger into the early autumn to mark the anniversary of Morny's death. As we leave, my father signs the visitors' book and enters the date, mistakenly writing '43. I am not surprised; that is where he is in his head.

As we drive back to Naples, I reflect on the indiscriminate, humbling power of war, and its aftermath, the way it plays havoc with people's destiny. Morny, who had spent his whole life preparing to inherit the dukedom, carried the title for less than two years; my father, the son of a younger son, never expected to become Duke, but from 16 September 1943 the responsibilities of his life were mapped out by the legacy which accompanies the title. I wonder whether he might concede that part of him wishes that he had not inherited it; but in any case, the answer could never be a simple 'yes' or 'no'.

In April 1944, as the SS *Strathnaver* steamed up the coast of Italy carrying soldiers from the 1HCR, Captain the Marquess of Douro would have passed the beach where his cousin had landed and seen the hill where he lost his life. By this time the Italian campaign had been going on for nine months and the German retreat had reached a point halfway between Naples and Rome. The Anzio landings had taken place at the beginning of January, and the first shots had been fired in the fight for Cassino, which would become the emblematic battle of the campaign. The whole country had become a battleground and many of the civilian population were suffering terribly. My father says, 'When we went into Naples, I was horrified to see children short of food, and covered in sores – desperately malnourished.' Their staging-camp was up in the hills, about ten miles from the city, and he and his regiment were still dressed in their desert combat khaki, with full regimental kit. The uphill march was forgotten the next morning. 'It was wonderful to wake up surrounded by olive groves rather than sand.' It was a perfect spring day and the camp was full of Italians selling walnuts and apples. Valerian took off in a jeep to try and find Morny's grave, but in the chaos of war the trail ran cold. He could not have known that it would be another sixty-one years before he would pay homage to his fallen cousin.

There was a lull before the regiment was sent off to the front and, with the weather often warm and sunny, the atmosphere was more like a holiday camp. The routine of daily drill and inspections continued – 'kits and lines', as they called them. There were lectures – some given by Valerian – and night patrols to prepare the troops for a terrain very different to that of the Middle East. Salerno's facilities were in full use: the showers washed off the grime of the camp and the Opera House provided a melodious escape from military chores. One outing was to the comic opera *The Barber of Seville*; the tale of the hero wooing and winning the heroine from the lecherous clutches of her guardian was warmly applauded.

Diana, in Jerusalem, was waiting nervously for news. 'I didn't get many letters', she remembers. My father is a little defensive about this, but unnecessarily so: 'We all knew how hard it was to write regularly,' she says, 'and quite often letters never reached you anyway.' In any case, though I am sure she kept my father's letters – my mother is a 'keeper' not a 'thrower' – for now, they have slipped out of sight. My father does not have any of my mother's: some were lost in the war, others discarded in the endless round of moves which characterised their life afterwards. My father was as anxious about Diana's safety as she was about his. Writing to his sister (another 'keeper'), he told her, 'Diana is well but has rather a harrowing time ... her father being GOC [she] is an obvious target. However she is heavily guarded.' My mother's regime in Jerusalem after her marriage was stricter than before – she always travelled in her father's car to the office and could never go out without being accompanied by an armed 'minder'. With the letters to Valerian went regular supplies of cigarettes, 'Turkish, non-tipped and in little red tins of fifty', my father remembers. Once she entrusted a bottle of whisky to a Russian who claimed to be heading for 1HCR's area of operation. It never reached its destination.

Valerian's regiment got their orders to the front at the beginning of May. Their path was impeded by the destruction left by the Germans: bridges were blown, many roads destroyed. When my parents and I set off for the next leg of our journey, our own passage is hampered only by the daredevil driving of some of my fellow motorists and the challenging confusion of road signs. Little can be done about the former, but my father's navigational skills come into play as he pores over a map and gets out his compass, which he carries with him at all times. We are heading for Palena, a destination that my father has been intent on reaching again ever since the end of the war. Perched in the Apennines, on the Maiella range of mountains, it was the scene of the regiment's baptism of fire in that phase of the Italian campaign. On our drive we pass by Cassino. In a 1944 letter to Eliza, Valerian described the scene as it was then: '... the most terrible sight I have ever seen. There is literally nothing left. There is not a living tree for miles around, just black skeletons. The ground is all churned up as if by a giant plough gone mad.' The great monastery was later rebuilt, and it looks to me more like a fortress commanding the entire area; it is easy to understand why so many lives were lost in the battle for its control.

Our route to Palena takes us inland and as we gradually climb, we leave behind the full-blown, blossomy spring of the western coast of Italy and reach the cooler, more mountainous terrain of beech woods, still dotted with snowdrops but with primroses and violets beginning to emerge as well. When, at last, we reach a signpost that says 'Palena' my father exclaims excitedly. We are bidden to be at the town hall at ten o'clock the following morning, so we spend the night in the nearby village of Pescocostanza, sitting at the bottom of some well-used ski runs.

Before we left England the Italian Ambassador had been in touch with the Mayor of Palena about our impending visit, and we had been alerted to what we might expect: 'They are going to make a big fuss.' The following morning, on the outskirts of Palena, I spot a police car parked on the verge, and as I instinctively slow down to pass it, two immaculately attired Carabinieri officers stand to attention and salute us. They are formally acknowledging 'the old hero's' return.

Valerian first entered the village on foot in May 1944; the roads were impassable so the Squadron left their armoured cars at base. Then it was like a ravaged ghost town; rubble filled the streets, and the smell of dead bodies poisoned the mountain air. In November 1943 the Germans had occupied the village and forced the entire population to leave – men, women and children. The Germans abandoned the village when they realised they could continue to control the area from various vantage-points in the mountains. However, before they left they blew up many of the remaining buildings. A very different sight meets us now. As we drive to the centre of the village, escorted by the Carabinieri, we can see the Mayor and other descendants of those hapless wartime inhabitants gathered outside the town hall. We are ushered in by the Mayor, in his full regalia, and other village dignitaries. I realise that this is just as big an event for them as it is for my father.

'We thank the Duke for his visit, which is a very important event for a small community like Palena ... Thanks to the crucial help from the Allied Forces, and their heroic conduct, we are now free to live in a democracy far from those dark and hopeless days of barbarism and disregard for human life, days when mankind failed. Today it is an honour and a privilege to have an opportunity to thank one of those heroes.' The Mayor's speech is warmly applauded by the assembled villagers. My father, as always immaculately dressed, today in a dark blue jacket with gold regimental buttons, takes a blue and white spotted silk handkerchief out of his pocket and wipes a tear from his eye. I know he would never cast himself in an heroic light, but as his generation dwindles, and he outlives many of his comrades, he must stand for many. The Mayor seems young enough to be my father's grandson but an even younger model steps forward. Palena has adopted the practice of having a junior Mayor, a twelve-year-old, who echoes the words of his elder and adds another layer of hope for the future. 'Fortunately we did not know the war. Although we have studied it in books, it is difficult to understand its horror from this alone. Now I realise that if war kept you so far from home, it cannot be a good thing, and we must never allow such things to happen again.'

We are all touched and charmed. My father is presented with gifts and my mother with some beautiful flowers. My father recovers his composure and in turn presents the village with a framed photograph of himself, dressed in his full regalia of Colonel-in-Chief of The Dukes. He thanks the Mayor and the village for their kindness and he recounts some of his memories of those dark days: the strangeness of coming into a village that was totally deserted, his horror at the devastation left by the Germans and of some sweeter memory. 'A few days after we arrived a woman appeared from the ruins – out of the mist, as if by magic. She told us that her name was Maria, and if we would feed her she would look after us – wash our clothes and cook for us. She was like an angel of mercy. I've always wanted to tell her how important she was to us. Does anyone know who she might have been?' There is silence in the hall and then an elderly man in the audience shouts out 'That's Maria "La Pesceija".' For one precious moment my father thinks she is still alive, that he may be able to thank her in person. But Maria died in 1980, and as the story unfolds it becomes clear that the people of Palena remember her as their own local heroine.

There is tremendous excitement in the hall. Maria has instantly become the crucial human link in the common but divided memories of my father and the village. She was related to several of the villagers, including the Mayor. Photographs are produced which show a strong, handsome woman who I can immediately believe capable of running the domestic lives of a group of young Englishmen. And Maria plays an important part in another story of my father's wartime days in Palena. To the delight of the audience my father tells them about her finding him a sleek, small black stallion: he needed a horse which could avoid the roads where the Germans, perched in the mountains, were waiting to pick them off. It was his job to get the provisions and he would go at night to a village four or five miles away where the Indian muleteers kept the pack of mules. Having loaded up the mules, they would stealthily find their way back to Palena. 'What I didn't realise', he says, 'was that mules come into season, so my little black stallion, the first thing he did was to try to mount all the mules!' In the end he had to be about 200 yards ahead and hope the muleteers could keep him in their sights. The audience love the story and roar with laughter, wanting more. My father tells them that when he moved on, he felt quite emotional about leaving Maria – he could not think what he could give her to thank her for all her kindness. In the end, he tore one of his Captain's stars off the shoulder of his uniform and the armourer, who normally looked after the weapons, made it into a brooch.

My father is enjoying these exchanges as much as the villagers are, but there is another important, symbolic task: to honour the fallen and lay a wreath at the village's war memorial. Everyone lines up outside the hall to walk the few hundred yards to the monument. I insist that we drive; part of the way is uphill and I worry that my father will tire himself. But, determined as he always is to defy the physical limitations of his age, he springs from the car and strides off to join the group, leaving my mother and me to bring up the rear. The procession, crowned by the Communale banner of the village, is led by the Mayor and two veterans of the war, both of whom had been Italian resistance fighters. The bugler sounds the Last Post; my father lays the laurel wreath adorned with the Italian colours of red, white and green, steps back, and everyone stands to attention.

The formal part of the programme is over but we are invited to lunch in a restaurant perched on the outskirts of the village, overlooking the road along which my father marched when he first entered it. Briefly the cloud lifts and we see the peak of the mountain; it is easy to imagine how dangerous the road would have been when the Germans had positions all along the mountainside. The lunch – a daunting seven courses – is presided over by the Mayor and attended by local dignitaries including the Carabinieri. More wartime tales are told and Maria, our interpreter, works overtime. Before we take leave of our hosts, we are showered with presents of books and photographs, and everyone, women and men, embraces my father. Any British reticence or formality that he may have harboured has melted in the warmth of their welcome and he embraces them back.

In the afternoon we drive to Lama, the next village along the valley. The road carries us close to where there would have been several German observation points and my father glances up the mountainside. 'The Germans were shelling us all the time during the day, so we found a deserted house under a cliff which acted as a shield and my squadron stayed there for the three weeks we were in Palena.' Many of the night patrols would have to find their way along mined footpaths; sometimes they reached the snowline. On one occasion a naturalised Austrian who was in the First Household Cavalry was killed by an enemy ski patrol. 'We went back to bury his body and it turned out that the German patrol was in fact from an Austrian Division of the German army. They had already buried him and covered his grave with two broken skis and the words "In Memory of a Brave Austrian".'

My father and his squadron were briefly in Lama before they moved into Palena and it was the setting for a spicy encounter. One day he spotted some Pointer puppies in a house and decided to see if he could buy one. He got to the first floor and found an extremely pretty girl, elegantly dressed, in a room bare of everything but a bed and chair. 'I went and sat on the chair and she sat on the bed – a few paces away – and asked me, in good English, if I could help her. I wondered what was coming!' It turned out to be a long story. The girl and her brother had been suspected of being fascists and her brother was now in jail; she wanted Valerian to intercede on his behalf. Ever the gentleman, my father took all the details and promised to do what he could, but she must have sensed that he had some niggling doubts about her story. 'I went towards the door to leave but she stood with her back firmly against it and put her arms round my neck: "Stay with me", she pleaded.' My father, with I suspect the briefest of pauses, gave her a chaste kiss on the forehead and left, reiterating that he would do what he could. He rejoined his troops, who were waiting for him in the street, unaware of the encounter. 'I thought I had got away with it until they all started to laugh and when I looked up to the first-floor window of the house, she was leaning out and waving, with her luscious bosom on full display!' A nasty aftertaste came later. When my father reached the next village he asked his friend Gavin Astor (later Lord Astor of Hever), the Intelligence officer, to check up on the brother. As it turned out, not only was he a leading fascist, but the glamorous seductress had been the mistress of the German Kommandant.

We leave Palena with an air of melancholy hanging over us: my father has spent so many years remembering and wanting to return, but now he knows he will never come back. We stop for one more look, and to receive a valedictory present: a pot of acacia honey that is one of the specialities of the region. The gift symbolises a day that has been infused with sweet and touching gestures from the people of Palena. We stop in the woods for my mother to pick some wild flowers, and it reminds my father that when he rode through these very woods on the little stallion that Maria had found for him, they were filled with little blue flowers. When we reflect on our visit to Palena, it is clear that my father has relished every minute of our packed day in this remote area, as wild and beautiful as the Highlands of Scotland. His regiment was on the move most of the time it was in Italy, but in spite of its vulnerabilities and the danger, the routine and rhythms of its few weeks here provided some kind of respite. When future generations of villagers look at the wall of the Mayor's office and see the photograph of the British 'Duca', it may seem out of place; but perhaps the 'young Mayor' will recall the visit, may be able to explain that this man played a small but significant part in the history of the village and returned over sixty years later to pay his respects to the people and the place.

A week after leaving Palena in June 1944, Valerian wrote a very important letter.

Dear Mrs McConnel

Thank you so very much for your letter. I only hope you will forgive me for not answering before. I am a very bad correspondent at the best of times and we have been very busy lately.

I cannot tell you how glad I was to get your letter as the fact that you didn't really approve at the beginning had been a source of worry to us both. It is a great relief to know from you personally that you are on our side.

I don't need to tell you how much I miss Diana, especially in this lovely country. It is really dreadful sometimes.

I am afraid it must be very much worse for her for I, at least, have a lot to occupy my mind at times.

Some of the places I have been to here are indescribably beautiful and it is at these times that I miss her particularly because I know she would appreciate the wonderful flowers, the trees, the mountains and the streams even more than I do ... The country people have been wonderful to us and we recovered many ex-POWs, when we advanced, whom they had been hiding ... in one case a junior NCO who took a small patrol to a village, was chaired round the streets for two hours by the entire population behind a brass band and then had to make a speech! The fatted calf (carefully hidden away from the Boche) was killed everywhere.

Thank you again so much. love from Valerian

Now, at last, Valerian had been able to show Diana the 'wonderful flowers, the trees, the mountains and the streams'.

The following day we are on the move again. This time our sights are on Florence, but before we hit the autoroute that snakes up the west side of Italy, we pass through Sulmona, a ravishing medieval town in the most dramatic setting, surrounded on all sides by mountains. It was June 1944 when my father was last here and he heard news of his close friend Gavin Astor. Gavin had been ambushed on his way to Palena and was missing, believed dead. Since my father was such a close friend, he felt it was his duty to write to Gavin's mother with the terrible news. To his great delight and relief, when he reached Sulmona he discovered that Gavin had survived the ambush, been taken prisoner and (it emerged later) managed to get onto very good terms with his captors. After the war the German doctor who had tended his wounds asked him to be godfather to his first child. I find it reassuring that there are some war stories which can shed a warm light.

As we drive further north my father exclaims with delight as he recognises the names of the towns and cities that were the staging-posts on the regiment's slow progress north: Assisi, Gubbio, Arezzo. Occasionally they would get a billet in a house; a grand one boasted an ancient English nanny. Sometimes they came across tempting orchards of fruit, but were warned to beware: the Germans had hung hand-grenades from the trees. In one place a family gave my father a goose as a parting gift, no doubt intended for the pot. But he called it Bella and it became a pet, sitting in a basket on the back of his armoured car, a pointer in another basket on the other side. 'The dog and duck', his men called his vehicle.

Anticipation builds as we near the city. My father's bold claim has always been, 'I was the first officer into Florence'. If that was true, why did the history books not record the fact? 'It was early August 1944 and the regiment were a few miles south-east of Florence', he remembers. 'The Germans were meant to be withdrawing and my squadron leader asked me to go and have a look round. I drove in an open jeep and we got a tumultuous reception. People were cheering and throwing flowers and we arrived in a huge square where an enormous crowd was gathered.' Remarkably, that brief visit was the only time my father has ever been to Florence. The following morning we stand in the city's main square, the Piazza della Repubblica, but it strikes no chord in his memory. Neither does the Piazza della Signoria, the political heart of Florence.

I can see my father feels rather dispirited by our failure to find the square, as if he too needs the place to reaffirm the reality. We decide to tackle another entrenched memory. The afternoon is bright, sunny and clear – the exact opposite of the conditions on the night in late summer 1944 when my father had his terrifying drive. Eventually the trauma faded, but it has never completely left his psyche and when we planned the trip to Italy I knew we had to find what he remembered as the 'road to Rimini'.

Once again we pore over a map, and by a process of elimination decide that the road in question must be the route from Florence towards Arezzo and then over the mountains to Rimini. Its treacherous bends are well-known to local people and my mother declines to accompany us – our flight to Naples has been as much vertiginous torment as she is prepared to take on one trip. My father and I set off in our solid hired car and for quite a while I am almost bored by the ordered, calm, flat countryside; but then we start to climb and gradually the incline becomes steeper and the bends more frequent. 'We were in a convoy, nose to tail, and I could not see anything but could feel the armoured car twisting round the bends and could hear the almost constant sound of the German shelling.' As we get higher the hairpin bends become more violent, the drop more dramatic; I begin to understand how frightening it must have been. 'Every second of the drive I imagined that they would be hit, roll off the road down a precipice and land at the bottom of a ravine, engulfed in flames and we would all burn alive.' I am pretty cool-headed on high, winding roads – a veteran of driving over the Atlas Mountains, in winter – but I am relieved when we reach the top, the Passo del Magliore, and we both climb out of our car. It is quite a bleak spot, but the view in every direction is stunning – a wild, craggy landscape with little evidence of human life. 'I think it was the feeling of helplessness that made it so frightening. In the heat of battle you react spontaneously, and you have some control over your environment, can take evasive action – defend yourself in some way. The night-time – being cloaked in darkness – made it so much worse.' We breathe deeply on the high mountain air. I take a photograph and we climb back into the car for the descent. A milder ritual is enacted when I stop to pick some mountain flowers for my mother. She is as delighted to receive them as she is glad not to have accompanied us.

The following day it pours with rain, but this is our last chance to find 'the square'. There is one more possibility: a large piazza just outside the central part of Florence but very near a road which leads to Arezzo, the direction my father arrived from. The Piazza Santa Croce, dominated by a fifteenth-century basilica where many of Florence's greatest citizens are buried, has always been used for religious and civic events. In the taxi on the way there I am willing it to be the right place. My father walks cautiously into the middle, stick in hand, and looks around. Somewhere in his mind a light of recognition is turned on and he is back there in August 1944. The square was bathed in sunshine and filled with the noise of jubilant crowds. Diana in his thoughts, he bought two silk scarves for her from a tiny shop, and was then 'whisked off for a boozy lunch in a grand house in the corner of the square'. His hosts all spoke English and he had the best lunch he had eaten for a very long time.

My father still has the two scarves. He gave both to my mother, but at some later point she tactfully returned them to him, since they were not her style. Before we left England, my father had opened his large mahogany chest of drawers and after rifling through his collection of neatly folded cravats, handkerchiefs and scarves, he found them. One, of pale yellow with a deep pink paisley pattern, is faded and fragile but still incredibly soft and, more importantly, instantly evocative for my father of a sunny day in Florence over sixty years ago. He wears it even now.

Before our flight home, we have one last duty. We started the week by paying our respects at Morny's grave; we finish it by going to the war cemetery just outside Florence. My father always searches in military cemeteries for graves of soldiers from both his own regiments, The Blues and The Dukes. He spots several – some young men still in their teens. The rain is bucketing down and it is hard not to feel melancholic as we walk down the aisles of graves, reading some of the moving inscriptions on the 1,632 gravestones. We decide to take shelter in a small building which houses both the lists of all the burials, and a book of remembrance.

My parents cast their memories back to the autumn of 1944. Before Valerian had left Palestine, he and Diana agreed that they would try to co-ordinate their returns to England. Diana may not have known exactly where the regiment was at any one time, but she would always see details of the main troop movements. 'Try to get on a ship that will join my convoy', he begged her. They had spent so little time together – even by that autumn it was still less than a year since they had started seeing each other seriously.

At last, at the end of September, 1HCR got their orders to return home. On the train from Arezzo to Naples, twenty officers and their bedrolls were packed into baggage trucks that normally carried eight horses. An extra item was hidden in Valerian's bedroll:

I and my friends had become very used to drinking the local wine and before we got on the train we bought a barrel of local red vino which was exceptionally good. I remember the shape of the barrel, about three foot long and one foot high, not like a normal barrel. We had heard to our horror that the ship we were going home on was dry – by this time the Americans were in the war and they had imposed their rules.

When they reached Naples, where they were to embark on the *Monarch of Bermuda*, it fell to Trooper Pearson to smuggle the contraband into the cabin. Once Valerian and the other officers in his cabin were sure that no suspicions had been raised, like excited schoolboys they broke open the barrel, only to discover, to their horror and huge disappointment, that it had turned to vinegar. They now had the greater problem of getting rid of the evidence; the wine was so rancid that when they tried to pour it down the communal bath – shared by fifty men – it was clear that the smell would be impossible to disguise. In the end they waited until darkness fell, heaved it up onto the deck and threw it over the side of the ship. With bated breath they waited for the cry 'Man overboard'. They got away with it; but they had a dry journey ahead of them.

When they had been at sea for a couple of days, they were joined by another convoy which had come up through the Suez Canal. Valerian knew there was a possibility that Diana might be on one of the ships, but when he approached the Purser the officer laughingly dismissed the chance. 'I am not going to contact every ship,' he said. Eventually my father persuaded him to try the one about 300 yards astern. So the message was transmitted in Morse: 'Do you have a Lady Douro on board?'. By a wonderful stroke of luck the message came back 'Yes'. For the rest of the journey my parents had a regular 'date'. 'At six o'clock every evening Diana went to the bow of her ship, I to the stern, and we would send each other "lovey-dovey" messages – to the great amusement of those who could read Morse code, which was just about all the troops on the ship!'

My father loves telling this story and both my parents relish the detail. The romantic tale has entered family legend, revisited at celebratory gatherings, including my parents' diamond wedding anniversary in 2004. As we leave the cemetery for our drive back to Florence and our flight home the following morning, I look back to see the cypresses, planted in perfect symmetrical attention, which stand guard at the entrance. There are eleven, and I wonder whether one died or whether they invoke the eleventh hour, on the eleventh day, of the eleventh month. 'Remember': that is all we are asked to do. A few minutes later a white dove flies across our path, a few feet above the red poppies that are growing, scattered, in the verges by the side of the road.

There were several postscripts to our trip. My father invited one of his brother officers from his squadron to come to lunch. Malcolm Fraser arrived bearing treasure: his original small pigskin diaries from the war. I searched his tiny, neat entries for any clues – I still had a niggling worry about my father's claim to be the first officer into Florence and was thrilled to discover that my doubts were misplaced. On 2 August 1944 the regiment were camped about fifteen miles south-east of Florence and the following day they moved east towards the Adriatic. Florence was not fully liberated until 12 August, but ten days earlier the Germans had left the eastern part of the city. To the crowds in the Piazza Santa Croce he would have been the first Allied officer they had seen.

However, the diaries cast a shadow over our nerve-racking drive along the 'road to Rimini'. There was no record of the regiment ever having been on that route. We considered the possibility that my father might have been on a recce and I tried to make the dates work but they did not add up. Eventually, having read through Malcolm's detailed notes, I came across a reference to a 'nightmare' journey in the dark which took five hours to cover eight miles; it was towards Rimini but it was right over beside the Adriatic. I realised that the route we took was the wrong one; our 'moment' on the pass at the top of the mountain had been a hollow triumph. But somehow it did not seem to matter. Driving my father to the summit had been a small gesture from daughter to father. It had helped to purge the nightmare and dispel the ghost for ever.

Of the memories that we carried home, none were more touching than those of Palena, whose inhabitants' kindness and welcome echoed that of Maria all those years ago. A few months after our expedition, a book was published in Italy which included an account of our visit. This gesture added to my father's great delight and pleasure at having made the trip; but the real treat was the discovery, when he opened the book, of a photograph of a badge – described in the caption as 'Le Croci de

Guerra de Maria' – the cross of war of Maria. My father instantly recognised it as the Captain's 'star' that he had pulled off his shoulder and given to her.

One day a carefully wrapped parcel, posted in America, turned up at my parents' house in Hampshire. It contained the star with a note from Mario Pescetti, Maria's son, generously offering it back to my father. It was tempting to keep it as a modest addition to the family's military memorabilia, but when the twenty-eight-year-old Valerian gave it to Maria in Palena in 1944, it was intended as both a badge of honour and a lasting thank-you. Maria may have treasured the gift but she did not know that the young soldier would never forget her kindness; instead, it was the twenty-first-century Palena that would hear an old man relive some of his memories of those war-torn days. We decide that young Valerian Wellesley's Captain's star should be given to the new Household Cavalry Museum, which was opened in June 2007 by the Queen. Maria's son was thrilled to know that his mother's story had earned a small place in history. I had been emailing Maria's grandson, who wrote: 'What our Fathers and my Grandmother experienced during the war is beyond my comprehension. What I do know is that I'm grateful for all they did and proud to be Maria's grandson.' And I replied, 'I am proud to be my father's daughter.'

SEVEN

Heirs and Graces

When I travelled to Italy with my parents, I knew that, first to find, and then to climb the hill where Morny died would be one challenge too many for them. But after I returned home, I realised that my own mission felt incomplete. I wanted to stand on the spot where the 6th Duke died. So, one late August day, I returned to Salerno to try to identify the small hill.

Not surprisingly, today's inhabitants of Salerno have turned the page, leaving few marks of those turbulent times. Nowadays the hillsides round the town are studded with villas and hotels looking out over the Mediterranean, but in September 1943 after the Commandos had spearheaded the invasion, wave after wave of troops landing on the beaches were greeted with fire from machine-gun posts set up on the hills above. And it was a complicated time for Italy: four days before Morny landed, the country had surrendered to the Allies, and the population had been faced with the challenge of seeing foe as friend.

Piegollele, the village where Morny's No. 2 Commando unit had their headquarters, is now virtually a suburb of Salerno. As I drove up from the coast along the winding road that leads to the village, I thought about the last days of Morny's life. The hills and mountains reach right down to the coastline; there are few places which could have provided respite from the fierce and constant fighting where much of the advance was by the light of the moon. The accounts and maps of the courageous battle for the Pimple give some clear landmarks – the Church of San Nicola, another hill dubbed '41 Commando' and one called 'White Cross'. Today's caretaker of the church was not old enough to remember the war, but his parents had taken wounded soldiers into their house and he grew up hearing stories of the intense battle for control of the area. The local people called the hill 'Pignolillo' – easy to see how it became known as the Pimple – and though it was not marked on my map, by a process of elimination its location became clear.

Two days after Morny died, the Commandos finally won their battle for the hill. When fresh Allied troops arrived there they found it deserted, but strewn with bodies. Today an electricity pylon straddles the site. I felt a little guilty that I had taken the easy route up, sitting comfortably in a car, but I climbed the last bit of the hill, clutching tufts of grass to stop myself slipping in the dry earth. As I advanced the last few yards, brambles grabbed at my ankles and small lizards streaked ahead of me.

At the top I stood and thought about my cousin Morny. I had known so little about him before I began my quest and now there was an odd kind of intimacy to be standing on the spot where he lost his life. He was a real soldier hero, the kind that our ancestor would have been proud to have as a descendant. Morny was an experienced officer, and when he went up the hill for the second time he must have known that the enemy positions were virtually impregnable. Was his courage fortified by an inspiration that reached down from his great-great-grandfather? When Jack Churchill found his body in its shallow grave, also buried nearby was the German officer with whom Morny had fought in close combat. Pistols rather than swords, but in other respects these honourable deaths were re-enacting the grim battle rituals of the Peninsular Wars. The crest of the Pimple is covered in miniature oak trees – as if a handful of acorns had been scattered to mark the spot where these brave young men fought and died.

The guns stopped firing in Europe on Tuesday, 8 May 1945. My father was with his regiment in northern Germany. The night before, he celebrated by spending the evening with his brother-in-law, Tommy Clyde, who, with the Second Household Cavalry Regiment, was based a few miles away. 'We had dinner, then played bowls in a local skittle alley. I crawled into bed at dawn only to be woken a couple of hours later by the most enormous noise of gunfire. I thought, "Oh my God, the war has started again!"' In fact, it was a few minutes before eight – the official time of the ceasefire – and the gunners were letting off shells into a deserted area of marshland, determined that they should be the ones to fire the last shots of the war.

The feelings of most Allied soldiers were of relief rather than elation; in any case, many of their comrades were still fighting in the Far East. When victory over Japan was finally declared on 15 August my father was home, waiting anxiously by my mother's side for the birth of their first child. After several false alarms, the baby was born on 19 August 1945.

They christened him Arthur Charles Valerian – Charles was a name my mother had wanted for her first son; even before her marriage, she had fantasised about children she would call 'Charles and Jane'. It was also the name of my father's great-grandfather, Lord Charles Wellesley, second son of the First Duke.

At the time of Charles's birth, my parents were staying at Stratfield Saye with my grandfather, the 7th Duke. Gerry's sixtieth birthday fell two days after Charles was born; he already had two cherished Clyde grandsons, but to have a Wellesley heir lined up two steps behind him would have been the best possible birthday present. A few months later, just after the end of the war, Diana and her father-in-law were present at the unveiling in Stratfield Saye church of a memorial to Captain the 6th Duke of Wellington. The ceremony was attended by many estate farmers and employees, and not simply out of duty: Morny was a popular figure there. It was only two years since Morny's death, and the family succession tree was growing strongly in another direction.

When Morny gave his life in the fight against fascism, a tragic irony circumscribed his death. His father, the 5th Duke, known to my father's generation as 'Uncle Charlie', had been a prominent member of several pro-Nazi organisations, including the controversial 'Right Club', a secret society which was set up in May 1939 – less than six months before the start of the Second World War. The founder of the club was Archibald Ramsay, the Conservative MP for Peebles and South Midlothian. An 'Open Letter' addressed to Ramsay, which appeared in July 1939 in the widely read magazine *John Bull*, targeted his activities outside of Westminster, describing a meeting in London of a 'pro-Nazi organ-ization' at which 'you [Ramsay] are supposed to have ended a fierce diatribe against the alleged "Jewish control of the Press" with the fol-lowing words: "We must change the present state of things, and if we don't do it constitutionally we'll do it with steel." Wild applause greeted you – and the listeners rose to give you the Fascist salute.'[1]

Not only was the 5th Duke one of sixteen wardens of the Right Club; Ramsay himself revealed in a written account that the Duke had been the 'Chairman at most of the few meetings we held', and also acted as Chair of the Co-ordinating Committee, which recruited for the club and kept in touch with the other, so-called, Patriotic Societies. In this same justification for the society, written in 1943 for MPs and published in 1952 as *The Nameless War*, Ramsay declared:

The main object of the Right Club was to oppose and expose the activities of Organized Jewry, in the light of the evidence which came into my possession in 1938 ... Our first objective was to clear the Conservative Party of Jewish influence, and the character of our membership and meetings were strictly in keeping with this objective. There were no other and secret purposes.

Our hope was to avert war, which we considered to be mainly the work of Jewish intrigue centred in New York.[2]

The club had its own badge: an eagle killing a snake, with the initials 'PJ' – Perish Judah. On the day after the war began, Ramsay penned his own version of a patriotic song, and distributed it to members of the Right Club:

> Land of Dope and Jewry
> Land that once was free
> All the Jew boys praise thee
> Whilst they plunder thee.
> Poorer still and poorer
> Grow thy true-born sons
> Faster still and faster
> They're sent to feed the guns.

The membership of the club consisted of imprudent patriots, virulent anti-Semites, neo-Nazis and pacifists; all members were against a war with Germany, and many believed Hitler was the only man who could hold back the advance of Bolshevism. Its most notorious member was William Joyce, who later, as Lord Haw-Haw, broadcast pro-German propaganda and was executed for treason in 1946.

The 5th Duke never had the chance to defend his name: when Ramsay cited the role of 'the Duke of Wellington' in his statement for MPs, it was two years after Uncle Charlie's death, and three weeks before Morny was killed. But the evidence is there for all to see: Ramsay consigned the names of the members of the Right Club to a leather-bound ledger, later to become known as the 'Red Book'. Sensationally, and accidentally, the existence of the society and the Red Book itself were discovered in May 1940 by MI5. In a dawn raid, Tyler Kent, an American working at the American Embassy as a cipher clerk, was arrested and charged with espionage. Kent had been passing on to the Germans messages between Churchill and Roosevelt. It turned out that he was a member of the Right Club, and a month before his arrest Ramsay had deposited the locked ledger with him for safe-keeping – believing, as he said later, that 'Jews might cause his own house to be burgled in order to get possession of it'.[3]

The Red Book then disappeared, but towards the end of the 1980s it was discovered lying at the bottom of an old filing cabinet in a lawyers' office. It is now lodged with the Wiener Library in London, where any member of the public can ask to see it. The stout volume, made by Waterlow & Sons Ltd, has 'Private Ledger' embossed in faded gold on its spine. The heavy lock, now no protection for the women and men whose names appear in the book, was broken by the Secret Services after they had raided Tyler Kent's flat. The Duke of Wellington appears as number thirty-four on the list, with a mark beside his name which indicates he was a warden. Ramsay's vision for the growth of the society was ambitious: there are 193 gold-edged pages in all, and an index in which he had begun to list the different occupations, or roles within the club, of the membership – 'Members of Parliament', 'writers', 'speakers', 'stewards'.

Shortly after Kent's arrest, Archibald Ramsay and a number of other prominent members of the society were detained under Defence Regulation 18B. I was surprised to discover that there was no available evidence to suggest that the 5th Duke had been officially reprimanded, let alone questioned. Thinking that it might be possible to get access to a secret file under the FOI (Freedom of Information) Act, I contacted MI5 through its website. In their first reply they merely stated that all the historical information they could release was accessible on their website or held in the National Archives. When, in another email, I pressed them, suggesting that it was very unlikely that a file would not exist on the 5th Duke's involvement in the Right Club, they replied that after further research, 'we now regret to inform you that there is no trace of a record for the 5th Duke of Wellington in the Service archives.' Did my great-uncle manage, through his Establishment contacts, to avoid any kind of surveillance or censure, or was there originally a file which had later been destroyed? His name exists for all to see in the Red Book; but, over sixty years later, the details of Uncle Charlie's involvement in the unsavoury activities of the Right Club remain a closed book.

I doubt that the 5th Duke's membership of the Right Club was known to his sister-in-law (twice over), Nesta. Born Nesta FitzGerald, her mother was Amelia Catherine, one of two daughters of Henri Louis Bischoffsheim, a prominent and distinguished member of London's

Jewish community. Her father was the Irish Knight of Kerry. Nesta had married first Dick Wellesley, who was killed in the First World War, and then Geordie, the youngest Wellesley brother.

I wonder, too, whether Charlie's wife knew of his role in the pro-Nazi organisation. Lilian Maud (Maudie) Glen Coats married Charlie, the then Marquess of Douro, in 1909. An heiress, she was the daughter of George Coats from Paisley, who had made a fortune out of manufacturing silk and cotton thread. A few years before the marriage, Coats had bought a large estate on the River Dee in Aberdeenshire, called Glen Tanar. For blood-sport-mad Charlie, prospects of shooting the grouse, stalking the deer and fishing for salmon must have added to the allure of his future wife. The estate could boast that when Lillie Langtry, Edward VII's mistress, stayed there, she was so bored when all the men were out shooting that, to the horror of the butler, she amused herself by sliding down the banisters on a silver tray. When Coats was made a peer in 1916, he styled himself Baron Glentanar.

In the early 1920s the Douros moved into Stratfield Saye, which had lain empty since the 3rd Duke's death in 1900. Uncle Charlie made full use of the sporting facilities on the estate; but he made few changes to the house. He did, however, dismantle the organ in the hall. He then, with the aim of improving his rabbit shoot, scattered the pipes round the park, providing on-the-surface burrows for his prey. My aunt Eliza tells me that her mother, long before she separated from Gerald, had very little time for Charlie and would describe him as 'having blood on his hands'. As a child Eliza took this literally, and every time she saw her uncle she expected to see a trail of blood behind him. However, she was extremely fond of her aunt, who seemed pretty and kind and wore make-up, which seemed very exotic to Eliza. Maudie had her own sitting room with a piano and lots of enthralling feminine clutter.

By the time Charlie inherited the dukedom on the death of his father in June 1934, events were moving fast in Europe. With the memories of the horrors and losses of the First World War still fresh in their minds, many of his generation were prepared to go to great lengths to stop it happening again; as the bearer of a famous title, Charlie was a prime target for anyone who wanted a top-drawer endorsement for a pro-fascist plan. No one can know whether he ever suffered remorse for his activities, but the last six months of his life must have been uncomfortable. In the spring of 1941 the existence of the Red Book had become known publicly when *The New York Times* ran an article about fifth columnists in Britain.

Archibald Ramsay, though still interned in Brixton Prison, sued for libel against the paper. In July 1941 the court found in his favour, but he was awarded only a farthing in damages.

On the same day a question was tabled in Parliament asking the 'Secretary of State for the Home Department if he will publish the list of members of the Right Club in the possession of the Home Office'.[4] A civil servant's private briefing for the Minister advised that it 'would be quite wrong to publish the names of the members, many of whom are no doubt simple-minded people who did not know the activities of the leaders of this organization' and went on to name 'the Duke of Wellington' as one of the 'fairly well-known' names on the list.[5] In the absence of any solid information about the Red Book, many people in the country believed that the membership consisted entirely of 'traitors'. I imagine that Uncle Charlie was aware of this, and knew that it would be only a matter of time before his association with the club became known publicly. A conspiracy theorist might question whether the Duke's death, just over four months after the trial ended, and attributed in obituaries to 'pneumonia', was entirely due to natural causes.

Whatever Maudie knew, it is hard not to feel a strong measure of sympathy for her. Less than two years after her husband's death, living alone at Stratfield Saye, she received the devastating news of Morny's death. In reply to one of the many letters of condolence she wrote: 'In his young heart he was like one of King Arthur's Knights dedicating himself to King and Country.' She mourned the loss of her son like any mother across the land whose child had sacrificed themselves in the service of their country. And she was dispossessed of a maternal claim to the future line of dukes. Unlike Elizabeth, 2nd Duchess, and Evelyn, 3rd, neither of whom had children, she had nurtured and groomed an heir, who held the title only fleetingly before dying on the battlefield.

In addition, with the succession of her brother-in-law Gerald, she had to move out of Stratfield Saye and was distraught at leaving behind so many memories. 'When the furniture men come lumping around', she wrote to a friend, 'I want to trip them up and very often I bare my fangs with irritation, for instance, when the telephone breaks down and the staff take to weeping at the thought of leaving here when they have always said it was a beast of a house. It is the House *we Loved*.' While her daughter, Anne, stayed on in a house on the Stratfield Saye estate, Maud bought a property in Richmond. It was here that she died in May 1946. Her sister, Mrs Adams, took a harsh view of her demise. 'She told me,' wrote James Lees-Milne, 'Maud Wellington had died as a result of "faithful repression" by the Wellesley family, into whom she had married.'

One of Maud's obituaries refers to an interesting family case that arose after Morny's death: 'The daughter, formerly Lady Anne Wellesley, who married in 1933 the Hon. David Rhys, youngest son of Lord Dynevor, succeeded as Duchess of Ciudad Rodrigo, and became a Grandee (first class) in Spain, when her brother, who was unmarried, was killed. Her husband by virtue of her succession became Duke of Ciudad Rodrigo and a Grandee (first class) in Spain also.'[6] Duque de Ciudad Rodrigo was the title awarded, in 1812, to the First Duke (then the Earl of Wellington) by a grateful Spanish nation following his siege and storming of the city of that name. With the title went the gift of two large Spanish properties in Andalucia. The year before he died, Morny wrote a will which bequeathed the Spanish estates to the person who would on his death become 'Duke of Wellington and Ciudad Rodrigo'. In Spain a title can pass through the female line, and Morny's next of kin was his sister Anne. When he was killed at the Salerno landings, under Spanish law Anne formally became 'Duchess of Ciudad Rodrigo' and her husband, David, the Duke. To my grandfather's great alarm, it seemed as if the Spanish properties would follow the title. However, when the will was subjected to vigorous review by both the Spanish and English courts, Spain ceded to England, and the Duke of Wellington was formally declared the heir. However, technically Anne and her husband remained the 'Spanish' Duchess and Duke of Ciudad Rodrigo. There ensued a discreet negotiation between Gerry and his niece, which focused on a financial inducement for her to forgo the title in his favour. Family records do not disclose the amount that was finally agreed; my father tells me the reunion of the titles of Wellington and Ciudad Rodrigo was a costly affair.

Though the First Duke never visited the Spanish properties, his son the 2nd Duke had every intention of getting there. He was foiled by the threat of capture by bandits who ruled the hills that enclosed the route from Malaga. When he was told that it would need a whole squadron of cavalry to protect him, he did not consider this to be appropriate use of the army. An agent working for the family at the time wrote of his concerns about a possible visit:

Suppose the Duke and Duchess and her companions had all been there – what a haul for a squad of fourteen bandits and cut-throats! They would have laid hold of the ladies and spirited them away, not with the gentlest or most persuasive, but with resolute and efficient, manners; they would have hurried them up among the wild ravines behind the great mountain wall of Parapanda. From there it was not iron or fire, but only gold, and much gold, that would or could rescue them.[7]

Maybe the same reasons prevented Henry, the 3rd Duke, from visiting the place, though he had an opportunity when he attended, in 1885, the funeral of Alfonso XII in Madrid. Arthur, the 4th Duke, was the first of the line to visit the estate, in 1900, shortly after inheriting the title. By then the railway between Madrid and Granada had been built and it was only the last ten miles that were in any way hazardous. He took his whole family with him, and my grandfather gave my father a vivid account of the last leg of the journey, which he covered with his father and brothers on horseback, while his mother and two sisters travelled in a carriage. Word of their arrival spread round the area and great crowds gathered in the villages along the route for the unusual sight of a group of English aristocrats.

Ever since that visit the property in Andalucia became, to many different members of the family, one of their favourite places in the world. Although there are now more buildings in the Vega, the view from the house remains, as described in 1869 by a correspondent of *The Times*, of 'unequalled loveliness'. Though there is no documentary evidence to back this up, my grandfather always said that the First Duke was offered the Alhambra, but chose instead the estate. If this is true, his descendants should be grateful.

Just before the Salerno landings, when Morny's ship was docked at Gibraltar, he sought leave from his Commanding Officer to visit the property in Andalucia for the first time as Duke of Wellington and Ciudad Rodrigo. The dashing young soldier on his way to war left a big impression on everyone on the estate. But later a local gypsy woman, who had been in the crowd which turned up to wish him well, said she had seen the angel of death hovering over his head.

It was in 1947, at the time of the legal wrangling over the Spanish titles and property, that my grandfather gave Apsley House to the nation. When he inherited the dukedom Stratfield Saye was in a terrible condition, and he needed to funnel his resources into restoring it. The house had been in decline since Gerald's father Arthur, the 4th Duke, inherited it in 1900, and chose with his wife Kathleen to live instead at Ewhurst, an estate near Stratfield Saye which the First Duke bought in 1837. Family history does not relate why the 4th Duke made the decision. Perhaps he did not like Stratfield Saye. Or could it have been that he did not get on with his brother? To me it seems almost sacrilegious that, less than half a century after the First Duke's death, his gift from the nation was to be closed up by a grandson. It would fall to a great-grandson, Gerald, to address the effects of so many years of neglect in the house.

It is true that when Arthur Charles Wellesley married Kathleen Bulkeley Williams in 1872, the 2nd Duke was still alive, and the heir was Henry, his eldest nephew and Arthur's brother. Kathleen and her husband started their family without any expectation that one day they would both have to don ducal robes and regalia. It was only after it became clear that Henry and his wife Evelyn were not to have children that succession became a real prospect.

However, while Stratfield Saye House deteriorated, the 4th Duchess made Ewhurst into a wonderful home which all her children, and eventually grandchildren, came to be very fond of. (Gerald would be bitterly disappointed when, after inheriting the title, he failed by two days to remove the property from auction – the decision to sell that part of the Wellington estate having been taken by Morny's trustees only months before his death.) Kathleen also created a home for a large collection of rare birds. My father had talked about his fascination for his grandmother's aviaries and how she helped foster his own love of birds. But I had not realised quite how impressive the aviaries were, or that Kathleen herself became a highly acclaimed aviarist, as attested in an ornithological magazine of the time. 'The Aviaries of the Duchess of Wellington at Ewhurst Park', the piece was headed, going on to describe the 'ten buildings that house this famous collection, with their ample, decorated flights and remarkable shrubbery'. In the midst of them Kathleen had created a 'sitting room', with comfortable seats and hung with pictures of birds, where guests could 'make friends' with the 'feathered occupants of the aviary'. The interviewer describes how the Duchess 'was able to call [the birds] almost to her feet'. There were macaws and toucans and birds with vivid blue plumage – 'Her Grace being very fond of blue'. Cranes and other large birds strutted 'majestically' over the lawns, and there was a pond which appeared to be full of bright blue water, an effect achieved by using a special solution of copper salt. Clearly Kathleen had triumphed in her ambition to construct not merely a house for her birds but an 'artistic home for them'.

*

My grandfather, Gerald, who was born in 1885 in Dublin (like his famous ancestor), had three brothers – Charlie (the 5th Duke) Richard ('Dick'), and George ('Geordie'), the youngest; his two sisters were Eileen and Evelyn, the eldest of the siblings and the first to get married. She chose Waterloo Day – 18 June – 1900 for her wedding, but her uncle Henry, the 3rd Duke, died ten days before and the celebration became a muted affair. 'The bride wore a robe of antique lace which was her great-grandmother's (Lady Sophia Cecil's) wedding gown', reported *The Times*.

Through this Sophia Cecil there enters into family lore a romantic tale of true love, immortalised by Tennyson in his poem 'The Lord of Burleigh':

> But a trouble weigh'd upon her,
> And perplex'd her, night and morn,
> With the burthen of an honour
> Unto which she was not born.
> Faint she grew, and ever fainter,
> As she murmur'd 'Oh, that he
> Were once more that landscape-painter
> Which did win my heart from me!

The distressed heroine of the poem had fallen in love with a simple 'landscape-painter' who turned out to be the 'Lord of Burleigh' – the Earl of Exeter. Before inheriting the title, Lord Exeter escaped a wife of whom he had tired, and debts which he could not pay, and ended up in a small village, living with the Hoggins family under the guise of 'Mr Jones', a landscape painter. He fell in love with Sarah, the daughter of the house, and they married but when, after succeeding to the earldom, 'Mr Jones' had to return home to claim his inheritance, Sarah was shocked to discover she was the châtelaine of a magnificent stately home. Sarah – the 'Peasant Countess', as she would become known – died in 1797, leaving three children, of whom Sophia Cecil was her only daughter. Sophia married Henry Manvers Pierrepont and the only child of that union, another Sophia, became Lady Charles Wellesley, mother of the 3rd and 4th Dukes.

When Lady Evelyn Wellesley wore her great-grandmother's wedding dress, the Boer War was at its height, and two of her brothers, Charlie and Dick, were in South Africa with their regiments. Earlier in the year Dick had been wounded at the battle of Paardeberg and Charlie, a

Second Lieutenant in the Grenadiers, had set off in March, after parading at Windsor in front of Queen Victoria. By the time both boys had returned safely to England, Victoria's long reign was over. At the time of the Queen's funeral Gerry and Geordie, the younger Wellesley boys, were still at Eton, and joined fellow Etonians in lining the hill from the Long Walk to the gates of Windsor Castle.

The 4th Duchess was ambitious for all four of her sons, particularly her favourite, Gerry. By the start of the Second World War three were married, all to rich women – Charlie to Maud, the cotton heiress, Dick to Nesta, and Gerry to Dorothy, the provenance of whose fortune, like Maud's, was cotton. When it seemed clear there was going to be a war Geordie, the youngest brother, already an officer in the Grenadier Guards, joined the Royal Flying Corps – the precursor of the Royal Air Force. When the notion of 'military aviation' was first mooted in 1910 it had been dismissed as 'a useless and expensive fad', but after its establishment in 1912 it attracted to its ranks quite a number of dashing, adventurous young men. Long before the war, Geordie had won himself a reputation for bravery. As a very young officer in the Grenadier Guards, he had been walking along the towpath of the Thames when he saw a young woman jump from Putney Bridge into the water. He leapt in fully clothed and managed to bring her back to the shore alive. For this act of bravery he won the Royal Humane Society Medal.

Two Wellesley brothers went to war in 1914 – Dick and Geordie. Within weeks of the start of the conflict, it had claimed one of them. Dick, fighting on the Western Front, was killed in October at Ypres. If Mary, his posthumous daughter, had been a boy, the child would have become Morny's heir. Dick's widow, Nesta, was comforted by her brothers-in-law, none more attentively than Geordie, and two years later *The New York Times* announced: 'Lord Wellesley weds a Wellesley'. Nesta and Geordie had been unable to get married in Britain, where it was illegal to marry your dead brother's wife, so Nesta sailed to New York in early 1917 with her two small daughters, and the couple married quietly in the chapel of St Thomas's Church.

The Wellingtons, with their Edwardian attitudes, were unsettled by the nonconformity of Geordie and Nesta's marriage, and the previous year had disapproved of the wedding, with its whiff of Bohemia, of their youngest daughter Eileen to an artist, Cuthbert 'Turps' Orde. However, an even greater distress was caused when, after the early and sudden death in January 1922 of their eldest daughter, Evelyn, their son-in-law, Bobby James, with unseemly haste married his sister-in-law's (by marriage) half-sister, Lady Serena Lumley, the Scarbroughs' only child. The rift between the Wellingtons and the Scarbroughs widened when, at this same time, their son Gerald's marriage to Dorothy broke up. But the Wellingtons never allowed their disapproval to spread to the next generation, and their kindness to all their grandchildren, particularly Valerian and Eliza, was unfailing.

The long and successful union of the 4th Duke and Duchess – they were married for fifty-seven years – came to an end with Kathleen's death on 24 June 1927. After the funeral she was cremated and the casket with her ashes was laid by her husband in the family vault at Stratfield Saye. When they married, he had been plain Captain Arthur Wellesley, though on the death of his uncle, the 2nd Duke, he was given the courtesy title of Lord Arthur Wellesley. A creditable career in the army was foreshortened when he inherited the dukedom in 1900 and needed to attend to the running of the Wellington estates. He then devoted much of the rest of his life to public service, albeit on a very different scale to that of his grandfather: his stage was the county, rather than the country. Like the First and 2nd Dukes before him he was made a Knight of the Garter, and at the coronations of both Edward VII and George V he bore the Standard of the Union.

The 4th Duke inherited the longevity gene of his grandfather, dying on Waterloo Day 1934, aged eighty-five. According to his son Gerald, who was with him at the time, 'he died so quietly and peacefully that neither I nor the two nurses were able to say the exact moment of death'. The funeral was, at the Duke's own request, a modest affair attended by near relatives and close friends. The 4th Duke had been three years old when his famous grandfather died. He had told his own grandson, Valerian, about the games at the feet of a kindly old white-haired man, as depicted in a picture by Thorburn, which of all the paintings at Stratfield Saye is my father's favourite. For my father to be able to say 'The little boy in blue was my grandfather' confers on the picture a special status. Of the First Duke's grandchildren, one outlived the 4th Duke; his sister Lady Mary Scott died in 1936.

The other little boy in the picture – dressed in brown – often stayed with his uncle, the 2nd Duke, at Stratfield Saye. In the late 1860s one guest reported to his wife: 'Young Wellesley, the heir, is here – a very pleasing, cheery youth'.[8] For Henry, the burden of succession as 3rd Duke seems not to have sat heavily on his shoulders. He was six years old when the First Duke died, and his settled upbringing – largely at Conholt in Hampshire, a house his mother Sophia inherited from her father – was not overshadowed by the certainty that one day he would have to step into the shoes of a great man. It appears that he had neither an inferiority complex, nor an anxiety about how others might judge him; he had little inclination towards public service and pursued interests that gave him pleasure – largely the turf, and country sports. There are irreverent caricatures of Henry at Stratfield Saye which emphasise his portly physique and ruddy complexion, suggesting that he spent many happy hours in his clubs.

As plain Lieutenant-Colonel Henry Wellesley, he married Evelyn Williams on 7 March 1882; two years later his uncle, the 2nd Duke, died, and the couple moved into Stratfield Saye. The 3rd Duchess was clever and accomplished, and a skilled organist. An organ was installed in the hall of the house for her and since she was tiny, and physically disabled, a special chair was made so she could reach the pedals. Evelyn was almost certainly more interested in the Wellington inheritance than her husband; she both oversaw a guidebook about Stratfield Saye and meticulously chronicled a catalogue of the pictures at Apsley House. She worked on the latter for many years, and must have greatly regretted the fact that the two-volume work was not finally completed and published until the year after her husband died. 'It is a work which does the greatest credit to the compiler,'[9] wrote one reviewer.

After eighteen happy years with the 3rd Duke, four years after his death she married another Wellesley – Frederick, grandson of the First Duke's younger brother, Henry. She was Colonel Fred's third wife – he had divorced the first two – and since they had twenty-seven years of marriage, it seems likely that it was another love-match. Interestingly, she was the translator of a book about Marie-Louise of Austria, Napoleon's second wife, which was published in 1910. She lived well into her eighties and when my father was about fifteen he was taken to meet her and remembers her great charm and warmth. She died in March 1939, and chose to be buried beside her second husband; she had, however, done her duty by her first. In the Stratfield Saye church the east window is dedicated to his memory and his bust sits in a niche, staring across at that of his uncle, the 2nd Duke.

The 2nd Duke of Wellington suffered a public and undignified death – on a platform at Brighton station on 13 August 1884. It was an inglorious end to an unfulfilled life. He had been ill for some time and, according to the report of his death in *The Times*, his doctor had suggested that he should have a 'change of air'. He was staying in a suite of rooms at the

Bristol Hotel, on the sea-front. On the morning of his death he felt unwell and, fearing he was about to have a relapse, decided to return to Stratfield Saye. He was talking to a friend while waiting on the platform for his train, when suddenly he 'reeled and fell'. His body was carried into the waiting room and the station-master sent out a call for a doctor, who pronounced him dead. His choice of Brighton for a change of air may not have been due entirely to the healthy sea breezes. My father remembers being told of a well-substantiated rumour that the 2nd Duke had a mistress there. After his death, one of his chequebooks was found showing regular payments to a lady who was not known to be in his employ.

After the Duke's physician had verified the cause of death as a heart attack his body, which had remained at the station for a night, was carried to London on a train to lie briefly at Apsley House before it made its last journey to Stratfield Saye, and its final resting-place in the family vault. The funeral service followed the pattern of his revered father, the First Duke, with the psalms sung to a chant written by his composer grand-father, Lord Mornington. To the strains of the 'Dead March' from Handel's *Saul*, his coffin was carried out of the small church and his remains were laid to rest alongside those of his mother Kitty and his brother Charles. Apart from Bessy, his long-suffering and devoted wife, the chief mourners were his nephews, both Colonels in the army: Henry, now the 3rd Duke, and Arthur, who would become the 4th. But after the death of the 2nd Duke, never again would it be so hard to be the Duke of Wellington. As he once wrote in a visitors' book when he was still 'Douro', 'J'ai payé pour mon Père'.[10]

'Think what it will be when the Duke of Wellington is announced and only *I* come in!'[11] This was the prospect that haunted Arthur, the 2nd Duke, long before he inherited the title. Suffering from the syndrome that afflicts many children of great figures, his case was compounded by the fact that, on utterance, his name would instantly invoke not merely the memory of his great father but also the dazzling glory of his heroic deeds. In the opinion of one of his friends, 'Never has there been an instance more striking of the disadvantage of great birth than that which the present [the second] Duke of Wellington affords. He would have been one of the greatest men in England if he had not been so completely overshadowed by the reputation of his father.'[12] It is likely that this is an exaggeration but it is striking how often those who knew the 2nd Duke expressed similar views. 'You are no fit judge in the case', was the Duke's typical response to such friendly criticism:

> In the first place, I deny that Nature gave me the talents of which you speak, and in the next, had she done so, there were warnings enough constantly before me to prevent my devoting them to the service of the public. My father's thoughts were given up entirely to the country, and the consequence was that he whom all the world may be said to have envied, was often heard to say there is nothing in life worth living for. I very early made up my mind not to follow his example in that direction, and have never for a moment repented of the resolution.[13]

'My father never showed the least affection for any of us', the 2nd Duke would say, 'Charles, Jerry [adopted nephew Gerald Valerian], and I, were taught to go to his room the first thing every morning after we were dressed; and without interrupting his correspondence, for we always found him writing, he would look up for a moment and say, "Good morning," and that was positively all the loving intercourse that passed between us during the day."[14] The stern, unbending father persisted into the adulthood of the sons. On one occasion when the Duke met his eldest son dressed in 'plain clothes', he took no notice of him. Realising the problem, Douro (his courtesy title was Marquess Douro) 'rushed off, quickly put on his uniform and appeared again in his father's presence. 'Hallo, Douro! how are you? It is a long time since I have seen you."[15] When, as an old man, the Duke was asked if he had any regrets, and confessed, 'Yes, I should have given more praise',[16] I wonder if he had his sons in mind.

When his father was alive, Douro mixed military duties with a political life, becoming MP for Norwich in 1837, a seat he held until the death of his father in 1852. Characteristically, he openly declared that, at the time, he considered Norwich to be the most corrupt borough in England, and though he himself stood fast against bribery, he was not above some dirty tactics; when a crucial number of voters were threatening to go over to the other side unless he agreed to their terms, he was party to locking them up until after the booths were closed. Unlike his father, to whom he claimed 'everything new must be bad', he had a more radical approach to life, even believing that the poor should be provided for by taxes. In 1828, when some Midlands seats vacated by corrupt practices were being disposed of, he thought they should be given to Manchester and Birmingham. When this view reached his father, who at the time was Prime

Minister, his immediate reaction was: 'Douro's opinion, is it? Douro is a d——d radical.'

Considering his inadequacy as a parent, it is all the more remarkable that after the First Duke's death the 2nd Duke dedicated himself to preserving and promoting his legacy, appointing himself, as Richard Ford wrote in 1853, 'trustee of his fame' and 'guardian of his memory'.[17] The 2nd Duke edited eight volumes of his father's 'Supplementary Despatches'.

The fact that the 2nd Duke was very similar in appearance to his illustrious father can only have added to the discomfort of stepping into his shoes. 'The likeness was very striking when he stood under the picture which hung over the mantelpiece in the drawing-room,'[18] wrote one friend. Another of his contemporaries described him as being 'not unlike what his father had been in middle life: a thin, hollow face, the configuration of the head of the same sort; but smaller than his father's; a very pleasant, and kind smile; having rather the manner of an "enfant gâté"; who being born to everything that the world can give, did not derive much enjoyment from the gift."[19] Unlike his father, he was not known for his sartorial style: one friend described how he would often wear 'an old soft felt hat and an aged cloak', topped off with a pair of 'goggles' – the whole effect making him 'a figure of a very noticeable and eccentric kind'.[20]

Though they looked alike, the 2nd Duke lacked his father's strong constitution. He believed in homeopathic medicine, and would initiate his friends into its efficacy.[21] His reluctance to become an achiever in any conventional field of life meant that he channelled his energy towards more unusual pursuits; and many of his contemporaries viewed him as a natural eccentric. The writer Augustus Hare was staying near Stratfield Saye in the summer of 1875 and accompanied his hosts on a visit to see the house. He later described the Duke, 'dressed like a poor pensioner', receiving us 'in his close little room', which was filled with various relics of the First Duke, including 'the last pheasants the great Duke had shot'.[22] Guests staying at Stratfield Saye found that many of the traditions established by the First Duke continued: one such was the absence of a smoking room, usually to be found in grand houses of the time. If, after the ladies had gone to bed, the men wished to smoke, they were expected to go to the housekeeper's sitting room.

In the family, stories about the 2nd Duke tend to revolve around his eccentricities. Then, as now, extensive lawns surrounded Stratfield Saye house, and the grass would normally be cut by a nineteenth-century version of a mower, pulled by horses. The Duke objected to the dents that the horses made in the grass, and decided to replace them with a small elephant. Apparently he was delighted with this innovation, believing that he saved money by not having to provide so many shoes for the horses; the cost of housing and feeding the elephant, which lived in its own quarters next to the stables, appears not to have entered into this calculation. He collected animals, including a herd of cashmere goats, whose hair he used to make coats and cloaks as gifts for his friends. One of the recipients confessed later that her coat was 'so stiff that it really could not be worn'.[23] Nowadays, 'Llama Cottage' on the Stratfield Saye estate is evidence of another species from his menagerie.

The 2nd Duke's interest in animals was not confined to his own home: he once attended a donkey show at Crystal Palace, where he insisted on striding uninvited into the area reserved for judges. When accosted – 'Sir, may I ask, are you a judge?' – he instantly retorted, 'A judge of what?' 'Of Donkeys', came the reply, to which the Duke answered, 'Certainly I am, and a very good one too; leave me alone.' After the initial consternation induced by this exchange, a member of the judging panel recognised the Duke, and a message was passed to him to say that it would be an honour if he would consent to act as one of the judges. He was also President of the British Goat Society, and believed that 'milk from the goat was very much better than that yielded by the cow'.[24]

The 2nd Duke was an accomplished horseman, and in 1853, the year he became the Queen's Master of Horse, he bought a large site not far from Apsley House on which he built a riding school. The building itself gained some plaudits, one suggesting that it had 'architectural merit seldom looked for in such buildings'.[25] As well as for equestrian events, it became a fashionable venue for bazaars, banquets and shows, including, in the last years of the Duke's life, the annual 'St Bernards Club Dog Show' and the 'British Bee-keepers Association'. It also hosted political meetings, one of which, in 1872, was a lively gathering of Chelsea residents who wished to denounce the Republican sentiments of their MP, Sir Charles Dilke. The meeting threatened to turn into a riot when Dilke's supporters invaded the building and tried to set fire to the platform.[26] The school did not survive into the twentieth century; some years after Henry inherited the title, he sold it and it was knocked down to make way for flats.

Six years after the demise of his father, the 2nd Duke had the melancholy duty of being at the deathbed of his brother Charles who died, aged fifty, on Saturday, 9 October 1858. Lord Charles Wellesley's health had been declining for some years; he suffered from glaucoma and by the end was blind. The two siblings were very close, both in age and in the strength of their affection for each other; no doubt the vicissitudes of being their father's sons strengthened this attachment. Charles would always understand the sometimes crushing effect of living in the shadow of the Great Duke. He was less serious than his brother, and more conventional in his tastes and habits. The good relationship between the brothers was evident in the discussions about their father's will. The First Duke left no up-to-date will, and according to the lawyer whom the brothers hired to advise them, when it came to deciding how to share their father's most treasured personal effects, the process became quite complicated; not because of their acquisitiveness but rather because the lawyer found it hard to persuade 'either to appropriate anything which he could prevail upon the other to accept'.[27]

The 2nd Duke valued his circle of friends and sought out an interesting mix including artists, poets, actors and politicians of every hue. He was drawn to intellectuals and people with talent, but hated cant; for this failing he targeted Methodists, whom he labelled 'Snivellers'. He had a good but rather whimsical sense of humour. Like his father before him, he was a prodigious letter-writer. Armed with a sound classical education, he could both recite and translate Horaces's Odes. However, only days before his death, when a friend encouraged him to publish some of his translations, he wrote confessing that he had 'no copy of anything', adding in a postscript, 'There is something contemptible about a sonneteering Duke'.

He may have been more radical than the First, but the 2nd Duke inherited some of his father's mistrust of social progress. Once, when the American Ambassador was staying at Stratfield Saye, the 2nd Duke was of the view that he should be accorded no particular preference. 'I maintain that he ought to go in [to dinner] merely as an ordinary guest.' Lady Dorothy Nevill, who was a very close friend of the Duke, was staying, and she cautioned him: 'Then, Duke, you want war with America, for without doubt Mr Motley, as diplomatic representative of that great Republic, must be sent into dinner first of all, otherwise you will be offending, not only him, but his country as well.' The story reveals the role that, I suspect, the 2nd Duchess often played in disputes of this nature; she agreed with Lady Dorothy and the Duke gave in, muttering, however, under his breath, 'brand-new countries and new-fangled non-sense'.

Elizabeth – 'Bessy' – the 2nd Duchess was described by Lady Dorothy as being a 'typical *grande dame*' and an 'admirable hostess'. As a highly accomplished harpist, she would often perform for her guests, and she was one of the first women in England to play the concertina. She had a reputation for being a glacial beauty. One man remembered seeing her at court. 'She had ... one of the finest and most classical faces I ever saw. I remember her arresting my attention at one of the balls. She was dancing with Prince Albert in the "uncrowded" quadrille, looking more like a magnificent Greek statue than a being of flesh and blood; but after you had seen and worshipped her for some time, you became aware that her expression was perfectly unchangeable: it was a beautiful body, but there was no soul.'[28]

The last years of the 2nd Duke's life were dogged by ill-health. Like his brother Charles, he fell victim to glaucoma and a few years before his death, in an attempt to halt the progress of the disease, he underwent an operation to remove one of his eyes; but gradually the sight in the other deteriorated. He directed the anaesthetist, 'Now, Sir, pray understand that I don't fear death but I abominate pain. If in your endeavour to spare me the latter you introduce me to the former I will, should we meet in another world, freely forgive you; but if you let me suffer and I remain in the flesh, God help you.' Afterwards, to an inquiry about his eyes, he replied, 'Thank you, one of them is in excellent spirits in Harley Street.'[29] When he had to give up fishing and shooting he retreated to the card table, where he would play whist, often with a neighbour who was older and even blinder than he was. Old age made him irritable, dispensing anger to whomever happened to be nearest. Towards the end, his loyal wife Bessy was his eyes and ears.

After she was widowed, and moved to live at Burhill House in Walton-on-Thames, Bessy kept pet dogs, including a small Maltese Terrier, who suffered the misfortune of being run over by her footman. She was so upset by the loss that she had him stuffed and mounted by Queen Victoria's taxidermist. It's a melancholy thought that Bessy's advance into old age was accompanied by animals in glass domes rather than visits from the offspring of the children she so desperately tried to have. She died aged eighty-four, twenty years to the day after the death of her husband, and chose for her remains to be laid by his side in Stratfield Saye church.

I imagine that Bessy never quite recovered from a profound and painful disappointment at not having been able to give birth to an heir for both the father-in-law she loved so much, and her husband. I am sure, too, that the 2nd Duke had deep regrets that he never had the chance to give children of his own a father's love – something that had been so lacking in his upbringing. There is touching sincerity in some words the 2nd Duke wrote, a few days before he died, to friends he had invited to stay at Stratfield Saye: 'I have arranged a special room for your baby for I know you won't be happy without him.'[30]

I wonder what hopes and dreams Kitty had for her cherished first child. The 2nd Duke was born on Tuesday, 3 February 1807, a tidy ten months after Kitty and Arthur's Dublin wedding. Careful preparations for his arrival had been made at 11 Harley Street (the Wellesleys' first marital home): a 'mahogany crib-bedstead' had been delivered to the house, with a set of curtains, two fine blankets, a marella quilt and two mattresses of the 'best curled hair'. Kitty would have been worried about the birth; in those days thirty-five was an advanced age to have your first child. And it is evident from a letter Arthur sent later to his mother-in-law, who had been by her daughter's side, that there were complications. 'I hope', he wrote, 'that considering the superior interest that I have in her safety and welfare, I may be allowed to take the opportunity of expressing my appreciation and acknowledgement for the great attention and kindness which you have shown her in the late disturbing and critical moments.'[31] They named the child Arthur Richard.

A few weeks after the birth there was a change of government, and Sir Arthur, who had been combining his military duties with being an MP at Westminster, was appointed Chief Secretary for Ireland. Kitty had cause for optimism: she had provided her husband with a healthy son, and now she had the prospect of a calm spell in her beloved homeland with her husband by her side. Perhaps Kitty even dared to imagine she could recapture something of the early years of their courtship in Ireland. But any such ideas were soon dashed; within weeks of taking up his post in Dublin, Arthur wrote to the Secretary of War, 'I am determined not to give up the military profession'.

For the next two years, while the Wellesleys' home was the Chief Secretary's lodge in Phoenix Park on the outskirts of Dublin, this 'determination' was the focus of Arthur's energy. For Kitty, her child was the centre of her life and, remarkably, given her age, by the summer of 1807 she knew that she was pregnant again – evidence, perhaps, of a brief romantic interlude around the time of their first wedding anniversary. It was the birth of their second son, Charles, on Saturday, 16 January 1808 that was to prove more significant to Wellington's direct descendants: he was my great-great-grandfather and his sons, Henry and Arthur, became in turn the 3rd and 4th Dukes. Kitty had produced for her husband an heir, and, crucially, one spare. 'Little Arthur' and 'Charley' would become her comfort and her joy, and provide something to cling to through the long years when her husband was away at war.

EIGHT

Alone and Sad

Wednesday, 12 April 1809 was a painful day for Kitty. Not only was Arthur setting off for war but there had been a violent argument between them. Sadly for Kitty, she had inflicted this unhappiness upon herself. Some time before, she had lent money to her youngest brother Henry, probably with the promise of swift repayment. When Arthur discovered the reason his wife had insufficient funds to pay all the household bills, he was furious. He believed the debts brought shame on his name and implied to the outside world that he was mean. That the loan had been to a Pakenham – the family who had originally turned him down because he was too poor – may have rubbed salt into the wound. As a young man, Arthur himself had borrowed money, but that seems not to have worked in Kitty's favour. The episode probably confirmed his growing suspicion that he had married the wrong woman. By now he may even have caught up with gossip about Kitty's pre-marital tryst with Lowry Cole – conveniently overlooked by the matchmaking Mrs Sparrow. Years later he confided to a close friend that he had 'received the impression that he had been grossly deceived, and never afterwards got rid of it'.[1]

Whatever fanned the flames, his anger brought out the timidity in Kitty, which served only to heighten his wrath. Many years later, when Arthur's letters to her about the incident were discovered by their grandson Henry, the 3rd Duke, he considered them so unkind to the grandmother he never knew that he destroyed them. Like me, he probably recognised that Kitty had a soft heart and a generous nature, and apart from the three Wellesley men in her life – Arthur and her two babies – Pakenhams took precedence. When Arthur set off for war, this confrontation hung over their parting like a dark and poisonous cloud. She could not know that he would be gone for five years and that the fall-out from this incident, when she had allowed her heart to rule her head, would invade her dreams and stalk her waking hours.

Arthur's gaze, however, was towards a bright horizon – to Portugal and Spain – and the challenge of ridding the Peninsula of Napoleon; 'as for private concerns', he later confided to one of his brothers, 'I never trouble my head about them'.[2] But for most of the five years he was away Arthur Wellesley carried with him, pasted into the lid of his dressing-case, a watercolour of his two small sons. No one knows whether he also took with him a portrait of his wife. I suspect not.

Just short of his fortieth birthday, he was one of the youngest Lieutenant-Generals in the army. There were those in Britain who resented his appointment, but it had been proposed by the Cabinet and approved by George III. India had taught him about soldiering – the importance of supply lines, the need for discipline and loyalty, the principles of battle strategies and tactics. The previous year, after the start of the Peninsular War, he had learnt another lesson: the role of politics and public opinion in warfare. Briefly he had commanded the first expeditionary force sent to Portugal to support the uprising against Napoleon's occupation of the Iberian Peninsula. Its initial success had ended badly for Arthur when, after being superseded by a more senior officer, he consented to being a signatory of the Convention of Cintra, an ill-fated armistice with the French which allowed them to remove their army intact from Portugal. When the British people and Parliament heard the terms they were in uproar. Lord Byron captured the mood: 'Britannia sickens, Cintra! at thy name.'[3] Arthur was held to account but, supported by all his brothers, he managed to clear himself.

The Cintra inquiry had provided both a brief respite from war and, for Kitty, the pleasure of being back in Dublin, when Arthur resumed his role of Chief Secretary. Even if Kitty harboured her guilty secret of the loan, she would have been happy to be near the Pakenhams, with her two babies, childhood friends and the house in Phoenix Park. Three gold hairbrushes were purchased by her husband in January – perhaps late Christmas presents for Kitty and her two small boys or a token that heralded his imminent departure. One of Arthur's last official acts before he left was a written directive to drain the 'Bogs and Morasses of Ireland'. But when, early in 1809, he left Irish soil, he would never return.

In London, whatever her private sorrows, Kitty tried to present a picture of the dutiful, stoical spouse. Writing to Richard, her brother-in-law, she acknowledged, 'I am but a Soldier's wife and the husband of whom it is the pride of my life to think, shall find he has no reason to be ashamed of me.'[4] She had every good intention to be strong, but over the next five years Kitty's mental state swung between anxiety about her husband's safety and elation at his victories. When Arthur did write to her, it would be about practical matters, and rarely did he tell her anything about his military exploits. She found comfort in her children, but for much of the time she was depressed and lonely. For periods, she recorded her life and thoughts in journals. These six marbled volumes have survived and reading them is the closest I will ever get to knowing what my great-great-great-grandmother was really like. The most poignant of all the entries consists of three plain words: 'Alone and Sad.'

Kitty's plan was to write about her own life on the left-hand side of the page and record her husband's activities on the right. I am sure she hoped that she might receive letters from him that would give her unique insights into his progress. In this, as in many aspects of her relationship with Arthur, she was disappointed. Her own preoccupations with domestic detail – trivial, tearful and at times self-pitying – are nevertheless a true record of frustrated devotion. Her story – the wife waiting at home – was repeated a century later and again for the Second World War. After my father went to fight in Italy in 1944 and my mother was left in Jerusalem, one of her comforts was that her job in Military Intelligence gave her some access to information about his movements. At times, Kitty was driven nearly mad by not knowing what was going on.

The first entry is for 15 July 1809. 'If I delay any longer, what I have proposed to do every day from the 8th of April, will probably never be even begun. Three months have passed of which I can give no account. I now begin to mark the time as it passes and will continue to do so till my husband returns.' Since he left, Arthur had crossed the Douro, captured the town of Oporto and, in early July, stepped over the border into Spain. In May Kitty had heard the guns firing in London to celebrate Oporto but she had not known any details; a friend who paid her a visit found her 'very anxious, but carries it off well'.[5]

Soon after, she prepared to leave London for the summer to stay in a house which her brother, Lord Longford, had found for her in Broadstairs, by the sea. On one of her last days in town Longford called on her with her old beau Lowry Cole in tow. 'A pleasant day,' she wrote in her diary. Did her mind wander over what might have been? Dutifully she spent her last evening with her mother-in-law, Lady Mornington, with whom she had a reasonable relationship; and then, escorted by her brother, moved to her summer retreat. She established a new routine: healthy outdoor exercise, teaching the children, going to the library, walking on the pier, writing to her husband, and going on outings. She spent a day at Deal where the British fleet was gathered. She was thrilled

ABOVE: The 2nd Duke (left) and his brother Lord Charles Wellesley, from whom my family are all descended. The First Duke's sons were very close both in age – they were only a year apart – and in their relationship.

Elizabeth Hay, 'Bessy', who married Douro in 1839. The First Duke loved her like a daughter, but to his great sadness, and even more to hers, she was never able to have children.

ABOVE: Sophia Pierrepont, my great-great-grandmother, who married Charles, and was the mother of the 3rd and 4th Dukes.

BELOW: Angela Burdett-Coutts, who proposed marriage to the First Duke in 1847. He declined, advising her 'not to throw yourself away upon a Man old enough to be your Grandfather'. When he died the family treated her as if she was his widow.

This caricature of Henry, the 3rd Duke, which appeared in *Vanity Fair* soon after he inherited the title in 1884, reveals his fondness for good living.

Evelyn, the 3rd Duchess, who was probably more interested than her husband in the Wellington legacy, meticulously catalogued all the pictures at Apsley House. After Henry's death, she married another Wellesley, the grandson of Arthur's younger brother Henry.

The 4th Duke and Duchess, my father's grandparents, hosted a grand ball at Apsley House in the summer of 1908, at which King Edward VII and Queen Alexandra were the guests of honour. My own grandfather, the 7th Duke, remembered it vividly and can be seen here between the heads of his father and the King.

ABOVE: Maudie, the 5th Duchess, and Lady Anne Wellesley, mother and sister to Morny, 6th Duke, in the conservatory at Stratfield Saye. The news of his death reached them only two years after Morny had become duke on the death of his father, 'Uncle Charlie'.

ABOVE: The 4th Duchess, my father's grandmother, photographed for British *Vogue* in 1917, knitting for the war effort. Her second son Dick was killed at Ypres a few weeks after the start of the conflict.

RIGHT: A watercolour painted by my great-aunt Eileen in 1902 when she was fifteen years old showing all the members of her family.

The 4th Duke and Duchess and their family, *c.* 1910. Back row (from left to right): Geordie, Gerry, Bobby James (Evelyn's husband), the 4th Duke, Dick and Charlie (later 5th Duke). Front row: Eileen, Nesta, the 4th Duchess, Evelyn and Maudie (later 5th Duchess).

LEFT: My grandfather, 'Gerry', the 7th Duke, as a young man. He started a career as a diplomat, but he always wanted to be an architect. After his marriage to Dottie he could afford to do so.

ABOVE: 'Mitey', born Lady Serena Lumley, was Dottie's half-sister, and a close friend and confidante to Gerry. After the death of both Dottie and her own husband Bobbie James, she might have become the 7th Duchess.

BELOW: A diptych showing my paternal grandmother 'Dottie' in the year she married, and nine years later, when the marriage broke up. This melancholy memento was put together by my grandfather, who wrote on it the lines from a Horace ode.

1914

The joys I have possessed, in spite of fate, are mine.
Not Heaven itself over the past has power;
And what has been, has been, and I have had my hour.
April 30. 1914. — February 9. 1923.

1923.

'Cissie' Dunn-Gardner as a child. She married Robert Ashton, and later the Earl of Scarborough. She was to have a malign influence on the lives of her daughters Dottie and Mitey, but she loved her son Scamp.

ABOVE: Robert Ashton, Dottie's father. He died on his yacht *Minerva*, with a letter from his daughter under his pillow.

BELOW: Dorothy was only nine years old when her father died. She missed him desperately through the rest of her childhood.

ABOVE: Scamp, the uncle my father never met (he died of tuberculosis in 1912), but who indirectly played a part in Valerian's joining his regiment, The Blues.

My father Valerian with his doting mother in Rome, where he was born in 1915.

Valerian as a toddler with his father, Gerry, who was a diplomat at the British Embassy in Rome at the time.

RIGHT: Valerian having his bath out in the open. His strict English nanny was shocked that 'Lady Gerald' allowed her son to run around naked on the terrace.

BELOW RIGHT: In the fierce sun of an Italian summer, Valerian's hair would go even blonder.

BELOW: Valerian in 1929 at Eton with a group of friends. 'I think we might have been drinking ginger beer'.

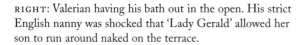

Eliza and Valerian, photographed at Sherfield on the island, which both children adored. 'It was our own little world.'

Valerian, David Parsons, Mary Coke and Eliza playing pirates at Penns.

Vita Sackville-West, whose relationship with Dottie was to have such a disastrous effect on the Wellesleys' marriage.

My grandmother with W. B. Yeats on the doorstep of Penns. His friendship and admiration for her work was her great consolation in life.

Penns-in-the-Rocks, painted by Rex Whistler in 1932. Dottie, who first saw the house with Vita, felt it 'had waited for her all her life'. Valerian and Eliza are on the 'Rocks', with Dottie's Great Dane, Brutus, while their dogs, Bess and Dan, sprint across the lawn. My grandmother can be seen leaning out of her window of her bedroom.

by the sight – 'above five hundred sail of transports, including fifty men-of-war. God Almighty protect our brave men, success attend them!' Her last sentence on that day simply said, 'I wrote this day to Sir Arthur.'

On the first Sunday that Kitty was on the coast, she went to church as usual and her meditations may have persuaded her to begin 'a regular plan of occupation tomorrow'. She knew she had to keep busy to keep sane. But the following day she confessed, 'Began the day wretchedly. God forgive and strengthen me!' It is clear from her journal that Kitty was battling against depression. 'Did not see any body I knew today except my Children & my Servants,' she wrote in one entry. Kitty's 'darling boys', on the other hand, loved the seaside. 'They were delighted walking on the pier. They proposed to make a necklace for me of the cannon balls!' There was a touching, down-to-earth normality in her relationship with her children: she taught them their alphabet; she gathered shells for them; she watched them play in the sea, exclaiming how they 'look beautiful when coming out of the water'.

Kitty spent a lot of time in the library, either choosing books to read or scanning the newspapers for news of Arthur's progress. One day she chose a book 'of which I have heard something I forget what'. In her journal the name of the book was erased; the reason for this was revealed the following day. 'Of all the improper books that were ever written, that one which I chose yesterday evening and whose name I have blotted out of the last page, is the most improper. I have carried it back to the library and, in the hope that my having had such a book would not have been perceived, I tried to slip it back into its place, but it would not do.' One can feel her embarrassment when she observed that Mr Muckle, the librarian, 'picked it out and, examining the number, had it marked down in the Catalogue. I never felt such shame!' This diary entry ended, 'Sir Arthur wrote the Despatch from Talavera de la Reyna ... he wrote also to me.'

These last words must have been inserted when she received the news of the battle, for her mood now was very low. 'I fear indolence is again creeping about me. I am fatigued by a regular course of insignificant occupations and dissatisfied with myself when Idle. These two last days I have been over fatigued by walking.' The day after she was still suffering: 'fatigue and cold oppress me'. She received a letter from Arthur but clearly it provided little comfort. On 2 August she was 'Ill and Idle. I have nothing to say of this languid day.' She longed for a hint of endearment – something that might make her feel she was forgiven, or, dare she hope, loved. She looked in vain. None of Arthur's letters from the battle-front to his wife survive. Maybe Kitty herself destroyed them, fearing a permanent reminder of her husband's coldness.

If Kitty had known of Arthur's exploits on 27 July 1809 her heart would have missed a beat, for he had his narrowest escape of the entire Peninsular War. His army had crossed into Spain, but so far had failed to engage with the enemy. Telescope to his eye, Wellesley was surveying the area round Talavera from the top of a tower attached to a farmhouse; suddenly he saw, just outside the walls, a unit of French soldiers. His party scrambled down the stairs at breakneck speed, jumped on their horses and galloped off with random French fire peppering their backs. Had the Frenchmen known they had General Wellesley in their sights, they might have taken more careful aim.

This near-escape was the prelude to the battle of Talavera, which was fought and won over two long days and a night. The battle began at sunrise on 28 July. A few hours later there was a lull in the hostilities as both sides tried to quench their terrible thirst, brought on by the unforgiving heat of the midsummer sun. By 11 a.m. the truce was over, and the scarlet and blue uniforms separated once again. This odd practice set a pattern for the rest of the Peninsular War. Arthur later recounted how the French advance-posts at the end of these intervals would shout, 'Courrez vite, courrez vite, on va vous attaquer.' Just over a hundred years later, my maternal grandfather in Flanders witnessed the equally strange sight of the Germans playing a Christmas football match with the British in no-man's-land.

Arthur's reward for Talavera was his elevation to the peerage. Kitty was not happy with the choice of name – Wellington – which she insisted to a friend 'recalls nothing'. Arthur on the other hand thought it was 'exactly right', as he wrote to his brother William, who had suggested it because it was 'a town not far from Welleslie in the county of Somerset' – where the family had originated. The title, Viscount Wellington of Talavera, appeared in the official Gazette on 4 September and a few days later Arthur signed his new name in a letter. I suspect he afforded less importance to this small mark in history than his request, in a postscript, for permission to hold a fox-hunt in Portugal.

During October Wellington (as he now was) started reconnoitring and planning his greatest strategic masterpiece of the entire campaign: the Lines of Torres Vedras. Unobtrusively he rode all over the Lisbon Peninsula with his Chief Engineer, who subsequently received a twenty-one-point memorandum outlining the plan for three lines of fortifications, consisting of dams, barriers, signal-posts and redoubts. The longest of the lines would run for twenty-nine miles from the River Tagus to the Atlantic Ocean. Remarkably, for the next thirteen months Arthur managed to keep these plans under wraps.

In England, the country celebrated King George III's Golden Jubilee. Kitty had donated money and helped to organise a dinner for the poor. She was impressed that her children were not frightened by the sound of the gun salutes. In the evening she was back in her refuge – the library – where she had supper and 'ended the day most loyally by singing and drinking punch'. A week later the family returned to London, where 'The Children delighted to find all their old play things'. But the unhealthy London air soon took its toll.

> It is decided that my poor Children have got the Hooping Cough. May God spare them to me: and may they escape the very dreadful consequences which I have known from this dreadful complaint. So uninteresting, so unvaried, is my life that to keep a daily journal is almost impossible and yet by not doing so I lose the pleasure of knowing how He and I were employed at the same time, which to me is a great pleasure.

When not looking after her children, who regularly – to the disapproval of her staff – slept in her room, she was knitting a blanket which she intended 'sending out to Lord Wellington – may it contribute to his comfort and save him from Cold!'. She read plenty of improving literature, *The Pilgrim's Progress* and the *Lectures* of a famous clergyman called Porteus. When she heard of her brother-in-law Richard's return from Spain to take up his post of Foreign Secretary she was offended that he had not paid her a visit and mortified that 'not one of his suite, all friends of Lord Wellington's, should have sent me even a line to tell me how he was'. A couple of the 'suite' were forgiven when they called on her, but still there was no word from Richard. Time dragged; on one day she simply wrote, 'Forgotten' in her diary.

Finally Richard did his duty and called on her, employing his charm to extract her forgiveness. 'Nobody has the power of pleasing more than he has.' By the middle of December, 'My Children Better' but she was 'Alone all day.' She had new friends, the Liverpools, and was gratified when Lady Liverpool 'approves my blanket', which was finally finished and dispatched to Portugal with the *Life of Cobbett*. She spent Christmas Day going to church, but otherwise saw no company. On 30 December, a Saturday, the entry read 'Alone and Sad'. The following day she signed off on the year, 'so ends a Melancholy Year! Heaven spare me from such another!'

Kitty made strenuous efforts to start the new year in a positive frame of mind.

> Began this year by wishing every happiness to my Husband, comfort to those who need it and a continuation of happiness to the happy. I have done none of the work, which I intended, today: but I have written, spent an hour with Lady Mornington and executed some of my Mother's commissions. William Pakenham came to town today. I look on it as a good omen that a Pakenham should have come to me the first day of the new year.

But despite her good intentions, Kitty's new-year optimism came to nothing, and once more she laid aside her journal. When she took up her pen again on 25 June she confessed: 'Near 6 months have passed in which it would hardly have been possible for me to have marked the events of a single day without some degree of Pain. Yet the time has not been totally lost. I have, in some degree, mixed with the world, made some acquaintance and tried to perform some duties – but so many of my resolutions, and these my best, have been broken.' She ended the entry with a promise to herself: 'From this day I shall keep an exact account of my time and deceive myself no more.'

For Arthur the first six months of 1810 consisted of a waiting game while the French army, headed by Marshal Masséna, marched slowly towards Portugal. On 10 July Ciudad Rodrigo, on the border with Portugal, surrendered to Marshal Ney, the Second-in-Command in the French 'Army of Portugal'. Arthur was unfazed by this apparent setback; according to Kitty's brother Edward, writing home on the same day, 'Lord Wellington looks as well as possible and I never saw him in such spirits'.[6] Arthur knew that soon he would be able to reveal to the French, and the world, his master-plan of the Lines.

For the summer of 1810 Kitty decided to take a house in Tunbridge Wells and, as evidenced in her calmer, neater writing, she experienced a peaceful period in her life. The house she had found 'wants nothing but to be clean to make it comfortable, but it wants that most dreadfully'. One of her neighbours invited her to dinner, but she declined – 'I could not bear her eternal pity of herself, nothing being the matter'. Others of Kitty's friends might have used the same words to describe her.

At dawn on 27 September, near the Portuguese town of Bussaco, Arthur was reconnoitring his outposts. The Allied army of 50,000 men – British and Portuguese – were lined up on a ridge facing a force of 65,000 thousand. The entire area was cloaked in thick fog, but at 6 a.m. the

French began their attack. One of the officers in the field found Wellington's orders 'so decided, so manly . . . He has nothing of the truncheon about him; nothing foul-mouthed, important, or fussy: his orders on the field are all short, quick, clear, and to the purpose.'[7] After five attempts to dislodge the Allies the French withdrew, and by the evening the battle of Bussaco had become another notch on the Peninsular post of honour.

It would be nearly three weeks before news of the victory reached Kitty. Meanwhile the seaside life continued – rides on donkeys for the children, a book auction where Kitty indulged her taste for poetry with volumes of Milton and Spenser, but failed to get a 'beautiful Shakespeare', and a conjuror performance – 'or, rather, sleight of hand player: his tricks are really surprising'. A Doctor Mayo called on her and gave her advice which, she believed, 'will be absolutely necessary for me to follow'. Part of his advice may have been to take regular exercise; weather permitting, she started to ride daily. She also steeled herself 'to the most disagreeable of all operations, sitting for my picture'. The chosen artist was Josiah Slater, one-time pupil of Sir Thomas Lawrence.

After Bussaco, Wellington planted an olive tree in the garden of the convent where he had stayed (the tree survives to this day), and discreetly withdrew his army, with the French at his heels. But by 10 October, as Kitty waited for news, the army was safe behind his Lines. When Kitty returned to London with the boys a few days later she found 'a letter which has indeed most deeply wounded me. No matter – I was originally to blame, but I think I could have felt more forgiveness, more indulgence: it is now, however, at an end for ever.' Clearly, Kitty had written to her husband seeking some kind of reconciliation; if so, none was forthcoming. Arthur's letter would have been composed before the battle of Bussaco; perhaps it even contained a punitive list of instructions in the event of his death. Kitty suffered the double torment of reading his wounding words while not knowing whether he was still alive. She passed a 'very wretched night' but was saved from another one by 'the happiness which this day was to bring. My Husband and brothers safe and victorious, thank Almighty God.'

She distracted herself by going shopping, purchasing 'a rug for my own room, a cover for the drawing-room table' and some 'stuff' for her mother. If shopping was one way of dealing with her depression, organising her paperwork was another. The first day of November saw her 'arranging my papers in a large tin box which I found it necessary to get, Bills and other Papers having so much accumulated in 4 years'. She was having problems sleeping and a friend came up with the solution of a

'Hop Pillow'. Regrettably, it did not work – 'the smell was too powerful'.

In Portugal, Masséna was sitting it out, waiting for reinforcements. When he had discovered the secret of the Lines, he had been angry. He demanded to know why he had not known of their existence. He was infuriated when told that the explanation was "Wellington has made them"'. Masséna would have been riled further when he heard of a grand ball that Wellington gave for his officers and the leading citizens of Lisbon. On 9 November Kitty's brother Edward, writing home, affirmed: 'The Mafra ball has given confidence to the capital and pride to the Portuguese army – *Viva*!!!'

Kitty received regular requests from Arthur: 'books', 'shirts', 'tea' and 'stockings'. The autumn months brought her low with another deep depression. On 11 November she wrote: 'The desperate dejection, which has oppressed me thus some days passed, will destroy me. I must pray for a calmer mind, for power to calm myself.' Her mother was staying with her and she was beginning to find her presence oppressive – resenting the fact that she was never able to see her callers on her own but on this day, in any case, 'nobody came'. Her sleep was terrible and she was ashamed to think that the 'best part of the day is over before I have begun the business of it'. She recognised that company removed the 'dreadful oppression'; she was even grateful for a visit from her mother-in-law, Lady Mornington. She continued to sit for her 'odious picture', and made determined attempts to be social. The Liverpools – he was to become Prime Minister two years later – were extremely kind to her, particularly Lady Liverpool, whom Kitty described as 'an angel'.

Drawing was another way of passing the time. She had been to see an exhibition of Nollekens' statues and decided that she might copy one. Shortly after, the artist sent her a small statuette of Arthur as a present and, armed with new brushes, she took up a long-abandoned hobby: 'considering how many years it is since I have drawn, the beginning is very promising.' But much of her time continued to be spent in moods of solitary introspection, and Christmas was a quiet affair, attending church with her companion Martha and her cook, who was in trouble with her mistress a few days later when she cut the 'boys' fine eye lashes'.

For Arthur, Christmas 1810 in Portugal was full of sport. The relationship between the Portuguese citizens and their French invaders was driven by hatred but, with the two armies in deadlock, day-to-day relations between the British and the French were extremely civilised. Their officers exchanged compliments and banter across the rivulet which separated their lines and when a greyhound belonging to an English officer chased a hare across the line, it was sent back with a polite message. Knowing that the French were lacking in medical back-up, Arthur offered help to a wounded French General. The gesture was politely dismissed.

The damp, fog-laden days in the Peninsula were getting to Arthur's bones, if not his spirits. Kitty's new year was heralded by a request from her husband for a 'larger Blanket, which he shall have as soon as it can be made: bought worsted & bespoke needles for it'. In London on New Year's Day there was a heavy fall of snow, the first that winter. Kitty's own spirits were unusually buoyant. 'Lady Liverpool kindly asked me to spend the day with her. I did so: the company, a set of stupid Lords, who were anything but pleasant. I behaved very ill and expressed what I thought of them.'

At the end of the second week of January 1811, Kitty enjoyed a 'remarkably pleasant day' dining with the Speaker; she even appreciated the company, including a 'Lord St Helens', whom she liked 'very much'. She revealed an aesthetic appreciation of her surroundings: 'The room, in which we dined, is under the House of Commons: it was a Chapel & is still preserved in the old stile of Gothick architecture. It would have been worth dining there had there been no other inducement than to see the room.' But a few days later she made the decision not to attend a function where she feared Ld. Wellington's name being introduced. I did not wish to encounter the public gaze.'

'I never will read "Corinne" again: it really hurts me,' she wrote in her journal on 4 March. The novel, written by Madame de Staël, had been published in 1807. It tells the story of an English lord who meets, on his travels in Italy, a beautiful, independent-minded and successful poet. Corinne becomes the man's mistress but he abandons her in favour of a less complex woman. I assume that Kitty was 'hurt' by the manner in which the heroine is discarded. In the middle of March Kitty was suffering from a terrible cold, and had received no new letters from Portugal. When the silence was broken, once again she was on the receiving end of unkind words: 'If I have not done all that was expected of me, at least what I have done was not wrong. I must try to make up my mind to repeated disappointments.' Physically and mentally she was at a low ebb. Dr Mayo called on her and prescribed 'what I hope may relieve me'.

A few days later she was managing to pull herself through. 'Much better today. I will not give way to this preying dejection,' she wrote, 'both my Children & I suffer from it ... Dr Mayo has been of great service to me, so has my dear and excellent friend, Lady Liverpool.' It is not surprising that the boys were affected by her moods; they were both sensitive children and they had a very close relationship with their mother. Despite her best intentions, 'I can hardly account for the Languor, the depression, which preys upon me! I really feel incapable of exertion or even occupation.' Clearly she confided her innermost thoughts to Mayo. 'To effect a cure I know that a wound must be probed,' she wrote in her journal. 'When that wound is in the heart, how torturing is the process.' Mayo seemed to be counselling her and often spent many hours by her side. 'Wrote to Portugal today. When shall I feel at ease?' she pleaded despairingly.

'Mr Hume called on me: he is an agreeable man but not a man of true principles.' Kitty had been shocked to hear Arthur's physician say 'there are cases when suicide is no crime!'. Some months before she had confided to her diary that she had considered taking her life; now she could see that it would be a terrible thing to do. To distract herself, she went shopping – for a pianoforte; her eldest brother was in town and called on her practically every day. But her moods could easily be hijacked: 'I have received a note from Lady Liverpool today that has distressed me: she has mentioned several houses to Lord Wellington, all of which I think too large for our fortune. I wish she had not done it. She perseveres in saying she is right: I cannot think so.' When, at the beginning of April, her friend Olivia Sparrow threw a ball, she could not face going. 'I cannot bear the questions and observations to which I am subjected.'

In Portugal, on 2 April 1811, the French were celebrating the birth of a son, the King of Rome, to their Emperor and his new wife, Marie-Louise. Genially, they warned the British not to be alarmed when they heard the 101 cannon-shot salute. But a week later Wellington issued a proclamation. 'The Portuguese are informed that the cruel enemy ... have been obliged to evacuate, after suffering great losses, and have retired across the Agueda. The inhabitants of the country are therefore at liberty to return to their homes.'[8] Wellington's grand plan, the Lines of Torres Vedras, had achieved its objective and the last Frenchman had been driven out of Portugal.

A few days later, on 16 April, Arthur, with a tiny band of officers, set off at a high gallop to visit the section of the army that he had sent south to try to reinforce the city of Badajoz. When he got there he found the British laying siege to the city, a treacherous new Governor having surrendered it to the French. Back at the northern army, everyone was nervously awaiting the return of their Commander-in-Chief. Most men under his charge admitted, 'we would rather see his long nose in the fight than a re-inforcement of ten thousand men any day ... there was not a bosom in that army that did not beat more lightly, when it heard the joyful news of his arrival, the day before the enemy's advance.'⁹ Once again the battle – Fuentes de Oñoro – was won, but in Wellington's opinion, only just: 'If Boney had been there, we should have been beaten.' Once again the French were on the run; at dawn on 10 May an officer rushed into Wellington's room to tell him the news. 'Ay, I thought they meant to be off; very well' – all said without pausing from his early-morning shave.¹⁰

In London, Kitty had spent weeks waiting for good news from Portugal. 'This day began with alarm & ended with happiness. Our troops have succeeded in driving the enemy from all of their positions ... All our friends are well.' But her demons would not leave her in peace, and most days were filled with loneliness and introspection. As ever, there was one thing in her life that could draw her back. 'I am now resolved to keep Gerald [her nephew] in my room and to watch him every night till the wakeful habit shall be broken.' At this point Kitty abandoned her journal and did not pick it up again for eighteen months. I assume she could not bear to go on writing about her routine. After all, it had become a pointless exercise – attempting to chart what her husband was doing alongside the chronology of her own life – when she had virtually no information from the man himself. It made her feel inadequate and unloved. Of course, to date she was lucky that all the men she really cared about – her husband and brothers – were still alive. There were many women in the country who were not so fortunate.

Arthur was absent from the next Peninsular battle. Albuera was fought and won without him, but at a terrible cost to his army. When he visited the scene on 21 May 1811, five days after the battle, he was appalled by the extent of the carnage. In one distinguished regiment they 'were literally lying dead in their ranks as they had stood'. Of the enemy, 'the slain were all naked, the peasants having stripped them in the night'.¹¹ On a visit to the wounded he told them, 'I am sorry to see so many of you here.' Their answer was simple: 'If you had commanded us, my Lord, there wouldn't be so many of us here.'¹² One of Wellington's men later remembered another exchange. '"Whore's ar *Arthur*?" "I don't know. I don't see him." "Aw wish he wor here." And so did I.'¹³

One of Wellington's cavalry officers who kept a journal described, in June 1811, his Commander-in-Chief's day:

> Lord Wellington rises at six every morning, and employs himself to nine (the breakfast hour) in writing. After breakfast, he sees the heads of departments, viz: Quarter-Master and Adjutant-General, Commissary-General, Commander of artillery, and any other officers coming to him on business. This occupies until 2 or 3 pm, and sometimes longer, when he gets on his horse, and rides to near six – this, of course, is interfered with when the troops are before the enemy. At nine he retires to write again, or employs himself until twelve, when he retires for the night. His correspondence with England, and the Spanish and Portuguese government, is very extensive.[14]

Both Edward and Hercules, Kitty's two brothers in the Peninsula, were amongst Wellington's most trusted officers. Edward proudly reported that, though 'quite the Commander of the forces, [he] is positively my brother in all our dealings'. In August, in another letter to his eldest brother, Lord Longford, he gave a hint of the Pakenham family's ongoing concern about their sister: 'I am pleased to hear that our Kitty (under all the circumstances of various anxiety) keeps up so good a countenance – the more so as I am in hopes that it will give her a degree of firmness which may render her more happy, and at all events give domestic calm, which heretofore her stock of philosophy was not equal to command.'[15]

Kitty spent the summer of 1811 at Broadstairs and coped with one of the boys suffering a serious illness. Richard, her brother-in-law, was frequently in the area and appears to have provided a supportive shoulder to lean on. She wrote to him on 10 November, just before returning to London, to thank him for his help 'when the situation of my child was most desperate ... on this subject I am not able to dwell. My boy is almost miraculously preserved and his dear and excellent father will, I trust, receive intelligence of his recovery, almost as soon as that of his danger.'

At this time Edward Pakenham came down with a fever in Spain, writing to his brother Longford of Lord Wellington's 'kindness' during his illness. He travelled back to England to convalesce with his sister. But a family tragedy struck the Pakenhams early in December. Kitty's brother William, recently given command of a ship, was patrolling the coast of Ireland against a French invasion when a violent storm sank it, with the loss of all hands. Fortunately Kitty had Edward with her to console her; he reported that she 'is calm to a degree that only could proceed from goodness and religion'.

After six months of minor military engagements and plenty of merriment – dinners, balls and hunting – early in 1812 Wellington's army were camped near the walled city of Ciudad Rodrigo. The weather was so cold that the water froze in the men's canteens.[16] The siege began on 8 January and eleven days later the Allies were in the city. George Napier, one of Wellington's trusted officers, was severely wounded and had his arm amputated. His mother received a letter from Arthur written immediately after the battle. She replied: 'I can with truth assert that *nothing* has had so much the power of consolation to me as your letter ... for the very cool composure of mind evinced by the admirable style of a letter, written to a simple individual by a General at the very moment of victory.'[17]

Wellington's compassion could extend to the troops. After Ciudad Rodrigo, when he heard that some wounded men had been left lying outside by their officers, he rode thirty miles through the night and ordered them to be taken into the officers' quarters. Next night he rode back to check that his orders had been obeyed. When he found the men outside again, he court-martialled the officers.[18] It was after this battle that Wellington became a grandee of Spain – the Duke of Ciudad Rodrigo – and in England was raised to an earl.

By April, Edward Pakenham had been nursed to health again by Kitty and was on his way back to Spain. Before the siege of Badajoz, Hercules wrote to Lord Longford, 'I have not written to Kate by this mail, being on the eve of a storming business in which our Division will most certainly be engaged; anything I said on this head must increase her anxiety ... I never saw Wellington look better.' When one of his officers tore down the French flag hanging from the tower and replaced it with his scarlet jacket,[19] Wellington knew the day was won but the carnage of the battle affected him deeply, and he broke down in tears. In the aftermath, Wellington was appalled by the drunkenness and looting, and found it hard to thank his troops.

In England, on 11 May 1812, Prime Minister Spencer Perceval was shot dead in the lobby of the House of Commons by a merchant whose business had been ruined by the war. London's gossips speculated about Richard Wellesley's chance of being summoned by the Prince Regent, but scandal and unpopularity hung over his head. Instead, Kitty's friend, Lord Liverpool, got the job, and was soon to be faced with another conflict when, a few weeks after he became Prime Minister, America declared war on Britain. As usual, Kitty left London with her boys in June to stay at Tunbridge Wells.

Arthur, writing at the end of June to his brother William, confessed that he was 'never so fagged. My gallant officers will kill me. In the course of a fortnight that we were before Salamanca I don't believe I have been in bed, or rather laying down, altogether 48 hours. I am always on foot at 4 in the morning ... I am now writing under a tree while the troops are marching.'[20] It was unseasonably cold – many years later Arthur remembered, 'I never suffered more from cold than during the man-oeuvres of the days preceding the battle of Salamanca.'[21]

At the battle of Salamanca, on a great plain between the two – Lesser and Greater – Arapile hills, Edward Pakenham was back in the saddle commanding the leading column of attack. 'Ned, do you see those fellows on the hill?' said Arthur to his brother-in-law. 'Throw your division into column and have at them. Drive everything before you.' 'I will, my Lord,' replied an emotional Ned, 'if you will give me your hand.' When he galloped off, Wellington turned to his staff. 'Did you ever see a man who understood so clearly what he had to do?' How Kitty would have loved to have observed this moment between one of her brothers and her husband.

After the battle Wellington was rapturously received when he entered the city. But Goya watched Wellington as he rode back to his camp and sketched what he saw – an unshaven, hollow-eyed man with damp hair plastered to his forehead, and a little shaken from a spent bullet that had grazed his thigh. The battle earned Wellington praise from one of his opponents, General Foy, who considered that 'he has shown himself a great and able master of manoeuvres ... it was a battle in the style of Frederick the Great'.[22] Edward Pakenham wrote to his brother Hercules, 'There never lived such a warrior.'[23]

Wellington continued his sweep through Spain, entering Madrid on 12 August. Lowry Cole, Kitty's old flame and one of Arthur's ablest officers, described the scene. 'They cut pieces off the skirts of his coat to keep as relics, and women of the first rank ran into the streets and embraced the soldiers.'[24] If they could not touch the man, they would kiss his horse instead. Thereafter he was more likely to ride around Madrid in a carriage accompanied, one of his more gossipy officers claimed, 'by two or three of the prettiest girls ... Lady Wellington would be jealous if she were to hear of his proceedings. I never saw him in his carriage without two or three ladies.'[25] Wellington's audience room was always crowded, but rarely with male petitioners.

Many of Kitty's friends were all too aware of her permanent state of apprehension. Miss Berry paid her a visit at the end of August. 'I went to Lady Wellington's, the new Marchioness [Arthur had been made a Marquess on 18 August]. She appeared to have suffered a great deal from the uncertainty which everybody had been in for more than a fortnight, and she spoke with an enthusiasm and a worship of her hero which was truly edifying. She goes to London today to be present when the *Te Deum* is sung in the Portuguese ambassador's chapel in honour of the victory.'[26]

In September 1812 Kitty resumed her journal. Her first words were devoted to her consolation in life. 'Took my boys to the Paper mill.' Two days later she attempted to explain the last blank months:

> Once more, and with what different feelings, I begin my journal, regretting, uninteresting as the events of my life are, that I have discontinued it so long. In the course of the last 12 months what various events have taken place: how different do I feel, altho' my situation exhibits no change – my Husband still abroad, my Children at home. My health nearly as it was: delicate, not positively unhealthy, but my mind strengthened, my habits different. I can now occupy myself and look forward without terror at the future. Of the public events which have taken place I will say nothing. My object is to compare in what I am engaged while He, the object of my thoughts, is engaged abroad.

Kitty was in trouble with the Wellesleys. 'At one o'clock went to the Poles [her in-laws the William Wellesley-Poles]: found Mr Pole very angry with me for not having gone to the Ball last night: it was given in honor of Lord Wellington's victory and taking possession of Madrid, the news of which arrived here on Saturday last, 5th – I could not go.' Kitty could not face it: the humiliation, when she could not answer even the most basic questions, of everyone realising how little contact she had with her husband. She filled the page with trivial detail of the rest of the day – lessons for the children, letters received, drinking the 'water', walking, writing letters, buying flowers for herself, raspberries for the boys, dining, telling Arthur and Charley 'stories', putting them to bed and finally, at night, writing 'from 10 to $\frac{1}{2}$ past 11'. In the course of the day she had heard that Hercules, who had been wounded at Badajoz, was getting better and had been shown a 'very <u>flattering</u> letter to Lord Wellesley. I hate those kind of letters, of which copies are kept.' Kitty was direct, outspoken and wary of the sycophancy that surrounded her husband.

The unsuccessful siege of Burgos, which had begun on 19 September, finally ended on 21 October. One of the Irish regiments which had recently blotted its copybook had asked for the privilege of leading the assault. They were cut to pieces. When Wellington went to visit the wounded, one of the soldiers, who had lost both his legs, exclaimed: 'Arrah, may be yer satisfied now, you hooky-nosed vagabond.' To his surprise, the General smiled and sent for a surgeon, and the soldier survived to tell the tale as a resident of the Chelsea Hospital.[27] The siege exacted a terrible toll on Wellington's army. One of the casualties, Edward Somers-Cocks, was a great favourite of Arthur's. At the funeral of the young officer Wellington was so upset that nobody dared speak to him.

'This morning the best I have yet begun.' It is a relief when Kitty's diary entry begins on a positive note. The lessons for her children were going well – she was giving them geography lessons with a jigsaw of Europe (perhaps she used their father's battles as landmarks); she sent Arthur particulars of a possible house, and was content to spend the evening alone. The following day the loyal 'Doctor M' called on her, she bought skipping ropes for the children and when the end of the day brought a report that Burgos was taken, for once she knew it was 'not true'. She had her brother Hercules staying, and was nursing him through his convalescence, changing 'the position of the Harp and Bookshelf to make it more convenient to Hercules'. Most evenings they dined together, sometimes followed by a game of chess, and she entertained him by playing the harp. Bathtime for the children had its hazards: 'My poor Watch set a-floating in the bathing Tub!'

Towards the end of November, Kitty sent an account of the boys to an old friend:

> I wish you could see the delight, hear the shout of joy, with which they fly out of the house after the confinement of a day of rain. They are absolutely wild. Woe to the old lady who happens to be turning the corner as Charley dashes round it! After running about the Common as long as they like, they return to me glowing with exercise and health. They are beautiful and good and a thousand times happier than they would be confined to town.[28]

Two days later she confided to her journal, 'They found a difficulty in settling to business today, which they would not have found had they been occupied yesterday: they are dear Boys and my greatest comforts.' Kitty wrote her last diary entry the following day, 21 November. The boys would remain her 'greatest comforts', not only for the remaining sixteen months of the war, but for the rest of her life.

In Spain the retreat from Burgos was undisciplined and chaotic. When Wellington met the officer in charge of the baggage, he exclaimed, 'What are you doing, sir?' 'I've lost my baggage.' 'Well I can't be surprised ... for I cannot find my army.' But there were serious consequences to the disorder: Wellington wrote a very sharp letter to his officers which, to the embarrassment of the government, was leaked to the press. In it he did not question the officers' gallantry but he demanded 'minute and constant attention' to orders. Five thousand men from the Allied army were lost on the retreat and 20,000 French prisoners sent home. And the Allied army were back in Portugal.

On New Year's Day 1813 Wellington was honoured by the Royal Horse Guards when they made him their Colonel. In March he became a Knight of the Garter. He had no idea whether the ribbon should be worn over the right or left shoulder, and had to ask the Garter King of Arms. On 13 March a ball was held at Ciudad Rodrigo to celebrate Lowry Cole's investiture with the Order of the Bath. Dinner was half-cooked in advance at headquarters and delivered, with the glass and crockery, on the backs of mules. Wellington worked until 3.30 p.m., rode the seventeen miles in full dress kit, danced, had dinner, and then, still in a good mood, rode back at 3.30 a.m. by the light of the moon. He was at work a few hours later.

April 10 1813 was Kitty and Arthur's eighth wedding anniversary. Kitty wrote to her sister Bess, 'My husband is blessed wherever his name is heard. He may possibly soon return to a wife who will no longer worry him because he, soft as well as strong, complying as well as firm, everything that is gentle and domestic; being obliged to live his soldier's hard and wandering life – I am grown wise, My Bess, and rejoice that I have lived to be seven years a wife.' The somewhat incoherent letter suggests that Kitty had a completely unrealistic view of Arthur's likely state of mind after his return. It goes on to detail her concern that she will not be able to provide adequate entertainment to her friends, Maria Edgeworth and her father, since 'I have not box at the Opera or Play, thinking that if I had it to spare, £250 a year may be spent in a more satisfactory way.'[29] When the Edgeworths arrived, they were enchanted to see their old friend. 'Charming, amiable Lady Wellington! As she truly said of herself, she is always Kitty Pakenham to her friends. 'After comparison with crowds of others, *beaux esprits*, fine ladies and fashionable *scramblers* for notoriety, her dignified graceful simplicity rises in one's opinion, and we feel it with more conviction of its superiority. She showed us her delightful children.'[30] Maria was amused when Kitty recounted stories of other women trying to counsel her about her clothes. 'My dear Lady Wellington,' said one lady, 'How many times a day do you think of your dress?' 'Why three times – Morning, evening, and night besides *casualties*.' 'But this won't do, you must *think* of it seriously – at other times and when you go into the country always dress to keep the habit my dear Lady Wellington.'[31]

On 22 May 1813, Arthur crossed the border from Portugal into Spain. He 'turned round his horse, took off his hat, and said "Farewell, Portugal! I shall never see you again".' As he marched through Spain, in the villages, the church bells rang, girls beat tambourines and everyone was dancing. A month later Wellington had fought and won the battle of Vitoria; with this victory, the Emperor's hold on Spain was broken. Beethoven wrote 'Wellington's Victory' in his honour.

When King Joseph, Napoleon's brother, fled the scene he left behind him his baggage train, which included a collection of rolled-up canvases, the property of Ferdinand VII, the real King of Spain. One hundred and thirty-four years later, my grandfather gave the majority of these pictures to the British nation.

Kitty did not show her face at the Vitoria celebrations in London, for which, as usual, she was criticised. She defended her absence in a letter to an old friend:

> If I did appear, I must be a conspicuous object. My feelings for Lord Wellington's victory cannot, I think, be doubted and surely need not be exhibited. Indeed, I believe that a woman can very seldom succeed in *exhibiting* without *exposing* herself ... the displeasure of one or two of Lord Wellington's family on this subject ... induces me to mention it in writing. Did you ever hear of a really great man whose wife did not like keeping at home in the absence of her husband?[32]

The 'great man' kept moving, and by the end of July he was near the Pyrenees. On 26 July he was standing on a small bridge with one of his ADCs, Fitzroy Somerset, writing new instructions for his Quartermaster-General when suddenly the Spanish villagers shouted that the French were coming. Fitzroy galloped off leaving Wellington, who rode to the top of the nearest ridge calmly to survey the enemy. When his brother William heard the story he wrote, 'I agree with you that the finger of God is upon you; but I shudder at the risks you run, & I wish I could persuade you to feel very much depends on your life ... for the sake of Europe & of us all, you ought not to run unnecessary risks.'[33] But his men too were becoming reckless. After the fall of San Sebastian on 31 August, one of the officers wrote, 'If Lord Wellington had told us to attempt to carry the moon, we should have done it.'[34]

On 7 October 1813 Wellington and his army crossed the River Bidassoa into France. As another officer put it, they had 'infringed upon the sacred territory at last'.[35] While her husband settled down to spend the winter in St-Jean-de-Luz, Kitty was starting to make preparations to move house – from Harley Street to the more fashionable Hamilton Place. Hounds were sent out from England and Wellington was able to indulge in his favourite pastime of hunting, sporting the sky-blue and black jacket of the Salisbury hunt. For the first time in the Peninsular War, Christmas was celebrated. 'Every man contributed some money, meat, or wine', remembered one of the soldiers. 'A sheep or two were bought and killed. Pies and puddings were baked, etc. Plates, knives, and forks were not plentiful, yet we managed to diminish the stock of eatables in quick time. For dessert we had plenty of apples; and for a finish, two or three bandsmen played merry tunes, while many warmed their toes by dancing jigs and reels.'[36]

In March 1814 Wellington was out reconnoitring with General Alava, his Spanish liaison officer, who always asked the Duke the same three questions:

'When do we start?'
'Daybreak.'
'What do we have for dinner?'
'Cold beef.'
'Where do we sleep?'
'Don't know.'[37]

When Alava was hit by stray shot on his backside Wellington laughed (his laugh was said to be 'easily excited . . . loud and long, like the whoop of the whooping cough'),[38] only to be hit himself seconds later. A spent bullet had struck the buckle of his sword belt, severely cutting and wounding his thigh. When they laid him on the grass they did not know how bad it was. Maria Edgeworth reported that Arthur wrote to Kitty 'four times in one week . . . without even mentioning the wound'. When Kitty heard about the incident, her response to an old friend was, 'I have always seen him in my mind protected by a transparent, impenetrable, adamantine Shield, and settled that he could not be *even touched*; so precious a life'.[39]

On 12 April, an hour after the Allies had entered Toulouse, Wellington was dressing for dinner when news arrived that Napoleon had abdicated.

'You don't say so, upon my honour, Hoorah!' and with these words he spun around snapping his fingers like a flamenco dancer. In the city, the statue of Napoleon which had stood on the roof of the town hall was in pieces, and the workmen were chipping away at the Ns and Bs on public buildings. At dinner everyone toasted Wellington as the liberator of Portugal, Spain, France and, last of all, Europe. After a standing ovation which went on for ten minutes, Wellington 'bowed, confused, and immediately called for coffee'.[40]

Soon after, Napoleon attempted suicide; he had told his brother Joseph that if Paris fell he would do so. During the retreat from Moscow he had carried with him a phial of opium. His valet and surgeon helped revive him and after being violently sick, he exclaimed: 'Fate has decided … I must live and await all that Providence has in store for me.'[41] He then signed the treaty with the Allies.

When the cheering died down on the Continent, Wellington finally turned his gaze to England and the family he had not seen since he set sail for the Peninsula in April 1809. As he embarked on the ship that carried him home, a whisper hung in the wind: as Napoleon was banished to Elba, he muttered that when the violets returned next spring he too would be back.

On 23 June 1814 Arthur set foot on English soil for the first time in five years or, to be precise – as Kitty might have calculated – five years, two months and eleven days. At the Ship Inn in Dover his first wish was for something he had been missing: 'an unlimited supply of buttered toast'.[42] He had left as Sir Arthur Wellesley; he returned now as Britain's newest duke. He was mobbed at Dover and cheering crowds lined the route all the way to London. When he reached Westminster Bridge a group of fans tried to take the place of his horses so that they might carry their hero the last mile to his home. The upright figure in the carriage spurned the adulation and instead quietly switched to horseback, riding on alone.

What were my great-great-great-grandmother's thoughts as she stood nervously waiting for her husband, a small boy grasping each of her hands? Arthur had recently written to her to tell her that his next post was to be as Ambassador to Paris, thereby avoiding the complications – familial and otherwise – of Westminster politics. He wanted to know whether she wished to join him in Paris. 'I have no hesitation in deciding to go,' she wrote back; '… there are no difficulties which I do not feel myself equal to overcome, no duties which I am not willing to perform and I may venture to add that you shall *never* have reason to regret having allowed me on this subject to decide for myself.'[43] She was determined to try and live up to what he might expect of her: to be a supportive consort, understanding wife and dignified Duchess.

As for the two boys, they had been two and one respectively when their father left. They knew him only from the stories their mother told of his exploits in battle, and from his image on portraits and busts. When very small, little Arthur (or Douro as he would be known), had longed for a nose as big as his father's and, according to Kitty, 'every day he used to feel his nose and that of the bust ... at last, quite out of patience and not perceiving any increase, he exclaimed with the strongest expression of impatience: "My nose is such a time a-growing."' Now he could touch the real thing.

For Kitty, the tragedy of the reunion would be the dawning awareness that she could never mend the relationship with her husband and that for the rest of her life his first duty would be not to her, but to the nation. And Arthur's triumph at Waterloo a year later would seal her fate; for if Wellington was a hero now, his final victory over Napoleon would place him even higher in the regard of the country.

NINE

Prince of Waterloo

S tanding proud in the park at Stratfield Saye in Hampshire is a cedar of Lebanon, a tree which the First Duke planted himself when he arrived in 1819 to take up residence in the house that was a gift from a grateful nation. A silent witness to seven successive generations of Wellesleys, the tree is now over seventy feet high and its branches stretch out over the estate that was considered by many of Wellington's contemporaries to be utterly unsuitable: the house 'wretched' – a 'miserable imitation of a French château', its site 'the worst place possible for the view'.[1] The Duke himself had reservations about the house, and a number of architects were commissioned to draw up plans for a grand palace to be built on higher ground in the park for the Prince of Waterloo, the title bestowed upon him by the Belgian King. Fortunately for all his descendants, the palace was never built; instead Stratfield Saye remains to this day a family home.

During the thirty-three years that the Great Duke lived at Stratfield Saye he turned it into a house that could claim to be one of the most up-to-date in the country, with a central heating system and water-closets in most of the bedrooms. When Queen Victoria went to stay there in 1845 she was able to describe it as 'very comfortable'. But by the time my grandfather Gerald, the 7th Duke, moved in a century later, the ravages of time and neglect had reduced it to a house which, in his words, was 'bitterly cold, dark and uncomfortable'; it became the focus of his life's work to turn back the clock. By the time my father became Duke in 1972, thanks to my grandfather's efforts, the First Duke's spirit and presence had been restored to the house. After further improvements and structural renovations, my father opened the house to the public. The circle was completed; nearly 160 years after the battle, the nation could finally see the generous gift it gave the victor of Waterloo.

It was Benjamin Dean Wyatt, Wellington's architect, whose task it had been to find a suitable country home for the Duke. Soon after

Waterloo Arthur's brother William had reported, 'The Duke of Wellington is now in treaty for Lord Rivers' place in Hampshire. Wyatt says the purchase is very eligible. I think it will not return 2 ½% but in other respects it may be eligible. The Duke must see it before he buys it.' Two years later Wyatt was writing to Wellington that he had 'no hesitation in saying, that the estate possesses great beauty & dignity; & is capable of being made a princely Place'. I suspect that after two years of discussions, the architect was becoming desperate to conclude a deal and Wellington had still not been to see the estate. A dozen other houses had been considered and rejected; they included Uppark, where the future Emma Hamilton had danced naked on a table, and Bramshill, the setting for the tragic death of a bride on her wedding day. (The guests were playing blindman's-buff and the young girl hid herself in a chest which clamped shut with its spring. Her skeleton was not discovered until many years later.)[2] In another case, Miserden in Gloucestershire, Wellington objected to the house's proximity to a fashionable spa: '*I am not* desirous of placing myself so exactly within a morning's ride of Cheltenham.'[3]

Finally Wyatt persuaded Wellington to look at Stratfield Saye; by the end of 1817 the nation had bought it for £263,000, less than half the generous kitty of £600,000 which Parliament had voted to Wellington in honour of his Peninsular victories and Waterloo. It is hard to say why Wellington liked what he saw at Stratfield Saye. Certainly the avenue of elms – now long gone – by which the house was approached, would have appealed; it was one of the most beautiful in the country. Later, he was enchanted when he found white violets growing in the park.

The house has an interesting pedigree. The main part was built in 1630 by William Pitt, ancestor of Pitt, the Elder and Younger, and Comptroller of the Household to James I. Little was done to the house until the time of Pitt's grandson George, who became the first Baron Rivers. He inherited the house in 1745, and though he was away for many years serving as Ambassador to, successively, Turin and Madrid, according to an account from his steward he 'saw with the prophetic eye of Taste much capability around him and immediately began to reform its "antiquated appearance"'. Others were less complimentary about Lord Rivers' talents, describing him as a 'model of a modern fine Gentleman – well-bred, accomplished, and debauched'; he was rumoured to ill-treat his wife, who was considered to be 'the most charming in the world'.[4] But he landscaped a beautiful park; he planted numerous trees, including two plane trees that frame the view from the house of the River Loddon.

One of Rivers' daughters, Penelope, adds some spice to the history of Stratfield Saye. Married to Lord Ligonier, she met and fell in love with the famous Italian poet Vittorio Alfieri when he was on a trip to England. They would have secret trysts in a romantic cottage near a lake in the park. When the lovers were discovered, her husband fought a duel in Green Park over the affair, but took pity on his opponent when he realised he was no marksman. When Ligonier divorced his wife, Alfieri planned to marry his Penelope but, according to one account, he changed his mind when she confessed she had also been sleeping with a groom for three years. Sadly, with scant regard for this zesty tale, the First Duke pulled down the cottage.

Penelope's brother, the second Lord Rivers, was not interested in the estate and was looking for a buyer when Wyatt came on Wellington's behalf. The house was sold as a 'job lot', including furniture, curtains and carpets, so all Wellington had to do was purchase some beds and ship over from Paris all the paintings and furniture he had acquired when Ambassador to France and, later, Commander-in-Chief of the army of occupation. And while he still expected to build a new palace on the estate, Wellington did little to the house until after Kitty's death in 1831.

Kitty's attachment to the house helped persuade Arthur not to build his palace. She took to Stratfield Saye for the very reasons that others thought it inadequate: she loved its comparative simplicity and lack of grandeur. She had the good sense, too, to choose the best room in the house for her sitting room; it has windows which rise up from the floor, displaying the glorious view of the lawn sweeping down to the River Loddon and the park beyond, and it probably reminded her of a happy childhood in the day nursery at Pakenham Hall in Ireland. Tellingly, her suite of rooms, at the north-east corner of the house, were as far away as was possible from those of the Duke; his territory, on the ground floor at the south-west corner, consisted of a small bedroom, dressing room, and bathroom – all close to his study. The footmen had to tread at least 200 yards carrying messages to and from the couple; no doubt when their relationship was at its worst, the servants clocked up miles to maintain a dialogue.

In their thirteen-year marriage Kitty and Arthur had scarcely lived under the same roof for more than a few weeks at a time, and it is hard to pinpoint a period that could be described as happy. Stratfield Saye was their first real home together; but moving in did not bring them any closer. When Wellington came home for good, there was a hint that he was determined to make his relationship with Kitty work better, or at least to make his domestic life more harmonious. He confided to his sister-in-law (William's wife), 'After all home you know is what we must look to at last.'[5] But even one of Kitty's closest friends had to concede that Kitty was her own worst enemy; 'the duchess has been more hurt by her friends than her enemies,' wrote Maria Edgeworth, 'and more by herself than both put together', but she was optimistic that 'if she does not quite wash out his affections with tears they will be hers during the long autumn of life'.[6] However, if Arthur started out with good intentions, they did not last for long. One visitor who stayed with the Wellingtons a year after they moved into Stratfield Saye gives a gloomy account of his visit: 'The house is not very comfortable, the park ugly, the living mediocre, the whole indeed indicating the lack of sympathy existing between the Duke and his Duchess'.[7]

Arthur escaped the uncongenial atmosphere by attending to his duties as Master-General of the Ordnance in Lord Liverpool's government. As the only military post in the Cabinet, it was an appropriate appointment, and for the next six years it enabled Wellington to reposition himself as statesman rather than soldier. The Britain to which he had returned at the end of 1818 was simmering with discontent. The euphoria of Waterloo had long evaporated: 200,000 ex-soldiers flooding back from the Continent had merely added to the country's economic problems. London's Regency revelries were deceptive: the working class needed more food and the burgeoning middle class wanted reform. Shelley's 'Song to the Men of England' took up the cry:

> Men of England, wherefore plough
> For the lords who lay ye low?
> Wherefore weave with toil and care
> The rich robes your tyrants wear?

The political agitation culminated in Manchester on 16 August 1819 when a peaceful crowd of 40,000 demonstrators, including women and children, were charged by troops and eleven people were killed and hundreds wounded. The Peterloo Massacre, it would be called. Wellington, who harboured a deep distrust of the 'mob', supported the strong measures that were put in place to quell any further social uprisings, but a revolutionary plot against the Cabinet came to light in early 1820. The Cato Street Conspiracy, as it became known, was almost comical in its ambition: the whole Cabinet was to be killed, and the heads of Castlereagh and Wellington paraded on spikes round the city. One of the conspirators, James Ings, had earlier intended to kill Wellington when he left the Ordnance Office, stabbing him in the back when he reached Green Park. In the event Wellington was saved when he met Lord Fitzroy Somerset (married to his niece Emily), and together they walked through the park back to Apsley House.

Strangely, it was this conspiracy that led to the greatest crisis in the Wellingtons' marriage; at its height Arthur threatened Kitty, 'If you are to continue to ask & obtain information of what I do from any Servant or dependant of mine or anybody else excepting myself I'll not live in the same House with you.' The first shot had been fired after the Cato conspirators sought to justify their plan to assassinate Wellington by referring to his harsh attitude to the masses, as exemplified in the way he treated his wife. Arthur convinced himself that the rumour came from Kitty and her family, and as he warmed to this theme in a letter to her, he went on, 'your whole conduct is one of watching & spying [on] me, and that you have employed my own Servants in doing so'.[8] He was prepared to concede, however: 'I really don't believe you have any bad Intention.'

In May 1821 the issue arose again, and this time the Duke was in no mood for conciliation. Kitty had sent him a letter containing a list of people to whom he had not given charity. Her purpose was to check whether certain applicants had indeed not already had money from him; but he took it that she was questioning his generosity, and furthermore that she had been talking to his staff. This he called 'the meanest trick'. Kitty protested that she had obtained information from a third person because she was at Stratfield Saye and he at Apsley House: 'I am as incapable of any mean or dirty action as you are yourself.' She went on that she hoped 'I may not again be subjected to offensive accusations for which there is positively no grounds whatever'. But, as their letters crossed, the whole affair escalated, culminating in his threat to move out. Kitty's distress is evident in one of her letters, which reads like a farewell note:

> I hope that I forgive you. I would and I am sure I could have made you happy had you suffered for me to try, but thrust from you I was not allowed, for God's sake for your own dear sake for Christ sake do not use another woman as you have treated me never write to a human being such letters as those from you which I now enclose they have destroyed me.
>
> God in heaven bless you my husband and bless and guard and guide you and my Children.

It was not the first time that she had contemplated suicide; in 1811 she had been pulled back from the brink by the thought of her children. If Arthur repented of his harsh words and wrote to calm her, such a letter has not been preserved.

The whole episode reveals a great many of the problems that lay between them. It was two years since they had resumed life under the same roof after his sojourns abroad and their incompatibility was evident in every aspect of their lives. He wanted an elegant, sophisticated, calm, efficient consort; instead, in his eyes, he got a badly dressed, financially incompetent, anxious woman who, to his great irritation, would stare at him adoringly. He never confided in her, not even to tell her about his diary engagements, so she had to resort to asking his staff about his plans.

The following year, in 1822, Arthur would pour his heart out to Harriet Arbuthnot, his closest friend and confidante. As she recounted in her journal, he spoke of 'the distress it was to him to be united to a person with whom he could not possibly live on any terms of confidential intercourse', that 'he had repeatedly tried to live in a friendly manner with her' but 'it was impossible, that she did not understand him'. He went on, 'Would you have believed that anybody could have been such a *d——d fool*? I was not the least in love with her. I married her because they asked me to do it & I did not know myself. I thought I should never care for anybody again, & that I shd be with the army, &, in short, I was a fool.' He catalogued her faults and failures, and complained that 'she made his house so dull that nobody wd go to it while, whenever he was in town alone or when he had been *en garçon* in France, everybody was so fond of his house that he could not keep them out of it.'[9]

Unquestionably the Duke was exaggerating. But many of his women friends were openly critical of Kitty's role of hostess at Stratfield Saye. 'She invariably called all the party "the Duke's company," and sat apart from her guests, dressed, even in winter, in white muslin, without any ornaments, when every one else was in full dress!' This account came from Lady Shelley, one of the silliest and most doting of Arthur's admirers. She went on, 'The Duchess talked principally to the tutor, or to one of their country neighbours, and seemed to be uneasy at being taken to dinner by a Royal person or an Ambassador. She seldom spoke, but looked through her eyeglass lovingly upon the Duke, who sat opposite to her.'[10]

Privately, some of his guests dared to denigrate an invitation to stay at Stratfield Saye. 'I have been obliged to promise the Duke of Wellington to visit him in the country tomorrow,' wrote Princess Lieven to her friend Prince Metternich. 'You have no idea how much it bores me and puts me out. He has unfortunately taken it into his head that his house is the most comfortable in the world. Well, there are two very definite draw-backs to that comfort. It is always cold there, and his wife is stupid. What's to be done.'[11]

The Duke enjoyed having visitors to stay but sometimes complained of the lengths he had to go to entertain them. 'As the Duchess does not like cards on a Sunday, I was then obliged to amuse them as I could till they went to bed. Really the call upon me for amusement is so constant that I am tired of having people in the House.'[12] The Duke did play cards, but according to Lieven, 'He knows as little about it [piquet] as I do; and the only difference between us is that I play badly and know it, and he plays badly and thinks he plays well. It is incredible how his pride has a share in everything that he does.' [13]

Early in July 1821, when news reached England of the death of Napoleon in lonely exile on St Helena, Wellington commented, 'Now I think I may say I am the most successful Gen[era]l alive.'[14] A few days later came the coronation of George IV. Douro ('little Arthur') was one of eight eldest sons of peers who were given the honour of holding up the King's train. His father's role as Lord High Constable of England was more demanding: at one point he had to ride his horse backwards down the Great Hall of Westminster. Arthur's outfit and those of his two sons reputedly cost £1,000. Kitty, on the other hand, conscious of social deprivation in the country, decided to wear cornelians rather than diamonds, which cannot have earned her any credit in the eyes of her husband. But, unlike the King's wife, she had her place in the Abbey; the previous year George IV had failed in his attempts to divorce Queen Caroline, but she was barred from attending the ceremony. 'Close the door,' cried the Lord Chamberlain as the Queen tried to force her way into the Abbey. That night she fell ill, and three weeks later she was dead.[15]

Much of Kitty's time was taken up with small domestic matters. Writing from Stratfield Saye to Lady Shelley, confessing that 'I am quite sorry we are deprived of your company', Kitty ended her newsy, friendly letter, 'I am sorry to tell you that our bonny black hen died one day, but not till she had laid a multitude of eggs, and left us a family of black pullets. The black cock is in health and spirits ... The boys return to Eton in a few days.'[16] She missed her sons sorely when they were away at school, and longed for the holidays. When he was nine years old Charley wrote: 'My dear Mama, You must have everything ready as ready as possible or dread the most severe punishment from me.' His elder brother was equally emphatic when, aged thirteen, he sent her instructions for the medieval tournament that was to be held in the spring holiday of 1820. 'You shall get up every morning at eight o'clock precisely if you are good and obey my orders, but if you are bad ... you shall get up at 6 o'clock without any fire or warm water and then stand in the corner with a fool's cap upon your head till breakfast time.'[7]

In later life Lady Shelley recalled the Duchess at Stratfield Saye being 'a slave of the boys when they came home for the holidays. I have seen her carrying their fishing-nets, their bats, balls, and stumps, apparently not perceiving how bad it was for them to regard a woman, far less their mother, as a simple drudge, fit only to minister to their pleasures. In consequence her sons pitied, without respecting her.'[8] Not only do I believe Shelley was wrong about Douro and Charley's view of their mother, but I also find it touching that Kitty wanted to be involved so closely with the boys' holiday activities, and not delegate fetching and carrying to a servant or tutor.

The boys' tutor, who accompanied them to Eton, was the Revd Henry Wagner, who in later life was for many years the Vicar of Brighton. Believing that Kitty spoilt the boys, the Duke would have approved of Wagner's strict and stern outlook. His own relationships with his sons were fraught with complications. He had not been around at all for the long years of the Peninsular War and even when he did return, for another five years he was based on the Continent. By the time he had the chance to get to know them they were already twelve and eleven, and beyond the age when he might have felt able to indulge them. He had very clear memories of his own youthful misdemeanours and inadequacies, and was determined that his sons would not tread the same path.

At Eton the boys lodged with Mr Wagner but had all their meals at their father's old house, Raganeaus. A contemporary later recalled, 'I think Lord Charles Wellesley was the favourite; and though he was deaf, yet he had such a fat, good-natured, smiling face, that everyone liked to talk with him. Lord Douro strongly resembled his father, and had the fine Roman nose, but not the eagle eye, or iron look. Yet Douro was a manly fellow, and one of the best swimmers and divers in the school.'[9] One of Douro's most admired feats was to dive headlong into the Thames from a high point on the river-bank (known to the schoolboys as 'Lion's Leap') and then surface halfway across the river.

Prompted by Wagner, the boys wrote regularly to their father, who would return their letters with comments and corrections. In July 1822 Douro wrote about his Latin verses:

My dear Father
   The Subject of our verses was Rain. I treated it in this manner. In the beginning of the exercise I introduced a traveller, who seeing a storm approaching sought for shelter in a neighbouring wood,* I then described the different signs which appeared to warn him to shelter himself, and the effect the Rain had upon different animals,* I described the swallow delighted at the rain, which gave sorrow to other animals, and souring* up to the very skies, to catch the first drop that fell.
   I remain dear Father
   Your affectionate son
      Douro[20]

The letter, when returned, had three comments:* '1. Want of stop. 2. The same. 3. Soaring.'

From boyhood Douro was made keenly aware of his role as eldest son and heir. His position made him vulnerable to the approaches of unwanted company and while still at Eton there was one such incident. The Duke wrote at length to him, exhorting him to 'avoid evil company' and reminding him that he had 'a great station and name to fill'. He advised his son,

It is a common but true proverb, that a man is known by the company he keeps, and you may rely upon it, that if you keep bad company thus early, you will never be able to shake them off ... good and wise men will shun you and you will never become distinguished for any thing excepting the low, vulgar, & contemptible pursuits of your companions, who, even if they should not have misled you, will have tarnished your Reputation.
   God forbid that I should be understood to advise you to keep company with none but persons of your own Rank and Station in life. In all stations there are persons of good and bad Education, manners and habits; and I earnestly entreat you to associate with the former alone, and to avoid the latter, be they of what Rank or Station they may.[21]

Kitty had copied the original letter, to make sure her son could decipher it, so it was to her that Douro replied, though using language that does not read as if it was meant solely for his mother: 'I once thought him the most severe disciplinarian that ever lived, and consequently avoided and feared him accordingly ... but now he appears in my eyes the greatest man that ever lived.'[22]

As her husband's social world and its inhabitants became increasingly hostile to her, it seems that Kitty's relationships with young people got stronger. One of the young girls she was fond of was Elizabeth, the eldest daughter of the trusted physician Dr Hume. Not only did Elizabeth become one of Kitty's protégées, she was also Douro's first love.[23]

Dr Hume was an important figure in the Duke's life, not least because in 1822 he saved it. Wellington's hearing had been affected when he attended a noisy artillery review, and he summoned a specialist who administered a treatment that went gravely wrong. Hume came urgently to Apsley House to find the Duke huddled in a chair wracked with a violent fever; he had an inflammation in his left ear which, had it not been for Hume's intervention, would have reached his brain. The Duke never recovered his hearing in that ear. That Hume had saved his life did not spare him from the Duke's derision. 'All Doctors are more or less *Quacks*! and there is nothing more comical than that Dr Hume should have made you believe that I am an *Idiot*! rather than the truth, that he as well as others of the Medical Profession is a little bit of a *Charlatan*.'[24]

In 1825 Douro accompanied his father on a trip to the Continent. Mrs Arbuthnot reported that the Duke complained 'that he shewed no curiosity or eagerness about any thing. During the whole month they were absent he did nothing & slept almost the whole way in the carriage.' But Mrs Arbuthnot was more sympathetic. 'I think the Duke judges him too severely. He is but 18, just let loose from school, falling in love with every woman who gets near &, I think, is just at the age when young men generally do nothing ... but he is remarkably gentlemanlike & pleasing.'[25]

In the autumn of 1825 Douro and Charley were sent together to Christ Church, Oxford, accompanied once again by Wagner. They were registered respectively as a 'Nobleman' and 'Gentleman Commoner' with allowances of £800 and £500 apiece; their father complained that 'when I entered the world I had just the same for the whole year, which I now give Charles every quarter'. With advice that he certainly did not follow in his younger days, the Duke advised them 'that there is but one certain and infallible mode of avoiding Debt, that is, first to determine to incur no expense to defray which the money is not in their pocket'.

Neither of the Wellesley boys finished their degree at Oxford after an episode which involved a classic catalogue of spoilt undergraduate bad behaviour: late-night drinking, gambling, damaging college property and, finally, breaking open the college gates 'in the dead of night with great and premeditated violence'. Charley was rusticated. The Duke, while furious with his son for involving 'me and others in the disgrace which it inflicts upon you', felt that the punishment was too severe for a misdemeanour which he believed was partly caused by the college authorities' failure to supervise their charges, and allowing them to have 'suppers in their Chambers every night, at which large quantities of Wine are drunk and at which other irregularities are committed'.[26] After an explosive correspondence with the Dean, who refused to admit to any responsibility, the Duke felt he had no alternative but to withdraw the boys; and though Charley had to sit out his penance with the stern Revd Wagner, they both ended up going to Trinity College, Cambridge, where they eventually managed to obtain degrees.

In 1826 Wellington travelled to St Petersburg for the funeral of Tsar Alexander 1. He wrote to Mrs Arbuthnot from Russia saying that the houses 'are always warm & cannot be otherwise. We should do well to follow their example a little. It is done by double Windows and by warming the Stair Cases & Passages.' On his return to England he had outer windows made for many of the bedrooms at Stratfield Saye, which were to be removed for spring and summer.

The following year, when Canning's government was in trouble, Kitty wrote from Stratfield Saye a sad letter to Mrs Arbuthnot:

> Do you recollect what day this is? It is the Duke's birthday! On this day last year we dined with you, we were together! He was lately returned from Russia, and in high spirits and in high favour! And now I am here alone, and most anxious, while [he] is probably with you! Pray for me, Mrs Arbuthnot, it will be praying for me to wish everything good to him. He feels far more deeply & often more painfully than he allows himself to express, and I cannot but apprehend that he often suffers that which none suspect.[27]

I imagine Kitty sitting on her own at Stratfield Saye, waiting anxiously for some word from her husband. Her sons were away; to pass the time she would have bent over a tapestry or her easel, or tried to distract herself at the piano. Whatever her anxiety, she would not have missed her daily walk to feed Copenhagen, who ranged in his own paddock close to the house. In 1826, in a good mood after his Russian trip, Arthur had suffered Kitty to be present at his birthday dinner; just being able to write 'we were together' would have given Kitty untold pleasure. Her husband's absence now was painful to her but she retained the sense that she knew him best; she could allude to his deepest self, to the part that 'suffers that which none suspect'.

When the King received the Duke at Windsor Castle on 9 January 1828 he was in bed, dressed in a dirty silk jacket and an old scruffy nightcap. 'Arthur, the Cabinet is defunct,' he exclaimed, and proceeded to impersonate various Ministers. His performance was so clever and funny that the Duke found it 'quite impossible to restrain from fits of laughter'. But the agenda for the meeting was no laughing matter: the King was asking the Duke to form a government. The *Manchester Guardian* did not question Wellington's military talents, but was utterly dismissive of his suitability for the highest office in the land: 'With a strong bias to arbitrary power, and an utter ignorance of the principles of philosophical legislation, and in great measure of the state of the country also, he combines inveterate prejudices, very mediocre abilities, and an un-teachable disposition'.[28] Wellington would not have been unduly disturbed by these opinions: he had a healthy disrespect for the press. 'I hate the whole tribe of news-writers, and I prefer to suffer from their falsehoods to dirtying my fingers with communications with them,'[29] he wrote to Sir Robert Peel, the Home Secretary.

Three weeks after the Duke became Prime Minister, the Wellesleys celebrated a small family milestone. 'Yesterday the Most Honourable Arthur Marquis of Douro, eldest son of his Grace the Duke of Wellington attained his majority', proclaimed *The Times* of 4 February 1828. It announced several parties that were being held to celebrate the occasion, including two in Ireland – one at his uncle Longford's Pakenham Hall, the other at Dangan Castle (which had long ceased to be a Wellesley residence). Others were held in Basingstoke and Reading, the latter 'for friends of the "True Blue Cause", to which 'any repentant Radical will on this occasion not be refused admission'. No doubt the private celebration at Stratfield Saye was an opportunity for Kitty to gaze dotingly at the son who so resembled his father. A few months before she had written to Lady Shelley, 'I hope you like my Douro upon further acquaintance! Is he not the living image of his father?'[30]

And politics and the army were to be the son's destiny too. As a schoolboy he had become an Ensign in the 81st Regiment and in 1827 he graduated to being a Cornet in the Royal Horse Guards. As for politics, on the day after his twenty-first birthday his name was proposed as a candidate for the constituency of Weymouth; his father declined the offer on his behalf. In any case, Douro and Charley, and their cousin Gerald, were all still at Cambridge.

*

When my father left Oxford in 1938 the army would have been his career, even if war had not been imminent. But when peace was finally secured and the mopping-up operation began, he became thoroughly demoralised, feeling that his professional life had been reduced to the 'desk job' he had always dreaded. As 1946 began, he was based in Germany, desperately missing Diana and their small son, who were living in a cottage on the Stratfield Saye estate. 'Have you had any photographs taken of Charles? If you haven't I wish you would. I long to have one.' A few weeks later he was writing, 'This winter has been for me the worst I have ever known, from the point of view of loneliness, boredom and general frustration.' Valerian believed he might be posted to Haifa and was ready to refuse, whatever the consequences. 'I reckon I have a strong case for not going, and I am quite prepared to be court-martialled if I refuse to go. I have always up till now been prepared to put the army in front of any personal issues but in this case I am not prepared to, as I reckon personal and family issues come first.'

In March 1946, with leave imminent, he was more cheerful. Diana was instructed to look out his evening clothes: 'my newest double-breasted dinner jacket with a plain roll lapel and the trousers that go with it ... a plain white soft ribbed evening shirt ... the one with the longest sleeves, an ordinary starched collar – not stick-up points ... my patent leather Wellington boots, some black socks if I have any ... some links and last but not least a dark red carnation, and we'll have a party!'. Diana and the baby were able to join him in Germany in the autumn of 1946, where they lived for a year in married quarters.

When the Douros returned to England they were based at Windsor and once again Valerian was considering his career, and the possibility of becoming a full-time farmer on the Stratfield Saye estates. In the summer of 1950, his Commanding Officer informed the King that Valerian was thinking of leaving the army. 'I remember we went to a party at the Wallace Collection[31] and the King and Queen were there and I got a message that the King wanted to see me. "I like to have people I know in the Household Cavalry. Can I persuade you to stay?" Loyalty to the Sovereign is a vital part of my father's code of conduct, and though the King did not 'command' Valerian to stay on, it was clear that he wished him to. And so he did.

Peacetime presented its own challenge. But in 1956 Valerian once again found himself in a war zone, when he was sent to Cyprus as the Commanding Officer of his regiment, The Blues. Cyprus had been a Crown Colony since 1924, but until the mid-1950s the British Army regarded it as a backwater; during the Second World War my father had felt as if he were kicking his heels when he was sent there for training. When Britain withdrew from Egypt in 1954, the island assumed a new strategic importance; this prompted the growth of an insurgent movement, EOKA, from within the majority Greek population which sought union with Greece. In many ways the character of the conflict that followed was similar to that which my parents had encountered in Palestine during the war: a well-organised, ruthless attempt to remove the British from the territory they occupied.

Valerian arrived in Nicosia early in 1956 and Diana followed him a month later. Before they found their own house for the family, they stayed for a few weeks at Government House with Field Marshal Sir John and Lady Harding, the new Governor-General and his wife. Valerian's morning routine here began with a swim in the pool in the grounds of the house. Usually he would stop for a chat with Neophytos, a Greek Cypriot on the Governor's staff who was keen to practise his English. One morning he was nowhere to be seen; Valerian thought nothing of it and set off with Diana to Limassol to pick up their car – a much-prized Bentley – which had arrived from England. Later in the morning, driving back to Nicosia, they heard a huge explosion and wondered about EOKA's latest target. When they got to Government House the place was swarming with security personnel. Neophytos's absence had raised suspicions, and in the course of a search a bomb had been discovered under the mattress of the Hardings' bed. It was carried 'through the house on a shovel like a dog's mess' and thrown into a pit for a controlled explosion. But for a faulty timer, it would have gone off in the middle of the night, killing the Hardings and perhaps my parents who were sleeping in the bedroom next door. With admirable insouciance Sir John announced, 'I slept better than usual last night.'

My father had said publicly before he left that 'the children would stay in England unless the position in Cyprus showed a marked improvement'. If anything, the bomb incident reinforced the view that it was important for the Commanding Officer to set an example for the regiment, so in early April 1956 my mother flew home to bring the family out to the island. By now there were four of us: Charles, Richard, myself and John, whose second birthday was celebrated a week after we arrived. For the next two and a half years our home was a house called Templestone, perched on the hills above Kyrenia. Family outings to deserted spots we called 'Snake Island' and 'Three-mile Beach' were made on a small boat called Kittiwake, which was based in the harbour at Kyrenia.

Of all my father's memories of the period he was commanding the regiment in Cyprus, none is more painful than the murder of the popular regimental doctor, Gordon Wilson. 'I had encouraged everyone under my command, particularly the medical staff, to try and help the local population.' One day Wilson was on his way to visit a Greek Cypriot family who lived in Nicosia. He was sitting in his car at a set of traffic lights when he was shot in the head. 'I felt appalling about it – felt I had sent him to his death.' Valerian's Second-in-Command volunteered for the grim ritual of identifying the body. 'To this day I feel rather ashamed that I let him', my father tells me.

Valerian slept with a pistol under his pillow for the duration of his posting; an armoured car stood guard round the clock at the family house. On trips home the papers would be full of all the terrorist activity, and when my parents got back to the island it took a few jittery days before they readjusted. There was a stretch of road in the middle of Nicosia called Murder Mile, and my father remembers being on his own there one day after a British soldier had been killed and the old city was closed down. 'As I walked back to my car there was nobody on the streets but I could feel the eyes of thousands of people watching me.' In the spring of 1958 Valerian handed over command to his successor, and we all went home, though not without regrets; in spite of the danger and volatility on the island, my parents, and those members of their family who can remember it, look back on the Cyprus posting as two magical years.

After a brief spell in command of an armoured brigade, in 1962 my father was dispatched, family in tow, to Germany. His job, with the well-aimed acronym CRAC (Commander Royal Armoured Corps), put him in charge of three armoured car regiments whose role was to be the first troops to confront the Soviet army should it cross the border. The weather in Germany was bitter that autumn, and East–West relations plummeted too. We arrived there just before the Cuban Missile Crisis. My father remembers the tension of the time and the procedure he was to follow in case of war. 'I would have received a telegram with the codeword "Quick Train". I had the key to the safe where I would find our instructions, and we would have had to be out of the camp in two hours and on the border, by the gap in the Harz mountains, where we would try and hold the Russians until the main Allied army was assem-bled.' When the crisis subsided, for the rest of his term there the atmosphere was one of an uneasy truce which observed military for-malities, while covert operations continued to guard and maintain nuclear launch sites.

By 1964 my father was a Brigadier, and as his term of command in Germany came to an end he found himself at a crossroads. 'I sometimes wonder whether I chose the right road', he confesses rather wistfully. A plum army job was on the horizon: 'I might have become the Major-General commanding the Household Cavalry Division.' But as my grandfather got older, more of the responsibility for running the family estates began to fall on the son. The Major-Generalship would have required his full attention, and after much soul-searching he felt that his prime allegiance was to his Wellington inheritance. With a strong measure of regret he accepted his final posting as Military Attaché to Spain; and so his last tour of duty was on the Peninsula where the First Duke had won many of his famous victories. It is a strange irony that part of the First Duke's legacy to his great-great-grandson was to deny him the chance of fulfilling his military ambitions.

On becoming Prime Minister in January 1828, Wellington was forced by his Cabinet to resign his position as Commander-in-Chief of the Army. Kitty's new role as consort to the Prime Minister made very little differ-ence to her life; not only did she continue to spend most of her time at Stratfield Saye, but her wardrobe failed to rise up her list of priorities. Even Douro, who adored his mother, was critical; writing of a head-dress she had worn, he admonished her, 'You may be sure I should never have found fault with it if I did not know *for certain* that the person whom you most wish to please is extremely hurt at your dress being inconsistent with and beneath the station you hold in the world'.[32] She still revered her husband. When a jeweller asked for her opinion of a wax impression of his profile for a snuffbox, she commented, 'The Hair grows rather *up* from the forehead, being naturally inclined to curl, it never lies flat and covers very little of the forehead, which is rather broad, open & beautiful.'[33]

In late March 1929 the precious 'forehead' was dramatically exposed. 'I did intend to have written to you on Monday last, but I was quite unable!' wrote Kitty to Charley, who was in Florence with his brother. 'Even now I cannot think without horror that the precious life of your father should have been endangered by the violent spirit of an Enthusiast,

for such is Lord Winchilsea, however sincere, however upright his intentions may have been.' A few days earlier Wellington had challenged the
Earl of Winchilsea to a duel, after being accused by the Earl of an
intention to introduce Catholics into the newly opened King's College
in London – 'his insidious designs, for the infringement of our liberties,
and the introduction of Popery into every department of the State',
Winchilsea had railed. The dramatic confrontation took place in the
early hours of Saturday, 21 March on Battersea Fields. When, acting as
Wellington's second, the Minister of War Sir Henry Hardinge gave the
order 'Fire!', the Duke spotted that Winchilsea's arm stayed firmly by his
side, and he fired wide; the Earl then discharged his pistol into the air.
Wellington accepted the Earl's retraction only when it included the word
'apology' rather than 'regret'.

   In fact the whole affair was a clever ploy on the part of Wellington to
harness public opinion in his favour, his ultimate goal being to push
through Catholic Emancipation, against the wishes of the King, and the
majority of both his countrymen and his party. As Kitty reported in her
letter to Charley, it worked. 'Last week the Mob were roaring, hooting,
abusing your father; now they are cheering him again.' A few days later,
as Prime Minister, Wellington addressed the House of Lords. The Duke
was no orator, but on this occasion he spoke without any notes and with
a passion and sincerity that impressed both his Westminster audience
and the country as a whole. 'I am one of those who have probably passed
a longer period of my life engaged in war than most men, and principally,
I may say, in civil war; and I must say this – that if I could avoid, by any
sacrifice whatever, even one month of civil war in the country to which I
was attached, I would sacrifice my life in order to do it.'[34] On 13 April
1829, exactly halfway through the Duke's tenure of the premiership, the
Catholic Emancipation Bill was given the royal assent. It was the peak
of Wellington's political career. Arthur Wesley, just in time for his sixtieth
birthday, had paid his dues to his Irish origins.

                                         *

When, at the age of fifty-eight, my grandfather inherited the dukedom,
Stratfield Saye was in a terrible state. Fortunately Gerry was already
passionately interested in the life and legacy of his great-grandfather and,
as an architect, in the restoration of buildings. He knew he would spend
a lifetime carrying out work on the house and found a fitting way
to chronicle these endeavours: 'I have chosen for my recording of my
alterations and rearrangements at Stratfield Saye, an unused volume of
Mrs Arbuthnot's journal,' he wrote. 'Mrs Arbuthnot knew Stratfield Saye

and in common with all the Duke's friends despised it and thought it unworthy of her hero ... I do not think she would mind her book being used to record a description of efforts to improve it.'

'The house was bitterly cold, dark and uncomfortable', were the first words of his description. 'The only illumination was from oil lamps suspended about four feet from the ceiling. They were all old, gave very little light and blackened the ceilings ... the light was not enough to read by, so everyone went to bed at about 9.15.' Gerry's disgust at the state of the house is evident: 'Whereon space could be found there were stuffed birds and animals'; 'the general impression of clutter and discomfort dominate'; and of the room his brother Charlie had used for a gun room, 'There was a wash hand stand, the basin of which was usually full of dirty water. The room smelt of grease.' Over the next twenty-seven years my grandfather dedicated himself to the task of bringing the house back to life.

The project may have been a Herculean challenge, but the house was also a huge treasure-trove. 'After church we unpacked in the attics brown paper parcels tied with string by fingers of the Great Duke's time, and not hitherto opened,' wrote James Lees-Milne when he stayed in the house a few weeks after Gerry had moved in. 'This was very exciting. We blew away the dust and undid the knots of string, never cutting. Regency wall sconces emerged.'[35] If the First Duke could have chosen to which of his descendants to give the pleasure of unpacking these parcels, it would have been Gerry. However, the First Duke would have regretted the obsessive idolatry of his memory, even amongst his own family. Gerry's share in this was gently mocked in Lees-Milne's diary. 'He showed me the Great Duke's Garter robes unpacked for the first time since his death and in perfect preservation, even the long brown curl with the wig-maker's name attached to the label. Gerry held up the Great Duke's underpants to the light, looked intently at the fork, and said solemnly, 'I am glad to see no signs of sweat – or anything else,' as though this were the occasion for personal congratulation.'[36]

Gerry had an unequivocal approach to old houses, declaring, long before he inherited Stratfield Saye, that 'The owner of a really beautiful old house has to live for it as well as in it, for its possession involves the shouldering of a responsibility for the debt which the present owes to the past and which can only be repaid to the future.'[37] The First Duke had amply provided for the future: in the 1830s and 1840s his additions included a conservatory, one of the earliest forms of central heating and the water-closets. He also spent the income from his tenants on improving the estate. 'I am a rich man', he would say, 'and the next Duke of Wellington will not be a rich man. I am therefore determined that he shall receive his patrimony in the very best order. If he cannot keep it so, it will not be my fault.'[38]

When my grandfather died on 4 January 1972 he had fulfilled much of his ambition for Stratfield Saye, and my father decided it was time to open the house to the public; there had long been a natural curiosity to see inside it. When the First Duke was living there he became so exasperated by uninvited visitors that he had a special sign made: 'Those desirous of seeing the Interior of the HOUSE are requested to ring at the door of entrance and to express their desire. It is wished that the practice of stopping on the paved walk to look in at the windows should be discontinued.' Before opening the house, my father restored two more rooms and carried out significant structural work. He also added a twentieth-century feature – a swimming pool – which was elegantly housed in the conservatory. In the First Duke's time the conservatory was filled with orange trees, whose scent would infuse his morning constitutional when the weather was too foul to go out.

For most of my parents' married life, until my father became Duke, their home had been Park Corner, a pretty Queen Anne house on the estate. They continued to live there for the months when the 'big house' was first open to the public, but soon this arrangement became impractical. For my mother, moving out of Park Corner was a real wrench; having to leave her walled garden behind was the hardest part. Cuttings were taken and some plants dug up, but after being there for twenty-five years, many of the shrubs were too big to uproot. But to leave Stratfield Saye empty, as it had been in the early part of the twentieth century, was never an option. Then, when attempts were made to let it, *The New York Times* referred to the house as 'one of the most celebrated "White Elephants" in existence'.

One of the duties that fell to my father when he inherited the dukedom was the annual presentation of a flag to the Queen, as 'rental' for Stratfield Saye. This is not mere tradition, but an absolute requirement, as laid down by Parliament when the nation bought the estate for the First Duke in 1817 – 'One tri-coloured flag for all manners of rents, services, exactions and demands whatever'. A new tricolour, with the date, is made every year, and is hung in the Waterloo Gallery at Windsor. Similarly, the Duke of Marlborough renders yearly to the Sovereign a flag with fleurs-de-lys for his rental of Blenheim. There was a time when a spare Stratfield Saye flag was always ready, in case an accident should occur on the journey between the shop in St James's and the castle. When the 4th Duke died on Waterloo Day, the flag still had to be at Windsor Castle by midday. In 1990 my father had the honour of being created a Knight of the Garter (in the footsteps of the First Duke, 2nd and both his father and grandfather) and in recent years he has presented the flag on the same day as the annual Garter service in St George's Chapel.

Many visitors to the house felt it was as if the Great Duke had only recently left. My father is a poor sleeper and sometimes, if he woke in the night, would go and sit in the Library. 'I could really feel the First Duke's presence there. I would sit in one of the chairs he designed himself [with a bookstand that slides across from one of the arms] and would derive real contentment from the thought that I was sitting in the spot where so often he had sat.'

When members of the public visiting Stratfield Saye spotted my mother pottering about the grounds – weeding, cutting flowers, or picking up litter – they sometimes mistook her for the gardener. To her this was a compliment rather than cause for offence. Often, her work would be in the 'American Garden', which was created by Kitty with plants from Britain's former colony. In the First Duke's time, a modest claim to fame of the Stratfield Saye gardens was their dahlias, propagated and nurtured by the Duke's gardener, Mr Cooper. In the late 1830s Miss Mitford, writer and local resident, went in search of one she was missing from her collection. Her journey was in vain, but she waxed lyrical about the avenue of elms:

> No cathedral aisle was ever more perfect; and the effect, under every variety of aspect, the magical light and shadow of the cold white moonshine, the cool green light of a cloudy day, and the glancing sunbeams which pierce through the leafy umbrage in the bright summer noon, are such as no words can convey. Separately considered, each tree (and the north of Hampshire is celebrated for the size and shape of its elms) is a model of stately growth, and they are now just at perfection, probably about a hundred and thirty years old. There is scarcely perhaps in the kingdom such another avenue.[39]

Like the First Duke's friends, most of the people who visited the property were unimpressed by the appearance of the house – 'merely a comfortable and convenient nobleman's house, hardly responds to the fame of its owner,' wrote Miss Mitford. The most damning condemnation came from a starchy, evangelical curate: the 'house is perhaps the ugliest in the world ... the Duke of Wellington has not much taste I think and no idea of personal comfort. He lives as if he were campaigning.'[40]

A far greater attraction, during his lifetime, was Copenhagen, the famous chestnut charger the Duke rode at Waterloo and who retired from the battlefield with his master, to be pensioned off in a paddock at Stratfield Saye. Here he was occasionally ridden by the boys, and regularly fed with bread by the Duchess. After her death, Copenhagen continued to approach every lady with, it was reported, the 'most confiding familiarity'. He died in 1836 at the grand old age of twenty-eight, and was buried with full military honours. Mrs Apostles, the First Duke's housekeeper, planted an acorn above the grave, and the tree grew vigorously. Later, the 2nd Duke marked the spot with a gravestone, which carries a verse he wrote himself: 'God's humbler creature though meaner clay / Should share the glory of that glorious day'. When Copenhagen was alive he had to suffer the indignity of having little bits of hair cut off his mane or tail to be made into jewellery for admiring ladies; even Kitty wore a bracelet made from the hair of her hero's charger. But in his prime Copenhagen could hold his own. After Waterloo, when Wellington dismounted, he gave his horse an appreciative pat on his hindquarters, only to have Copenhagen lash out in irritation.

No less than Copenhagen's grave, the great oak growing beside it has become a notable feature of the grounds of Stratfield Saye. Trees have played an important part in the history of the estate, from the time when Lord Rivers laid out the meticulously ordered elm avenue until my father's tenure, when he began a programme of replanting to replenish the landscape and restore the park to something of its former glory.

One early autumn afternoon my father and I go off for a drive round the park, to revisit landmarks on the estate that means so much to him. He sports a strong pair of boots, moleskin trousers, a pale blue cotton shirt, a camel-coloured cashmere cardigan and a tweed waistcoat, all enlivened by a faded red and yellow cravat; round his neck hang binoculars and a whistle to call the dogs – Yasmin, a golden labrador and Roo, a brown cocker spaniel – who accompany us on our tour.

The First Duke himself stands guard at the main entrance to the park: a bronze statue of our ancestor on a tall column, his back to his home, his gaze eastwards towards the Continent and the field of Waterloo. Over eighty feet high, the monument towers over us all. Designed by Baron Marochetti, Wellington stands in his Field Marshal's uniform, his hat in his left hand. My father reminds me that when he was a small child, on approaching the monument someone would always say, 'I wonder whether he will have his hat off to greet us. We would try and catch him out by sneaking up on him without him seeing us.' Even years later when I was an excited child, we never caught him out. The statue was erected in 1865 by the 2nd Duke and, as the inscription reads, 'the tenants, servants, and labourers on the estates of his father, as a token of affection and respect'. In the 1890s, in the time of the 3rd Duke, an old retainer who occupied one of the lodges that flank the entrance differentiated the First from his two successors by referring to 'He that's up there', as she looked towards her old employer.

Behind the gates an avenue of Wellingtonias, planted in 1873–4, compete in scale with the monument. These trees were first introduced into Britain from America in 1853 (the year after the Duke's death), when the species was given the name *Wellingtonia gigantea*. 'Wellington stands as high above his contemporaries as the Californian tree above all the surrounding foresters,' wrote the botanist who chose the name. Some Americans were outraged that the world's largest tree had been called after an English war hero and argued that *Washingtonia* would have been more appropriate. The botanical world finally settled on *Sequoiadendron giganteum* or Sequoia, but on this side of the Atlantic Wellingtonia is still the preferred name. Wellington himself would likely have deferred to Washington, whom (according to his son) he considered 'the purest and the noblest character of modern times'.[41]

As we drive down the avenue we spot a cluster of white fungus growing in the grass and stop to check it out. My parents have always loved foraging on their walks or expeditions; on foreign territory that might involve furtively digging up a small plant, gathering some seed or taking a cutting – my mother is never without a plastic bag in her pocket into which to consign the booty. In Stratfield Saye park and nearby woodlands, they have found several species of mushrooms over the years – inkcaps, cèpes, chanterelles, blewits. This time we are not so sure. 'If you break the skin and it oozes, you know it's poisonous,' says my father. The flesh does not break drily and we take no chances. Soon, away from the avenue, we pass through a wood that has always been known as Switzerland. In 1810 Lord Rivers' steward explained that the covert reminded 'the passenger of the romantic Alpine scenery'. Near Switzerland is the site where Wellington thought of building his Waterloo Palace. 'Thank God the plans were scrapped,' says my father. 'I am sure the family would have ended up turning the palace into a museum.' The grandiose designs now hang in a passage in Stratfield Saye house, a constant reminder of the First Duke's good sense.

Near the proposed site of the palace we are looking at the remains of a small group of umbrella pines, the seed for which was sent by Lord Brougham to the First Duke from his villa in Cannes, which was built in 1834. Once political adversaries, Lord Brougham and the Duke became close friends. The trees are reaching the end of their natural life; originally there were four and the two survivors look as if they are soon to be firewood. As my father gazes across the park towards the house, he spots a bird circling in the sky, and reaches for his binoculars. 'A buzzard', he pronounces. We watch it scanning the earth for its prey and I consider the apparent contradiction between the pleasure my father derives from observing wildlife in its natural habitat and his enjoyment of shooting. When very young he was fascinated by the birds that flew round his grandmother's exotic aviaries; as a nine-year-old, his Wellington grand-father taught him to shoot. He rapidly mastered the skill and, once into adulthood, was acknowledged as one of the 'best shots' of his generation, a claim he holds to this day. In his mind, the two different interests sit comfortably alongside each other: the hunter and the nature lover.

'As I have got older, increasingly I have enjoyed fishing more', he tells me. In a letter to Diana just after the war he had been rather dismissive of salmon fishing – 'dry-fly fishing for trout is a much more skilled business', he had written. But when he came back to live in England, summer holidays at Knockdolian became a regular fixture, and not only did he grow to love the place, he also became an expert salmon fisherman. My parents still spend six weeks every year in Scotland. One recent September when I spoke to my father after he had been out on the river, I asked him how his day had been:

> I've just caught the hardest fish I've ever landed. I was fishing from the bank and had been in the pool for about half an hour when it took midstream. I played it for about ten minutes but was worried about how I was going to land it and didn't want it to get into some rocks downstream. Of course, just as I was beginning to tire it out, that's exactly where it ended up! I had to put down the rod and clamber down the bank, and, on my hands and knees, get hold of the cast, at which point I discovered the fly had slipped out of its mouth! I somehow managed to get two fingers under its gills. It was quite small – about 5 pounds – but beautifully fresh. It had come up the river with the spate. It was a triumph – I do feel rather pleased with myself.

This was six months after he had had a hip replacement operation, in his ninety-third year.

The 'best shot' accolade could never have been given to the First Duke. Once, when shooting with the Shelleys, he peppered a dog, a gamekeeper and, finally, a woman hanging out her washing. When she exclaimed, 'I'm wounded, milady', Lady Shelley retorted, 'My good woman, this ought to be the proudest moment of your life. You have the distinction of being shot by the great Duke of Wellington!' Lady Shelley's remark confirmed the Duke's opinion that she was a rather silly woman; but he himself had a cavalier attitude towards such episodes, believing that 'Bird shot never hurt anyone'.

The Duke, however, had a strong respect for the hierarchy in the field of sport, as the son of one of the gamekeepers at Stratfield Saye remembered:

> One day Jonathan, our head keeper, who had to tell everyone which way he was to walk and where to stand ... orders the Duke which way he was to go. And His Grace never said a word, but away he goes, just as if he was a private soldier and keeper was Commander-in-Chief; and the Duke went straight on right through the wood, and when he came out on the other side, you never saw such a sight in your life as the Duke's nose, it was that full of thorns. Father had quite a job getting them out. And Keeper said: 'Why Your Grace, I can't think how you came to walk through all those bushes.' And the Duke said: 'You ordered me to go that way, and go I did.'[42]

The First Duke's favourite sport was hunting; one of Stratfield Saye's advantages was that he could attend the House of Lords in the evening and drive down to Hampshire late at night, to be up in time to be out with the hounds. He continued to do so until the last few years of his life.

My father and I are now near the cedar the First Duke planted when he arrived to take up residence. At the foot of the tree stands a plinth with a bust of the Duke. 'When the old Knightsbridge Barracks was demolished in 1966, there was a bust of the First Duke on the outside of the building and I persuaded the regiment to let us have it.' From here there is a good view of the house, with the River Loddon in the foreground. In the eighteenth century Lord Rivers widened the river, creating the impression of a lake, which became known as the Broadwater. By the time my father took over the running of the estate it had become a solid reed bed, with little rivulets of water running through it; one of his first projects was to recreate Rivers' view.

My father remembers how cold it was in the house when, in the autumn of 1944, he first took my mother there to meet her new father-in-law. 'No heating, no electric lights, brown water coming out of the tap! A lot of the rooms were derelict. We slept in the best guest room but at night the wind rattled behind the panels on the wall and shook the windows. Diana hated it.' When they went upstairs they had to take a candle to light their way, and one of my grandfather's favourite tricks was to blow it out. 'On the first morning we thought we would have a lie-in, but at nine o'clock my father came bursting in saying, "You're very late! What is happening?" He wasn't disapproving but it was quite unnerving for Diana meeting him. It was quite unnerving for both of us.'

> We used to all sit on the sofa together by the one oil lamp – my father doing the crossword, me reading, Diana knitting, all hugger-mugger. We had a fire but it was damn cold. When Diana was pregnant, there was one terrible moment when we were all sitting in the drawing room and she suddenly said, 'I am going to be sick'. My father said quick, quick, take her through the gallery and out where the dogs go'. So we rushed and she didn't quite make it and she was sick on the floor. Poor Diana was fighting with the door to let herself out!

There is a picture of Stratfield Saye in the time of the First Duke showing, in the foreground, Douro, Charley and their cousin Gerald as Eton schoolboys, fishing rods in hand and dogs scampering beside them. The First Duke had no fondness for dogs, though he had a small terrier called Vick when he was a young man at the Academy in Angers; and while in India, reputedly, another one got lost and trekked over 100 miles to be reunited with him. My father, on the other hand, since being given his first Labrador, Bess, when he was thirteen, has rarely been without a dog by his side. Dogs from the Stratfield Saye strain of Labradors are recognised as being top gun dogs and in his nimbler days my father would regularly attend field trial championships to see descendants of Juno, the first of the strain, winning prizes. He presented a puppy to the Queen in 1978, and another went to France's President Giscard d'Estaing.

In the First World War part of the park was used as an extension of nearby Bramley ammunition dump and the army built the roads across the park, with lay-bys (which still exist) where the ammunition was stored. In the Second World War much of it was ploughed up to grow food for the war effort. The park has never been purely ornamental. 'The First Duke was told that it was excellent land for wheat and beans,' says my father. When he was running the estate, he juggled the programme of tree-planting with the agricultural needs. 'I love the golden poplars – you can see them from a long way away,' says my father, gazing at the display of autumnal colours.

We spot a heron in the sky and a small group of deer appear from the wood and spring across the fields to disappear once more from sight. My father glances at his watch – a 'field-and-stream' make, with a compass. It is nearly time to get home for lunch. 'I keep my watch five minutes fast. I *know* it's five minutes fast but it helps. You always have to appear five minutes before everyone else when you are an army officer. It wasn't part of my training but I came to the conclusion that it was a good plan, because when I was young I tended to be idle about getting to places on time. I have become punctual but I was not as a young man. My father was obsessively punctual and maybe I have inherited some of it from him.' One of my own abiding images of my grandfather is of him standing in front of the fireplace in the drawing room at Stratfield Saye, looking at his half-hunter watch, waiting for us to arrive for lunch. Occasionally we would tease him by creeping up and standing outside the room until just after we were meant to be there.

As we wend our way homeward, my father remarks on other features of the landscape for which he can take credit. Ponds where ducks and geese return in the evening; coverts of trees that shroud the deer and provide twilight sanctuary for barn owls and hen-harriers.

My father has always preferred 'outdoors' to 'indoors', the 'countryside' to 'town'. He relishes his memories of escaping as a young boy to wander in the woods, gun in hand, or in search of an interesting, long-abandoned object. He is drawn to the natural world in its fullest manifestation. He has often travelled with my mother, to search out the best salmon fishing – living in a tent in Siberia or a log cabin in the wilds of Canada. He is intolerant of failure in his sporting endeavours, and has been known, even in his tenth decade, to reveal a barely disguised irritation if my mother's firm and straight casting has secured 'top rod' status for the day's fishing. It is their joint love of landscape – and all that grows and lives in it – that has been one of the mainstays of their long marriage. Their favourite home-grown 'expedition' has always been to inspect a new area of planting, or anxiously surveying the damage after a terrible storm like the hurricane of 1987, when many trees came down in the park. They are still replenishing the landscape, many of the family and their friends tending to favour presents that can be planted. In the First Duke's time, one of his friends remarked acidly that the park seemed 'rather barren'; by the time my father took over the running of the estate, once more it had assumed that appearance. Now, as my father looks out over the Stratfield Saye landscape, he says, 'It gives me great pleasure to think that I planted a lot of the trees that I can see.' The 8th Duke's legacy is to the land.

TEN

'That Damned Infernal Family'

The walls of the dining room at Stratfield Saye are hung with portraits of men, and a light sprinkling of women. From a young age I learnt to recognise the images of my great-great-great-grandfather – a magnificent large painting by John Hoppner of the Duke in India dominates the room – but my curiosity did not extend to the other pictures. In fact the room is filled with family, not only Arthur's parents but also his grandparents, a sister and all his brothers: Henry, Gerald, William and Richard, the eldest. Now, as I look closely at the faces of these Wellesley men, with their striking similarity of features, I know that Arthur's brothers were all successful in their own right (three became peers), and undoubtedly all helped him in his career, particularly Richard, who, destined for great heights, found his life eclipsed by the heroic achievements of his younger brother. Not surprisingly, their relationship was the most complicated of those of all the siblings. Richard never quite overcame his jealousy of Arthur. Only a few years before he died, Richard scribbled in the margins of a new book about the history of India: 'In 1797 ... Arthur was Lieut-Colonel of a regiment, not distinguished by anything but his connection with Lord Wellesley [Richard]. This is no disparagement to the Duke of Wellington. History is spacious enough for the fame of both brothers without injury to either.'¹ Regrettably for Richard, this was not to be.

Looking back to the early days of Richard and Arthur's relationship, there were strong bonds between them. In 1786, when they were both in Paris with their mother, they all went on an expedition to one of the palaces outside the city. Lady Mornington became aware that there was a secret between the two boys and, getting Arthur on one side, demanded he tell her what it was. He refused, insisting that if it had been his own secret he would, but he was not prepared to betray his brother. Lady Mornington became furious and despite Richard's entreaties on his brother's behalf, Arthur was left to walk all the way back to the city.

Eventually he 'arrived whistling most unconcernedly; and from this period it was understood that he retained a painful sense of his mother's tyranny and injustice'.[2]

The secret was almost certainly about a dazzling young French actress called Hyacinthe Roland whom Richard had recently met and fallen passionately in love with. For the next eight years she was his mistress, and became his wife only after she had borne him five children. Queen Elizabeth the Queen Mother was descended from Hyacinthe and my father tells me that she derived great pleasure from this fact. I am not surprised; with her passion, wit and beauty Hyacinthe stands out as a beguiling member of the Wellesley family.

In the early days of her love affair with Richard, Hyacinthe delighted in her French origins: 'I am not cold and vulgar, like an Englishwoman.' She sized up Lady Mornington behind her back and nicknamed her '*La Croûte*', which translates from the French as a combination of 'cross-grained, unfair, unkind, snobbish'. She included in this category her sister-in-law Anne, a portrait of whom, with two small daughters, also hangs in the room; it provides a refreshing contrast to the strong male presence.

Born in 1768, a year ahead of Arthur, Anne was educated at home by a French governess. Spotted at the theatre in 1789 by the diarist Fanny Burney – 'Lady Mornington and her beautiful daughter Lady Anne Wellesley' – in June of the same year she was dancing the minuet at a ball at St James's Palace to celebrate the recovery of King George III from one of his bouts of illness. But in spite of this gaiety and social success, some part of Anne's life was unhappy; in September she wrote to her friends, the celebrated Ladies of Llangollen:

> I have been in a state of mind for this year and a half passed which has rendered me totally unfit for holding any *rational* correspondence with a *rational* being. I have gone thro' a great deal my dear ladies since I saw you – more misery than I expected would have fallen to my lot. However, wretched as I have been, I would bear it all again in the same cause. I dare say I need not be more explicit upon this subject, for, as you say you have heard of me, I conclude the world has not been more silent to you about my affairs than it has to others.[3]

This 'cause' may have been a rumour, supposedly put about by a 'mischievous' Arthur, that she had run off with a footman. If she had an unsuitable romance, the world would certainly have been talking about it. In any case, within four months of writing this letter, on 7 January

1790, she contracted a safe marriage to Henry Fitzroy, a younger son of the first Lord Southampton. On the day of her wedding Anne's parents-in-law were described as behaving 'with great civility, Lady S particularly, but not a farthing either to set them up or to enlarge their income'.[4] Anne, like her brothers, had a keen intelligence and inbuilt pride, but she resented the restrictions of her gender and was jealous of her brothers' success, and the wealth that went with it. Throughout her life she would regularly ask them for money, reminding them that she had never had their opportunities.

This resentment may have started at her wedding, when Richard gave his sister away, but stopped short of providing her with a dowry. By this time he had three children of his own, and his modest means had been stretched by having to pay off the creditors of his maternal grandmother, Lady Dungannon, who was by all accounts a spirited character. The previous year, after leaving Ireland and being installed in an apartment at Hampton Court, Lady Dungannon had run up big debts. As a result she was conducted, by two bailiffs and six 'Marshal Men', to a 'Spunging house' (a halfway prison), where her daughter and grandson, Lady Mornington and Richard, found her happily conversing with her fellow inmates. Lady Mornington was 'shocked and provoked by her mother's want of feeling or shame',[5] and she was summarily dispatched in disgrace to a convent in France to rehabilitate herself, accompanied by 'Lady Mary Wesley'.

The account of Lady Dungannon's misdemeanours appears in the journal of Lady Eleanor Butler, one of the Ladies of Llangollen. In the published diary, 'Mary' is identified in a footnote as William's daughter. William did have a daughter called Mary, but the year was 1788, and since he was married in 1784 she would have been very small, and the Ladies would never have referred to her as 'Lady Mary' since her father had yet to be ennobled. 'Mary' has to be Lady Dungannon's grand-daughter, the Wellesley brothers' second sister, who was born in 1772. Mystery surrounds her; many of the Wellington biographers, including the authoritative Elizabeth Longford, make no mention of her, referring to his four brothers and 'one' sister. Why are there no records of her in the family archive and why, unlike her elder sister Anne, was she not presented at court?

The only public notice of Mary is a melancholy one. The deaths column in *The Times* of 4 March 1794 announced, 'Yesterday, the Right Hon. Lady Mary Wesley, sister to the present Earl of Mornington'. What was the cause of her death? I suspect she may have suffered from some mental or physical disability, which at the time would have carried social stigma and confined her within the boundaries of family life. She was probably buried in the vault of the Grosvenor Chapel, alongside her father; but if so, after the vault was closed up, no one in the family knew that her remains were there and they failed to inscribe her name on the plaque in the church. No image, no memorial, no place on the family tree – until now.

The day after the announcement of Mary's demise there appeared a notice of another family death: 'At Lisbon, the Hon. Henry Fitzroy, fourth son of Lord Southampton'. Anne had travelled to Portugal with her husband, who was suffering from consumption, in the hope that the climate would improve his health. After his death, Henry Wellesley, who was fond of his sister, took leave of absence and went out to Lisbon to accompany her home. What happened next reads like an episode from Baroness Orczy's *The Scarlet Pimpernel*. 'On her [Anne's] way back to England in company with her brother Henry, she was captured at sea by a ship of French revolutionaries, brought before one of their tribunals, and suffered nine months' imprisonment.'[6] This was the footnote that I came across; it was extraordinary to discover that two of the First Duke's siblings had suffered so directly at the hands of the French Revolution. Henry's own journal reveals the full drama.

We had been at sea about three weeks and were within twelve hours sail of Falmouth when, at daylight on the morning of April 23, we discovered a large frigate, apparently French, in chase of us. We had every prospect, however, of escaping, when we were met by another frigate coming from the land with English colours flying and surrounded by several smaller vessels. This we of course took for an English man-of-war with her convoy, but before coming within hail she hauled down her English colours and hoisted the French tricolour flag, and although we immediately surrendered to this superior force she poured a broadside into us which luckily passed through the sails and did not injure anybody on board. She proved to be the *Thamar*, French frigate, and had captured all the vessels which we had taken for her convoy within two or three hours' sail of our coast.

Since February 1793 England had, once again, been at war with France. Louis XVI and Marie Antoinette had both been executed and the horrors of the guillotine were still haunting the psyche of the aristocracy. It is easy to imagine Henry and Anne's fear when they were captured, and it can have been no comfort to hear the assembled French fleet singing the 'Marseilles hymn' at sunset every evening. After three days the prisoners

appeared before Jean Bon St André, one of Robespierre's closest associates, and according to Henry 'a thorough specimen of revolutionary
brutality'. Their hearing took place in a large room filled with officers
wearing the tricolour, Bon St André sitting on a platform.

> As soon as we entered (addressing himself principally to my sister) he began
> a violent attack on the King and Mr Pitt, styling them 'votre George and
> votre Pitt que vous adorez tous a genoux'. After indulging in this strain for
> some time, alluding frequently to the King's iniquity, he concluded by
> saying that England was on the verge of ruin, 'car George est un imbécile
> et Pitt est un scélérat'. He then dismissed us, saying that we should of
> course be treated with all the humanity for which the French nation was so
> justly celebrated.

This 'humanity' led to nine months of confinement, but it seems that
Henry was unaware what danger they were in. At the beginning of 1794
Richard had denounced in the House of Commons the principles and
practices of the revolution in a long, eloquent and widely acclaimed
speech; and the Committee of Public Safety realised that with two
Wellesleys in their hands they had an opportunity for revenge. A Victorian biography of Richard reveals how near they were to the blade of
the guillotine. 'So rare an opportunity of vengeance was too tempting to
be neglected, and without trial or inquiry Mr Wesley and his sister were
consigned to the scaffold. Their names actually stood upon the list for
the next holocaust in July when, happily for them, on the eve of their
impending doom Robespierre fell, and with many others they partook of
the unexpected reprieve.'[7]

Despite their reprieve, Anne and Henry were kept as prisoners by the
French until the beginning of 1795 when Anne was freed and Henry
dramatically escaped. He gathered some other prisoners around him,
bought a twenty-three-foot boat and set sail for England. But the weather
was treacherous, and had it not been for the seafaring skills of a smuggler
in the party, they would all have drowned. As it was, three of Henry's
companions died. It is a reflection of the rising profile of the family that
The Times for Monday, 19 January noted, with only a small measure of
inaccuracy, Henry's return. 'Mr Westley [*sic*] brother to the Earl of
Mornington, landed a few days since, at Megavissey in Cornwall, having
escaped with some other prisoners, from Brest.' Henry did not forget the
smuggler who had saved his life. He helped him get command of a store
ship, but when the man went to take up his post he was so drunk that
the Comptroller of the Navy 'turned him out of the room'. Thereafter

his 'propensity for drink' made him a difficult recipient of Henry's charity, though not of his eternal gratitude.

While Henry and Anne were languishing in France, Richard monitored their progress. His fears for their safety probably played a part in his decision, in the autumn of 1794, to marry Hyacinthe. Richard's biographer, Iris Butler, thought he may have felt the 'need to be sure of something and someone'. Hyacinthe for her part sought security for her five children, the last of whom was born that year. The wedding, at St George's, Hanover Square, would certainly not have been as the result of pressure from her in-laws. At this point the brothers were civil to her but the women in the family regarded her with a mixture of wariness and snobbery, and were deeply disappointed when Richard chose to formalise the union, none more so than the dowager Lady Mornington. She had not visited Hyacinthe when she was her son's mistress, and had no intention of doing so now.

Richard had been hankering for an important role since he entered politics in 1784 and, in 1797, four years into his marriage, he was offered the job of Governor-General of India. By accident rather than design, Arthur was already in India, commanding the 33rd Regiment, and Henry left his job as a précis-writer at the Foreign Office to accompany Richard as his secretary. William, a Westminster MP, took care of the family affairs in England and Gerald, ordained in 1793, in the post of Chaplain, Reader and Preacher at Hampton Court, minded the family's spiritual welfare. In India the success of the Wellesley triumvirate would result in the British Crown gaining, in Richard's words, '250,000 *squares miles of territory*, 35,000,000 *subjects, and £6,000,000 annual revenues*'.[8] Despite Richard's prodigious talents, it also left him so 'sultanised' that his arrogance and vanity would ensure that he never managed to attract and retain a following. For Arthur it would prove his making and set him up to be the liberator of Europe.

Richard begged Hyacinthe to accompany him to India, but she was terrified of a journey on the high seas which could take up to seven months and, more crucially, she could not bear to part with her children, or to leave them with 'une folle comme ta Mère, une coquette comme ta soeur et un étourdi comme M Pole'. Caught in a mother's eternal dilemma, Hyacinthe chose the needs of her children against those of her husband. While Richard was away for seven long years they wrote to each other frequently. The correspondence reveals a relationship which was intense, passionate and highly sexual, but it was also one of love and friendship. In an age when marriages were so often born out of convenience and convention, theirs was a genuine love-match.

From the moment Richard left English soil, Hyacinthe missed him desperately.

> It is impossible to explain to you how lonely I have been since you left. I wander up and down in the house from morning till evening without finding him whom my heart looks for ... The only place I care to be is in the bedroom where I embraced you for the last time, and I stand at the window of your dressing-room and imagine that I see you throw yourself in to your carriage and disappear from the eyes of your unhappy lover (*amie*) distraught with pitiable grief.[9]

With her husband gone she was now at the mercy of his family: 'Your mother and sister will do nothing for me unless it is for their own benefit.'[10] She gave him a medallion made of the hair of the five children intertwined with her own, which she had worn herself before sending it off. Wear it 'under your shirt',[11] she entreated him. Their separation tormented her with paranoia and passion in equal measure and their exchanges, though frequent, were distorted by the time delay of six months. Richard's family were giving her a hard time and society in general was wary of her: her past was obscure, all her children were illegitimate and, maybe the greatest sin of all, she was French. Richard warned Hyacinthe about the consequences of not joining him and was irritated by her grumbling and jealousy. 'My dearest, my dear soul, rest assured that I love you with all my heart, that I long for nothing more fervently than to be once more in your arms, but in the name of God and of human and Christian mercy, do not add to my sufferings here by outbreaks of jealousy as unjust as they are ridiculous.'[12]

When Richard had been in India for four years, he was rewarded with an Irish marquessate. He deplored the nationality of the title – the 'gilt potato', as he referred to it – and became ill from fury and depression. In his own words, he suffered an 'almost mortal' collapse. Enormous and painful boils broke out on his body and he was 'reduced to a skeleton, yellow, trembling, without appetite, unable to sleep, too weak to walk twice round my room ... in my mind I suffer martyrdom. Cursed forever may they be who are the sole cause of the only serious illness I have ever had in this country ... and if I die let the world know they have caused my death. And may the earth, heaven and hell avenge me on their despicable heads.' Strangely, after all this melodrama and venting of spleen, Richard seemed to calm down and reassured Hyacinthe, 'Don't be alarmed about my health'![13]

In England, while Hyacinthe may not have been formally accepted into society, the Prince Regent was happy to visit her and exchange gossip about other members of the Wellesley family. 'I don't like Pole,' he said, 'and I am very glad his wife cuckolds him so often and so publicly.'[14] 'Pole' was the second brother, William, who at the age of fifteen, after a brief stint as a midshipman in the navy, had struck lucky when a distant relative called Pole made him heir to his estates. William honoured his benefactor by styling himself 'Wellesley-Pole' and his new-found wealth may have helped him secure the hand of Katherine, one of the twin daughters and heirs to Admiral John Forbes. They married in May 1784 and had three daughters and one son.

Whether the hints about Katherine were true, or malicious gossip, William himself certainly had a roving eye. Hyacinthe, in another letter to Richard, referred to a famous actress of the day. 'As for Mr Pole, I think he is even nearer ruin than usual. He is neither beautiful nor young enough for Mdlle. Descamps to stick to him for his *beaux yeux* only.' Descamps was an actress noted for her performances at the Haymarket Theatre; she was also supposed to keep her admirers at a chaste distance, so it may be that William loitered in vain at the stage door.

It is probable that for the first two years Richard was in India, he remained faithful to his wife. Aware of the strength of her husband's sexual appetite, Hyacinthe was quite sanguine about the odd transgression, but she could not bear the idea that he might fall in love with another woman. When anonymous letters started turning up which implied that this had happened, she became distraught, and wrote of her 'irreproachable and unexampled life in a situation which earned her the esteem and admiration of all'. Richard, with typical elegance and fervour, wrote back: 'I have never loved any woman save you, since I have known you; I have never had any female friend except you at any time. I have never placed any confidence in any other woman. I have none in any woman now, and I never will have. I have not lost even the smallest measure of confidence in, or attachment to you.'[15] Richard's protestations have a hollow ring: by this time – 1804 – he was certainly being unfaithful to Hyacinthe.

In England, Lady Mornington had been landed with two more daughters-in-law of whom she disapproved. On 2 June 1802 Gerald married Lady Emily Cadogan and a year later Henry, home from India and suffering from ill-health and loneliness, married Emily's sister Charlotte. 'Dearest Henry's sudden determination to marry and form the same odious connection that Gerald had done, affected my spirits beyond all description,'[16] wrote Lady Mornington to her eldest son. She considered that the Cadogan girls had bad blood, since their mother had run off and been divorced by her husband.

Though he may have married for love, Gerald was probably not insensible to the fact that an alliance with the Cadogans would bring with it both the living of St Luke's, Chelsea, and a house. In spite of his clergyman's collar, he too had a reputation with the ladies. Before his marriage, the Prince of Wales told Hyacinthe that he considered Gerald 'one of the greatest roués he had ever met, that Henry was infinitely amusing and knew all "les filles"'.[17] Hyacinthe's view was that he was marrying Charlotte only because he was lazy and had just happened to meet her at Gerald's house. Some thought Charlotte was a terrible flirt, and of 'very little beauty'. Hyacinthe gained some comfort from Lady Mornington's disapproval. 'It seems to be decreed', she wrote to Richard, 'that none of the Wellesleys should make grand marriages.'[18]

In 1805 Richard sailed for home expecting to be received as the conquering hero, but he left under a cloud that would come back to haunt him. Though his rule of India had achieved great things for the British Empire, he had clashed with the directors of the East India Company, who considered India to be their domain. He resigned before he was recalled. Arthur had gone home a few months earlier, so towards the end of Richard's time in India he had no one to moderate his moods or hone his judgement. He had been away for seven years and the world and the family had moved on. Arthur, rewarded for his military prowess on the subcontinent, returned to England a Major-General. All the other siblings had now established their own families and were progressing well with their lives and careers. England had gained a glorious victory against the French at Trafalgar and, in Nelson, been given a true hero of the time. Through no fault of Richard's, India had become the sideshow; the real drama was on the continent of Europe. India had reenforced his vainglorious attitude to life, and deprived him of the one person who might have kept his feet on the ground – Hyacinthe.

Just before he landed at Portsmouth, Hyacinthe wrote to her husband that she 'lives for and longs only to find herself again in your arms and to replace our five interesting and beautiful children under your protection'. He in turn was 'dying to embrace you ... chère amie, toujours à toi et pour toi'. These were the last tender words Richard would ever write her. He stepped onto English soil on 7 January 1806, two days before Nelson's funeral. McCullagh Torrens, Wellesley's nineteenth-century biographer, sets the scene:

Lady Wellesley and her children awaited him on landing, and several private friends pressed round him with kind welcomes. The Port-Admiral was there also, and certain military officials eager to see the little man of whom they had heard so much, and being able to say that he had shaken them by the hand, a familiarity the thought of which had never occurred to him. There was in short, no lack of fuss, and even of affection; enough to content any ordinary general or envoy returning home. But he was neither. He had been playing King.[19]

Richard tried to contain his vanity and disappointment but the effort became too much and at dinner later that day he exploded, uttering expletives that shocked the assembled company. Hyacinthe, no doubt embarrassed by his behaviour, made a fatal mistake. She laughed and said, 'Ah! you must not think you are in India still, where everybody ran to obey you. They mind nobody here.' Richard rose from the table and left the room. Knowing so much of her husband's complicated, sensitive psyche, Hyacinthe should have poured balm on his wounded ego, but her sharp wit had become part of her survival kit. Richard could not find the generosity of spirit to forgive her and she was hurt by his apparent lack of interest in her or the children. Richard and Hyacinthe would never rediscover the pleasure and passion of the early years of their relationship; from now on they were a couple at war.

In 1809, just as Arthur was about to set off for the Peninsular War that would keep him from Kitty and his sons for five years, a huge scandal engulfed the family. 'Early in the year 1809 I resigned my situation at the Treasury in consequence of a domestic occurrence', noted Henry in his journal. The gossip-mongers fell hungrily upon the 'occurrence'. Mrs Calvert, a social doyenne of the day, breathlessly breaks the news in her diary: 'Lady Charlotte Wellesley, the wife of Mr Henry Wellesley, and mother of four children, has run away with Lord Paget, also a married man with a lovely family. The town rings with it. Indeed, it is too shocking to think of.'[20] Lady Mornington's fears had materialised.

Lord Paget was a distinguished cavalry officer who, when Henry had neither the time nor the energy, had given Charlotte – 'Char' – riding lessons. The prospect loomed of a duel between Henry and Char's brother, Lord Cadogan, but, according to a contemporary account, the two men ended up agreeing 'that stinking Pole Cat [Char] not worth the shedding blood. Damn her! How Paget's stomach will heave in the course of six months, when she seizes him in her hot libidinous arms.' Charlotte suffered a barrage of other insults as her name was dragged through the mud: 'liar', 'whore', *maudite sorcière*. These words were all used by different men involved in the scandal when they felt that Charlotte Wellesley was not following their advice. The newspapers had a field day; there was even a rumour put about that 'Sir Arthur Wellesley had pursued the fugitives, overtaken them on the Oxford Road, and inflicted a dangerous abdominal wound upon the ravisher of his ailing brother's wife.'[21] Henry was already ill with a liver complaint when his wife left him.

After several stages of threats and equivocations, the affair finally ended up in the Sheriffs' Court, Middlesex, where Henry's barrister painted a picture of his client's wedded bliss before Henry Paget intervened: 'it promised the perfection of human happiness'. Lord Paget's counsel in turn waxed lyrical about the soldier returned from battle, who could have 'died in the bed of honor, and the tears of his country would have streamed upon his grave'. The poetic sentiments failed to impress the jury, who brought in a verdict for the plaintiff, with damages assessed at the extremely high figure of £24,000. Henry was forced to introduce into the House of Lords a Private Bill to dissolve the marriage and enable him to marry again, which he eventually did six years later, when Lady Georgiana Cecil became his second wife. The children of Henry Wellesley's first marriage were sad victims of their parents' break-up: one of them, Gerald Valerian, who was born in a no-man's-land between his mother's relationships, was adopted by Arthur and Kitty and was brought up as if he were their own son. In later life he became Queen Victoria's trusted Dean of Windsor.

Over the next few years (with the exception of Gerald, the English parson, who was living a quiet but busy life with Emily, producing a lot of children – 'am intolerably poor, but, that excepted, as happy as possible'), the Wellesley brothers danced to their own ambitious tune. They worked as a team, and when one was in trouble they all circled round. As with the fall-out from Richard's reign of India, when Arthur was under attack for signing the Convention of Cintra they presented a united front. They handed jobs over to each other; in October 1809 William took over from Arthur as the Chief Secretary for Ireland; in 1810 Henry succeeded Richard as Envoy Extraordinary to Spain. But if in public they were supportive of each other, in private they vented frustration and sometimes fury. Arthur to William in 1810: 'I wish that Wellesley [Richard] was *castrated*; or that he would like other people attend to his business & perform too. It is lamentable to see Talents &

character & advantages such as he possesses thrown away upon Whoring.'²² But from December 1810, for two crucial years Richard was Foreign Secretary, and was able to provide his younger brother with considerable support for his Peninsular campaign. William Cobbett, the radical and champion of the Whigs, abhorred the influence and involvement of the family in public life and railed at 'the arrogance of that damned infernal family'. The Wellesleys had come a long way to command that kind of public disapprobation.

Unquestionably it was Richard who had led them, but with Arthur's assault on Napoleon's control of the Peninsula the centre of power in the family began to shift. After the battle of Salamanca in August 1812, when Arthur was promoted to be an English marquess, the title Richard had coveted while in India, as news of the victory reached London, jubilant crowds appeared on the streets. Richard drove out to have a look and was spotted by the mob who, delighted to have a stand-in for his brother, pulled his carriage all the way to St Paul's and back to his house. 'The fear stole over him', wrote his Victorian biographer, 'that the part of pre-eminence in great affairs he had aspired to play had come to an end. The younger brother to whose advancement he had so much contributed already outstripped him in the race of fame, and would to-morrow take precedence of him in rank as a Peer.'²³ Three years later, after the battle of Waterloo, the race was truly over.

The brothers had traits in common: quick-wittedness, strong wills, ambition and, above all, ties of blood and common experience. But at this stage of their lives, it is easy to pinpoint their different natures. Richard had a brilliant mind, but his vanity and arrogance contributed to lack of discipline both in his political tactics and in his personal dealings. He had described his parents as 'frivolous and careless personages' – references to his father's talents being restricted to music and his mother's lack of sensitivity and affection – but there is evidence in his own personality of a clash between romance and reality. Arthur's streak of artistic sensitivity had been closed off when he abandoned his violin. Richard's disturbed spirit, which Hyacinthe identified as being common to all the brothers – 'Vous êtes tous d'un caractère assez tourmenté'²⁴ – resulted in symptoms which suggest he suffered from manic depression. Arthur's iron discipline derived partly from his military training but, through the long years in India, though he had learnt a huge amount from his brother, he had also observed that Richard's unrestrained ego was his Achilles' heel. Unlike Richard, Arthur was aware of the value of strategic retreat. Iris Butler wrote of the two brothers: '[Richard] could always see what had to be done, and Arthur could always do what had to be done. When they combined, as in India, they moved mountains.'[25]

Henry, who also owed a great deal to his eldest brother, was able to command respect from his subordinates but was instinctively better at receiving orders than giving them. His sound judgement and sensible negotiating skills would ensure him a successful career as an Ambassador to the Court of St James's and a peerage when he was created Lord Cowley in 1828. William, who became Lord Maryborough in 1821, was in many ways the most controversial of all the brothers. Not without intelligence, he lacked the power of persuading people to trust him and many considered him unlikeable. He was opportunistic and not a little devious, and though he became Arthur's trusted confidant during the Peninsular War and remained close to him for the rest of his life, he would just as happily have aligned himself to Richard, if the dice had fallen in a different way. Of all the Wellesley brothers Gerald was the gentlest and most amiable.

I doubt that my great-great-great-grandfather would have scaled the heights that he did without the help of his brothers. But it was inevitable that Arthur and Richard would reach the point where their relationship ruptured – Richard unable to tolerate the glories of his brother, Arthur intolerant of his brother's more aberrant behaviour. Yet when, towards the end of their lives, the chance came to bury their differences, they both reached out and seized it. As John Severn (the historian who has studied the interacting lives of all five brothers for many years) has written: 'Arthur, the indolent youth, and Richard, the cash-strapped and awkward genius, had made it to the top largely because of the assistance they had provided one another. It made no sense to nurse wounds inflicted in the heat of political battle and fraternal rivalry. Without one another, their lives were incomplete.'[26]

Richard and Hyacinthe's marriage ended when, in February 1810, three years after Richard had bought Apsley House as their London residence, she accepted the terms of a separation and moved out. 'The sacrifice is consummated,' wrote Hyacinthe in her last letter to her husband. 'I leave your house with horror.' She was a broken woman, her spirit and joie de vivre destroyed by the infidelities and insensitivity of her husband, but her sharp tongue survived: 'Continue to live with vile and depraved characters who, by flattering your extravagant vanity, dominate you, dishonour you and ruin you.'[27] But four years later, when one of her daughters, Anne, abandoned her marriage and bolted with Lord Charles

Bentinck, the repercussions of the whole scandal dealt Hyacinthe a final blow;[28] despite the challenges of her relationship with Richard, she prided herself on having brought up five intelligent, respectable children. On 5 November 1816, during a visit to the home of her youngest daughter, she died. All five of her children, Anne included, were devoted to her and were distraught at her death. It might have been a consolation to her troubled spirit to know that through Anne's marriage to Charles Bentinck, one of her great-great-great-granddaughters would be Queen Elizabeth, the Queen Mother.

Around the time of Hyacinthe's death, Lady Mornington's early antipathy to both her Cadogan daughters-in-law was soundly vindicated. Once again the scandal involved Lord Paget (since Waterloo, the Earl of Anglesey). 'He [Anglesey] had intrigued first with Lady Emily, his wife's sister, after having got his present wife from Sir Henry Wellesley,' wrote a member of the family later, 'and then through jealousy because Lady Emily would not give up Lord Wallscourt, a young Irish Peer just of age, whom she had introduced into her house as a visitor to her daughter, but in fact for her own purposes, Lord Anglesey betrayed her to her husband, Dr [Gerald] Wellesley, showing her letters and securing from her proofs which he afterwards placed in the Doctor's hands.'[29] Emily left her husband, but it appears that the dalliance was short-lived and for Lord Walscourt, possibly fatal: he died in October 1816 aged only twenty-one. Wishing to protect his children, Gerald refused to divorce Emily. Whatever the other consequences of Emily's infidelity, to Arthur's great fury Lord Liverpool, the Prime Minister, turned down Wellington's request that he appoint Gerald to a bishopric. Had Liverpool agreed, all five brothers would have sat in the House of Lords.

Richard was back in political favour when, in 1821, a black year in Kitty and Arthur's marriage, he was appointed Lord Lieutenant of Ireland. It was while he was in Ireland that Richard at last wrested a great prize away from his younger brother, but this time it was nothing to do with affairs of state. Marianne Caton was the eldest of four 'belles' from Baltimore – the granddaughters of the last surviving signatory of the Declaration of Independence. Marianne was renowned in her home town for her looks and her accomplishments. At the age of nineteen she chose from her many suitors the eldest son of the richest merchant in America, a Robert Paterson, whose sister Betsy happened to be the first wife of Jerome Bonaparte, sometime King of Westphalia and brother to the Emperor. Soon after becoming Mrs Paterson, Marianne sailed to

Europe with her seemingly 'boorish' husband, two unmarried sisters and, perhaps most important of all, letters of introduction into the highest echelons of British society.

Before long she had met, and according to contemporary accounts, conquered the victor of Waterloo; soon her fame spread round the drawing rooms of Paris and London. When she was formally presented to the Prince Regent, he exclaimed, 'Is it possible that the world can produce so beautiful a woman!' After a ball in Brighton in January 1817, even *The Times* carried news of Marianne and her sisters, 'who danced in a manner to rivet the attention of his Royal Highness the Prince Regent'. Not everyone was so complimentary; some sneered at her 'yankee' roots. But she had the Duke of Wellington in her thrall and, on the second anniversary of Waterloo, managed to persuade him to take her and her sisters on a conducted tour of the battlefield. The following year Arthur gave her sister Louisa away in marriage to one of his ADCs, Colonel Hervey.

By 1818 it was reported that the 'Duke of Wellington looks horribly ill, *si dice* that it is not the present *combinazione* but love; that he declares he never knew the meaning of the word until he saw Mrs Paterson, & her departure for America *déchire son tendre coeur* in a terrible manner'.[30] Soon Marianne and her sister Lady Hervey had been widowed and the three sisters, the 'American Graces', were once again together in England. Wellington entreated his friends to look after Marianne. In 1820 Princess Lieven reported, 'Yesterday, Wellington wrote to tell me of the arrival of Mrs Paterson, the American, and to ask me to introduce her to the pleasures of London. The style of his letter radiates happiness.'[31] Others are more mischievous: 'She [Marianne] shook all over when I went into the room, but if for grief at the loss of Mr Paterson, sentiment at the recollection of the Duke, or the coldness of the room she received me in, I do not presume to judge.'

The sisters were invited by Wellington to stay at Stratfield Saye. Was Marianne surprised to find her portrait hanging on the wall of the Duke's study? Princess Lieven had spotted it when she stayed in the house two years earlier: 'The Duke took me into his study', she confided to a friend; 'there were two portraits in there, one of Lady Charlottte Greville and one of Mrs Paterson, the American. How can one have two passions at the same time, and how can one bear to parade them before the world at large'[32] Richard too would have seen the painting of Marianne and was aware, no doubt, that she was now a highly eligible widow; it may have been pure coincidence that he was a visitor to Stratfield Saye during the sisters' stay. Seeing Marianne in the flesh, he was 'much struck by her extraordinary personal attractions'.[33]

The Duke must have rued the day he introduced them; in the autumn of 1825 he received notice of Richard and Marianne's impending nuptials. Mrs Arbuthnot was at Stratfield Saye when the news came through: 'he [the Duke] told me he had given her credit for more real good sense than to make such a preposterous match. I told him I was not the least surprised for that she had come to this country on a matrimonial speculation; that it was pretty well for the widow of an American shopkeeper to marry a Marquis, the Ld Lieutenant of Ireland and a Knight of the Garter, and that I was not at all surprised.'[34] Arthur tried in vain to warn Marianne off his 'profligate' brother, who had 'a violent temper' and 'not a shilling in the world', but the marriage went ahead on 29 October in Dublin. The Prince Regent, now King George IV – his excitement when he watched her dance the quadrille forgotten – was furious that her Roman Catholicism had invaded the Viceregal Lodge: 'In my palace Mass shall not be heard,' he thundered.

Marianne and Richard's union became, in many respects, a successful one, and years later she did the greatest service to the two warring brothers, Arthur and Richard, by brokering peace between them. But when, in 1828, Wellington was asked to form a government, the relationship between Richard and his younger sibling was probably at its most complicated. Richard had never been in competition with Arthur's military prowess, merely jealous of the glory it brought him; soldiering was Arthur's trade, politics was Richard's. Richard was even mooted in some quarters as a possible Premier. However, it never crossed Richard's mind that the appointment of his brother would not immediately open the doors to his own re-entry into the Cabinet. For William too, any resentment he may have felt towards Arthur for not using his influence during Liverpool's premiership, paled into insignificance beside the ill-feelings he had for him when he became Prime Minister. He was furious to discover that Wellington was not prepared to offer any of his brothers 'advancement'.

By the time of Arthur's premiership his sister Anne was living a contented life with her second husband, Charles Culling Smith, whom she had married in 1799. With two daughters from her first marriage to Henry Fitzroy, they had had their own share of family scandal when, in 1821, after the death at Apsley House of Georgiana, married to the Lord Worcester of the day, Worcester had then pursued Emily, Anne's daughter by Culling Smith. It was illegal to marry your dead wife's sister and great pressure was put on the couple to separate, but to no avail. The Duke was furious with Anne for allowing the marriage to go ahead, and never quite forgave her. But it was her only son Frederick who would cause her real heartache. In 1828 he was a successful soldier serving with the 80th Regiment in Malta. His twenty-sixth birthday fell on 1 June and Anne wrote him a congratulatory letter on unusual lime-green vellum. It is the kind of letter that any child away from home, whether in infancy or adulthood, would love to receive from their mother. There is gossip and words about the June landscape at their home being 'more beautiful than I ever saw it'. She compliments him on his popularity and achievements. 'I pray to God to grant you many many happy returns of a day which has proved such a happy one to us in giving you to us, my dearest child.' Frederick had met someone who had told him of his mother's experiences in revolutionary France – clearly the first time he had heard such stories. No doubt they were events that Anne was happy to forget, but she acknowledged that, 'It is true that I did *get the better* of the *Directory* which consisted of *Masons Bricklayers Butchers* etc – & thank God I had the means of conveying food & clothing to many of the Poor Sailors who really were starving. I will tell you all about it some happy Evening over our fireside when you return.'[35]

Tragically, Frederick never returned. 'At Malta, on the 19th June, in the 27th year of his age, Major Frederick Culling Smith, of the 80th regiment': the sombre news in *The Times* of his death must have devastated Anne. It is poignant to wonder whether Frederick ever received his birthday letter. Charles Greville, the well-known diarist of the day, suggested that Wellington was lacking in feeling over Anne's bereavement, but Greville was embittered by disapproval of the Duke's affair with his mother Charlotte. Emily Worcester, who eventually became the 7th Duchess of Beaufort, preserved some of the letters Wellington wrote to her mother, and though there is a tendency for them to focus on practicalities and arrangements, there is no hint of unfriendliness or hostility.

Anne's eldest daughter, Caroline, is something of a mystery. The only reference to her in books of the peerage, which record copious details of the men and marriages both of the Wellesleys and the Fitzroys, is her name, 'Anne Caroline Fitzroy', date of death 14 December 1835 and the letters 'du' – died unmarried. Priscilla Burghersh, Wellington's much loved niece, the daughter of William, Lord Maryborough, wrote to her uncle Arthur in 1824 asking him to try and procure a 'pension' for Caroline to enable her to marry. Surprisingly, and sometimes controversially, quite a number of Wellesleys were on the pension list, including the Dowager Lady Mornington and Anne Culling Smith and her husband Charles. Wellington declined, probably feeling that it would be inappropriate for another member of the family to benefit from the state. Was this the reason she never married? She remains one more female member of the family who has left no trace.

It fell to another of Wellington's large band of nieces and nephews to be the real thorn in his side during his premiership. 'Wicked William', as the family always refer to him, was William and Katherine Maryborough's only son. His dissolute, wild character was all too evident. His uncle Arthur agreed to have him on his Peninsular staff, but he was soon sent home and, with mounting debts, William alighted on the idea of marrying an heiress. Catherine Tylney-Long was the richest commoner of the day and had numerous suitors, including the Duke of Clarence, the future William IV. Wicked William, young and handsome, saw off his jowly royal rival and played his ace when he fought a duel after being accused by another suitor of being a gold-digger. On 14 March 1812 they married, the bride wearing a necklace worth £25,000, the bridegroom inauspiciously forgetting to procure a ring.

For the next few years William systematically went through his wife's fortune, acquiring Wanstead House, described as 'the noblest Palladian House in England', and throwing lavish parties, the like of which, it was said, had not been seen since the time of Cardinal Wolsey. In 1823, having had three children, the couple fled to Italy to escape his debtors. There Catherine suffered the further humiliation of witnessing William seduce the wife of a Guards officer, a Captain Bligh. With the lurid details (including the seduction on the slopes of Mount Vesuvius) supplied by indiscreet Italian servants, the Duke found himself acting as peacemaker. He had known Helena Bligh since she was a child and had entertained her parents just after Waterloo. But Helena's subsequent pregnancy and the birth of her illegitimate son put paid to the Duke's efforts. The crisis deepened when Catherine, beset by ill-health, had a fatal spasm after reading a letter from her estranged husband demanding the return of their three children. In accordance with Catherine's will, and to Wicked William's great fury, the Duke agreed to become the guardian of the three children. There then followed eighteen months of legal wrangling, with William desperate to get his hands on his children's moneys and using every threat to achieve this – particularly that of 'exposing' his whole family in the press, culminating in a mad, sinister boast that he would kill his uncle if his appeal against the guardianship failed. When he dropped the assassination threat William diverted his energies to a colourful pamphlet about his uncle which, when the Duke became Prime Minister in January 1828, was prominently displayed as part of *The Rambler's Magazine or Frolicsome Companion*. The Duke's moral rectitude was questioned by linking his name to a string of women. It subjected most of the Duke's nieces to the same innuendoes; no member of the Wellesley family was spared.

William then turned his attention to the sisters of his deceased wife, laying an affidavit against them which contained accusations even more lurid and libellous than those levelled against his uncle. He accused the Misses Long of 'gross improprieties, licentiousness and indelicacies of behaviour of which they have frequently been guilty' and of selecting a playfellow for his sons who was 'having intercourse with his aunt'; claimed that his daughter's governess and her sister were prostitutes, living with the Misses Long's uncle, who had had an incestuous relationship with the younger Miss Long; that all the rest of the Longs were drunken blasphemers; and finally that the two Misses Long were having a 'libidinous relationship' with each other. At this point the Duke, who, impressively, found time to deal with these taxing family matters while handling matters of state, broke off communication with his nephew, writing a remarkably measured letter which refers to the awkwardness of the position he had put him in. It ends with the words, 'It is not desirable that there should be much intercourse between us. Believe me ever yours most affectionately Wellington.'

After Wellington became Prime Minister, Kitty took over the guardianship of the children. Her dedication as a mother emerged again, and ensured that in the twilight of her life her troubled relationship with her husband enjoyed a calm, affectionate period. But her care could not prevent William from kidnapping his youngest son, James, whom he then used to try and entice the eldest (also William) away from Kitty. She was pelted by verbal taunts in letters which arrived regularly from father and son; they called young William 'an old *school girl*' (rather than an Old Etonian) and a 'Toad-Eater to the Duchess of Wellington'. Kitty, who loved nothing better than to heal a damaged child (particularly if it was a Wellesley), believed that you should not give up on somebody 'while you can discover as much Heart as you can rest the point of a pin on'. The younger William never really overcame the traumas of his early childhood, but Kitty's care and affection got through to him, and when the illness (probably cancer) that overtook her last years became serious, he secretly bought her a wheelchair so that she could dine downstairs.

Even this young tearaway was moved by the sight of his great-aunt circling the dining table – 'Don't you think she looks better for the drive?'

My grandfather selected most of the pictures that now hang in the dining room. The only non-family portrait, Lady Charlotte Greville, an early amour of the First Duke, hangs next to that of Mrs Paterson – latterly Marchioness Wellesley. Stratfield Saye, the house that some of Wellington's contemporaries derided as not being fit for the nation's hero, has portraits of eighteenth-, nineteenth-, twentieth- and twenty-first-century Wellesleys. The First Duke took pride in his honorary role as head of the family; he was protective of those members who showed him loyalty and affection and amazingly tolerant of those who did not. In spite of his complicated relationship with Richard, I think my great-great-great-grandfather would be content to have all his brothers near him. For me, though, there is one sad omission in the room. The 1st Duchess hated having her portrait painted, so the woman from whom we are all descended, the much-maligned Kitty, is absent from the feast.

ELEVEN

No.1 London

As Kitty's illness took hold of her small frame and it became clear she was dying, at last, and for the only time in their marriage, Arthur became a devoted husband. While a friend was paying him a visit at Apsley House, Arthur was called away to his wife's room. When he returned his face showed signs of emotion: 'It is a strange thing', he remarked to his friend, 'that two people can live together for half a lifetime and only understand one another at the very end.' Kitty had run her thin fingers up his sleeve to see whether he still wore an armlet she had given him many years before. 'She found it', said Arthur, 'as she would have found it any time these twenty years, had she cared to look for it.' Maybe he had worn the armlet all those years; but perhaps it was Kitty's first chance to discover this.

A few weeks before Kitty's death, Maria Edgeworth paid a call on her old friend and found her lying on a high white day-bed, in a room filled by some of her husband's trophies. 'Always little and delicate-looking,' Maria wrote in a letter to her mother, 'she now looked like a miniature figure of herself in waxwork.' As she approached Kitty, a small 'death-like white hand stretched itself out to me before I could reach the couch, and when I got there I could not speak.' When Maria's gaze drifted towards some of the treasures in the room, Kitty raised herself up on the bed and exclaimed weakly, 'All tributes to merit! There's the value; all pure, no corruption ever suspected even. Even of the Duke of Marlborough that could not be said so truly.' Maria was no admirer of Wellington – in particular she resented the way he had treated his wife – but she was touched by Kitty's youthful 'enthusiasm' for her 'hero'. 'There she lies fading away, still feeding, when she can feed on nothing else, on his glories, on the perfume of his incense.'

Kitty, used to doing everything for herself, wrote, 'I have been compared to the cat turned into a Lady, who bounced out of bed to catch a mouse that crossed the floor.' In early April it appeared that Kitty was improving a little, but Arthur knew that the end was not far off and wrote to Mrs Arbuthnot that he would 'not go out of town again'. Kitty's brother, Lord Longford, visited her on 23 April and reported that she had been in cheerful spirits.[2] She died at 10.30 on the morning of Sunday, 24 April, exactly two weeks after the twenty-fifth anniversary of their wedding in Dublin in 1806. 'This End was quite unexpected so soon,'[3] wrote Wellington to Mrs Arbuthnot. Many thought it a blessed release. 'So the poor little Duchess of Wellington is gone at last!' wrote Lady Wharncliffe. 'I am told she suffer'd but little, & was latterly so happy at the Duke's kindness & attention to her, that she said she never knew what happiness was before. Poor little soul, how well for her that she *did* die then! I am glad for his own sake, as well as hers, that he did his duty by her at last. I hear he sat up with her the last night.'[4] Douro, too, was by her bedside.

The original announcement in *The Times* stated that Kitty had died at Stratfield Saye and implied the Duke was in London. Two days later the paper published a correction: 'We are authorised to state that the decease of the late Duchess of Wellington did not occur at Strathfieldsay, but at Apsley-house; that during her protracted illness she was attended by the Duke with the most unremitting attention, and that her hand was in his when she expired.'[5] Arthur was well aware of public criticism that circulated about his treatment of his wife. His friend and biographer Gleig, writing later, summed up the way many of Wellington's friends viewed the marriage: 'There was no natural congeniality between them in tastes, habits, or pursuits; and, unfortunately for both, the Duchess, while she doted on her husband, never appears to have thought it necessary to adapt her own views of things to his.' However, Gleig conceded that Kitty's death 'touched' Wellington keenly; 'when she ceased to breathe, he evinced great emotion'.[6]

Kitty was the first member of the family to be buried in the small church in the park at Stratfield Saye. The Duke followed her coffin, and spent some time alone in the vault after it had been laid to rest there. I wonder what his thoughts were. Did he reflect back to the time when, while still in India, he had allowed Mrs Sparrow to persuade him that marriage to Kitty Pakenham was still a mutual love-match? Did he recall Kitty's plea to go to Ireland to see her before he made the commitment? 'I do not think it fair to engage you before you are quite positively certain that I am indeed the very woman you could choose for a companion, a friend for life', she had written to him. Did he accept that, in not heeding her words, he alone had been responsible for the disastrous union?

Perhaps if the Longfords had accepted Arthur's original proposal of marriage when he was still a young Captain, he and Kitty could have developed together; instead, when Wellesley came back from India, he was a changed man with different ambitions and priorities, while Kitty had remained within the safe haven of the Pakenhams' settled Irish life. At the time of her marriage Kitty was already a woman in her mid-thirties, and her character, unaffected by matrimony, was unable to adapt to a different beat of the drum.

Many historians have used the word 'tragic' about this marriage, and of course they mean for Wellington; but if the adjective is apposite, it should refer to Kitty. Had she married Lowry Cole, she might have had the domestic peace and happiness she craved. There is no doubt that her romance with Cole was serious. Cole was generous about the man who had wrested his love from him: 'I never served under any chief I like so much – Sir John Moore excepted – as Lord Wellington.'[7] Cole went on to become one of Wellington's most respected Generals, but was absent from his greatest victory. Shortly before Waterloo he had written to check whether he could stay home on leave without the risk that he might miss 'active operations'. Duly reassured, on 15 June 1815, the day before the campaign began, he married Lady Frances Harris, whom he had known for ten years. Kitty might have benefited from Lowry's softer heart but the man who took his place at Waterloo, the famous Sir Thomas Picton, fell in the heat of the battle.

How different would Arthur's life have been if he had not married Kitty? I wonder whether he would have become such a consummately successful soldier if, during the five long years he was away in the Peninsular War, he had been distracted by fond thoughts of a wife he had left at home. When he did return to England, I suspect it suited him to have an excuse to seek out the company of other women, often as confidantes and intellectual companions, occasionally, I assume, as lovers. But as Wellington's fame grew, so did the list of his alleged liaisons. The most notorious instance of an attempt to gain advantage from one of his sexual exploits was when the courtesan Harriet Wilson attempted to blackmail him before publishing her *Memoirs*. It is not certain that Wellington used the actual words 'Publish and be damned', but he was unfazed when the book appeared with fanciful details of their encounters. Although Wellington had a number of affairs, I do not believe that he would have wished to make a lifelong commitment to any of his lovers. Within him lurked the desire to be an independent spirit; he liked his own company and was content to draw on his inner resources. 'I like to walk alone', he had written to his brother Henry in 1801.[8]

I feel sad that Kitty did not spend her last days at Stratfield Saye, where she could have lain and gazed out of the window at the tranquillity of the park and the River Loddon flowing through it. In the end, though, I know that she would have been comforted to have her favourite view of all – the features of her beloved Arthur. And that her hand was in his when she took her last breath. Not long before her death, she wrote to a friend, 'With all my heart and soul I have loved him from the first time I knew him (I was not then fifteen) to the present hour.'[9]

At the time of Kitty's death, Apsley House was still relatively new. Completed in 1778, it was designed by Robert Adam for Lord Apsley, who became the 2nd Earl Bathurst. Originally red-brick, it stood on a site which was formerly home to an apple stall, near the toll-gate at the top of Knightsbridge (later this would earn it the name 'No. 1 London'). Richard Wellesley became the second owner when, recently back from India, he bought it in 1807 for £16,000. Less than ten years later, finding himself in straitened circumstances, Richard sold it on to his younger brother Arthur – for a tidy profit of £26,000. As with Stratfield Saye, Benjamin Dean Wyatt was involved with the purchase: 'It certainly is an excellent house, and in very good repair,' he wrote to the Duke. Though Arthur may have paid over the odds, it was a canny move to acquire Apsley House, with its convenient location for the palaces of Westminster and St James's. When Wellington became Commander-in-Chief of the Army after the death of the Duke of York in 1827, it was also close to his office in Horse Guards. At the beginning of the nineteenth century, however, the house was not well situated. 'Who will come especially so far out of their way as Apsley House is from every thing?' complained one fashionable young woman when she was invited to stay.[10]

When the Duke resolved not to build a Waterloo Palace on his Stratfield Saye estate, he diverted some of his energy and funds into making Apsley House a residence which was big enough both to entertain on a lavish scale, and to house his collection of paintings. The building of the Waterloo Gallery, ninety feet long and designed by Wyatt, coincided with the Duke's premiership; it was the only reason that for eighteen months Wellington resided at No. 10 Downing Street. As soon as the work was completed he moved back into Apsley House, which he found more comfortable and convenient. The Gallery became the setting for an annual dinner on the anniversary of the battle of Waterloo, when the

Duke gathered around him many of the officers who had fought alongside him on the battlefield.

The Duke suffered a shock common to many home-owners who undertake renovations. 'The Duke came here last night ... telling me that he had received the bills of his house & that Mr Wyatt had just exceeded his estimate three times over,' wrote Mrs Arbuthnot in her diary in February 1830. 'The sum was so enormous that he did not know how to pay it & had seriously been thinking of selling the house.' The Duke's rant continued with the injustices and ridicule of being 'cheated and imposed upon', that the whole thing was going to ruin his family and that he could not bear the sight of the house. She succeeded in calming him down, with some sound advice. In fact the attentive Mrs Arbuthnot was closely involved with much of the planning for the Gallery. But she failed to persuade the Duke not to hang the room with yellow silk, which she was not alone in thinking a disastrous choice that would do nothing to enhance the hanging of his collection of pictures in their gilt frames. (Wellington's stubbornness on the matter may have owed something to nostalgic memories of Peninsular wartime gaiety when, with his coterie of glamorous young ADCs, he danced round rooms hung in yellow satin.[11])

Many of the paintings in his collection were those captured at the battle of Vitoria, when they were discovered by Captain Wyndham in the baggage of Napoleon's brother Joseph, who was attempting to escape to France with loot from his spell as King of Spain. They were sent back to England for safe-keeping with Wellington's brother William, who was able to report that the consignment contained 'a most valuable collection of pictures'. One of the experts he called in to inspect them was the President of the Royal Academy, who pronounced that two of them – a Julio Romano and a Correggio – were 'worth fighting a battle for'. Wellington suspected that some of the paintings came from the Spanish royal collection and immediately asked his brother Henry, now Ambassador to Spain, to offer them back to the restored Spanish monarch, Ferdinand VII. The formal reply was not in fact received until after Waterloo, when Wellington's illustrious reputation may have stood him in good stead. 'His Majesty, touched by your delicacy, does not wish to deprive you of that which has come into your possession by means as just as they are honourable.' This gracious endorsement would ensure that neither the family, nor the British nation, would in future face any legitimate pressure to return the pictures to Spain.

The Duke had been showered with lavish gifts from home and abroad.

He kept most of these at Apsley House, preferring to leave Stratfield
Saye relatively unadorned by battle booty. Of all the works of art that
were given to him, none was more momentous than a huge statue of a
naked 'Napoleon as Mars' by Canova. Commissioned originally by the
Emperor himself, when he first saw it in 1811 he considered it 'trop
athlétique' and forbade public viewing. Eventually it was bought by the
British government and presented to the Duke by the Prince Regent.
The eleven-foot statue arrived at Apsley House in June 1817 and was
placed in the stairwell, where Maria Edgeworth saw it on a visit to Kitty.
'When he has a palace in the country I hope he will contrive a place large
enough for the great man who now looks shockingly ill placed.'[12] She
was probably right that Waterloo Palace was the sculpture's intended
destination; but since that palace was never built, the statue remains in
the stairwell to this day. Wellington's fans and fellow patriots liked the
story that when a visitor to the sculptor's studio saw the statue and
commented that the globe in Napoleon's hand looked too small, the artist
responded, 'Ah, but you see Napoleon's world did not include Great
Britain.'[13]

Apsley House bulged with the Duke's other treasures and trophies,
including a silver dinner service from Portugal, the silver-gilt 'Wellington
Shield' from London's bankers, and Field Marshal batons from six European armies. A note from Louis XVIII accompanied his offering of the
hundred-odd-piece Egyptian service: 'Do little gifts keep friendship
alive'. The Duke's favourite painting in his collection was Correggio's
'Agony in the Garden'. He was so attached to it that he carried the key
that opened it on his person and would not allow anyone else to clean it.
And opposite Apsley House in Hyde Park stood the colossal statue of
Hercules, made from guns captured at the battle of Salamanca, and
donated by the 'ladies of England'. Wellington was content with his
London residence, though he never referred to it by name even on letters
he simply wrote 'London'. I assume his reluctance owed something to
the fact that the house was named after a friend and contemporary, but
manners prevented him from renaming it. Perhaps it should later have
been called Wellesley House.

Kitty's death came a few months after the end of Wellington's premiership in November 1830. Fundamentally opposed to change, the Duke
had been unable to contemplate the much-needed reform of the parliamentary system, and his implacable position brought his government
down. Wellington's fall from grace did not save him from the fury of the

'mob' who, as Kitty's body was scarcely cold, stoned Apsley House. 'I think that my Servant John saved my House', Arthur wrote to Mrs Arbuthnot from Stratfield Saye, 'or the Lives of many of the Mob – possibly both – by firing as he did. They certainly intended to destroy the House, and did not care one Pin for the poor Duchess being dead in the House.'[14] One of the Duke's staunchest defenders was his coachman Turnham, an ex-Peninsular soldier, who was inclined, when visiting pubs, to take on the mob. Once, an unsuspecting individual called the Duke a knave. 'I had my two shillings' worth of brandy and water before me, scalding hot it was, 'cos I had the heartburn, and I slapped it in his face.'[15]

In the autumn of 1831 the Duke's mother, the indomitable Lady Mornington, died at the age of ninety. She was the most senior of all the Peeresses and could claim a unique link to the past, having, in 1761, taken part in the coronation of King George III and Queen Charlotte. The Duke was staying with Mrs Arbuthnot at the time, who as usual had an opinion about it, writing in her diary, 'If the people of England or, I might say, the King of England had proper feeling, the mother of the Duke wd have had some public honors at her funeral, but no notice was taken of it whatever.' Not for the first time, she was wrong. The King, as he had done for Kitty's funeral, offered his carriages, but the Duke declined, saying that his mother had expressed a desire for a private funeral.

For many years Anne Mornington had lived at Hampton Court in a grace-and-favour apartment where the Duke sometimes visited her; her son Gerald had been Chaplain there and her daughter Anne was also a resident for a while. One warm, sheltered corner of the palace was dubbed 'Purr Corner' by the Duke, for it was a favourite spot with the more elderly ladies who could be seen sitting in the sun and gossiping. Given Anne Mornington's early view of her younger son as 'food for powder and nothing else', the Duke's visits to his mother would have been made out of duty.

Lady Mornington had not been close to any of her children. Richard in particular may have privately evinced relief at her passing: at the time of her death he was still paying her an annual allowance. More controversially, she was also in receipt of a state pension of £600 a year [16] which had been referred to only months before in a leading article in *The Times*. 'Can it be believed', the newspaper asked, that 'the Duke of Wellington would allow his mother to be maintained, wholly, or in part, as *objects of charity*, by a distressed nation? Impossible. If they do suffer this, there is not a shopkeeper in London, who by honest industry has got a little before the world, that has not a nobler soul ... than [the] Duke.'[7] Since Lady Mornington's funeral notice made reference to her pension, it would appear that, as usual, the Duke was indifferent to public opinion.

Not long after the death of Lady Mornington, Apsley House once again became a target for the mob. This time, as he described in a letter to Mrs Arbuthnot, the Duke was in residence.

> They broke all the Windows on the lower floor looking towards Rotten Row, a great Number in my Room in which I was sitting, some in the Secretary's Room, and some in the Drawing Room above Stairs. All the blank windows fronting towards the Park and Piccadilly are likewise broken. They did not attempt to break in the Garden. We had Men with fire Arms ready to receive them.
>
> They are quiet now; but there is a considerable body in the Park about the Statue, and another attack is threatened for this evening. However, I do not fear it.
>
> My Garden and the Area between my Room & the Garden are filled with Stones. The Principal fire was directed upon my Room, which they reached easily from the Road.
>
> It is now five o'clock and beginning to rain a little; and I conclude that the Gentlemen will now go to their Dinners!'[8]

Out of concern for his paintings rather than for his own safety, and without bothering to mend the broken glass, the Duke ordered iron shutters for all the downstairs windows. 'I don't blame the men who broke my windows,' he commented. 'They only did what they were instigated to do, by others who ought to have known better. But if any one be disposed to grow giddy with popular applause, I think that a glance towards these iron shutters will soon sober him.'[9] It was these shutters, curiously, that earned him the epithet the 'Iron Duke'; they remained in place until a few years after his death, when his son, the 2nd Duke, removed them.

In spite of the fact that Arthur was not close to either his wife or his mother, their deaths within six months of each other must have affected him. But if he ever suffered from loneliness, he relieved it by keeping busy. He wrote to Mrs Arbuthnot, 'You are quite right. I don't care about being alone. I walk, play at tennis and ride and read and write all day, so that the Hours do not at all hang heavy upon my Hands.'[20] But the Duke's public unpopularity continued unabated and his friend John Croker noticed that he was staying away from London, 'where he can neither walk nor ride without being occasionally insulted, or, at least, hearing disagreeable expressions'. Croker went on, 'occasionally a black-guard hoots or says something gross, and this, I think, induces the Duke to prefer Strathfield Saye ... his spirits are very low.'[21]

As the passage of the Reform Bill continued on its way, the Duke received several warnings from well-wishers or mischief-makers. 'I think it my duty humbly to advise your Grace to be particularly careful of your person at this crisis ... you have everything to apprehend from the Radicals and the assassin,' wrote one. Meticulous in replying to every letter he received, his response to one of these doom-mongers was, 'The Duke has the firmest reliance that the law is able to protect him. The Duke knows of old that assassins and those who employ them are not the boldest of mankind.'[22]

One June morning, Wellington's nerves, and faith in the law, were soundly tested. 'Bonaparte for ever!' greeted him when he left an appointment at the Mint to ride back to Apsley House. Word had got around that he was there, and an angry crowd had gathered. Accompanied only by his groom, he set off on the three-mile ride home. In Fenchurch Street, where the mob tried to drag him from his horse, two Chelsea Pensioners came to his assistance; soon a man in a tilbury carriage drove behind him to provide some cover and two policemen joined the band of protectors. When the Duke spotted a loaded coal-cart he joked, 'Here's the Artillery coming up, we must look out.' When he reached Lincoln's Inn he tried to throw the crowd off but they stuck with him, their ferocity wavering slightly when another supporter, an apothecary, leapt on to the steps of Surgeons' Hall and shouted, 'Waterloo, Waterloo.' The ill-assorted procession reached Pall Mall, where members of gentlemen's clubs spotted the famous profile as he sat on his horse staring straight ahead – his '*visage de fer*' he called it. Women waved handkerchiefs from upstairs windows, offering sanctuary, but he knew he had to sit it out. 'If I were to get in, in what manner was I to get out again?' he later reflected. When finally he reached his own front door, still surrounded by the crowd, he turned to a man who had ridden the last leg of the journey with him: 'An odd day to choose. Good morning!' It was 18 June – the anniversary of the battle of Waterloo.

As so often, the Duke bounced back. Not only was Mrs Arbuthnot able to report to Lady Shelley that 'the Duke is uncommonly well and in high spirits, getting quite fat, and is better than I have ever seen him for years',[23] but by the start of the next year hostility began to recede. After a day out hunting at Stratfield Saye, when people had been 'kind' to him, 'opening gates, and that sort of thing', he observed, 'I'm getting up in the market.'[24]

Not long before Kitty's death, the Duke had complained to friends that his eldest son, without a 'by your leave', assumed that he could leave his horses to be fed and kept in his father's stables. Wellington felt ignored by his son: 'he is afraid of me and dislikes to be in the House with me'. (There was some truth in this: both boys – and their mother – would sometimes use the back stairs at Apsley House, to avoid bumping into the Duke.) Douro, in turn, believed that his father kept his mother short of money; he even offered Kitty part of his allowance when he came of age.

Douro's own first taste of politics had been under the prime ministerial mantle of his father: he was elected to Parliament for the seat of Aldeburgh in Suffolk in 1829, and stood as their MP until the end of 1831. But if it was tough to be the son of the Duke of Wellington in private life, it was even harder in public: Douro appears not once to have addressed the Commons. On a rare parliamentary duty, he served on a Select Committee appointed to inquire into the 'Laws and Regulations which restrict the sale of Beer by retail'. When he lost his seat through Reform reorganisation, he sought another one, choosing to seek selection in a borough which was, in effect, the backyard of his father's estate, the 'Northern Division for Hampshire'. However, when it became clear to Douro that he did not stand a chance, rather than risk further humiliation he stood down before the poll took place. But he did so without discussing it with his father, who was infuriated by his son's action since it prompted a wave of despondency in neighbouring constituencies.

When the reformed Parliament sat for the first time in January 1833, Wellington surveyed the new intake from the Peers' gallery and commented wryly, 'I never saw so many shocking bad hats in my life.'[25] One family consequence of the new government was that Richard was back in favour, in the first instance as Lord Steward of the Household and then in his old job as Lord Lieutenant of Ireland. Douro, however, was left with time on his hands, and his idleness was a constant irritation to his father; in fact both sons were the object of Arthur's wrath. 'My Determination is to have no quarrel with either of my Sons,' he wrote to Harriet Arbuthnot, 'but I am convinced that if ever I am employed again, in the Command of an Army for Instance, I shall be under the necessity of disgracing them both. What I mean is that they are both so inefficient and foolish that I can employ neither.'

Wellington's relationship with his sons continued to give him no comfort, and neither of the young men showed any signs of providing him with a daughter-in-law, let alone an heir. For a while after the death of Kitty, Charles acted as his father's Private Secretary, sharing the role with Algernon (Algy) Greville, brother of the diarist. Charles was living at Apsley House and every morning would go into his father's office to find out what his day's work was, but they had no personal communication. If there was a dinner party Charles could join his father, but they never dined alone. 'Why what would be the use of it? He would sit at table and never speak one word to me the whole time', he told Lord Hatherton, who was married to his cousin.[26] If the Duke went out to dine, the cook would take a holiday and neither he nor Douro would get anything to eat, even if they were unwell. Hatherton reported that the 'Duke is fond of his sons, but I never saw them riding or walking together in my life, and I believe they seldom converse'.

When the boys were briefly at Christ Church, Oxford, the Duke had been even more critical of the Warden's conduct than that of his sons, eventually removing them. So he was both surprised and delighted when he was elected to be Chancellor of Oxford University. The appointment ruffled the feathers of other public figures, not least his brother Richard. 'What will Lord Wellesley say?' he wrote mischievously to Harriet. At the grand installation in mid-June 1834 Wellington, robed in black and gold, was greeted by the students with uproarious applause and stamping feet:

> Till on that plain when last the eagle soared,
> War's mightier Master wielded Britain's sword,
> And the dark soul the world could scarce subdue,
> Bowed to thy Genius, *Chief of Waterloo*.[27]

When these words were recited by the poet who won the English Prize, the hall erupted. 'Such peals of shouts I never heard; such waving of hats, handkerchiefs, and caps, I never saw; such extravagant clapping and stamping, so that at last the air became clouded with dust,'[28] wrote his old friend Croker. Through all the ceremonies the Duke stared straight ahead, apparently unmoved; but one observant bystander noticed 'a certain tremulous motion in the mouth'. For someone who deeply regretted his lack of formal education and urged young men to go to university, the compliment paid him by his juniors meant a great deal to him. Ever the perfectionist, he had carefully rehearsed his Latin speech, but made two small mistakes, for which he afterwards castigated himself.

The installation was to be the last time that Mrs Arbuthnot would witness public adulation of her friend and hero. Two months later, the Duke was staying at Hatfield with the Salisburys when news arrived of her death. 'He threw himself in the greatest agitation on the sofa ... and the letter on the floor: and then rose and walked a few minutes almost sobbing about the room, after which he retired,'[29] wrote Fanny Salisbury in her journal. Many people thought that Harriet had been his mistress, but she was quite simply his best friend; Lady Salisbury, herself one of Wellington's closest confidantes, described her as 'a woman of strong understanding, considerable information and perfect discretion'.

Wellington went immediately to comfort Charles Arbuthnot – 'Gosh', as he was affectionately called – who wrote to the Duke shortly after: 'I believe I may say that you never had such a friend before & you will never have such a one again ... I am writing all my thoughts to you, for we were three, & you will understand – O my dear Duke you feel for me I know – you feel for yourself also.' This unusual triangle of friendship was reduced to the two men comforting each other. Wellington took the widower under his wing: Gosh became the Duke's trusted confidant and adviser, and lived for much of the time in his houses.

One of the consequences of the deaths of Kitty and Harriet was a belief (among some members of the female population) that Wellington needed the comfort of a woman's love and companionship. Aged sixty-five, he had become the most eligible bachelor in the land. Young girls set their caps at him. One put it about that she had rejected a proposal from him; another, whose singing voice he greatly admired, pursued him relentlessly for seven years. It is likely that the Duke enjoyed some aspects of his new-found freedom and allure – after all, he had not enjoyed much of it as a successful young man, since he had married Kitty within months of his return from India. But in affairs of the heart Wellington could be immature, and this is nowhere more evident than in a bizarre liaison that developed within weeks of Harriet's death.

Miss Anna Maria Jenkins was a young orphan and religious fanatic who first wrote to the Duke at the beginning of 1834. Encouraged when he replied immediately, she then called at Apsley House on the third anniversary of Kitty's death, leaving a marked bible: 'Except a man be born again ... he cannot enter into the Kingdom of God'. The Duke declined to respond. However, three weeks after Harriet's death he wrote to her – as 'Mrs Jenkins'. Her reply pointed out that she was single, and suggested that he paid her a visit. It was the start of an entanglement which, when the details emerged many years later, baffled historians and the Wellesley family alike; the 3rd Duke thought the letters were forgeries. In all, Wellington was to write nearly 400 letters to Anna Maria Jenkins over a period of seventeen years.

I too find my ancestor's behaviour bewildering, particularly when I read Anna Maria's account of their first meeting: 'HE [God] must have influenced the Duke of Wellington to love me above every other lady upon earth from the first moment he beheld me,' she wrote. She went on to describe how the Duke seemed to be without the power of speech until 'he was compelled to exclaim: "O, *how* I *love* you! how I *love* you!" repeating the same over and over and over again with increasing energy.'[30] When next they met, Anna Maria claimed that Wellington declared, 'This must be for life!'. Did he really intend to make her his wife? It seems improbable. By all accounts she was a beautiful girl who, having saved the soul of a convicted murderer the year before, wanted to bring this great prize – a national hero – closer to God and perhaps, as a by-product, gain herself a coronet. Even allowing for some exaggeration in Anna Maria's account, whether his goal was marriage or seduction, my great-great-great-grandfather undoubtedly pursued her. She claimed that she had never heard of the battle of Waterloo, and his title meant nothing to her. He was a religious man, and her designs on his soul may have hit their mark. He was susceptible to flattery, lonely and infatuated by her; these feelings did not last long, but he continued to write to her until a year before he died.

It was fortunate that soon after the Duke first met Miss Jenkins, public duty rescued him from having too much time on his hands. The Whig government under whose rule Reform had come to Westminster was dismissed by William IV, who then summoned Wellington. The Duke declined to form a government, but agreed to act as caretaker while Robert Peel, who was in Rome, returned to England. 'His Highness the Dictator', wrote Earl Grey disparagingly, 'is concentrating in himself all the power of the State, in a manner neither constitutional nor legal.' All these accusations were true: Parliament was not sitting, but for three weeks Wellington held all the senior offices of state with the exception of the Chancellorship. 'I believe that the business was never done better!'[31] he later boasted. He took his role seriously and, with shades of military manoeuvring, moved round Whitehall, making sure that the wheels of government kept turning. Some were not pleased, complaining of 'the unceremonious and somewhat discourteous mode in which without pre-vious notice he entered the vacant offices, taking actual possession'. Others could see the funny side: 'At least we have a united government', joked one commentator.[32] When Peel arrived home, Wellington handed back the offices of state, graciously agreeing to stay on as Foreign Secretary.

Wellington's social activity continued to belie his years. He threw balls and dinners in London, and entertained at Stratfield Saye and Walmer Castle, his official residence as Warden of the Cinque Ports, an office he had held since 1829. He was in a mischievous mood in the autumn of 1835, when he invited his radical neighbour, Sir John Cope, to stay at Stratfield Saye at the same time as Queen Adelaide, and amused himself by making him kiss the Queen's hand. Sir John, for his part, was unimpressed by the food on offer: 'The very worst turtle soup I ever tasted, and the Punch as bad'.[33]

After the death of Harriet Arbuthnot the Duke looked more to Fanny Salisbury for some of his political and social gossip. He gave her an edited version of the Miss Jenkins affair; it is not clear whether Fanny in turn told him that Douro had made a declaration of love to her.[34] If she did, I imagine that it can only have served to irritate the Duke even more about the behaviour of his eldest son; and perhaps it was this which prompted Douro to make another long trip abroad. But after nine months of travelling, he suddenly turned up at Apsley House in the middle of June 1836, and without having written a single letter to his father. The first the Duke knew of his presence was when, after giving the list of guests for dinner that evening, the servant added, 'and Lord Douro, your Grace'.

The Salisburys were dining there that evening, and Fanny wrote in her diary: 'The Duke is very much afraid he has formed some connection abroad which may prevent his marrying, for which the Duke is very anxious.'[35] In fact, so anxious was he that some time that year he wrote a letter to Douro, pointing out to him his obligation to marry and provide heirs. Given the lack of harmony and accord in their relationship, it seems likely that Douro was all too sensitive to this pressure and that it had contributed to his inability to procure a bride for himself. At one point he had his eye on the daughter of Lord de Rothesay, Louisa Stuart, and he asked a friend to give an opinion, not of her beauty, but of the 'sense and sensibility of the young lady'. Douro was worried that Louisa was lacking in both heart and head, and that her mother was a 'catamaran'.[36] 'Lady Betty', however, was quite clear what she wanted for her daughter – '*la madre* [the mother] wants rank, especially Lord Douro.'[37]

Charles, too, was not spared his father's views on his responsibility to get married: Fanny Salisbury wrote that the Duke had 'made him the very handsome offer of enabling him to marry whom he chose'. The journal does not reveal the extent of this inducement, but clearly it was not enough; it would be another eight years before Charles walked down the aisle. Both boys were nearing their thirties; more pertinently, Wellington was nearing the end of his seventh decade.

The beginning of 1837 found the Duke at Stratfield Saye, having managed to avoid the influenza epidemic. He was fit and strong enough to hunt; on one occasion when Croker was staying with him he rode for fifty miles.[38] Never deterred by bad weather, if the Duke drove to the meet, he would take the reins of his curricle himself. He seemed indefatigable; when Fanny Salisbury told him that she thought he got too little rest, he replied 'Whether a man has a little more sleep or a little less, what does it signify?'[39] In the Peninsular War he could take a nap in the lull of a battle, and in peacetime his view was that 'If it's time to turn over, it's time to get up'. When the weather was very cold he had a habit of sleeping with his head under the bedclothes. One early morning at Apsley House, when a housemaid was in his room lighting the fire, she spotted the supine figure shrouded in bedclothes and assumed he was ill. The rumour shot around Whitehall, and Ministers started turning up to inquire after his health.[40]

By the middle of 1837 it was William IV's health that was causing concern. To the King's great relief he managed to live long enough to see his successor, Princess Victoria, come of age on 24 May; he could not bear the idea of her mother, the Duchess of Kent, being Regent. By 18 June the King was still hanging on – 'Only let me live through this glorious day,' he said to his physicians. The Duke had wanted to put off the annual Waterloo dinner but the Sovereign insisted he went ahead. According to one guest, it was a 'gloomy affair' and 'The Duke was much affected when he drank the King's health'. Wellington left Apsley House early and went to Windsor to present his rent flag for Stratfield Saye; when the tricolour was brought to him, the King buried his face in it. Two days later he died.

The young Queen did not at first show the same adulation to the Duke as her predecessor, preferring to court the Whig Prime Minister, Lord Melbourne. Wellington was invited to her first formal banquet, but merely because he was, as his place-card said, Chancellor of Oxford. 'I keep the card as a real curiosity,' wrote the Duke to Arbuthnot the day after. But from the start of Victoria's reign, the Duke had been impressed by her, commenting after a Privy Council meeting that 'if she had been his own daughter he could not have desired to see her perform her part better'.[41]

At the Queen's coronation on 28 June 1838, when Wellington bent to pay formal homage to his Sovereign, there was 'a great shout and clapping of hands'. Likely the young Queen did not notice; she was too distracted by the fact that few of the people taking part, with the notable exceptions of the Duke and the Archbishop of Canterbury, knew what they were meant to be doing. But Lady Salisbury, sitting in the nave, saw that Lord Melbourne 'coloured, and grew pale again'. The ceremony over, as the procession left the Abbey once again applause erupted for the Duke, who 'looked back to see if the Queen was coming, with an air of vexation, as if to say, "This is too much; this belongs of right to her"'.[42] That night the whole country celebrated. 'A ball was going on at Apsley House, which was beautifully illuminated', remembered one of Wellington's great-nieces many years later. 'The windows were open and the dancing visible while the music was inaudible, which produced a strange effect on our young minds.'[43] It was the first of many times through Victoria's long life that the house would be lit up to celebrate great events of her reign.

'Everybody says the Duke of Wellington is broken down and will soon go,'[44] wrote one of Arthur's Peninsular Generals, William Napier, during that summer. Others, such as Charles Greville, noticed that old age was beginning to take hold of the Duke: 'He is much deafer than he was, he is whiter, his head is bent, his shoulders are raised and there are muscular twitches in his face.'[45] Wellington himself complained of the 'rheumatism in my shoulders and neck'; he was more bothered about the ailment than a French libel which Croker had drawn to his attention. 'I consider such an affair not worth the trouble of writing even this note,' he wrote back. 'I have been abused, vilified, slandered since I was a boy.'[46]

In February 1839 the Duke at last had a piece of news which gladdened his heart: Douro announced his engagement. Lady Elizabeth Hay – Bessy – was the eighteen-year-old daughter of the Marquess of Tweeddale, an old friend who had served under Wellington in the Peninsular campaign and, perhaps more crucially, been loyally supportive through all his political confrontations, including the battle over Catholic Emancipation. The Duke wrote to Tweeddale: 'No connection which Douro could form could be more agreeable to me. We have for many years been connected in Service; and by friendly Relations; and I entertain no doubt that the closer connection about to be formed between our families will tend to our mutual satisfaction. You will find me disposed to make every arrangement which may be desirable for the Comfort Happiness and Honor of Lady Elizabeth.'[47]

The engagement of his eldest son prompted the Duke to make formal arrangements to secure the future of his art collection. A Bill came before Parliament which would ensure that 'certain most valuable and costly ornaments and other presents which had been made to him by the different potentates of Europe' would be preserved in the family for ever as heirlooms. Wellington also showered his future daughter-in-law with gifts. 'The trousseau of the bride elect of the Marquis of Douro – the Lady Elizabeth Hay – is likely to be one of the most splendid that has added value to the dowry of modern belles', reported an American magazine. 'We hear that his Grace the Duke of Wellington, having found in his cabinets quantities of diamonds which he had forgotten or never thought of till now, has declared that the bride shall have them all.'[48]

Douro, like his father susceptible to the charms of the female sex, would certainly have been struck by Bessy's beauty; but she had not yet been presented at court, so it is possible that there was some element of 'arrangement' in the betrothal. If so, Douro seemed perfectly content with his side of the bargain, writing to his intended a few weeks before the wedding: 'Dearest Bessy, I fear I can write you nothing more original than I am most unhappy at your absence ... you have left everything in London miserable; there never was a worse day; nobody can enjoy it but ducks for the wet, and pigs for the dirt; I have caught your cold too; indeed I don't see how I could have escaped, that is if colds are contagious.' He goes on to give her advice as to how to deal with her new father-in-law.

> Pray do not neglect to write to the Field Marshal on Sunday at farthest; He will like much to hear shortly from you often, for he likes to be in everyone's confidence and to have his advice asked in things which are *not* his business. Consult him about your difficulties of the breakfast; tell him that you lay your indisposition to flurry and anxiety, and that his kindness to you has been a great support to you; or something of that kind in your own short unaffected style.[49]

He ends the letter: 'Believe me to be, dearest love, yours most affectionately Douro.'

The Duke relished his forthcoming role. 'I met the Duke at Lady Peel's party,' wrote his friend Lord Stanhope, who chronicled many of his encounters and conversations with Wellington, 'he looked very well indeed. Talking to Lady Shelley on his son's marriage, I heard him observe on his new part of *un beaupère*, and add with a laugh, the French expression, *Le beaupère là n'est pas beau.*'[50]

The wedding took place at St George's, Hanover Square, on Thursday, 18 April. Predictably, the presence of the Duke produced a large crowd of onlookers but there were loud cheers for the bride too. The congregation included a full complement of Wellesleys: Gerald, since 1827 Prebend of Durham, performed the ceremony and the Duke and his three other brothers, Richard, William and Henry, were all witnesses, their signatures in the marriage register surviving to this day. Douro's voice rang out clearly with his marriage vows, and everyone in the church could just catch the timid 'I will' from the 'youthful and beautiful' bride. The Tweeddale house in Belgrave Square hosted the wedding breakfast, the centrepiece for which was a wedding cake weighing a hundred pounds, garlanded with alternating armorial bearings of the two families, and bunches of roses, shamrocks and thistles. Bessy may have found the whole experience overwhelming, for one guest commented that, at the breakfast, she was 'indisposed, and could not appear'. However, it was widely reported that the Duke was in 'excellent health and spirits'. At last Douro had done something which met with his father's approval.

When, in January 1853, after the death of the First Duke, Apsley House was briefly opened to the public, the world was able to see in the Duke's small bedroom two crayon heads of Lady Douro by John Hayter. They 'hung', wrote Richard Ford, 'in such a position that his last look might fall, and his first might light, on the noble and graceful features betokened by so many busts and pictures – the best ornaments, in his eyes, of Apsley House'.[51] Ford went on to describe 'the Lion's Den' – 'it bears the look of the well garnished comfortable library of a man of business'. He noted that everything seemed to be designed to ensure quiet and – one of the Duke's obsessions – 'exclude draughts'. Ford's first impression was of confusion 'conveyed by the multitudinous objects heaped on tables and sofas, but soon order and method is evident in the apparent chaos'. No one had ever been allowed to move anything – the Duke had his own system.

As at Stratfield Saye, the 2nd Duke left most of Apsley House as it had been when his father was alive – even, for several years, the iron shutters. But he did remove the boards which had been placed on the front railings to prevent curious onlookers peering through – 'I don't think a crowd is ever likely to assemble to see me get on to my horse,' he said. Bessy, thirty-two at the time of her father-in-law's death, stepped easily into her role of hostess at Apsley House. The Duchess, first as one of her Ladies-in-Waiting, and then two terms as Mistress of the Robes, was close to Queen Victoria. In 1857, while her husband was still Master of the Horse, on the occasion of the Queen's birthday the house was illuminated by a gas-lit display which spelt out the words 'Long Live the Queen.' In June 1860 the Queen and Prince Albert attended a concert at the house where, on arrival, they were met at the portico. 'After saluting the Duchess, the Queen received from the noble host a bouquet of choice flowers', reported *The Times*. When, three years later, the Prince of Wales married Princess Alexandra of Denmark, 'The front of Apsley-house was almost covered by a large and brilliant device in gas, representing the Prince of Wales's plume between two letters "A.," surrounded with wreaths of laurel, while underneath was a broad band, or riband, of jets, enclosing the legend, "Long may they live"'.[52]

Occasionally, the 2nd Duke lent the house or its garden for a cause or event that met with his approval. In the summer of 1864 two well-known Victorian actors, Mr and Mrs Alfred Wigan, gave a series of readings, including scenes from *The School for Scandal* and *Hamlet*, and poems by Thomas Hood. Shortly after the Wigans' readings, the Duchess threw a 'close of the season' party, where the 'gallery and saloons wore their accustomed aspect of splendid festivity', but the special attraction of the evening was an 'al fresco' exhibition of sculptures. It seems the Duke had an interest in lighting and pyrotechnics: an account of the evening described the illumination of the works of art. 'The colours applied were vivid shades of red, amber, blue, green, and white, the ever-changing and floating beams of coloured light on the various groups producing a most charming effect.' [53]

The garden was put to more practical use when, in 1871, just after the end of the Franco-Prussian War, the Duke allowed a French inventor to exhibit a 'house which may be packed and carried in a common country cart, and set up by two persons in less than half an hour'. The constructions were intended for use by 'French peasants and poorer class of citizens', whose homes had been destroyed during the war. Despite his generous gestures to those wishing to take advantage of the prestige his London residence could offer, the Duke was fussily protective of the house. A friend who wanted a tour of the mansion received from the Duke a 'pass' for the visit: 'Admit Mr Hare to see Apsley House on any day *on which the street outside is dry*'. Hare was careful to select a fine day and took the extra precaution of arriving in a cab. However, the servant who admitted him, as Hare recorded in his journal, laughed as he produced a pair of huge slippers to go over his boots. The servant informed him that, 'His Grace left these himself, and desired you should wear them when you came.' Hare commented in his journal, 'Yet the floors of Apsley House are not even polished.'[54]

After the Duchess stood down as Mistress of the Robes in 1880, and the 2nd Duke's health deteriorated, the house fell quiet. It remained so when his nephew Henry succeeded, but it was during his residency that the 3rd Duchess, Evelyn, did her work on cataloguing the pictures. In her introduction to the two volumes, she revealed a challenge that confronted her in this task: 'The late Duke of Wellington [2nd Duke] ... exasperated at being told that experts, admitted to view the gallery, frequently attributed pictures labelled with the names of certain artists to other painters, had all the labels and numbers removed, saying, with characteristic humour, "Hang it, let them choose for themselves." The chaos thus produced materially added to the difficulties of identifying the pictures for the purposes of this work.' When Henry died in 1900, the 4th Duke and Duchess resumed entertaining on a large scale. As *The Times* announced in July 1901, 'After the lapse of a quarter of a century, the famous reception rooms of Apsley-house, Piccadilly, were yesterday afternoon once more thrown open, the occasion being a garden-party given by the Duchess of Wellington.'

The major social event at Apsley House during the tenure of the 4th Duke was a ball, given in the summer of 1908, attended by King Edward VII and Queen Alexandra and other members of the Royal Family. Over 700 invitations were sent out. Of the royal party, none had a closer connection to the Wellingtons than Prince Arthur, Duke of Connaught, said to be Queen Victoria's favourite son, who was born on 1 May 1850, and so shared a birthday with his godfather, the First Duke, after whom he was named. A famous picture by Winterhalter in the Royal Collection depicts the Prince as a one-year-old baby receiving a gift from his famous godfather on his first birthday. On another occasion the Queen sent her small son over to Apsley House where, hand in hand with the Duke, he was given a tour of the house. In 1908, over half a century later, very little had changed, particularly in the Waterloo Gallery, where at eleven o'clock that evening the King led off the quadrille with the Duchess of Wellington, and the Queen with the Duke. The garden was lit with Chinese lanterns, the house filled with roses and sweetpeas, and the sideboards in the dining room displayed three equestrian statuettes of figures whose ghosts hung over the evening – Queen Victoria, the Great Duke and Napoleon.

A framed print showing the start of the state quadrille hangs in the downstairs 'gents' in the private apartments of Apsley House. My grandfather, then a young man of twenty-two, can be seen in the back-ground; in later life he delighted in pointing himself out to his descendants – 'I am probably the last survivor of everyone at the party', he would tell us. The ball, attended by all his siblings, Evelyn, Charlie, Dick, George and Eileen, excited some interest on the other side of the Atlantic, not merely because of the grandeur of the occasion but also because, in the words of *The New York Times*, 'it proved the Waterloo of a certain well-known American woman' who some said had been snubbed by the Duchess of Wellington. One lady who was invited had cause, later, to regret the invitation: 'Mrs Marshall Roberts's Collarette Disappears at Duchess's Supper Table'. She had been careless enough to remove the jewellery and, as she later reported to the police, 'as far as I can recollect, put it by my plate'.

In 1912 the 4th Duke discovered in the cellars of Apsley House thirty-seven boxes, all sealed with the royal arms. It turned out that they contained a huge number of royal papers and correspondence. When George IV died the First Duke, as his executor, decided that he should guard the privacy of the King's reputation by removing all the papers and storing them at Apsley House. Wellington had been well aware of the King's clandestine marriage to Mrs Fitzherbert and was not surprised when, shortly after the monarch died, he spotted her miniature, half-concealed by a nightshirt, on a black ribbon round the King's neck. It explained why the King had left instructions that he should be buried undisturbed. Three years later Wellington would enact his last duty to George IV when, with his own hands, he burnt all Mrs Fitzherbert's letters from her 'husband' in the grate of her fireplace. But when Wellington's grandson unearthed the royal papers in the bowels of Apsley House, they had not been touched since 1830 and the 4th Duke deliberated for some time as to whether he should return them to the Royal Family, uncertain as to whether the First Duke would have approved. I wonder if my grandfather Gerald, with his burgeoning interest in his ancestor, was consulted; if so, I suspect he would have advised that the Royal Archive was the best place for them. They were duly returned.

When Valerian and his sister went to stay for a few months at Apsley House with their grandparents, after the break-up of Gerry and Dottie's marriage, the house left a deep impression on my father. 'I remember it extremely well because it was incredibly frightening and dark,' he recalls 'We had gas lights and candles in the rooms. We lived on the top floor, and I remember getting into the most appalling trouble when I peered over the balcony and jumped out on my grandmother, giving her the most awful fright as she came round the corner!' But his favourite game of all was sliding down the banisters. 'I had to be very careful at the end because Napoleon is holding his hand out with Victory on it and if you weren't very careful you'd collide with her as you reached the bottom of the stairwell!' Of course, to a very small boy, standing at the feet of the famous Canova statue and peering up under the fig-leaf was another thrill. 'It's very rude, isn't it', he would exclaim delightedly.

Valerian's grandparents were not remote figures – he was close to both – though, as was the custom of the day, he and his sister would often see them only at tea-time, when they were taken by their nanny down to the Piccadilly drawing room for cakes and stories and games. 'We didn't have breakfast with them, but nor did we with my parents', he remembers. 'We used to have lunch with my grandparents sometimes, in the Portico Room. There was a lift which brought the food up from the kitchens, through a central well of the house, and a footman then carried it to the table.'

The footmen were 'all very smart', my father remembers. 'They had chocolate-coloured coats, red waistcoats, and trousers with a red stripe down the side'. The most memorable of all his grandfather's staff, however, was the night-watchman. 'He was called Mr Donovan and he sat in a large oval-shaped leather chair at the front door. He was from the Irish Guards and had been awarded a MM for bravery in the First World War. He was a huge man with a kiss-curl that hung down his forehead.' The 4th Duke was continuing a practice of the First Duke to favour the employment of ex-soldiers. One visitor to Apsley House in 1842 described how, after he had rung the bell, the gates were rolled back by 'a fine, hale old soldier, whom his Grace had promoted to the situation of porter'. The First Duke was not always so fortunate with his watchmen; when he was Prime Minister, he had in his employ one Charles Smith, described as 'a fat made man, with large black whiskers, dressed in a fustian jacket, with sleeves', whose duty it was to watch the back of Apsley House; but it emerged that he would regularly 'climb over the palings and run off to halls and other places, leaving the premises unguarded'.[55] He was caught out when he was a witness to an incident that occurred at a dance held at one of the 'places'.

My aunt Eliza was only a toddler when she and Valerian lived at Apsley House, and her memories are much mistier than my father's, but they both remember that in the nursery there was a cabinet filled with toy soldiers which they longed to play with, but which their grandfather never allowed. Perhaps they had been a gift from his own grandfather and were therefore, symbolically, more precious than other objects of far greater value in the house.

After the death, in June 1927, of the 4th Duchess, Apsley House seems to have retired once more into obscurity. By now, like Stratfield Saye, the house was in dire need of renovation and its future was the subject of much discussion in the family. Morny had once joked that, with careful reconstruction, Apsley House might make a 'jolly good restaurant, with a roof garden overlooking the Park and a cocktail bar on each floor'. When Morny himself became Duke and was recruiting in 1942 for the Commandos, one of his interviewees was surprised when, after receiving orders to attend a meeting in a house in Piccadilly, he found himself being interviewed by the Duke of Wellington on the second floor of Apsley House.[56]

During the Second World War, because of its central location, Apsley House was particularly vulnerable and was damaged in several bombing raids. The real concern was for the collection, rather than the building, as recounted by James Lees-Milne in his diaries:

> The Queen rang up the duchess a year ago [1942] to ask if it were true that the treasures in Apsley House had not been evacuated. The duchess admitted that it was true. 'Well then, I am coming round at 11 with a van to take them to Frogmore', the Queen said. And punctually she arrived with the King. With pencil and paper she made lists and decided what should be moved and what left behind. 'You mustn't be sentimental, Duchess. Only the valuable pictures can go,' she said.[57]

The Queen Mother confirmed this to my father at a Wellesley family party, when they were walking through the Waterloo Gallery. 'She remembered that the house had already suffered some damage from bombing and apparently all the pictures had been taken off the walls and were lying on the floor. She was very much aware that all the male members of the family were fighting abroad. It was a marvellous thing to have done.'

A cousin of my father's, Arthur James, who was in the Grenadier Guards, was so worried about the risk of incendiary bombs hitting the house that he organised a picket of Guardsmen to be stationed on the roof. After one bombing raid the housekeeper at Apsley House, Mrs Dowe, who had been the 4th Duchess's lady's-maid, was said to have been preoccupied about one particular detail of damage. 'Arthur told me', says my father, 'that Mrs Dowe was most upset that the fig-leaf had fallen off Canova's statue of Napoleon, and insisted it was repaired immediately!'

The decision to give Apsley House to the nation was made during the war, when Gerry and Valerian met in Cairo. 'My father knew that he could not afford to spend the money that would be needed to restore it, and he felt the responsibility of looking after the valuable collection was too great. He wanted my agreement in principle to donate it to the nation and of course I agreed.'

The offer of Apsley House, with most of its collection, was formally made at the end of 1944. But it was no foregone conclusion that the nation would receive the gift; it was announced that 'the Cabinet will decide whether to accept the offer'. Some quarters of the press described the gesture as 'generous and imaginative', but others were less complimentary, calling the financial commitment that would be required from the public purse 'a most terrible waste of money', and suggesting that my grandfather would make 'a very good bargain out of an impoverished country'.[58] The 'bargain' allowed the family to live in part of the house. In the end, the Wellington Museum Bill was passed in 1947, but my grandfather felt aggrieved for the rest of his life that the gift was the subject of such criticism. 'It is demonstrably untrue that I had made a good bargain', he claimed. 'For the money for which I might have sold the chattels and the freehold, I might have had a much better residence than I got in Apsley House – and a good bit over.'[59]

Nowadays, when the nation is regularly expected to turn out its pockets to prevent a single work of art from leaving the country, it may seem graceless to question the integrity of a proposal which handed over such a priceless possession including, among other great treasures, four paintings by Velásquez. But Attlee's post-war Britain was still living in a climate of austerity, with rationing and a shortage of housing. To many families suffering both the loss of loved ones and social deprivation, an issue which concerned the collection of a long-dead military hero did not seem high on the list of priorities. But unquestionably my grandfather's action saved the collection, which might otherwise have been scattered to museums worldwide. After extensive renovation the Wellington Museum opened to the public in 1952. Apsley House, or No. 1 London as many taxi drivers still refer to it, sits in the very heart of London. Every visitor to the capital will be likely to pass it at some point, but strangely it is overlooked by many.

My grandfather may even have preserved Apsley House itself; had it still been considered that 'gloomy' private mansion, as described in some earlier accounts, it might have been pulled down along with other houses in Hamilton Place and Piccadilly, to make way for the new traffic scheme at Hyde Park Corner in 1962. The problems of traffic in the area had long been the subject of discussion: in a debate in the House of Lords in March 1926 one Peer had commented, 'They might buy and remove Apsley House, and go out that way into Piccadilly. Or if they were sufficiently Philistine, they might entirely alter or re-model the present arches at Hyde Park Corner.'[60]

During the period of transition before it ceased to be a private house, my grandfather, on 9 July 1947, gave a coming-out dance for Fay James, the daughter of his close friend Lady Serena James – Mitey. It turned out to be an historic evening. Fay's sister Ursula, who married Lord Westbury in that year, remembers the evening well. 'The papers were full of rumours that Princess Elizabeth was about to get engaged to Philip Mountbatten,' Urusla told me. 'The Princess was coming to the party, and my mother rang the Palace to see if she should invite Mountbatten. She was told it wasn't official until midnight. There was a dinner at the Dorchester beforehand, and we were mobbed by the press when we left to go to Apsley House for the dance.' A few months later, at the wedding on 20 November, my father rode as an escort to one of the royal carriages. It was the first time since before the war that the regiment had donned ceremonial dress; for many, including my father, it was the first experience of wearing the elaborate uniform. 'I remember my helmet kept slipping back and when we went under Admiralty Arch I quickly passed my sword to my left hand, and adjusted the chin strap with my right. I emerged the other side without anyone noticing.'

Apsley House has had a bird's-eye view of many public processions, none more solemn and moving than the First Duke's funeral on 18 November 1852. One of my father's early memories is watching, as a five-year-old, the Victory Parade after the First World War, in which 150,000 servicemen took part. The house was emblazoned with a loyal 'Long Live the King', and the sight and sound of marching men, sun glinting on highly polished swords and breastplates, and the clatter of the cavalry as the horses' hooves struck the tarmac, was the most exciting thing he had yet experienced. For the Victory Parade after the Second World War, by then Major the Marquess of Douro, he commanded the contingent of The Blues, who as part of the Household Cavalry were at the head of the procession, just behind the guns.

My father was once again on ceremonial duty for the funeral of King George VI on 15 February 1952, having stood guard at the lying-in-state for twenty-two periods – 'more than anyone else', he remembers. 'Standing with your head bowed was very disorientating – you could only see people's feet.' The day of the funeral itself was bitterly cold, and The Blues were responsible for escorting the coffin from Westminster Hall to Paddington Station, where a train carried it to the funeral at Windsor. 'It was extremely difficult to adjust the pace of your horse to a slow march. When we got to Paddington and I had to give the order to salute as the train pulled out, my hands were so cold I could hardly move my sword. We rode back to the barracks as fast as we could go, and Maxted, my old friend and Corporal-of-Horse, invited me to the NCO's mess for a drink. He ordered eight whiskies, "four for us and four to warm our boots!", he said.'

At the coronation of the Queen in June 1953, when my grandfather was one of four Knights of the Garter holding up the canopy, my father was again involved in the royal procession, as the Gold Staff Officer. Meanwhile, my mother stood with other members of the family on the portico of Apsley House, with her two small sons, Charles and Richard, and me (nearly two) by her side. I have no memory of that momentous occasion, but fifty years later, at the Queen's Golden Jubilee celebrations, my parents and I climbed onto the roof of Apsley House to watch the fireworks exploding over Buckingham Palace.

Since my father became Duke in 1972, Apsley House has been my parents' London base, occupying rooms on the ground floor that were the private apartment of the First Duke. My father sleeps in the Duke's narrow Empire-style bed, which is rumoured to have once belonged to Napoleon. Unlike his great-great-grandfather, he is a restless sleeper and often prefers to return to Hampshire, where the tranquillity of the countryside is more likely to induce slumber than the roar of London traffic as it circles round the house. The room where Kitty spent her last days, surrounded by the trophies of her hero, is used by my parents as their drawing room. I read Kitty's melancholy Peninsular diaries in the library, which in the First Duke's day was his office and still holds his collection of books. Perhaps, somewhere on the shelves, the five-volume novel *Love at First Sight*, which accompanied the Duke on his return journey from India, hides among the more erudite volumes that filled his trunk on the way out, but if so, I looked in vain.

In the First Duke's time there were stables in the basement of Apsley House; towards the end of his life this meant that he did not have to suffer the indignity of the public watching him as he heaved himself on to his horse. When my father was Deputy Colonel of The Blues and Royals he too would regularly, when he was staying in London, go riding in the park with young officers from the regiment's Knightsbridge

Barracks. Occasionally his horse, called Oscar, would be brought to the house and he would mount him from a block outside the garden gate. When Oscar died he ceased the habit, but would still get pleasure from observing the regiment carrying out their ceremonial duties, particularly on one recent occasion: 'I was standing on the doorstep of the private entrance watching the Queen's Life Guard of the Blues and Royals riding past with the Sovereign's Standard. The young officer spotted me and gave the order, "Eyes Left". I wrote to his Commanding Officer saying how much I appreciated the gesture. He wrote back – "I will pass on your compliments but he had no right to do it."' The salute in question should be given only to the Sovereign. But perhaps the ninety-two-year-old 8th Duke of Wellington – as both ex-Deputy Colonel and ex-Commanding Officer of the Household Cavalry Regiment, and as a great-great-grand-son of the First Duke – standing on the steps of his ancestor's house, is a worthy exception.

In the First Duke's time, his son and daughter-in-law, Charles and Sophia, lived at Apsley House when they were in London, the children no doubt enlivening their grandfather's morning walks around the garden. When my father and aunt went to stay at Apsley House in the 1920s, they became the last children to live in the house while it still belonged to the family. Kathleen ('Granny') and Arthur ('Granfer', and grandson of the First Duke) provided stability and affection to the children at a time when they were confused and upset by their parents' separation. For my father it is an evocative thought that when his grandfather hugged him, those arms when small had reached out for the touch of an elderly white-haired gentleman who, in his turn, in spite of all his fame and glory, was simply 'Granfer'.

TWELVE

Thistles and Thistledown

W hen my grandfather died, he left among his possessions a black diptych photograph frame. It passed, along with other objects from his desk, to my aunt who recently, twenty-five years after his death, gave it to me, saying, 'I can't bear to have it in the house any more.' When I opened it I found two photographs. The one on the left shows a demure young woman, sitting in profile, head slightly inclined, her long hair pinned in a chignon, hands clasped calmly on her lap, a smile hovering on her lips. The photograph on the right is of a worldly woman, bandeau round her head, a long string of pearls hanging from her neck. To me, both images are beautiful: both depict my grandmother. Underneath the photograph of the young Dorothy Ashton are four lines in my grandfather's handwriting:

> The joys I have possessed, in spite of fate, are mine.
> Not Heaven itself over the past has power;
> And what has been has been, and I have had my hour.
> April 30, 1914 – February 9, 1923

I knew the date of my grandparents' wedding – four months before the start of the First World War; but until I saw these words, I could never have known the exact day that their marriage ended. February 9, 1923

When I look at the black photograph frame, it is disturbing to imagine my grandfather planning this private, melancholy memorial: acquiring the frame; placing the images in it; choosing the lines of poetry (from John Dryden's translation of a Horace ode); writing the exact dates and then closing the diptych, no doubt to hide it in a locked drawer. He never displayed photographs of my grandmother in any house he lived in. I suspect he never forgave her for the break-up, but did he ever take this sombre souvenir out, open it and look at the images of the woman who played such a tragic part in his life?

On paper the match between Dorothy and Gerald seemed auspicious.

She had the money to indulge both their interests and passions; he had the intelligence and artistic talent to complement her intellectual and literary aspirations. And from this distance, I judge the early years of Dottie and Gerry's marriage to have been happy ones. Their shared joy in the birth of their son and daughter; their mutual interest in the arts; the pleasure they found in creating beautiful homes filled with lovely objects. But the marriage of my paternal grandparents was a disastrous union which damaged them both and had painful consequences for the lives of my father and my aunt. I feel sure that when they married, they believed they loved each other and that together they could provide each other with the lifelong companionship and affection they both craved. What happened to derail a union that seemed to hold so much promise?

Dorothy Violet Ashton was born at Heywood Lodge, White Waltham in Berkshire on Wednesday, 30 July 1889 – a year after her brother 'Scamp' and two years after the wedding of her parents, Lucy Cecilia Dunn-Gardner and Robert Ashton. The licence for the Ashtons' marriage, which took place on 17 February 1887 at St Stephen's Church, South Kensington, reveals that 'Cissie' (as her family called her) was a 'spinster' aged twenty-six, Robert a 'widower' of thirty-eight. His occupation is cited as 'Gentleman' – their fathers', respectively, as 'gentleman' and 'cotton spinner'. By all accounts Robert Ashton was a rich man, probably a factor in Cissie's decision to marry him. He already owned or rented considerable estates in Cheshire and Berkshire, but soon a grand town-house, 21 Park Lane, was added to the property portfolio. With a smart London address and plenty of money to spend on entertaining, the new Mrs Ashton was soon moving in the higher echelons of London society. Undoubtedly, her desire for position and social acceptance owed something to the illegitimacy of her father, Cecil Dunn-Gardner, a son of Sarah, Marchioness Townshend, the leading character in a notorious nineteenth-century scandal.

In 1807 Sarah Dunn-Gardner, a seventeen-year-old 'Fenland heiress', was married off to Lord Chartley, the eldest son of the Marquess Townshend of the day. The union, however, was not to achieve both families' desired results. According to a contemporary account, 'Lord Chartley is a very effeminate young man, – sometimes He wore pink ribbons to His shoes – & having married a young Lady only a few months ago, He is said to be upon the point of separation from Her. – In Italy, while on his travels, some circumstances were observed in Him that gave an unfavourable opinion of Him.'[1] A year after the marriage Sarah left her husband, accusing him of 'impotency & not being formed as a man shd. be'. Without waiting for a divorce, Sarah eloped with her first love, one John Margetts – climbing through the same small window that her own mother, herself an heiress, had used to elope with the family solicitor, Mr Dunn.

The lovers had a big family – five children – but, wrote their grand-daughter Dorothy many years later, 'One day the beloved John missed his footing and fell dead to the ground. And had not Sarah loved him, loved him with an ardent passion that is given to few?'[2] When Lord Chartley, living in Italy as 'Mr Compton', succeeded to the title, not unreasonably Sarah called herself Marchioness Townshend; she was, after all, technically still married to him, and her children all took on the surname of Townshend. But when John, the eldest, who was using the Townshend title of Earl of Leicester, was elected to the House of Commons, this was one step too far and, in Dorothy's words, 'the scandal began to unroll before the eyes of the horrified yet delighted Victorians'. Sarah was summoned to the Great Hall of Westminster and tried for bigamy. When asked if her children were legitimate, she replied, 'No, I have no wish to claim this.' It seemed a strange answer but when questioned later she declared: 'They will have enough of their own, and titles without honour are only an empty puff.'

Lord Brougham, Whig and one-time foe of the First Duke, represented the Townshend family and succeeded in having all Sarah's children declared illegitimate, whereupon they assumed the maiden name of their mother. One of them, Cecil Dunn-Gardner, was my great-great-grandfather. Although, like all his siblings, he was bitter about the disgrace that hung over the family, he made good his life and joined The Blues (he was one of the few who returned from the battle of Balaclava); amassed a fine library – including a first folio of Shakespeare; and married a girl of Huguenot extraction who was called Emma, after Lady Hamilton. Emma was vivacious and artistic, uneducated and im-poverished; she was also lovely-looking, with a beautiful skin and 'shining golden hair'. My grandmother reveals that there was speculation that Cecil might actually have been the son of Lord Chartley – apparently he was often addressed in shops as 'my Lord'. I put that down more to canny deference than a correct mode of address. In any case, if given the choice, I am sure that both of us (my grandmother and I) would choose as our forebear the romantic, steadfast John over the effete, ineffectual Lord Chartley. Dorothy relished the spirited Sarah's presence in her family tree but also believed that a malign legacy had been passed down by her.

Valerian (centre, second row) with fellow members of the Oxford Bullingdon Club in June 1936, a few weeks before his twenty-first birthday.

RIGHT: Lady Rose Paget, one of the glamorous daughters of the Earl of Anglesey. My father had a 'walk-out' with her in 1938–9. Two engagements were broken off, but they remained close friends until her death in November 2005.

LEFT: Seen here at a point-to-point in 1938, my aunt Eliza was one of the most popular girls on the social circuit.

Valerian aged about sixteen with some friends on a beach at Le Touquet. The blonde girl next to him is the actress Dorothy Hyson. 'I fell madly in love with Dot. But she wasn't the slightest bit interested in me!'

Morny, the 6th Duke, my father's first cousin, in
the uniform of Captain in 'The Dukes'. Seconded
to the Commandoes, he died a hero's death at the
Salerno landings in September 1943, and was
succeeded by my grandfather.

Eliza married Tommy Clyde in November 1939.
'Because of the war my mother wouldn't allow me
to wear white, and the handbag I carried
concealed my gas mask.'

My father and grandfather dressed for a fancy
dress ball in 1935. 'This photograph was taken
10 years ago at a ball at the Austrian Embassy',
wrote Gerry when he sent it as postcard to
Diana, his new daughter-in-law. 'You can cut it
into two and keep the left half.'

Valerian and Gerry met up in Cairo at the
beginning of 1942. They sent this photograph
back to Eliza in England, with a joint letter
about the Cairo nightlife: 'We are watching a
girl dance a "danse de vent". She has nothing
on but a heart made of silver sequins!'

LEFT: A photograph of Valerian taken by my mother not long before their wedding in January 1944. He is standing in the gardens of her parents' house in the Talpiot area of Jerusalem.

ABOVE: My mother, before her marriage, in Palestine, where she would go with friends to swim and soak up the sun. The photograph was taken by 'G' Gerard Leigh, a fellow officer of Valerian's.

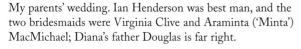

My parents' wedding. Ian Henderson was best man, and the two bridesmaids were Virginia Clive and Araminta ('Minta') MacMichael; Diana's father Douglas is far right.

ABOVE RIGHT: After their wedding, they snatched a brief honeymoon, but Valerian was on stand-by to return to Europe.

RIGHT: Valerian in the ruins of Palena in 1944.

James McConnel, my maternal great-great-great-grandfather, was born in New Galloway, Scotland in 1762, seven years before Arthur Wesley. With his kinsman John Kennedy, he became a founder of one of the most successful cotton-mill empires in Manchester.

Margaret Houldsworth, 'Peggy', who married James in 1799 when he was already thirty-seven. They had nine surviving children, two of whom settled in Australia.

The McConnel cotton-spinning trademark.

ABOVE: The Sedgwick cotton mill in Manchester built by McConnel and Kennedy in 1820. When my mother gave me this watercolour some years ago, I had no idea that it was part of my family history, or that the building still existed.

RIGHT: My great-great-grandfather William McConnel, one of James' and Peggy's children. After he took over the running of the family business, he bought Knockdolian in Ayrshire, which eventually my mother inherited.

On Wednesday, 2 September 1903 my maternal grandfather Douglas and his identical twin Malcolm fished in the same pool, with the same type of fly, on the River Stinchar at Knockdolian. Both caught their first salmon, and the two fish weighed within a few ounces of each other.

Douglas in 1901 with his parents, William Houldsworth (W.H.) and Florence, and his siblings, Malcolm (his twin), Merrick and his sisters Eryl and Muriel. Seven years later a tragic accident would claim Malcolm's life.

ABOVE: Douglas shaving in a trench during the First World War. His brother Merrick was killed at Passchendaele in 1917.

LEFT: My maternal grandmother Ruth and her mother Daisy. When the dark waters of the River Stinchar were in order, salmon could be caught by several different generations.

I am very attached to this formal photo of my grandmother, though in later life her more typical garb would be outdoor clothes for the gardening she loved.

Douglas was proud of his Matchless motorcycle, but my grandmother later remembered uncomfortable, and slightly hair-raising, rides in the sidecar.

Douglas and Ruth became engaged only weeks after he finally got back from the Western Front in spring 1919. They married the following year. Ruth's wedding present to her husband was a Kodak camera; his to her an elegant 'skunk stole'.

My mother Diana, who was born on 14 January 1922. Like her mother before her, she was an only child.

My parents with my brothers, John, Charles and Richard, and me on our boat *Kittiwake* in Kyrenia harbour, Cyprus in 1956

Gerry, my grandfather, with six of his grandchildren. From left: Richard, Charles, me, John, and Jeremy and Jonathan Clyde.

Gerry standing in front of the fireplace at Apsley House. In the background can be seen the portrait of his great-great grandmother, the formidable Anne, Countess of Mornington.

My family in 1994. Back row from left: Christopher, Richard, John and Charles.

TOP ROW: My father with
Stratfield Saye in the
background, and presenting
his rental flag to the Queen
in 2005.

MIDDLE ROW: My parents
after a successful fishing trip.
My father with his grandson
Gerald, in front of a
Waterloo cannon at
Sandhurst in 2007.

LEFT: My parents and me in
the garden of Park Corner
House, summer 2008.

'Was it not said that a curse fell upon the loves of all who descend from Sarah Townshend.'[3]

The Ashton history is less well-documented, though Robert Ashton, Cissie's husband, may have inherited his wealth from his 'cotton spinner' father James. Dorothy, for her part, decided that James, the grandfather she never met, was 'uninteresting', but I am struck by the fact that when my parents married in 1944, strands from two cotton families – the Ashtons and the McConnels – entwined.

Robert, my Ashton great-grandfather, was adored by his daughter Dorothy, who described him as 'a dreamer without purpose, a poet without words'. He was a natural eccentric, uneasy in normal social company, happiest when at sea on his yacht, the *Minerva*. One vivid experience from Dorothy's childhood was when, aged five, she travelled round Scotland on the yacht. 'There were brass cannon on board which had been used at Trafalgar, and whenever the weather was rough, these cannon would start trundling slowly up and down the deck, to my infinite delight, until some stupid grown up person lashed them to something solid.' When she wrote this nearly sixty years later, she confessed, 'Still now, in sleep, I hear the flap, see the bulge of the great cream-coloured sails, hear the scurry of her crew.'

When young, Robert's eccentric behaviour included jumping out of a four-storey window onto a blanket – just to see if he could do it. He had a mania for ballooning and to the horror of some of his more respectable relations, he and his brother would drift around the countryside 'dropping in' on people. At home he would sit in his study surrounded by 'compasses, telescopes, magnets of all sizes and shapes' and books – about the sea, the moon and the stars. He would tell his daughter stories of the legend of Atlantis, of the Sphynx, or the Golden Fleece'. They called him Oyster – 'he was so silent with grown-up people, and seemed to shut himself up whenever they were near'. He measured for Dorothy the 'length of the shadows of the moon'. He illuminated and enchanted Dorothy's young childhood, and then suddenly he fell ill, and in the last two years of his life she rarely saw him. When her mother told her he was dead she did not believe her, and on the evening before his funeral, as she lay in bed, she cried out to him, 'You must wake up quickly, they are going to bury you tomorrow.' Robert Ashton had died alone at sea with a letter from Dorothy under his pillow.

Did Cissie have a hand in hastening Robert's end? Before his death in March 1898 her energetic socialising had taken her across the path of the bachelor 10th Earl of Scarbrough. Family gossip suggests that she started an affair with him; whatever the truth, less than a year after Robert's death she called her children into her room and, kneeling on the floor in her dressing gown, held out her arms and announced, 'I am going to marry Lion' – their name for Scarbrough. Their new stepfather was a kind man who insisted that the two Ashton children call him 'Daddy', but assuredly he wanted an heir to inherit the family seats of Sandbeck and Lumley Castle. He did not know that his new bride, nearly forty years old at the time of their marriage, had lied about her age. Cissie carried this secret with her when she left the Ashtons' home in Kent and set off with her children for their new grand life. For now, she had got what she wanted: a title and riches to go with it. But for Dorothy, a sharp line was drawn. Abandoned by her introspective, clever father, with him went the endorsement of her own creative nature; instead she joined a family where the women – Scarbrough's sisters – were 'all very subdued ladies who spoke in thin, rather low voices'. One of these ladies declared that 'Dottie' was a suitable nickname for her stepniece. After her father's death, my grandmother developed a stammer which lasted for years.

There were compensations in Dottie's new life, chief among them the appearance of a small half-sister, Serena. For Lady Scarbrough, desperate for a son, Serena was a mixed blessing; though she conceived again, she suffered a miscarriage and it was rumoured that the baby was a boy. Dottie, however, instantly 'fell in love' with her sister. Other features of Dottie's childhood were more unsettling. Her mother's old Nannie, known as Wa-Wa – 'staid old pepper-pot shape of a woman' – would advance towards her with slow but relentless movements, uttering maledictions such as 'You're only a silly *Gurl*, half dwarf, get out of my sight, you drive your own mother half wild'. As was customary for girls of her background, Dottie's education was left to governesses, the last of whom – a German 'Fräulein' employed to 'finish' her – confounded Dottie's expectations when she revealed a good sense of humour, a love of the classics and an ability to keep a secret. When she persuaded Lady Scarbrough to approve a trip to Florence, Dottie was so thrilled she flew downstairs to kiss and thank her mother. 'Oh, go away, I cannot bear being kissed by a woman', was her response. In her memoirs, my grandmother wrote: 'The psychological significance of this strange remark did not at the time, fortunately, penetrate my comprehension.' Dorothy savoured every minute of her trip to Italy and the two months away 'flew by on the sandals of Mercury'. She loitered in the Cascine Gardens, inspired by the knowledge that Shelley wrote poetry there, and was 'overwhelmed' by the Michelangelo figures in the Medici Chapel. When she returned home, 'once and forever Italy had stolen my wits away'.

"'You,'" said the old man solemnly, "have the three bumps of temper, pride and combativeness more developed than anyone I have ever known."'[4] This was the pronouncement made by Sir George Goldie, the founder of Nigeria, when he met the eleven-year-old Dorothy Ashton. Goldie, an unconventional intellectual who defied the normal picture of a Victorian empire-builder, had a hugely formative influence on Dorothy's life and encouraged her to read and write poetry. He was the one fertile, intellectual presence in an otherwise arid, philistine desert where as a little girl she was punished for getting up early to read books in the huge library at Sandbeck. Secretly she started to write poetry and would go off on her pony, Nobbie, 'with toffee in one pocket and paper and pencil in the other'. And if she wasn't writing poetry, she was looking for wild flowers – 'Once I came upon sheets of the dark blue wild Columbine, there, as dropped from heaven, like the dark blue wing of a sunset cloud in winter.'[5]

'Early childhood was coming to an end,' wrote my grandmother about this period in her life:

> With its passing an inner melancholy began to settle upon me. Perhaps all children feel the same; perhaps it was simply the approach of adolescence. Yet I believe the cause lay deeper than this. I had long been convinced that I was an unmanageable, unattractive and plain child. Up till this time an almost violent vitality, an intense excitability about life, had carried me along. I had disregarded the snubs and the complaints administered by the grown-up people. But at last something seemed to slacken. I stopped, turned the gaze inward: something is happening – what is happening? What did actually happen was that from one day to another I discovered poetry. Pandora's box was open, all the miseries of the world flew forth. At the bottom remained, not hope, not comfort, but the incredible relief of actually writing verses myself.[6]

When Dorothy was growing up, she and her brother, Scamp, fought like mad, but a love for him was the one thing she had in common with her mother. Cissie's devotion to her son knew no bounds: many years later, Dorothy described it as 'desperate, passionate, unwise, that of a tigress'. Dorothy remembered her mother driving the two of them round the country lanes of Kent in her carriage. 'There were long white ends to the reins, and my mother wore long white gloves, to match, we thought. She looked very beautiful and radiant and young, with her golden-red hair piled up and a little hat on top of her head.' But even this idealised image of her mother is subverted by the recollection that it was always her brother who was 'wedged all warm between me and my mother'. In the games they played, sometimes they would fight a battle – 'I preferred to call it Trafalgar, while Scamp said Waterloo'. Scamp would taunt her; 'You're only a silly little girl', he would say. 'But we always made a point of never letting the sun go down upon our wrath.' When home from school, Scamp loved to frighten his sister with ghost stories and she would 'turn cold and sick with fear'. 'What is a ghost?' she would ask. 'They are spirits of bad men or murdered women and you can't get away from them anywhere', Scamp would exclaim gleefully. In the end Dorothy dealt with these malign presences in her own way. Lumley Castle was legendary home to a whole community of ghosts. Dottie stayed there for a fortnight without the rest of the family, and challenged herself to confront her fear 'till I should be frightened no more'.

If the loss of her father violently jolted Dorothy out of an innocent, carefree childhood, the death of Scamp cast a long shadow over the rest of her life. It was not simply that she lost him; to her his death was bound up in a toxic mix of love, obsession and rejection. To the horror of his mother, at the age of nineteen Scamp fell madly in love with a married woman, nine years his senior, called Baroness de Forest. For Dorothy, the memory of her brother in the violent grip of this passion never left her. 'I vividly remember one evening in my bedroom when my brother rushed in upon me impetuously. He looked pale and distraught and throwing himself on his knees by my chair, cried, "I can't bear it, she wants me to run away with her, which I know would be mad!"' Then Dorothy noticed his wrist was bound up with the blood still oozing. '"I did this myself," he said, "just to think of something else for one moment."'

When Scamp was still only twenty-three, the scandal exploded onto the pages of the newspapers. A year later, already suffering from TB, and desperately trying to recover his strength of will to give up his lover, he got a call from the Baroness. Dorothy wrote later: 'Another quarrel so upset him that he jumped out of bed and fell to the floor – the last haemorrhage. He died on his mother's birthday – 1912.' Scamp was just twenty-four years old.

Whenever I talk to my father about his mother, I am conscious of treading on difficult territory; there are so many aspects of her life which he finds hard to discuss. However, he and my aunt grew up hearing about Scamp, the brother Dorothy had loved so much and who had died long before his time – the 'Lost Leader', as his friends called him. This uncle they never knew became an iconic, romantic figure in their lives, and has remained so. Hanging over my aunt's mantelpiece is an idealised portrait of him as a boy; my father has several mementoes, among which are a miniature watercolour and Scamp's regimental sword. A large portrait of him also hangs in the hall at Stratfield Saye. To both my father and my aunt he is a positive way of connecting with their maternal roots. Neither of them knew where he was buried, assuming it would have been in one of the Lumley burial sites. It turns out that he was laid to rest alongside his father – the 'poet without words' – in the heart of the Cheshire countryside, in Ashton country.

I travelled with my father to the Church of St Lawrence, Stoak and we found the gravestones, a few feet apart. The cross that stood on Scamp's grave was broken and lying in the undergrowth, but the words on the stone were clear: 'The curfew tolls the knell of parting day'. Did Dottie choose the first verse of Thomas Gray's 'Elegy Written in a Country Churchyard' to be inscribed on her brother's grave? Cissie 'went utterly to pieces' and did not attend the funeral. When I told my aunt about the discovery of the graves she imagined her mother, four months short of her twenty-third birthday, beside the open grave of her brother, and near the remains of her lost father. 'Daddy', the ever-kind Scarbrough stepfather, was with Dottie, but for all his generosity of heart he was not her blood relative. While Scamp had been alive, he had been their mother's great solace. Now, more than ever, Dottie would know that her mother loved sons, and daughters were an unsatisfactory alternative. The following year Dottie published her first book of poetry, and in 1914 she married Lord Gerald Wellesley. 'Seize the day, M.A.', Goldie always told her. 'Seize the day.'

When the Gerald Wellesleys returned from Rome in 1918, bringing with them three-year-old Valerian and with another child on the way, they stayed briefly at Apsley House. Then, while they looked for a home to buy, they rented a house from Vita and Harold Nicolson. The Wellesleys' and Nicolsons' lives were already entangled. Dottie had first met them when she went out to Constantinople before her marriage. Vita noted in her diary, 'She is very rich.' Harold and Gerald were old friends and colleagues from the Diplomatic Service; Gerald had been one of the young men who squired Vita round the dance floor before she was married and she regularly went to stay at Ewhurst where Gerald's parents, the 4th Duke and Duchess, lived. Harold had for a time been in love with Eileen Wellesley, Gerald's younger sister. 'Would it have been better, I wonder, if Harold had stayed in love with Eileen and married her?'[7] wrote Vita before she married Harold in 1913. The following year, only months before marrying Dottie, Gerry had broken a brief engagement to Violet Keppel – with whom, he had earlier confided to Harold, he had been 'tremendously in love'.[8] In 1918 Vita and Violet, after fourteen years of intense friendship, became lovers. Violet's 1919 marriage to Denys Trefusis served merely to raise the stakes.

When Vita's affair with Violet threatened the Nicolson marriage, Harold found in Dottie a kind and caring confidante, and, realising that Vita too liked Dottie, he approved of their friendship. When Vita and Dottie went to stay with a mutual friend, Lord Berners, Harold wrote to his wife, 'Enjoy yourself. Tell Dottie she is an angel and very good for both of us.' But these were vulnerable times for Dottie. In March 1921 Robin Hollway, the brilliant young cousin (at sixteen, he had won a scholarship to Balliol) who had been so badly wounded in the war and, in Dottie's words, had 'perhaps the most remarkable brain I have ever intimately known, blew out that brain one morning in a bathroom in Half Moon Street'.[9] The verdict was 'suicide while in a state of unsound mind'. He was five years younger than Dorothy; from their earliest days of reading poetry to each other she had felt protective of him. His death, she wrote, was like the loss of her 'last brother'.

During this time, Dottie was a frequent visitor to the Nicolsons' home, Long Barn in Sussex. 'Slight of build, almost fragile, with blazing blue eyes, fair hair, transparently white skin',[10] was Vita's description of Dottie. Vita wrote a short story, 'The Christmas Party', which she dedicated to A(prile), her name for Dottie. It is a tale of revenge by an unconventional woman on her disapproving family. That autumn the Wellesleys and the Nicolsons went on holiday together to Italy. 'My word, they do squabble', reported Vita to Harold before he had joined the group. Harold's diary describes an incident in Venice. 'Vita says she doesn't like the Salute which makes Dottie very angry. In a state of tension we reach the Piazza ... the Doge's palace comes under Gerry's displeasure. Vita says she thinks it is a nice colour. Gerry says it is like a fat German lady with coarse lace underclothing, and he points to the Salute to show how much better other people do things ... We then go back to the gondola and go back in silence.'[11]

By the following year Dottie had become Vita's closest friend. It was also growing clear to the outside world that the Wellesley marriage was going very badly and weekends at Sherfield, the house in the country the

Wellesleys now owned, were fraught affairs. Harold wrote in his diary, 'Gerry says he has done no wrong and if Dottie wishes to run away that's her business. I do think Dottie makes a mistake in trying to be at one and the same time the little bit of thistledown *and* the thistle.'[12]

Just before Christmas 1922, Dottie wrote to her sister:

> I feel as if all the suffering of my life has culminated at last. There have been scenes all this week. He has gone to Ewhurst, & after the New Year he is going to live out of the house. So far so good. I can see no further than this – He is very upset, and <u>very</u> <u>kind</u>. He says he will never take my babies from me. For God's sake keep Mother away from me.
>
> I am going abroad in the New Year. I don't want to see her till I feel strong again.
>
> Darling little one I am sorry, oh so sorry to fail you at this moment. But the machine has just broken down, & can't move backwards or forwards.

'Tomorrow I dine with my darling Mrs Woolf at Richmond', Vita informed Harold on 12 January 1923. She continued, 'I love Mrs Woolf with a sick passion. So will you. In fact I don't think I will let you know her. Dots is away at Sherfield so the mouse is playing.'[13] A month later, Vita wrote again to Harold, who was at this time attached to the Embassy in Germany: 'I have got to go to Sherfield tomorrow, oh damn, *damn*, damn. But the enclosed letter [from Dottie] will show you the sort of state that wretched little thing is in ... But it is a great bore, especially as I do *not* want people to say I have anything to do with her marriage having gone wrong, which probably they would be only too pleased to say ... I do *not* want to be dragged into this, either for your sake or my own. We have had quite enough of this sort of thing, haven't we?'[14]

The day after, Gerry wrote to Mitey:

> You have probably by now heard the dreadful news that Dottie and I have separated. I am absolutely miserable & wish I could see you & talk it over with you. Ten days or a fortnight ago Dottie seemed much better. Last week for some unaccountable reason, for there was no sort of a quarrel, she had a relapse and on Friday morning she suddenly told me out of the blue that she was quite determined on separating for a year at any rate. In a matter of this kind a year seems to me like an eternity. I saw all argument and discussion was useless. That night as already arranged I went down to Sherfield & on Saturday morning I drove away from the house so sad that I was practically crying. She told me she was trying to sell Portland Place but she wanted me to stay there till it was sold. I do not think it is possible

for me to stay on in a big house with 5 or 6 servants running up huge monthly bills quite by myself.

A few weeks before, Harold had written to Vita warning her that no Wellesley would ever concede that another Wellesley was to blame for the break-up of the marriage, and that they might look around for a scapegoat and fix on her.[15] The Nicolsons had a very unusual marriage in which each of them had affairs, primarily, but not exclusively, homosexual ones. Vita herself was a predatory, powerful, possessive woman who wanted her lovers to become dependent on her. I believe that my grand-mother lost her heart to Vita, and was prepared to risk her marriage for the sake of that love. Maybe seeing the Nicolsons' unusual 'modus vivendi' gave Dottie a false sense of security, believing she could secure a similar arrangement with Gerry. I do not think that my grandmother made a conscious decision about her sexuality, rather that she was seduced by the intensity of Vita's interest. I think she craved love and affection, and yearned for someone with whom she could form an intense intellectual and emotional bond. The two women had a great deal in common. Both had difficult mothers, both had been brought up surrounded by the trappings of riches and grandeur, both were free spirits. And both were from worlds where men ruled, in more ways than one: in Dottie's case, her mother had regard and respect only for Scamp; in Vita's, though an only child, as a girl she could never inherit Knole, the house she adored, where she grew up.

April 30 1923 was the Wellesleys' ninth wedding anniversary. 'I am so depressed that I don't see how I shall ever live through the day', wrote Gerry to Mitey.

> Time does not seem to make this ghastly mess-up any better & I feel that I have lost everything that made life worth living –
>
> Perhaps I should not have spent this day here where I am alone – except for the children – & where there is so much to remind me of our past happy life together. After the children have gone to bed I shall have no companion but my thoughts.
>
> O Mitey. I hope your life will be happier than mine. But I know it will be for you can make people love you. I am beginning to understand that that is something which I will never be able to do.

Harold, in a letter to Vita, declared that he was 'sore and hurt about Gerry & feel it is her fault. I don't mean I *really* think it her fault, but the Gerry complex tries to get relief by projecting itself on to her.'[16] This enigmatic assertion is hard to decipher out of context, but unquestionably Gerry suffered from some confusion about his own sexuality, and he and Harold, as very young men, had shared a sentimental friendship. There was certainly an intimacy between them, and a relationship which lasted for the rest of Harold's life.

At the end of the year, Dottie wrote to tell her mother that she was 'presenting Gerry with a Deed of Separation – I do not know whether he will sign or not ... I can argue no more with anyone about this – All I can say is, that if you all knew what I know, you would sympathise & agree, that it is impossible for us ever to resume life together.' My grandparents' marriage was over. The Deed was designed, claimed Dottie, so that it did not 'preclude either of us from seeing the children almost as much as if we lived together'. However, my father's painful memories of listening to endless arguments about the holidays, and my aunt's even more perplexing accounts of being torn from one school mid-term and placed in another for the convenience of one or other parent, suggests otherwise. Gerry and Dottie never divorced – maybe it would have been easier for my father and aunt if they had; but divorce was considered a scandal in itself. Extramarital affairs were common and condoned among the upper classes, but only if they were discreet: appearances were everything. Perhaps there was a moral dimension to their decision – 'till death us do part'; maybe my grandfather entertained a hope that one day they might get back together.

My grandfather's letters to Mitey give an insight into the turmoil of his mind at the time of the separation. He never talked to either of his children about it; possibly Mitey was his only confidante. He was from a generation and a class which tended to keep emotions under wraps, but it is clear that he was profoundly affected by the break-up. For me, the saddest declaration is, 'For you can make people love you. I am beginning to understand that that is something which I will never be able to do.' My grandfather was loved, uneasily by his two children, certainly by his grandchildren, and unquestionably, both in spite of and because of his eccentricities, by his friends; but I suspect that the 'love' he refers to, which he thought he had with Dottie, never came his way again. In any case, Gerry and Dottie contrived to ensure that for the rest of the time they were on the earth together, their paths rarely crossed. Among the exceptions were their daughter's marriage in 1939 and the memorial service at Stratfield Saye for Morny in 1943. And, thirty-three years after the separation, Gerry attended Dottie's funeral.

After the separation, life was much more challenging for my grandfather than it was for my grandmother, whose decision it had been. Rightly, one of the terms of the separation was that Dottie should pay her husband an annual allowance, and for a period Gerry supplemented this income by writing an occasional column – 'Architectural Notes' – in *The Spectator*. 'Something must be done to arouse the dormant architectural perception of the nation', [17] was the rallying call of his first piece in March 1924. He took on subjects as diverse as 'The Problem of the Office Block' and 'Houses in Jane Austen Novels'. His writing reveals an eagle eye, a well-informed mind and an eclectic range of interests. His architectural nous was sufficiently assured to refer to Nash as a 'second rater'. With the end of his marriage, work for Gerry became a necessity rather than merely a pleasurable pastime, and he devoted a great deal of energy to his architectural partnership with Trenwith Wills. At the time, as Lord Gerald Wellesley, he was the only aristocrat since the eighteenth-century Lord Burlington to ply his trade as an architect. The success of the firm owed more to talent than titles, and Wellesley and Wills had a regular stream of commissions and invitations to submit work for competitions or exhibitions. In 1924 their entry for a competition run by *Country Life* for the British Empire Exhibition won first prize. Gerald's commitment to his profession was rewarded when, in 1929, he was made a fellow of the RIBA.

During the rest of the 1920s, in spite of the other attachments in Vita's life, she and Dottie continued to be intimate friends and, no doubt, occasionally lovers. One of Vita's other lovers was Geoffrey Scott, author of *The Architecture of Humanism*, whom she had met when on holiday in Italy with the Wellesleys. Scott fell passionately in love with Vita: 'Do whatever you think best about Dottie ... I'm terribly sorry you should have had such painful things to go through. I'm a bad surgeon myself and understand how wretched it all is.'[18] Later, Scott wrote, 'I sometimes think you react to people by the amount of passion or suffering they *display*.'[19] Dottie was one of the examples he gave.

Vita's affair with Scott was short-lived, but her relationship with Virginia Woolf was different. From the start Woolf was wary of Dottie, whom she considered a rival. To Dottie's dismay, the affair between Vita and Virginia began in December 1925, but she was compensated when, early in 1926, Vita suggested Dottie accompany her on a trip which took them through Italy to Cairo, and then down the Suez Canal, and across the Indian Ocean to Bombay. Vita wrote to Harold that Dottie was 'the most satisfactory person to travel with, as she is so thrilled; she says "Oh

look!" every time she sees a donkey. Which is the right attitude.'[20] Vita
was also writing regularly to Virginia, whom she was missing 'in a quite
simple desperate human way'. She reported that on one leg of the
journey, when they were steaming through the Indian Ocean, Dottie was
indignant about being forced to give away prizes: 'Really I do think it's a
little hard that because I happened to marry Gerry I should have to make
a fool of myself on a P. & O.'[21]

Neither woman fell for India. In Agra Dottie worried about snakes in
the hotel. Vita reported that she looked everywhere in her room, then
'jumped into bed forgetting the old tale of the snake said to be found at
the bottom of everyone's bed when they put their toes down'. When Vita
left her to go on to Persia, most mornings Dottie swam in the sea, where
sharks sometimes lurked. 'I remember one pursuing me to the shore', she
wrote, 'on to which I leapt with a beating heart.'[22]

When Dottie returned home, England was in the grip of industrial
action. 'I am just going up to fetch Elizabeth back & spend the last day
with Valerian', she wrote to Mitey. 'Isn't this strike a muddle? . . . Darling
you have convinced me that you love me, & it is a delicious warm feeling
to remember one has one relation one can rely on.' A few days later Vita
returned from her trip to be met at Victoria Station by Dottie, who
whisked her off in her Rolls-Royce to her flat in Mount Street, where
Vita, according to her own account, drank 'a bottle of champagne practically straight off, and fell into a swinish sleep'.[23]

> She walks among the loveliness she made,
> Between the apple-blossom and the water –
> She walks among the patterned pied brocade,
> Each flower her son, and every tree her daughter.

These are the best-known lines of a long poem called *The Land*; it
was started by Vita Sackville-West in 1923, finished in Isfahan in 1926,
published a few months later and dedicated to D.W. At Vita's funeral
these four lines were used on the back of the service sheet; later her son
Nigel described it as a 'eulogy of the flowers she loved most'.[24] The lines
come from a section called 'The Island'. When I read it, the roll-call –
apple blossom, kingcups, primroses, wind-flowers, fritillary, orchids,
irises, tulips, nut trees, roses – seemed familiar. By the time I reached the
lines '. . . And tulips in a flying cavalcade / Follow valerian for their
lieutenant'[25] – I realised that this passage is not only about my grandmother but also about the island at Sherfield – the house where my

grandfather put into practice his designs for the perfect home, the house my grandmother loved because, she wrote later, it was 'everything I could have wished for'. And the 'island' was the little haven where my father played as a small boy – where he kept his menagerie of animals (guinea-pigs and rabbits); where my aunt would roam as a toddler in the mysterious undergrowth; where the traumas of the adult world did not intrude.

I read 'The Island' for the first time when I was planning to visit both my father and aunt, and decided that I would take it to each of them as an offering. My father is not drawn to poetry. When young, occasionally he read his mother's verse, but I felt sure that this passage would resonate with him. His forget-me-not-blue eyes scanned the lines; he had never read them before and was moved by the lyrical evocation of his childhood memories. By coincidence, my aunt had been thinking of the small plot of land, protected by its moat, and of the flowers that grew on it; thinking of the place which represented a safe, happy piece of her childhood. Metaphorically, 'The Island' represents a fleeting period in my father's and aunt's young lives when the future seemed sweet and secure. In reality the words were part of the love and devotion that Vita showered on my grandmother: attention that was mesmerising, appealing and, for Dottie, inescapable.

In the winter of 1927 Vita Sackville-West suddenly appeared in Dottie's Mount Street sitting room. 'Will you come to Persia on Monday?' she asked. 'Of course', was Dottie's reply. This moment of spontaneity marked the start of what Dottie always regarded as the greatest trip she ever made. En route, when they were near a freezing-cold Hanover, she appeared wearing, Vita wrote, 'a very long fur-coat, down to the ankles, so thick as to make her quite round; she looks like a Russian grand-duke'.[26] Perhaps partly to pacify Virginia, still very much in favour, Vita sometimes wrote disparagingly of her travelling companion: 'I never realised what a luxury-child she was, being accustomed to seeing her always in England, where comforts happen automatically – she thinks Teheran uncivilized, – no electric light, scanty baths – what would she be like really roughing it.'[27] Dottie was blissfully unaware of the criticism, writing to Mitey:

Now the spring has come: at a bound, the thermometer jumping from 50 to 70 in a day. Rather wonderful. Puffs of pink peach, & almond blossom, flowering in this arid waste; & presently: irises, tulips, & wisteria in the gardens. Next week I go south to Isfahan, Shiraz, & the ruins of Persepolis the ancient capital sacked by Alexander. This appears to be a very wonderful ruin. Your Tid will go mad, & will make herself very ridiculous digging with a tiny trowel for Persian Iris, & relics of Darius the Great, King of Kings ... I leave the party at Isfahan motor back across the 600 miles of desert, mirages, & claret hills.

Dottie's return route took her via Constantinople, which, she confessed to her sister, she did not want to see again. 'It will be painful, but don't tell Gerry so. Things were so full of optimism all those years ago. I had today by the bag such delicious letters from Valerian and Elizabeth. She bursts into poetry, to my great amusement!'

At the end of 1927 Dottie wrote to Mitey, 'I have gone into partnership with Virginia Woolf, & am editing a series called The Hogarth Living Poets Series; by which I hope eventually to act as a signpost. And it's the greatest fun.' Virginia declared to Vita: 'Lady G. Wellesley has bought me. She paid £25 thousand down and the rest on mortgage, so I'm hers for life. I have use of the Rolls Royce and wine to taste.' The letter went on, 'Speaking sober prose, however, I wont belong to the two of you, or to the one of you, if the two of us belong to the one. In short, if Dotty's yours, I'm not. A profound truth is involved which I leave you to discover. It is too hot to argue: and I'm too depressed.'[28] Probably both women had entered into the arrangement to please Vita, and Leonard Woolf had to go along with it, despite the fact that his antipathy towards Dottie was, if anything, stronger than Virginia's. After visiting Dottie at Penns, he drove home at a dangerous speed, 'furious at her vanity, conceit, egotism, vulgarity; ill breeding, violent temper etc'.[29] In spite of their views (Virginia was no more generous about Dottie's work than she was appreciative of her money, writing in her diary that she 'lends me her own poems, which I promptly throw down the W.C.'),[30] the Woolfs managed to accept Dottie's money for four years, during which time she co-edited twenty-four volumes of poetry.

Harold thought that Vita's relationship with Dottie was an example of his wife's ability to have durable relationships, but Vita knew all too well the effect of her behaviour, admitting to Harold, 'You have no idea how miserable I have made Dotz.'[31] Vita's biographer, Victoria Glendinning, writes that Vita 'failed to take into account that the people who fell in love with her invested the affair with a far greater significance, and sometimes were ready to risk the stability of their lives for what they believed to be a great love. At the beginning of an affair, she exacted this total commitment; she attracted and was attracted by personalities who were temperamentally disposed to abandon themselves to love in this way.'[32] And once she had hooked someone, Vita never wanted to let go completely, so that her list of 'emotional pensioners' (as Glendinning calls them) steadily grew. One of Vita's lovers wrote to her, 'But you do like to have your cake and eat it, – and *so* many cakes, so many, a surfeit of sweet things.'[33]

At the beginning of April 1928, a new interest came into Dottie's life. Vita took her to see a property not far from Long Barn. 'The house, which is red brick William and Mary, stands up on a hill,' wrote Vita the day after to Harold.

> 'This is quite nice,' we said, 'and ordinary.' But then I went round the corner, into the garden, – I must tell you that the place was entirely deserted, – and I got such a surprise. A glade stretched away in front of me, and to the right were <u>huge</u> rocks, covered in moss, littered about in a wilderness of oaks and cedars! The trees grow out of the fissures in the rocks, so that their roots twine and twist over the stone; and there was one rock, with old steps cut in it, which had a squat little old cedar sitting at the very top of it. It was absolutely fantastic, – a mixture of the most absurdly romantic age, and Shakespeare scenery, especially a Midsummer's nights dream, and Walter de la Mare, and Piranesi, and Mrs Ann Radcliffe ... Dotz is wild about it, & wants to sell Sherfield.[34]

To my father's great dismay, his mother did exactly that. Within six weeks of seeing Penns, Dottie had bought it. 'Am I the ghost that has always haunted this house?' wrote my grandmother about Penns-in-the-Rocks.[35] When I visited Penns and passed through the white gate and onto the drive, bordered by a wood of chestnut and beech trees, I entered another world. The drive swoops and turns until it arrives at the house which, to my eyes, is anything but ordinary; but once you walk round the side and see the rocks, your heart is lost. They are 'huge' and primeval and, as my grandmother wrote, 'Perhaps an earlier man than the men of Stonehenge worshipped here some unknown god.' For me, standing on the rocks, I can conjure up my grandmother's spirit. She loved Penns – her home, her refuge and often the inspiration for her poetry. She was nearly forty when she bought the house and she lived there for the rest of her life, creating a glorious walled garden, the broad structure of which survives to this day.

Looking beyond the rocks and up the glade you see a little temple, in the spring surrounded by yellow azaleas and daffodils – some, no doubt, from many bags of bulbs my father gave his mother when she moved in. In this small folly, in my grandmother's words, 'dedicated to the muses and gods of the countryside', lies a small York stone engraved with the words 'Hilda Matheson Amica amicarum'.

Hilda entered Dottie's life through Vita who, in December 1928, had begun an affair with her. At the time, Matheson was Director of Talks at the BBC. From the start Hilda showed a level of sensitivity which marked her out as being very different to Vita's friends in the Bloomsbury Group. 'I am sorry about Dottie, really sorry I mean, I hate it that a happiness for me should mean an unhappiness for her,'[36] she wrote to Vita. But her happiness was short-lived and as Vita looked for her next adventure, Hilda and Dorothy sought out each other's company. Dottie told Hilda: 'I would so much like to see you. To talk. But is it a good plan? I don't want either of us to hurt one another inadvertently. I know we shouldn't do so intentionally. I have been a great deal alone since Vita left.'[37] Soon Hilda had lost not only Vita but also her job at the BBC, and Dottie offered her sanctuary at Rocks Farm, a property on her land. However, Hilda's role in my grandmother's life was to be a great deal more than as tenant on her estate. Even while Hilda's affair with Vita was going on, the two women had gone on holiday together – in summer 1929 to Florence and then Sicily in early 1931.

A year older than Dottie, Hilda came from a very different background. She was the daughter of a Scottish Presbyterian minister, read History at Oxford, and worked for British Intelligence in the First World War. Later she was recruited by Nancy Astor, the first woman MP, and for seven years served as her political secretary. When John Reith, the founder of the BBC, hired Hilda to be the first Director of Talks, the then wireless network was still in its infancy; she became one of its highest-paid employees. Unusually for the time, she was a respected professional woman – feared by some of her younger colleagues at the BBC, acknowledged as an intellectual force within the organisation. Unlike Vita, who never wished to be publicly identified as a lesbian, Hilda regretted that her sexual orientation had to be hidden. But when, in January 1932, Hilda resigned from the BBC under pressure from John Reith, the issue was nothing to do with her sexuality, but rather fundamental disagreements about programme policy. Hilda believed in 'love which liberates the heart and opens the mind'; she had a similar attitude to work.

Apart from their shared experiences of being cast off by Vita, Hilda was a good listener for all Dottie's other problems – loneliness, depression, her mother. Dottie in turn provided a sympathetic ear for Hilda's tales of her professional troubles. They shared a passionate interest in poetry and as Dottie strove to make Penns a haven for poets and other writers, Hilda's own friends and interests can only have added to the success of this venture. Virginia was as snobbish about Hilda as she had been graceless about Dottie. 'I hate to be linked, even by an arm, with Hilda. Her earnest aspiring competent wooden face appears before me, seeking guidance in the grave question of who's to broadcast. A queer trait in Vita – her passion for the earnest middle-class intellectual, however drab and dreary.'[38] In fact, Virginia abhorred the idea of being 'linked' with either of them: 'I cant have it said "Vita's great friends – Dottie, Hilda & Virginia". I detest the 2nd rate schoolgirl atmosphere.'[39]

Hilda was a kind and caring woman and though undoubtedly she was my grandmother's lover, I suspect, as time went by and Dottie's problems with depression and, increasingly, alcohol grew, Hilda became more companion and carer. Neither my father nor my aunt liked her. Though it was never discussed, both were wary of her intimacy with their mother, and regarded her as a rather ominous presence in the house. These were times when homosexual love was illegal, and lesbianism barely acknowledged. *The Well of Loneliness*, the trail-blazing lesbian novel by Radclyffe Hall, was published in the middle of 1928 and created a huge controversy, resulting in a court case which banned the book. To have a mother who, albeit privately, displayed scant regard for social convention was hard enough in a naturally bohemian family; for my father and aunt, Wellesleys firmly grounded in the English upper class, it was at times unbearable.

Gerry may have described Nash as a 'second rater', but in 1931, after living for seven years on the north side of Nash's Regent's Park, he acquired a lease on 3 Chester Terrace, on the east side. He had had his eye on the house for some years – not surprisingly, since it stands out as being smaller and more elegant than its companions in the row. Even the strait-laced 1938 *Survey of London* refers to it as 'attractive', and includes an illustration which reveals the back of a bust standing on a window-sill (I am quite sure it was of the First Duke). And in a gesture to a fellow architect, my grandfather placed on a plinth on the side of the house overlooking the garden a bust of John Nash. It is still there to this day and must have contributed to No. 3's aggrandisement: the building is now called Nash House.

The entrance to the house is on a narrow road which connects Albany

Street to the park, and the porch, with its three steps, became an irresistible staging-post for small children, or elderly walkers, on their way to and from their exercise in the park. Dogs often lifted their legs against the railings, and occasionally a fearless young adventurer would ring the doorbell and run away. Should Gerry happen to catch any of these trespassers in the act, he would give them a severe reprimand and the cry would go up from his neighbours, 'Come quickly – Lord Gerald's having one of his rows!'

One visitor described Gerry's house as being 'crammed with exquisite Regency furniture and memorabilia of the Great Duke'.[40] My aunt confesses that, much as she loved the house, she lived in fear of breaking some precious family relic, which would inevitably incur her father's terrible temper. At the time, Gerry was almost certainly the only member of the family who, fascinated by anything to do with his great-grandfather, was constantly on the lookout for any Wellingtoniana. There were those who thought that Gerry's 'incessant plugging' of the First Duke was a contributory factor in the break-up of the Wellesleys' marriage. Rumour has it that when an attempt was being made at reconciliation, Gerry turned up to see Dottie with a huge brown-paper parcel. When she undid the package, it turned out to be a red terracotta bust of the First Duke.[41]

In the autumn of 1931, Dottie rushed to Sandbeck, where her mother was dying.

> I went into her room. She was in a coma. I bent over her and spoke her name and mine.
> 'It's not true,' she said. Those were her last words.
> Something inspired came in that dreadful second.
> I said, 'We are all together now, the darling boy, all of us.'
> For one second she opened her dying beautiful eyes and gave me the one sweet smile she gave me in her life. After that the end.[42]

What was not true? That she had engineered the death of her first husband? That she had lied to ensnare Lord Scarbrough? That she had blighted the lives of both her daughters? The one truth about which there was no doubt was that she loved Scamp, her 'darling boy'. But Cissie's malign influence on Dottie's life reached out from the grave. A few days after her death, Dottie left Sandbeck, writing a letter, on black-rimmed notepaper, to Mitey. 'Daddy doesn't seem to want me at Sandbeck ... I am going back to Elizabeth at Penns. Mother's Will has hurt me dreadfully; I know you will understand this; from the human point of view. Had she left me all my father's jewels, I shouldn't have cared for them, but would have offered those things to you. I hope you have some? As it is I only want her little old Bible, & the silver dogs at Park Lane, which I loved as a child.' The brief obituary in *The Times* stated that Lady Scarbrough 'leaves a [*sic*] daughter, Lady Serena James'. The funeral at Sandbeck went ahead without Dottie. Once again a death had overturned my grandmother's life.

In one letter to Mitey Dottie added, 'P.S. Whatever happens you & I must never drift apart.' The intimacy and affection between the two sisters did fade a little; given my grandfather's close friendship with Mitey, perhaps conflicting loyalties intervened. In August 1934 Gerry and his daughter Eliza stayed for a few days at St Nicholas, Mitey and Bobby James's home in Yorkshire; the day after he left, Gerry's estranged wife arrived for a visit.

While Dottie's pen filled her notebooks with poets and poetry – by 1934 she had seven books of her own poems to her name – Gerry's hand guided his pencil across the sheets of minutely detailed architectural drawings. The Wellesley/Wills partnership, by now in offices in Baker Street (a convenient brisk walk from Chester Terrace), flourished through the 1930s. Their commissions ranged from designing a house in the burgeoning Hampstead Garden Suburb – their efforts are now described as 'being driven intellectually towards the Modern Movement but whose emotional taste was for something more aristocratic' – to creating a Folly in Wiltshire for the eccentric Lord Berners, an old friend of Gerry's. The Folly, a 140-foot tower, was the subject of several objections from local residents, but when finally completed in 1935 it was opened on Guy Fawkes Day to a fanfare of fireworks and a bonfire crowned by effigies of enemies. The tower owes its hybrid style – Classical and Gothic – to the fact that Berners insisted, after work had begun, that Gerry's Classical design be subverted by putting a layer of Gothic on top. The notice at the entrance was also Berners' idea: 'Members of the Public committing suicide in this tower do so at their own risk'.

Just as the Folly dominates the landscape, one Wellesley/Wills project which also lays claim to a prominent position on the horizon is the Church of St Mary and St George in High Wycombe, its distinctive green copper dome slightly at odds with its surroundings. Another of their commissions – Portland House in Dorset – is now Grade II listed and cited by the Twentieth Century Society as being an 'excellent and very complete example of the Hollywood Spanish style in Britain', and of 'the eclectic fantasy architecture of the period. It brilliantly reflects popular imagery of the day: a combination of the glamour of the cinema with the exoticism of the sunshine holiday.'

A more conventional accolade came Gerry's way when, in 1936, it was announced that he was appointed Surveyor of the King's Works of Art. Formally the appointment was from Edward VIII, but within months he had abdicated and Gerry was serving a new master, George VI. As well as having established a reputation as an architect, Gerry had by this time formalised his interest in his ancestor by publishing, with John Steegman of the National Portrait Gallery, *The Iconography of the First Duke of Wellington*. No doubt, as his credentials and erudition grew, so did his sometimes lofty outlook on life. His friends termed the word 'Gerriana' when exchanging the latest story about him. It was at the suggestion of one of these friends that an account of a trip Gerry made in 1930 was published in 1938 under the title *The Diary of a Desert Journey*. The highlight of his adventure was a visit to the remote Convent of St Catherine on Mount Sinai, where he memorably described 'the fragrant smell – presumably the true odour of sanctity – in the Bone House',[43] the eventual repository for the bones of all the monks after their term as corpses in the cemetery has ended. Equally evocative is my grandfather's description of a dancer at a wedding in Cairo, which he had gatecrashed:

> The danseuse or odalisque then advanced towards us and, coming up to each of us in turn, dangled her charms and waggled her rotundities at a proximity and with an intensity which made the performance highly embarrassing. There was not a cubic inch of flesh on the woman's body which did not quiver like a jelly to the tinkling rattle of hundreds of small glass tubes sewn on to her dress. The great hemisphere of her stomach churned and heaved round like a maelstrom.[44]

A hastily written black-and-white postcard of the gigantic Sphinx, addressed to A.V. Wellesley Esq., arrived at Penns, where Valerian was staying with his mother and sister. 'Shepheards Hotel Cairo April 18 I arrived this morning and have seen the things from the grave of Tutankhamun. They are quite marvellous – much better than I antici-pated. I am off Sunday on the next leg. Daddy.'

If Valerian and Elizabeth resented the presence of Hilda Matheson at Penns, from the summer of 1935 there was another visitor for whom they had little time. 'I couldn't bear Yeats. He wasn't very friendly to me', remembers my aunt. It was Ottoline Morrell who brought the famous poet to stay at Penns. A few days after the visit, Dorothy wrote in great excitement to her sister: 'When Yeats says to me: "You must sacrifice all to poetry," Well then I reply: "What of my children?"

He answers: "Whilst you are on this earth you must take care of your children."

I try to explain (if I can get a word in edgeways) that these two objects I have made my purpose. He booms on.

All very exciting, & it has made me very happy.'

Yeats, too, was smitten. 'You have brought a new pleasure and interest into my life,'[45] he wrote. 'Penns in the Rocks is the perfect country house, lettered peace and one's first steps out of doors into a scene umbrageous, beautiful.' From the day of their first meeting there developed a relationship which was to become hugely important in my grandmother's life. In spite of adverse commentary about her work (much behind her back), Dottie had received some decent reviews for her published verse, but Yeats singled her out for special attention. He wrote later in an introduction to a book of her poetry: 'Then I came upon *Matrix*, a long meditation, perhaps the most moving philosophic poem of our time ... and discovered that it was moving precisely because its wisdom, like that of the sphinx, was animal below the waist. In its vivid, powerful, abrupt lines, passion burst into thought without renouncing its uterine darkness. I had a moment's jealousy.'[46] My grandmother felt that, at last, her poetry was being judged in its own right. In one of her letters to Yeats she hugged 'the thought that you had recognized my poetry before you knew me'.[47]

Valerian's memory of Yeats is the tedium of listening to him intoning 'Innisfree'. Vita, too, was not impressed by Yeats. 'He is the sort of person who has no small-talk at all, but who either remains silent or else plunges straight into the things that matter to him. So little small-talk has he that he doesn't even say "How do you do?" when shaking hands on arrival. He just sits down on the sofa, looks at his nails for two minutes' silence, and then tells one stories about Manley Hopkins or Lady Gregory or Gogarty.'[48] Perhaps Dottie's relationship with the great man influenced Vita's decision, as Dottie described later, to 'chuck me out of her life'. But the distress this final fissure might have caused would have been relieved by the distinguished poet's attention. 'Perhaps you are too modest and too great a man to realise what our friendship (8 months old I think) has meant to an obscure poet,' wrote Dottie.[49]

Virginia Woolf, in a letter to a friend, commented: 'But isn't she [Dorothy], after Yeats' praise, considerably restored from her old bitterness? I always thought praise would do the trick.'[50] It was not praise, but approval that my grandmother yearned for. If people suspected that her good wine and soft beds[51] had anything to do with Dorothy's appeal, they may have been right; since the death of Lady Gregory there had been a vacancy in Yeats's life for an aristocratic, intelligent woman with a beautiful, peaceful home. A guest who stayed at Penns described the scene:

> Dottie Wellesley and the poet Yeats are alone here ... she is a very odd woman, morbid and unhappy and silly; but there is something disarming and nice about her, and I am enjoying the experience of staying here, and meeting Yeats ... she *adores* Yeats – in quite a touching way, she is so awed and grateful to him – but she is one of those people who can't listen, so that even though he is her Prophet, her train of thought never linked up with his once, so the conversation always had a double theme.[52]

'All this time am torn and distracted by practical and material affairs', Dottie had written to Yeats in July 1935. 'My boy, whose youth has rushed to his head, turns to me for everything, moral, practical, spiritual. I get tired. But this sudden and wonderful friendship between you and me gives me strength.'[53] On Christmas Day 1936 she told Yeats that 'both my own children have had flu. The boy badly. He yearns for the North West Frontier and the gallantries of his dreams.'[54] Yeats replied, 'Your son wants a framework of action such as a man who feels his poetry is vague & loose will take to writing sonnets.'[55] Dottie may stand in Yeats's shadow, but she does not slavishly follow all his advice. 'W.B.Y. is for ever trying to revise my poems. We have quarrelled about this. I say to him: "I prefer bad poems written by myself to good poems written by you under my name."'[56]

He mentor, she muse; it is unclear whether the intimacy between Yeats and Dorothy extended to a sexual relationship. Roy Foster, Yeats's biographer, thinks not: he writes, 'Much about their relationship concerned passions declared but safely kept in check.'[57] Nevertheless quite a number of their letters have erotic, passionate passages which suggest physical intimacy.

'It is not the Sudetenland that Hitler wants. Wait and see,' wrote Dottie to Yeats in October in a prophetic postscript to a letter. In September 1938, the world seemed on the brink of war. Hitler had threatened to invade Czechoslovakia unless Britain supported his plan to take over the Sudetenland. As Prime Minister Neville Chamberlain made increasingly desperate attempts to broker a deal with Hitler, Sunday, 18 September was declared a 'day of national prayer for peace'. Tension mounted and the evacuation of children from the cities was ordered. I was fascinated to discover that my grandfather was the pivotal figure in a small behind-the-scenes operation which took place at the height of the Munich Crisis; top-secret and endorsed by Chamberlain himself, had the mission come to light at the time it could have had serious repercussions. In the view of one security expert, it was in every respect 'an amazingly risky step for the Government to take'.[58]

My grandfather's account of the episode exists in the form of a memorandum, Chamberlain's own copy of which is now part of the Chamberlain Papers, owned by Birmingham University. Headed 'Memorandum by G.W. of Special Broadcasting Arrangements – September 27th–30th, 1938', the first two paragraphs set the scene for the operation.

> With a view to placing the services of Wireless Publicity Ltd. and the Luxembourg Broadcasting Station at the disposal of H.M. Government, I telephoned on the afternoon of Monday, September 26th, to Sir Joseph Ball. As the result I met him by appointment at 2.30 p.m. on the following day.
>
> During the discussion Sir Joseph told me that information received from Germany indicated not only considerable discontent and unrest in that country, but also complete ignorance as to the true state of affairs, in particular the attitude of Great Britain and France. It was agreed that any steps which could be taken to inform the German public of such matters, might prove of vital importance.[59]

Essentially the discussion revolved around the prospect of using Radio Luxembourg, based ten miles from the German border, to transmit 'black propaganda' into Germany, where eight and a half million of the 9 million private wireless sets were capable of receiving only local broadcasts. Approval for the clandestine operation came through at 7.15 p.m., with the hope that the first of these transmissions, involving the BBC, Downing Street and the Post Office, could be a direct relay of the speech that Chamberlain was due to make three-quarters of an hour later. With only minutes to spare the connection was set up, and the German people heard Chamberlain's voice. Over the next forty-eight hours German translations were recorded of speeches by Roosevelt, Chamberlain and the French and Czechoslovakian leaders, Daladier and Beneš, and the tapes were flown out from Croydon to Luxembourg, where the station broadcast them at regular intervals over the two days. The last of these broadcasts was of a speech delivered by Chamberlain in the House of Commons on Wednesday, 28 September. The day after, Chamberlain signed the famous 'piece of paper' and, as detailed by Wellesley in his Memorandum, 'On Friday morning I gave instructions for the German broadcasts to be discontinued.'

Wireless Publicity Ltd was a subsidiary of a company which, along with a number of other semi-secret organisations, was involved with the compilation and distribution of propaganda, and other behind-the-scenes subversive operations. Sir Joseph Ball was a shadowy figure who acted as Chamberlain's go-between with the Secret Services. In the view of one Intelligence Services pundit, Nicholas Pronay, Sir Joseph would never 'have entrusted such a very tricky operation which could have blown Chamberlain out of office if it had been bungled, to an amateur however able or even a rookie, especially when he had serving and experienced Intelligence officers under him and around him'.[60] The only conclusion that can be reached is that, at the time, my grandfather was working for MI6. On reflection, that is not at all surprising. He was a trained and able diplomat who spoke French, German, Italian and Russian; he moved in social circles where he rubbed shoulders with the highest echelons of the Establishment – the Royal Family, politicians and foreign diplomats; and his work both as an architect and as a commentator on the arts in general gave him the perfect cover.

I suspect that my grandfather's likely role within MI6 throws some light on how his brother Charlie managed to escape detention or any formal censure over his involvement with the Right Club. The brothers may have had a bad relationship but I am quite sure that Gerry would have abhorred the prospect of seeing the name 'the Duke of Wellington' being dragged through the mud. When, in May 1940, after the discovery of the Red Book, the membership of the Right Club became known to MI5, did Gerry use his contacts within the Secret Intelligence Service to secure some kind of amnesty for his brother? By now, carrying the rank of a Major in the Grenadiers, he was not far from home; during Dunkirk he was in France as an Intelligence officer.

In a strange crossing of paths, Hilda Matheson effectively took over where Wireless Publicity Ltd left off. In the middle of December 1938, in a meeting of the Cabinet, Chamberlain referred to the fact that a speech he had made the night before had been 'specially relayed from the Luxembourg station'. 'Presumably, we are back with Sir Joseph Ball and Wellesley's activities in MI6,'[61] wrote Nicholas Pronay and Philip Taylor in an article about the Munich operation. But the following year, the JBC – the Joint Broadcasting Committee – assumed responsibility for this type of media propaganda, and Hilda was appointed its director.

When not involved with her high-powered work for the government, Hilda was at Penns helping make plans in preparation for war. Yeats's last stay at the house was in November 1938, when he found Dottie arguing with Hilda about her insistence that trenches be dug as air-raid shelters: 'Under no circumstances will I sit in a dug-out with my employees listening [to] the gramophone'.[62] 'My dear Dorothy,' wrote Yeats after the visit, 'I thank you for those cheerful days and because I learned something as I always do in your house. Yours affectionately W.B. Yeats.'[63]

Early the following year Dorothy rented a villa in the hills above Beaulieu, in the South of France; 'W.B.' and Mrs Yeats were staying at a country hotel nearby. At one point the Yeatses joined Dorothy and Hilda, to meet Artur Schnabel, the pianist, and W.J. Turner, who were both guests in the house. 'I sat with the Austrian Jew on my right and the Irish Nationalist poet on my left', remembered Dorothy later. When Yeats said to her, 'I feel I am only beginning to understand how to write', Dorothy felt it was a sign that the end was near. 'Come back and light the flame', Mrs Yeats asked Dorothy when the time came. 'I sat on the floor by his bed holding his hand,' Dorothy wrote in her account, 'he struggled to speak: "Are you writ . . . are you writing?" "Yes, yes." "Good, good." He kissed my hand, I his.'[64] Yeats died two days later. For my grandmother, finally, a death had a calm and dignified bearing. 'So ended in the material sense this short and beautiful friendship,' she wrote in the published *Letters on Poetry, from W.B. Yeats to Dorothy Wellesley*, which she edited. In the British Library's copy of the book, by these words my grandmother has written: 'Pompous ass! (D.W.)'. I applaud her self-mockery.

Though for Dottie Yeats's death was a miserable blow, he had been ill for some time; but Hilda's, the following year, was a terrible shock. Her 'Amica amicarum' died of complications during a minor operation. It seems that the two women had quarrelled, which can only have added to my grandmother's grief. My aunt, shocked that her mother was not going to attend the funeral, went herself to the crematorium. Vita was decent enough to rush over to Penns, where she found Dottie 'completely incoherent and inarticulate'. She spoke to the doctor, who declared that she needed a nurse; but in his opinion there was 'no means of coercing or controlling a person who drinks'.

Dottie's drinking was the greatest demon in her life. Though she may never have acknowledged it, she was an alcoholic – an illness which, at the time, as the doctor's words illustrate, was misunderstood and misrepresented. By the time of Hilda's death, my grandmother's drinking was already out of control. Deprived of both her mentor and her companion, and with war fracturing normal communication with friends and family, she allowed alcohol to assume a vice-like grip on her life. Its effect on her behaviour was eventually to alienate most of the people who cared about her.

The beginning of the war was a watershed for Gerry, and in more ways than he could possibly have imagined at the time. Despite his age – he was fifty-four when it started – he was desperate to enlist. When the Grenadier Guards accepted him he was delighted. Mitey called him a hero, but he protested that he was merely 'a middle-aged man who suffers from a terrible Inferiority Complex at not having been in the last war, and is determined to be in this one'. He described himself as 'skittishly dressed in the uniform of a Second Lieutenant', adding, in another letter to Mitey, 'I believe I have the unique distinction of being the oldest Second Lieutenant in the British Army.' He could have claimed that it was likely he and Valerian were, for a few short weeks, the only father and son in the army who carried the same rank. At the beginning of the war my father was Cornet Wellesley – the Royal Horse Guards' equivalent of a Second Lieutenant. At the end of October, after disbanding his architectural practice and three weeks' training in Intelligence work, Gerry got his call-up and an immediate promotion to the rank of Major.

Before the conflict, relations between father and son had been strained, prompted chiefly by Gerry's displeasure that Valerian had not joined the family regiment, the Grenadier Guards; but when the war began, Gerry was desperate. 'If there is any news of Valerian do let me have it', he had written to his daughter the night before Britain declared war on Germany. 'He does not write to me or try & see me. It is so awful to think he feels like this about me when we may never meet again.' But war melted hostilities and when Valerian finally set off for the Middle East he sent regular, if not frequent, letters to his father.

Father and son were reunited in Cairo in February 1942. Later in the year Gerry wrote to Eliza:

> I am sorry to say that I am leaving Cairo next week to take up a job to help to govern a former Italian Colony. The capital is 8000 ft. above the sea & everyone is in a bad temper. They lead a country club sort of life & drink a

lot of bad drink. It may be quite interesting & if I don't like the job & my
employers don't like me which is more probable I come back here. It is
terribly remote from you all, & I am afraid there is not much chance now
of seeing Valerian again, before the end of the war in another 2 or 3 years
time. However, I am damned lucky to be employed at all &, as you know,
I look upon the darkest side of everything in the hope that it may not be
quite so bad after all.

He arrived in Eritrea on 26 June.

During the war, my grandmother was a very lonely woman. This was
evident from a strange series of letters addressed to Yeats after his death;
they were published in 1950 under the title *Beyond the Grave*. In one she
confided: 'This is a dream I had: I had written two letters, one to you
and one to Hilda, begging you both to come back to me at once. I could
bear the absence no longer. Someone opened the door. I asked: "Is there
no answer to my letters? It is a week since I wrote." Someone replied:
"How can they answer, you know they are both dead".'[65] Dottie even
resorted to writing to Yeats about flowers, 'although they meant nothing
to you'. 'Next comes the Winter-sweet of which I could write pages and
have written five lines. Its scent is beyond all compare. I saw it first at
the gardens of Stratfield Saye and determined to grow it myself. After
fifteen years of patience it now fills a corner in the walled garden where
we used to sit. I first saw it at its best when staying with Harold Nicolson
and Vita Sackville-West at the Legation in Teheran.'[66]

In April 1943 Dottie was one of a number of poets, including Vita,
who were asked to take part in a poetry reading in aid of the Free French
Movement, which was to be in the presence of the Queen and the two
young Princesses. Since the order of appearance was alphabetical, Dottie
was due to be the last, but when her turn approached it became clear that
she was in no fit state. When she was forcibly prevented from going on
to the stage she became violent and abusive, shouting at, among others,
Harold Nicolson, 'Take your bloody hand off my shoulder! Who are you
anyway?' Later, when she had returned to Penns, she was mortified by
her behaviour and repeatedly telephoned Vita, protesting that she had
not been drunk, and threatening suicide. 'How happy you and Harold
must be together,' Dottie said to Vita.

Word may have reached Gerry of Dottie's distressing performance, but
by the summer of 1943, he was playing an important role leading up to

the Allies' invasion of southern Italy. On 22 July 1943 Gerry wrote to his daughter:

You must have guessed long before now that I am in Sicily. I landed on the beach within a few hours of the assault troops from an assault landing craft. I then had to carry all my kit & much official stuff weighing 60 lbs for $1\frac{1}{2}$ miles up hill to an almond orchard with interspersed rocks. Here I waited for a whole afternoon being bombed & machine gunned almost incessantly. The next morning I got in early into Archimedes' Home Town & took over its government. The only rule to follow for censorship is:– 'If its interesting cut it out'. So I really cannot tell you anything of what I have been doing since. I have a great feeling that I am passing through the most exciting & horrendous days of my life, but I cannot pretend that I like the process, though for the last few days there has been peace from bombing & comparative peace from noise. When you are close behind the advancing troops the sight & smells are appalling. Oh the corpses! You cannot believe that women once loved them or that they dangled babies on their knees. However I am well & the campaign is going well and you mustn't worry about me. If it depended on the Italian people we should have peace tomorrow but M. will never give way. Let Mitey or everyone who would be interested know that I am alright. Later when things are quiet & censorship less strict I will write an account of my (very small) part in the campaign.

Gerry had waded ashore carrying, among other things, a copy of Baedeker's guide to Sicily, purloined in Cairo with the express purpose of being able to identify monuments which he wished to protect.[67] Less than two months later, Gerry heard the news of his nephew Morny's death at the Salerno landings. After a dignified period of mourning, he could admit that 'Inheriting two houses and a title was like having a birthday every day.' He had worshipped at the shrine of the First Duke, long before the prospect of a war which would place him at the head of the succession line. He was a youthful fifty-eight-year-old, strong, energetic and with all the knowledge and interest to spend the rest of his life restoring and conserving the legacy of his great-grandfather. If my grandmother's great consolation prize in life was her friendship with Yeats, inheriting the dukedom was my grandfather's.

Gerry first stepped over the threshold of Stratfield Saye House as owner on 20 November 1943, just two months after Morny's death. At the end of January his sister-in-law Maudie finally moved out of the house that had been her home for nearly twenty-five years. Just before Christmas of that year, Gerry's old friend James Lees-Milne went to stay. 'Found Gerry and his very handsome son and daughter-in-law (to whom I was introduced, titles and all mentioned by Gerry) cutting branches and clearing the shrubbery at the conservatory side of the house.' The Douros had just got back from their romantic voyage home, on separate ships but part of the same convoy. They had docked at Liverpool from where Valerian had set off in the summer of 1940 on the *Empress of Britain*. For both of them it was the first time on English soil for four years, but for Diana the time-lag would have seemed a lot longer: her last sight of England had been when her head was still filled with schoolgirl fantasies.

Soon after their return, the Douros drove over to Penns so that Valerian could introduce his wife to his mother. When they walked together into her sitting room, all she said to Diana was, 'I want to be alone with my son'. My father never forgave this and my mother never forgot. My grandmother had worried about Valerian every day that he was away in the war, and surely longed for him to be home and safe; but her view of the world had become so skewed and introspective that she could not conduct a normal conversation or even conjure up a basic set of civilities to welcome her twenty-two-year-old daughter-in-law. I am certain she did not plan a hostile reception for Diana, but how could my mother interpret it any other way? As the years passed, unquestionably this incident contributed to the fact that, apart from a brief encounter with Charles when he was a baby, Dottie never saw us, her Douro grand-children. (My brothers, Charles, Richard and John, were born, respect-ively, in 1945, 1949 and 1954; I was born in 1951. My youngest brother Christopher's birth was in 1965, nine years after my grandmother's death.)

When, during the war, she would hear an explosion and think of her son − ('Oh, don't think!') − Dottie would find a peace and calm walking round the grounds at Penns, the different levels giving her a 'sense of pilgrimage, the deep dells, the sudden crystal, almost opal light. Timeless as ever. Those were the only times I could forget the fury of the world.'[68] But in April 1949, writing her last letter to the ghost of Yeats, she confessed to him: 'Nothing could be so lonely as Penns now. All the old friends, as I have said, are dead and gone. I have found it hard to make others. They do not understand.'[69] She was unhappy 'because there is no one to gossip with or to say goodnight when one goes to bed'.[70] When she published all these letters, she ended the book with a poem:

Yeats, greatest of friends, I've not forgotten thee
Possessive of ancestral night! I give
Thee back unto ancestral night again.
Death's no concern of death.
My spectre walks alone, sole entity;
Thy spectre walks not – I the ghost
Not thou. For thee no pain.
The living are the spectres, like men walking,
I give thee to ancestral night again.[71]

My first cousin, Jeremy Clyde, born in 1941, saw his grandmother quite regularly. He remembers her as an intimidating figure, but one who clearly derived pleasure from the company of a grandchild. When Jeremy tried to enunciate grandma, she decided she wished her grandchildren to call her 'Gem'. She would treat him to spellbinding readings of *Through the Looking-Glass* and sometimes asked him whether he wanted to be a poet, to which, nervously, he always replied 'Yes'. But Gem's temper, inherited from her mother, identified by Sir George Goldie in one of her 'bumps', could be easily triggered. Once, Jeremy's younger brother Robin broke a red smoking-pipe and she bore down upon him with her stick, terrifying the wits out of him. Characteristically, she later deeply regretted the incident. I came across a small piece of evidence in mitigation for her action. Early in 1949 Gem wrote to Mitey thanking her for the 'lovely xmas presents ... My father's [Robert Ashton's] red Baltic pipe is a very beautiful piece of carving. I could still smell his cigarettes ... if you have any more of his personal objects do let me have them. I have almost nothing.'

Less than a year later, there was a terrible accident, and Robin drowned. When Gem heard the tragic news she kept on ringing, desperate to speak to her daughter. But Eliza could not face her. All she wanted from her mother was flowers from her garden. At Robin's funeral my aunt stood by the small open grave in the churchyard at Stratfield Saye, holding a tiny bunch of flowers from Penns; her mother had picked them that morning and they had been delivered by Goacher, the gardener. Tommy supported her on one side, my father the other. As she threw the flowers onto the top of the coffin, both men instinctively held her back. 'It took me six months to cry', my aunt told me; 'it took Tommy eighteen years.' They divorced in 1960, but remained close and supportive friends until his death in 1995.

*

My grandfather's latter years were as filled with events and people as my grandmother's were, in many ways, empty. On inheriting the dukedom, Gerry had stood down as Surveyor of the King's Works of Art, but now his public duties included, from 1944, being the Lord Lieutenant of London and then, in the footsteps of his great-grandfather, Lord Lieutenant of Hampshire. He contrived very successfully to blend friends and interests. Violet Powell (wife of the writer Anthony Powell) wrote about her stay at Stratfield Saye in 1958 for the AGM of the Jane Austen Society, of which Gerry was President. She had earned her place at the weekend by correctly answering Gerry's two test questions: 'Where in Jane Austen is there a scene of transvestism and where is the word "dung" mentioned?'[72] Violet had correctly identified an officer in *Pride and Prejudice* in a dress belonging to the Miss Bennets' vulgar aunt, and the appearance of a dung cart in *Persuasion*.

The Powells lived opposite Gerry when he was in Chester Terrace and, with the eye of a chronicler novelist, Powell painted in his memoirs a picture of my grandfather: 'His touch of haughtiness was scarcely, if at all, augmented by becoming a duke ... No amount of ragging on the part of his contemporaries ... could undermine this lofty demeanour'; but, Powell went on, 'Mere pomposity, however splendid, would never have brought Gerry Wellington his fame if he had not possessed many other qualities too, one of which was a powerful capacity for counter-ragging his raggers.' Gerry ended up with a plethora of art-orientated appointments, of which the first, soon after becoming Duke, was to sit on the committee appointed to look into 'works of art stolen by the enemy'. As a genuine connoisseur of the arts with ducal clout, he was in great demand.

As my grandmother advanced into her sixties, she became increasingly dependent on nurses and carers. My father rarely saw her – in any case, from January 1955 the family were posted to Cyprus. My aunt, ever the dutiful daughter, would visit her regularly, driving the 100 or so miles from her own home to listen to her mother's sad, self-pitying rambling conversations about all her problems. Eliza had the unenviable task of arranging, invariably against her mother's will, for her to go into 'homes' for a 'rest-cure'. Many of her friends fell away, but Gem's poetry and books continued: her last collection of poetry was published in 1955 under the title *Early Light*. At Christmas of that year she sent to her grandson Jeremy a book which had belonged to her brother Scamp – 'I would like you to begin now to have a shelf of books given to you from me'. At the end of the letter she recalled how, when very small, he had sat on her knee and 'shrieked with laughter at things we read'. Was there an echo there of her holding her young son Valerian in her arms, when life had been sweet and full of hope?

In *Far Have I Travelled* Dottie wrote, 'Had I been as robust or courageous as Freya Stark, Gertrude Bell, or Ella Maillart, I do not think I should have married, or have lived in England ... The wanderlust is ever with me. I would have trained as an archaeologist; but evidently I was intended to be a poet.'[73] My grandmother would, I believe, have been content with the last few lines of Kathleen Raine's introduction to the 1964 edition of *Letters on Poetry from W.B. Yeats to Dorothy Wellesley*, referring to Yeat's poetry in his last years. 'The soil from which great poetry grows is remote from these aridities which occupy the pens of critics; the beauty of a woman, the charm of her house and her companionship, friendship, dreams and kindness, these nourish immortal poetry.'[74] She would also I suspect, have derived some pleasure from the irony of her placement in the most recent *DNB*. Her entry comes immediately after that of the First Duke. He, however, would not have relished the association. 'I hate the whole race', was his verdict on poets. 'I have the worst opinion of them. There is no believing a word they say – your professional poets, I mean – there never existed a more worthless set than Byron and his friends for example. Poets praise fine sentiments and never practise them, their praise of virtue and fine feeling is entirely from the imagination: if they describe a fine action they quote some other author from whom they have taken the idea, to prove it was nature.'[75]

On Wednesday, 11 July 1956, Eliza got a call from the nurse who was looking after her mother. By the time she reached Penns it was all over. The funeral was a small and dismal affair. When in India, my grandmother had found that the Hindu burning 'held the calm, the peace, the silence that all funerals should have', and she left instructions that she should be cremated. Eliza, remembering the horror she had felt when she attended Hilda's cremation, did not allow anyone to go to the crematorium. My parents flew back from Cyprus to be at the service in Withyham Church. If more from duty than devotion, my grandfather was there and the Nicolsons were amongst the few people who attended. Vita described the scene to a friend. 'It was rather moving – just a little hole in the ground, and a tiny wooden box containing her ashes. All that was left of those blue eyes and that wild spirit!'[76] In December 1922, when her marriage to Gerry was rupturing, Dottie wrote a poem called 'Exiled', the last words of which were 'When I am dead, / Will you forgive me then?'.[77]

It is hard to find Gem's grave. When I do, the stone is covered in moss and lichen. Almost caressingly, I pass my fingers over the lettering: 'Dorothy Violet Duchess of Wellington'. I have brought for her what I would have done had she been alive: a small bunch of flowers from my garden. Conscious of the commonplace variety of the blooms – viburnum and winter jasmine – I inwardly apologise to Gem for their lack of originality. The sixteenth-century church stands on a hill above the main road, and on this bitterly cold winter day the wind is howling round the graveyard. If I were with Gem, we would seek shelter inside and sit on a wooden pew near the Sackville family vault, where Vita's ashes lie, in the pink marble sarcophagus that sat for many years on her writing-desk at Sissinghurst. There would be so many questions that I would want to ask Gem. Did she ever think she could have saved her marriage? Did she regret her relationship with Vita? Did she wish she had met me? I am sure the answer to the second question would have been 'no'.

Four years after the death of my grandmother, Mitey's husband Bobby James (whose first marriage had been to Gerry's sister Evelyn) died. By then, my grandfather had lived on his own for nearly twenty-seven years. It is a measure of his loneliness that he asked Mitey (my grandmother's half-sister) to marry him. Their close friendship stretched back to Gerry's wedding to Dottie, when Mitey, as a young teenager, had been a bridesmaid. They were devoted to each other, and as well as the comfort of companionship – someone (as Gem had said) to 'say goodnight when one goes to bed' – I feel sure that my grandfather also yearned for an elegant châtelaine to share the burden of running, and entertaining in, a large house. After one lunch party for the Queen Mother, Gerry confessed to Mitey:

> One cannot tell how one's own parties go off. All I can remember is that H.M. was offered one wedge of Brie on a plate instead of assorted cheeses on a large cheese dish, of which I have plenty in the house & which was given to others. I was frozen with horror, but of course could say nothing. She ate a large piece of the Brie, after a good helping of egg mousse, followed by roast beef & blackberry & apple tart ... She wrote me a four page Collins [thank-you letter] and said I had got together all her favourite people.

But Mitey had her own responsibilities and ties in Yorkshire: St Nicholas and its famous garden and, more crucially, a band of grandchildren who lived on her doorstep. Perhaps with a pang of regret, Mitey turned Gerry down. 'She would have made a wonderful duchess,' says her daughter Ursula. However, they remained very close up until the end of Gerry's life, with frequent visits to each other's houses and regular outings to racy musicals with dinners afterwards at the Ritz. My grandfather loved going on cruises – usually on his own, and never in search of new friends. On one of his last ones, he was surprised when a box of flowers was delivered to his small cabin. 'I tore it open & found it was from you,' he wrote to Mitey. 'No one else would have thought of it and I am very much touched and grateful.'

To many of Gerry's friends, his foibles and failings added to his appeal. James Lees-Milne, staying at Stratfield Saye in the spring of 1949, found his host 'at his most entertaining and charming, although fussy'. In his diary he described how 'he came into the drawing-room and saw me with my feet, in perfectly clean evening shoes, poised lightly on an ordinary footstool. He rushed up with newspapers, seized my feet, arranged the papers on the stool, and banged down the said feet, exclaiming, "It never occurred to me that anyone would actually put a foot on a footstool."'[78] Later in the same year, when Lees-Milne was again staying with his old friend, he cut and bruised his leg and hand when he was climbing into the car. '"Some people make a terrible fuss over a scratch", was Gerry's response. "Now the other day I fell, cut my head open to the skull, bled, was dreadfully messed about, and never turned a hair."'[79]

Lady Gladwyn – Cynthia – was another of Gerry's friends who often stayed at Stratfield Saye with her husband. When Gerry visited them in Paris (Lord Gladwyn, then Gladwyn Jebb, was Ambassador to France from 1956 to 1960), he always requested the same treat: 'I am a simple English gentleman living near Reading, and when I come to Paris I want to be as gay as possible, and have the club seats at the Folies Bergère and be as close as possible.'[80]

My grandfather had a wonderful voice. When he was well into his ninth decade, Cynthia Gladwyn described a car journey on the way back from the Wexford Festival, when everyone was singing arias from their favourite operas. 'As we drove through Dublin, Gerry became embarrassed by all the noise we were making. He turned pompous, showed all his double chins, said we must stop; and then, suddenly remembering something particularly good from the *Geisha Girl* ... started off again.'[81]

In one of his last letters to Mitey, he complained that he was 'feeling every minute of my 86 years and don't move much from the same armchair. Weren't you coming to London for Christmas shopping? If so, you must come here. I am going to Apsley House on Tuesday Nov. 2nd for a play but I feel that will be my last beano.' He ended the letter, 'I do hope I see you again before I die.' To his daughter Eliza, living in America, whom he missed terribly, he confessed, 'I feel it is high time I went as I don't much want to stay.' A few weeks later my grandfather broke his hip and was rushed into Reading General Hospital. When pneumonia struck him he was taken home to die at Stratfield Saye, the house of his ancestor, the preservation of whose legacy had been the focus of his life's work. He died on Tuesday, 4 January 1972. Like Gem, he chose to be cremated and his ashes lie in a porphyry urn in Stratfield Saye church, surrounded by a memorial that he designed himself.

Despite all the good things in his life – of which his seven grandsons and one granddaughter represented a significant part – I suspect that real contentment eluded him. On one of the Nicolsons' wedding anniversaries, Vita said to Harold: 'I would rather have our untidy busy ramshackle life, irradiated by the love we have had for each other for thirty-five years now, so indestructibly, than all Gerry's titles and possessions.'[82] Yet in all likelihood it was Vita who, however unintentionally, deprived my grandfather of a life 'irradiated by love'. Three years before he died, Gerry wrote to Mitey about his misery at the theft, from a hotel room, of a precious possession – 'Dottie had given me the watch in 1914 & it had lain under my pillow ever since'. For fifty-four years my grandfather slept with his head close to a wedding gift from my grandmother, his dreams accompanied by its muffled ticking. He may never have forgiven her, but I believe Gerry's feelings for Dottie never really went away.

Now, as I write this book, I wish I could talk to my grandfather about the First Duke. His knowledge and understanding of our ancestor was unique within the family, and there are so many questions I would want to explore. I wish, too, that I could gather some of the memories of my maternal grandfather. He died when I was nine: old enough to mind, but too young to appreciate what disappeared with his passing. Long after he had gone, the sweet smell of his tobacco lingered in Knockdolian, the house he had loved all his life.

When, after the Second World War, Douglas returned from Palestine, for two years he commanded Scotland's Lowland District, and then served as an ADC to King George V. When he retired in 1947, he set up and ran the Knockdolian Nursery Gardens, a role in which he took great pride. He ceded to his wife Ruth on all matters horticultural, but had a hands-on involvement with many practical aspects of the business, including the annual picking and packing of the daffodils, which he then drove himself to the market in Glasgow. In 1951 he started a column in the *Journal of the Scottish Rock Garden Club*, of which his wife Ruth was a prominent member; writing anonymously, he titled it 'Locum Tenens'. In his first column, he confessed that occasionally his wife 'permitted [him] to weed the middle of the paths and to pull up groundsel and chickweed, both of which I can recognise. Otherwise I may look and admire, but I am not to touch.'

In the country, unless the occasion demanded otherwise, Douglas preferred to wear his comfortable plus-fours, made of 'Knockdolian Tweed' – the design of which, inspired by the colours of the Knockdolian landscape, had been a gift from his son-in-law Valerian. He hated London, though from time to time he would venture forth in support of his wife or daughter. On one of these outings, having donned an old country mackintosh, he found himself in Piccadilly with time on his hands and thought he would go into the Ritz to have a drink. The doorman firmly barred his entry – 'I think Sir might be more comfortable somewhere else'. Unfazed, my grandfather took himself off to a less snobbish watering-hole, no doubt chuckling at the thought of how obsequious the man might have been had he known he was addressing a General.

Douglas was clever (among his hidden talents was the ability to read and write Gaelic), kind and modest, and he had a resolute set of principles and priorities which made him a very good soldier. His life, though threaded through by its own private tragedy, was attended by contentment and fulfilment and the end, when it came, was far too early. On Tuesday, 7 February 1961, at the age of sixty-seven, he died of lung cancer. Punctiliously polite, the day before his death he wrote to his niece Helen and her husband Teddy, apologising for the late Christmas 'thank-you'. A sports lover to the end, he was hoping they would join him in June to watch Test Match cricket at Lord's. The day after his death, his last 'Locum Tenens' column arrived at the offices of the journal.

After my grandfather's death my grandmother decided to move out of Knockdolian, which passed to my mother, though Ruth regularly returned to check on the plants she had left behind. She re-established herself in Farnham, where she created a glorious garden worthy of her considerable reputation as a horticulturist. When searching for archival treasures in my mother's stash of McConnel family memorabilia, I came across a small brown leather attaché case which had not been opened since my grandmother died. Among the contents were letters, shells, banknotes, postcards, pencils, pens, lists, envelopes of seeds, my mother's childhood drawings, fishing tackle, recipes, knitting patterns and endless other small examples of a life's flotsam. There were also black-and-white photographs, one of which was captioned 'D.F. McConnel shaving in trench during the First World War in France'; another was a 1919 portrait of a young, good-looking naval officer. Attached to the back was a tiny newspaper cutting recording his death in October 1966.

How significant was the young naval officer? My mother remembers hearing talk (but never from her mother herself) of a romance. Did Ruth end her relationship with him to marry Douglas, or was her engagement in 1919 a by-product of a broken heart? Was this sailor the reason that the wedding of my maternal grandparents was briefly postponed, or was the delay prompted by family concerns about the marriage of two cousins? No one will ever know. When Ruth died, tending her garden until the end, on Thursday, 27 November 1980, she took her own secrets and sorrows with her. She was buried alongside her husband in the McConnel family vault in the village of Colmonell in Ayrshire. The small alpine greenhouse was lifted from its home in Farnham and taken to Stratfield Saye, where my mother assumed the guardianship of this prized inheritance.

Stratfield Saye, as well as being home to many Wellesleys through the generations, has also nurtured in its soil plants, shrubs and trees that have provided solace, celebrated good moments and been a constant source of uncomplicated pleasure. My paternal grandmother, Gem, painted some exquisite small watercolours of her favourite wild flowers from the area around Stratfield Saye. Half hang in my bathroom in my parents' house; the rest, which belong to my aunt, are, coincidentally, in her bathroom. Another Duchess of Wellington found consolation in flowers. When Kitty died in 1831, she left behind her a delicate watercolour of spring flowers which, many years later, was found in the corner of one of the Stratfield Saye attics, lying next to her paint-box and easel.

THIRTEEN

Arthurolatry

When my father and I visit Walmer Castle, the residence of the Warden of the Cinque Ports – a romantic sixteenth-century fortress near Deal, with dramatic views out across the sea – I understand why the First Duke chose to spend so much time here. As he got older, his attachment to the place seemed to grow. The room where he slept and wrote was plainly furnished and methodically arranged, 'something like an officer's room in a garrison'. It was in this room, at 3.25 p.m. on Tuesday, 14 September 1852, that the Duke died at the age of eighty-three. When it was clear that he was slipping away his valet, Kendall, who had been with him since Waterloo, placed him in his favourite chair by the window looking out to sea, and to France.

In his last thirteen years, the Duke's life had been transformed by one simple, new pleasure: finally he experienced the happiness of an intimate family relationship, through the marriage of his eldest son. Lady Douro, as he always referred to his daughter-in-law, was charming, innocent and utterly devoted to the Duke; she proved the daughter that Mrs Arbuthnot had commented, years before, he was 'so unlucky' not to have. But there was the one great sadness in Bessy's life: her inability, despite repeated and agonising attempts which went on through the last year of the Duke's life, to have children. She was only thirty-two when the First Duke died, and I am sure he went to his grave hoping that a miracle might happen. Bessy would carry his great name, but with the sorrow of knowing she would never be able to perpetuate it.

In the early years of the Douro marriage there were no shadows, and the Duke delighted in his new role. He proudly took Lady Douro to court, where 'She was much admired by everybody, especially by the Queen.'[1] And a weekend guest at Stratfield Saye commented that it was 'pleasant to see the devotion with which he consults and anticipates every wish of his beautiful daughter-in-law'.[2] Bessy shared her father-in-law's love of music – they would go to concerts and the opera together; and for the Douros' first wedding anniversary, which fell at Easter, the Duke laid on a musical entertainment at Stratfield Saye that included a performance from the famous Giulia Grisi, one of his favourite opera singers.

Lady Douro would also ride with her father-in-law, accompany him on his walks in the park and enjoy the pleasures of his seaside retreat; after Parliament had recessed, the Duke would take up residence at Walmer. Though he was merely the 'tenant' for his lifetime, unlike his Hampshire home it had no ghosts; there is no record of Kitty ever visiting Walmer.

The Duke's penchant for simple living was taken one step further at Walmer. 'I have one room in this Residence,' he wrote to a friend, 'in which I sleep, dress and write all day!'[3] Characteristically, he installed his own private water-closet behind a door off his room; this involved attaching a small extension to the castle. A photograph of Walmer taken some years after the Duke's death reveals that he had more concern for his most private needs than he had for aesthetic appearances. He was so fond of the castle that he described it as 'the most charming marine residence I have ever seen. The Queen herself has nothing to be compared with it.' George Robert Gleig, to whom he made this remark, cites it as an example of one of his 'amiable peculiarities, that whatever happened to be his own possessed great attractions in his eyes'.[4]

At Walmer, as always, the Duke's routine was regimented and, apart from his most intimate activities, open to public scrutiny. 'He always rises at six o'clock, and walks on the platform', wrote the commentator and diarist Thomas Raikes,

> then returns to his room to dress, which ... takes a very long time. He is remarkably neat in his appearance, always wearing a white waistcoat and trowsers, under which is a good guard of fleecy hosiery against the cold; and a blue riding coat in the morning.
>
> At ten o'clock he appears at breakfast; he seems to eat heartily, and makes messes of rusks and bread in his tea, never meat or eggs. He converses the whole time, then retires, saying, 'Well, we shall dine at seven.' He remains in his room, writing letters, and despatches and making notes, some rather droll and concise ... About two o'clock, he generally gets on his horse, and gallops over the Downs, or perhaps, to Dover, where he is very active in attending to his business as Warden of the Cinque Ports.[5]

Not long after the Douro wedding, there was cause for anxiety over the Duke's health. Lord Stanhope, hearing him speak in the House of Lords, described how 'his words came out very slowly, and as it were drop by drop, and he seemed to have lost the modulation of his voice, which sometimes rose almost to a scream – sometimes sank almost to a whisper'.[6] But the Duke assured his new daughter-in-law that he could keep going with his parliamentary duties for another twelve months if need be. In November, however, not long after being deeply affected by the death of his close friend Lady Salisbury, he suffered a stroke; Kendall found him lying motionless on the floor of his room. Whatever the cause, it was exacerbated by the cold, damp weather and his habit of fasting if he felt slightly unwell. Earlier that day he had been out hunting; with his customary disregard for sartorial convention, he had put a fur collar round his neck and tried to keep the rain off by holding up an umbrella. There was genuine alarm about his condition but he managed to recover and within four days, though 'thin and pale in the face', he returned to London to attend a Privy Council meeting, where the Queen announced her betrothal to Prince Albert of Saxe-Coburg-Gotha.

Over the next two years the Duke had several more strokes: one, a few days after the royal wedding in February 1840, prompted a friend to declare that, for the Duke, 'the day of retreat is arrived'. The family gathered round him, and Douro sat by his bed all night. William, his brother, reported that 'he lay one may say insensible from near six o'clock till half past twelve – and in the course of that time he had eighteen very severe convulsions in which he must have suffered much – for the noise he made was dreadful'. But, for the Duke, retreat was not a familiar move and within days the doctors were declaring that 'they have never seen such an extraordinary power of rallying in anybody before in the whole course of their practice'.[7]

At the end of 1840 there was a postscript to the drama that had defined the Duke's life. Nearly twenty years after his death on his island prison in the middle of the South Atlantic, Napoleon's remains were disinterred and returned to France. There had been a delicate negotiation between the two governments about the repatriation, and the Prime Minister, Melbourne, had been prudent enough to suggest that 'it would be as well to inform the Duke'. When told, the Duke professed indifference to the whole matter; he knew that 'some day or other the French would be sure to make it a matter of triumph over England, but that personally he "did not care a twopenny damn about that"'.[8] The interment at Les Invalides went ahead on 15 December with great pomp and ceremony, and the British press reported every detail to their readers. Around this time the Duke's Spanish friend Alava had arranged for the French writer, Prosper Mérimée, to visit him at Stratfield Saye. The Duke was gratified that

Mérimée enjoyed his stay, but commented drily in a letter to his niece Priscilla, 'It must have been delightful to him to find our populace so much attached to the memory of Napoleon.' The Duke was back in his stride, and his letter-writing was as strong as ever; one cold winter afternoon he managed to pen twenty-five.

1841 started well for the Duke: he had his beloved daughter-in-law to stay at Stratfield Saye. But at the end of the month he suffered another attack and this time it was in the House of Lords. The Prime Minister wrote to the Queen telling her that it happened while Lord Brougham was addressing the House and he 'observed the Duke's face to be drawn and distorted, and soon afterwards the Duke rose from his seat and walked staggeringly towards the door'.⁹ Once again the family and physicians gathered around him, and once again he confounded them.

The Duke was more troubled by Lady Douro's health and well-being than by his own. In a decisive gesture, in October 1841 he paid off her debts. Did his thoughts go back to the time all those years ago when Kitty's fatal combination of generosity and inefficiency had so angered him that he never forgave her? It was just over ten years since Kitty's death; he had had plenty of time to consider whether he had always been fair. Perhaps he could already see strains on the Douro marriage, and wanted to avoid family history repeating itself.

In March of the following year Bessy seems to have suffered a miscarriage. She convalesced at Stratfield Saye, where her father-in-law made sure he gave her all the comfort and care his house could provide. He acquired a special wheelchair, and had rollers put on the feet of one of his chaise-longues. He implored her to follow her doctor's orders, for everyone's sake, 'above all for your own; and I will add mine'. In June he suggested that the Douros should use Walmer for a long period of convalescence. 'I should be more than compensated by the re-establishment of your Health and particularly the Restoration of the domestic Comfort and Happiness of yourself and Douro!'

The Queen suffered no such traumas or complications in childbirth. Just over nine months after the royal wedding, Victoria and Albert had their first child, a daughter; a year later, on 9 November 1841, the future Edward VII was born. As with most royal events, the Duke was soon in attendance. On arriving at the Palace after the birth, he is reported to have said to the midwife, 'Is it a boy?', to which he received the sharp reply, 'It's a Prince, Your Grace'. The Duke sent a brief bulletin to his friend Lady Wilton: 'A Prince at 12 minutes before eleven. He is as red as a Lobster.'¹⁰

The Queen had become so fond of the Duke that in November 1842 she asked him if he would lend her Walmer for a spell of bracing sea air. Various special preparations were put into effect, and she pronounced herself delighted by its simplicity. Others in her household were not so complimentary: the royal children's governess thought the castle 'a heap of comical rooms', where the 'doors and windows all chatter and sing at once, and hardly keep out the dark storm of wind and rain which is howling round'.[11] (The Duke savoured the time he spent at Walmer, but severe winter weather could dent his own enthusiasm. 'Wind, snow, sleet, and rain in succession. I wish that I was at home in my warm comfortable house in Hants',[12] he had written a year earlier, when he had workmen at Stratfield Saye – 'I cannot get them out of my house'.) By the end of the royal party's month-long stay the Queen had caught a cold; but she had been charmed by being able to walk along the beach unattended, and largely unobserved.

There were more melancholy events in 1842. Richard, the eldest Wellesley brother, died on 26 September. The Duke was staying at Walmer Castle and 'seemed much depressed throughout the evening and said little'. Encouraged by Marianne, Richard's wife, there had been a rapprochement between the two brothers the previous year. On the anniversary of Waterloo, Richard turned up at Apsley House but the Duke was not at home. 'I was very sorry that I was not in the House when you called upon me . . . I am very much flattered by your coming on this day; and above all delighted with your Note.' It is a sad reflection on Richard's life that he chose to be buried at Eton, probably the setting for his happiest and most fulfilling memories. At the funeral, an Etonian schoolboy was struck by the sight of the four remaining brothers – 'with their Wellesley faces so like each other'.[13]

The Duke's one surviving sister, Anne Culling Smith, died in 1844; his brother William the year after. William's obituary in *The Times* was unusually judgemental – 'an undignified, ineffective speaker, an indiscreet politician, and a man by no means skilful in the conduct of official transactions'.[14] Henry was the next brother to go, in 1847 in Paris, where, after a long and successful career as a diplomat, he and Georgiana had taken up residence. Gerald died in 1848 – his obituary, in contrast to William's, describing him as 'much respected by all classes of the community for his kind and conciliatory manners, and the unvarying benevolence of his disposition'.[15] Though he never gained the mitre, Gerald ended his days as Prebend of Durham Cathedral, where he chose to be buried.

In 1843 the Queen appointed Lady Douro as one of her Ladies-in-

Waiting. For her first spell of duty at Windsor, she took her harp, and after she had got over her initial shyness was persuaded to play duets with the Queen. She was not the first of the family to hold an office at court: her brother-in-law Charles, unattached and under-employed, had been appointed Clerk Marshal to the Stables in September 1841.[16] Maybe court life put a spring into Charles Wellesley's step. In the summer of 1844, *The Times* picked up on a piece of gossip. 'We understand that a matrimonial alliance is on the tapis between Lord Charles Wellesley, Clerk Marshal of the Household, youngest son of the Duke of Wellington and the accomplished Miss Pierrepont, only daughter of the Right Hon. H. Pierrepont.'[17]

As the newspaper predicted, the wedding between Charles and Sophia Pierrepont took place at St George's, Hanover Square, on 9 July 1844. The bride, wearing a veil of 'rich Brussels lace', was attended by six bridesmaids and her new father-in-law threw a wedding breakfast at Apsley House and lent the couple Stratfield Saye for their honeymoon. The Duke may have had some misgivings about the father of his new daughter-in-law. In his younger days Henry Pierrepont, grandson of the Peasant Countess, had been a renowned dandy and friend of the infamous Beau Brummell. White's Club in Piccadilly was one of the dandies' haunts; they would often be seen sitting in the famous bow window. A member of the more staid Guards Club opposite railed, 'Damn those fellows; they are upstarts, and fit only for the society of tailors!'.[18]

Among the family guests in the church at Charles and Sophia's wedding was Marianne, Marchioness Wellesley, Richard's widow. I wonder if the Duke spotted her when he walked with his son up the aisle behind Sophia and her father? Did a memory of lost love flit across his mind when he thought of the way Richard had wrested from him the affection of this beautiful woman? Might she even have become his second Duchess? The Duke continued to be flattered by the attentions of young and charming women and sometimes accepted their approaches because it amused him; he was always dismissive of what people might think, even a little defiant. 'What is the good of being sixty-seven,' he once wrote to the first Lady Salisbury, 'if one cannot speak to a young lady?'

The Duke once claimed to Mrs Arbuthnot, 'No woman ever loved me, never in my whole life.'[19] Of course, Kitty would have disputed this, but Arthur may have considered that her kind of love – obsessive and reverential – disqualified her. In the last weeks of her life, Kitty had the consolation of her husband's concern; but she would have grieved at being deprived of the pleasure of seeing her two sons marry, and of the joy of having grandchildren. A year after Charles and Sophia's marriage, Sophia gave birth to a son. One friend observed that when the child (whom they christened Arthur) was born, it was to the Duke's 'great delight and relief, for she [Sophia] was ill for some hours, and he was in as great an agitation as a young husband could have been'.[20] Tragically, the baby died on 7 July 1846, when he was only fourteen months old; the Duke was inconsolable. 'I found the Duke very low and I think more grieved for the poor child's death than the day before',[21] reported his niece Priscilla to her husband. But, as the Duke wrote, 'By the Mercy of God! the second son, an infant has recovered.'[22] The 'second son' was Henry, who would eventually become the 3rd Duke.

Apart from Priscilla, there were others whose comfort the Duke may have sought. Angela Burdett-Coutts, one year old at the time of Waterloo, was forty-five years his junior. A considerable heiress, conveniently she lived down the road from Apsley House at No. 1 Stratton Street. They had first met in 1839, and by 1846 had formed a close friendship. Her strong will and generosity of spirit appealed to him. Initially Angela had turned to the Duke for advice about the management of her eponymous bank, of which he was a client. By the end of 1846 she had stayed at Walmer, and they had exchanged presents. Burdett-Coutts' biographer, Edna Healey, had no doubts about the status of the relationship at this time. 'The Duke had become deeply attached and Miss Coutts was in love.' On New Year's Day 1847, the Duke wrote that he knew she considered the previous year to have been the happiest of her life and he promised that 'nothing shall be omitted on my part as your friend to make this year as happy as the last'.

The Duke was alone with his grandson at Stratfield Saye in a bitterly cold January of 1847, wishing Angela were there, in his 'catching-cold proof' house. But she was ill in London. When he returned to the city he praised her 'clear correct judgement: which with an excellent heart will always keep you right'. Perhaps this spurred her on, for on 7 February she took the unusual step of proposing marriage to him. 'My dearest Angela,' he wrote the following day, 'I have passed every Moment of the Evening and Night since I quitted you in reflecting upon our conversation of yesterday, Every Word of which I have considered repeatedly.' He viewed himself as her friend, guardian and protector and he entreated her, 'in this way, not to throw yourself away upon a Man old enough to be your Grandfather, who, however strong, Hearty and Healthy at present, must and will certainly in time feel the consequences and Infirmities of Age'.

He may have turned down her proposal but the bond between them seemed to grow even stronger. He was as devoted as any ardent young lover; he sent her little gifts, pressed sweet-scented flowers into his letters, persuaded her to wear his favourite colours, and tenderly gave her advice about every aspect of her life. At Stratfield Saye he had been 'looking out and measuring walls with a view to break out doors and make passages ... to make fresh communication with my Apartment'; a response to a 'recollection of what you said to me some time ago as to your wishes'. He went ahead with the plan, and the small staircase is still there, connecting the rooms she used to the Duke's own suite below.

In the summer of 1847 the Duke and Miss Coutts were inseparable. There were critics of what some people considered to be inappropriate behaviour for an octogenarian. The diarist Greville described the Duke's relationship with Burdett-Coutts as a 'strange intimacy' which was evidence of 'lamentable appearances of decay in his vigorous mind'. It is clear from the Duke's letters to Angela that he was capable of romantic love; perhaps they even give an insight into his early courtship of Kitty. Even when summoned by his Sovereign, he continued to dream of his absent amour. She was 'ever in mind yesterday at Windsor Castle'. 'I am become like you. I have you with me constantly!' When Angela went on a trip to France, she had not been gone a month before he was longing for the return of his 'companion ... whom I look at and caress, who is happy and delighted and smiles on me in return!'. He entreats her to 'keep your feet dry and warm' and reveals, 'If mine are very cold I rub them against each other at night as I have entreated you to do! I think of you when I am in the act of doing so and whether you have adopted that practice.'

Whatever the nature of their relationship, by the end of the year winter winds had cooled his ardour and she noticed that his letters were 'not as they had been before'. But he let her down gently: 'I know and feel, God Bless You! that I have only to say the word and that I shall have you at my side at all Times! Is that reflection very presumptuous? No. It is the truth, you delight in it as I do.' The intensity of his feelings may have waned, but her trust and kindness continued to be 'the delight of his life'. A small faded envelope, still at Stratfield Saye, contains the touching evidence of their mutual devotion: a lock of his silver hair, looped in a bow and entwined with strands of Angela's brown hair. The date on the envelope is 4 June 1848, a month after he entered his eightieth year.

His attachment to Angela Burdett-Coutts was enduring, and when, in the last year of his life he sent her some tickets to attend the House of Lords, he wrote, 'It does amuse me mightily at times to find a veteran eighty-two years old, deaf with all! turned into a lover!'[23] Is the word 'lover' to be taken seriously or did he use it as a mode of self-flattery? There were rumours in both families that they secretly married; if there is any truth to this, which seems unlikely, the secret went with them to their graves. What is certain is that when the Duke died, the Wellesley family were as attentive to her as they would have been to a widow; Charles escorted her to the lying-in-state at 'the most convenient and least observed moment' and Douro wrote that he was giving a copy of his father's death-mask 'to no other ladies but you; that is votre affaire'.

If the attentions of eligible young women were one of the solaces of the Duke's old age, his love of children was another. He adored his own grandchildren, often describing them in letters as his 'children', just as he referred to Lady Douro and Lady Charles as his 'daughters'. Not surprisingly, it was Walmer's idyllic seaside setting which encouraged the presence of many young companions in his sojourns there. 'When we assembled for dinner, we usually found the Duke, who had dressed early, engaged in a regular game of romps with the children, who came down on purpose for what they called the Battle of Waterloo, which commenced by one of them throwing a cushion at the newspaper the Duke was reading.'[24] One of these children was accused of lying: 'I really think that you ought to warn your little girl not to romance as she does. She has just told me that this morning she had a pillow-fight with the Duke of Wellington.' 'My Dear Sir,' the father replied, 'that is absolutely true.'[25]

To his small great-nieces or nephews he may have been 'Uncle Dukey', to other young children he was sometimes 'Mister Dook'. Unlike many adults, who were all too conscious of his great fame and power, children were drawn to him because he entered their world without any pretensions, and to them he seemed to be always up for some fun. 'I don't think it ever occurred to us that he was a great man, but simply that, of all the relations, he was the one we were most at our ease with, and whom our mother too seemed happiest with.'[26] This was the view of one of Priscilla Burghersh's children; another remembered that when the gardener at Walmer understandably objected to a raid on the fruit trees, he reminded his fellow raiders, 'Never mind, let's go to the Duke; he always allows everything and gives you what you like directly.' On one occasion, at Stratfield Saye, an ambassador turned up to see the Duke, to be confronted by the sight of his noble host having his nose plastered with butter by a little girl who was sitting on his lap. A chair was placed for His Excellency next to the Duke, but the child continued with her work.[27]

The artist Benjamin Robert Haydon witnessed a group of noisy young children clambering all over the Duke at breakfast one morning. 'One boy . . . roared, "I want some tea, Duke." "You shall have it, if you promise not to slop it over me as you did yesterday."'[28] Haydon was one of a pack of artists who were constantly after the Duke to sit for a portrait or bust. 'There is not a moment of the day or night that I can call my own,' wrote the Duke to a friend. 'These gentlemen are at breakfast, dinner, and supper, and all the evening my existence is at their pleasure; I cannot move along the passage, or on the staircase, or the ramparts, without meeting them.'[29] Wilkie, another of the Duke's famous portraitists, was sceptical of the Duke's protestations. 'He would be mortified if he were not asked to sit.'[30] But the Duke continued to lament his fate – 'having passed my Manhood acquiring celebrity; and of having to pass my old Age in sitting for Busts and Pictures to Artists, that they may profit by it.'[31]

In the winter of 1845, when Prime Minister Peel proposed the repeal of the Corn Laws, the Duke faced his last political challenge. Wellington's opinion, expressed to Henry Pierrepont, Sophia's father, was that 'Rotten potatoes have done it, they put Peel in his damned fright'. But he knew there was genuine cause for concern: famine threatened Ireland and there was growing support for repeal across the country. The Duke was, as ever, relishing his role. 'I am doing all that I can to relieve matters, and to keep the Ship afloat,' he wrote to Lady Wilton just before Christmas.[32] Eventually he determined that the priority was 'the peace of the country and the Queen'. He supported Peel and, when the Bill arrived in the Lords, he expertly steered it through the Chamber. The landed aristocracy and Protectionists felt betrayed, but the Duke never worried about alienating his own class and, in any case, by this time his great age and experience afforded him a strong measure of respect from all parties.

'You must permit us to pay you a visit at Stratfield Saye', the Queen announced in 1845. The Duke wrote to Lady Wilton that he had done 'everything I could to avoid the Subject: never mentioned the word Stratfield Saye and kept out of Her Way'. However, when confronted, 'I bowed and said that I should be highly Honoured, and added that I must go there immediately to have the preparations made for H.M.'s reception.' The Duke was apprehensive, however, that the Sovereign would find his residence 'small and inconvenient'. 'She smiled and continued to be very gracious, but did not give a Hint of postponing the Visit.' When he told his long-standing housekeeper, Mrs Apostles, she nearly had a nervous breakdown: 'My Lord, Your House is a very comfortable Residence for yourself, your Family and your friends; But it is not fit for the Reception of the Sovereign and Her Court.' Of this the Duke was all too aware, but, characteristically, knowing there was no way round it, he declared, 'Very True!' but 'what cannot be prevented must be borne; and we must make the best preparation in our Power'.[33]

Good humour infused the whole weekend and in her journal the Queen remarked, 'Stratfieldsaye is a low & not very large house, but warm & comfortable & with a good deal of room in it.' If she had any criticism it concerned the temperature in the house, which she found rather high – not surprisingly, since the Duke confessed, 'he was never warm at Windsor, excepting in bed!'. When it was all over the host admitted: 'I thank God! the visitation is concluded.' No doubt, Mrs Apostles' relief was even more palpable.

When at Stratfield Saye or Walmer, the Duke always went to church on Sunday and in the later years of his life he regularly attended the early service at the Chapel Royal in St James's. One visitor to London went there on a bleak winter morning in February 1848, hoping to spot its famous worshipper, and found 'a singularly interesting congregation'. The account continued: 'We saw before us a congregation of rank, fashion, fame, power, worth and wisdom such as is rarely witnessed. In a word, the congregation consisted in one single person – the duke alone!'

The older he grew, the more famous he became and wherever he went people craned to catch sight of him. 'His movements were so certain and regular, that he might be calculated on as a planet,'[34] wrote one observer. At noon on the dot he would get on his horse, out of sight in the underground stables at Apsley House, and by the time he got to Horse Guards a small crowd would always have gathered to see him dismount. The onlookers watched fearfully as the old man heaved himself out of the saddle. 'Yet nobody presumed to touch or even to approach him.' The Duke could not bear to be helped. One young officer remembered seeing him leaving a rather stormy meeting, clearly in a very irritated mood: 'The old butler, who was very shaky on his legs, went out to help the Duke on his horse, than which nothing provoked him more'. The old man was pushed away and tumbled into the gutter, 'the sight of which appeared to restore his Grace's equanimity'.[35] Grudgingly, Wellington understood the obligations that fame conferred upon him, but he was unsparingly cynical about the adulation of the 'mob'. Once, when he entered Apsley House to the cheers of onlookers, he touched the brim of his hat with two fingers (his customary gesture of acknowledgement), and then pointed ruefully to the iron shutters on the house.

As the Duke got older, inevitably his writing became slower and more illegible. But he had no sympathy for his correspondents. 'It was my business to write that letter. It is your duty to read it', he once retorted.[36] Ever since the disaster with his left ear, he had suffered from deafness, which got worse with old age. When he was still in the Cabinet, his fellow Ministers always went and sat next to him when they were about to say something. Others were less sensitive; one of Queen Victoria's Ladies-in-Waiting complained of an evening when she was 'bellowed at' for more than an hour. 'I never was so thoroughly frightened, and I went to bed with a headache.'[37] However, according to Thomas Carlyle, in old age the Duke's voice was 'aquiline clear ... perhaps almost musical'.[38] Unquestionably, the Duke's temper increased with age. Algernon Greville ('Algy') and Fitzroy Somerset, who both for some years acted as his secretary, feared to ask him questions on business. Instead, 'Lady Douro used to go to the Duke, and immediately brought them all that they wanted. He was always charming in his manner to her.'[39]

Some took advantage of the Duke's generosity; he rarely refused a request for money if he believed the applicant to be a worthy cause. On one occasion, Gosh found him stuffing banknotes into envelopes. 'What are you doing, Duke?' he inquired. 'Doing? Doing what I am obliged to do every day.' One officer's widow wrote from France to ask for £5 travelling money to enable her to return to England. 'I sent the money by return of post', reported the Duke to Lady Salisbury. Unfortunately the woman had been so overjoyed at receiving the money that she broke a looking-glass and wanted 'five pounds more' to repair it. In truth, the Duke was not that interested in money; his younger brother Henry had once accused him of caring 'less about money than any man I have ever met with'.

There was a final call to arms for the Duke when, in 1848, as revolution was blowing through Europe, the Chartists threatened to march on Parliament, to force the House of Commons to accept their petition demanding a range of democratic rights. As Commander-in-Chief of the Army, Wellington put into action a plan which flooded the capital with 7,000 troops, all hidden from sight and merely acting as back-up to the specially enrolled constables. But he had no intention of being responsible for provoking another Peterloo. On the morning of the demonstration, an acquaintance who spoke to him thought that 'his old eyes ... sparkled like a girl's at her first ball'.[40] The Cabinet had sat and listened enthralled as the old warrior, in his eightieth year, explained his plan. While the demonstrators assembled on Kennington Green, the Duke sat in his office at Horse Guards reading the morning paper. 'Tell me when they are within one quarter of a mile', he calmly instructed his ADC, as he fell easily into his old battle-speak. When told that the march was breaking up, he exclaimed, 'Exactly what I expected', and went back to his paper.

Around this time the Duke was especially solicitous of his daughter-in-law Bessy's health because she was considering drastic measures to try to correct her inability to have children. He wrote to her in 1849 praising her courage in contemplating an operation which a surgeon would perform in Edinburgh. 'I am anxious about one thing in the world; and that is that you should be the Mother of Children! For your sake for mine: and for others! but however desirous I am that this should come to pass; I am unwilling that you should suffer.'[41] If she went ahead with it, he assured her that he would not reveal the reason for her trip to Scotland, not to anybody, the Queen included. Whatever the operation, it was to no avail.

In July 1850 Sir Robert Peel died, after falling from his horse. The political alliance between him and Wellington had been a complicated one; very different in character and background, they were never friends, but they came to respect each other, and as Wellington delivered his tribute in the Lords, his voice broke and his eyes filled with tears. A few weeks later there came an even greater blow. On 16 August 1850 Gosh, the Duke's loyal friend, died. Arbuthnot had been ill for some time, but when the end came the Duke could not bear to think he was about to lose him. 'No, no; he's not very ill, not very bad,' he said as he seized the doctor's hand and peered into his face. 'He'll get better. It's only his stomach that's out of order. He'll not die.'[42] The Duke wept as Arbuthnot's coffin was lowered into the ground in Kensal Green Cemetery. Ever since the death of their beloved Harriet, Gosh had been the Duke's trusted confidant and companion. He read most of the Duke's correspondence and acted both as sounding-board and punch-bag for his friend's opinions or outbursts. The housekeeper at Walmer would see them walking along the beach, and relished the sight of 'our two dear old gentlemen so happy together'. The Duke was always solicitous of his friend's health. 'Now, Arbuthnot,' he would say as the evening fell, 'you've been out long enough. The dew is falling, and you'll catch cold; you must go in.'

In the last few years of his life, the Duke formed a very important friendship with the second Lady Salisbury whom, as Lady Mary Sackville, he had known since a child. She was eleven years old when they first met and an indication of her early hero-worship was that she kept 'the glove I wore when first I touched the Duke's hand'. Her 'arthurolatry' (as I call it) surpassed all others: each of her children carried his name, including her daughter, whom she christened Mary Arthur, and the Duke stood godfather to all of them. When Lady Salisbury was in London, the two would often be seen walking in Green Park – 'quarter-deck exercise, with a footman following some 20 paces behind'. When they did not see each other he wrote chatty letters, almost daily, and often about her children. 'I am delighted to learn that Mary Arthur has teeth! It appears to be early!'[43] Lady Salisbury shared his love of Walmer, and when he arrived for his annual visit in the summer of 1850, he enthused to her: 'I never saw the Castle looking so well. The Fields at the back of the beach were quite green, the sky without a cloud, the sea calm and blue; and everything in tranquillity!'[44]

In the last full year of his life, the Great Exhibition became for the Duke a wonderful source of interest and enjoyment. Two weeks before it opened he went with Lady Douro to have a look at the preparations, pausing at one of the foreign stands just as they were unpacking a pair of silver equestrian statuettes depicting the Duke and his old rival Napoleon. 'The news instantly spread that the Duke of Wellington was within "the French territory," and in a few moments, probably for the first time in his life ... the Duke was *surprised* and surrounded by a body of French-men.'[45] The exhibition opened on 1 May and the crowds cheered and wished him happy birthday. He and his fellow veteran Lord Anglesey, who all those years ago scandalised the world by running off with Wellington's sister-in-law, walked arm in arm down all the aisles, applause greeting them as they reached a new section. The Duke became a daily visitor, fascinated by the displays of new artefacts and inventions, and he urged all his friends to visit, often escorting them or advising on the highlights. Part of his enthusiasm stemmed from being something of an amateur inventor himself; his devices included a teapot/water jug, an umbrella/sword, and a cape that was so compact he could carry it in his pocket. After one of his visits to the exhibition the Duke wrote to a friend, 'The Police advised me not to enter, and if they had not exerted themselves to take care of me, I should never have got out! They rushed upon me from all directions – Men, Women, and Children, all collecting into a crowd and endeavouring to touch me!'[46] For many, the Duke was the most interesting exhibit of all.

A few weeks later, he was complaining about having to attend a fancy dress ball given by the Queen. The Duke admitted to reading 'in order to know what was the Costume between 1660 and 1680'. He was appalled that his daughter-in-law, Lady Douro, was going to have to wear a wig and his Field Marshal's uniform left him looking, by his own admission, like a 'state coachman'. Nevertheless, he was happy to show off his outfit to a group of his great-nephews and nieces who turned up to see him at Apsley House just before he set off for Buckingham Palace. 'Uncle Dukey' added to the children's delight by demonstrating how to dance a minuet.

The autumn of 1851 saw the beginning of the Duke's last new friendship with a woman. Mrs Jones of Pantglas was sixty years his junior, and, as usual, there were some raised eyebrows. After his death, his relationship with Mrs Jones was described as 'unbecoming'. But the liaison was without impropriety; again, it was Mrs Jones's children and the joys of his seaside retreat which provided the main topics for their letters. When Mrs Jones had to go away and leave her children he promised that whenever he went into Dover, he would look in on his 'young friends'. After one inspection he reported, 'The sun was shining upon their rooms, which were very airy and comfortable.' And, after one of Mrs Jones's visits, 'My dear Mrs Jones: I thank you for writing to me and particularly for recollecting my sea girt Castle, my walks upon the Platform, of the Waves and Ramparts, my beautiful garden and its sheltered walks, while you are flying on your Railroad!'[47]

As 1851 drew to a close the Duke was, typically, complaining about the inefficiency of the postal service and the tyranny of the railways, describing the timetable as 'the book of knowledge'. As always he had been on the lookout for new and interesting inventions, and the Salisburys had been given a gift of a 'baby jumper', possibly a device he had spotted at the Great Exhibition. 'You will observe', he wrote, 'that it is intended to be screwed into the ceiling of the Nursery', but the Duke was concerned that the screw might not be strong enough, and urged them to check it carefully before it was used. The jumper was a great success.

For the Duke, the year ended peacefully and contentedly. His grandchildren had measles, but by Christmas he was able to tell Mrs Jones that 'My daughters are both here and the children quite well'. In the same letter he thanked her for her good wishes and hoped 'that I may keep my health and my strength! I should be an awkward sort of old man if weak and doubled up!'[48] But despite the warmth and affection for the Charles Wellesley family, once again it was Lady Douro's health and well-being which were his unceasing preoccupation, particularly when he wrote to Lady Salisbury. After a train journey with Lady Douro the Duke, referring to Lady Salisbury's pregnancy the year before, wished 'there existed the same necessity for her [Lady Douro] coming by that conveyance as existed at that time for yours! But I have no reason to believe that is the case!'[49]

At Stratfield Saye the new year dawned with sunny skies and plentiful demands on the Duke's time. At the end of January, on a visit to the Queen, he took a stroll round Windsor, intending to visit a battalion of Grenadier Guards which was quartered in barracks there. A retired farmer spotted him asking for directions and 'went up to him and politely gave "the old gentleman" his arm, offering to conduct him to the place he wanted, and away the Duke and our old English farmer went through the streets arm in arm in familiar chitchat to the barracks'.[50] On his eighty-third birthday, as the Duke walked with Lady Douro to her house in Upper Brook Street, cheering crowds followed them. As usual the Duke was circumspect about his popularity. 'Cromwell's reflection occurred to me. They would readily pull me to pieces if convicted of exciting undue influence ... Alas! we are but men!'[51]

The Duke threw his last ball at Apsley House on 14 May 1852. Given his lifelong service to the Crown, appropriately it was for two members of the Royal Family: the Queen's aunt (the Duchess of Cambridge) and her daughter Princess Mary, who was making her debut in society. And London's hostesses continued to use all their charm in persuading him to attend their own parties. 'If you cannot Dine, Dear Duke, will you honour me with your company here on Saturday evening? *Pray do* – it will be so kind and *so charming* if you will come to us on Saturday evening *as early* as you please, or *as late* as best suits your other engagements.'[52] Escorting elderly ladies was another matter. 'I visited three dowagers,' wrote the Duke to Lady Salisbury, 'and did what was about equally agreeable, read through the Cape despatches! ... I shall have another dowagering this night.'[53]

There was no duty in hosting the annual Waterloo dinner at Apsley House. All day there had been a stream of dignitaries calling to pay their respects and extra police were laid on to control the crowds. When Prince Albert arrived in the courtyard, the Band of the Grenadier Guards played the 'Coburg March'. At dinner, after the Queen's health had been proposed by the Duke, the Prince rose to his feet and enjoined his fellow diners – eighty-four in total – 'Gentlemen, I have only to give you the "Health of the noble Duke our distinguished host," and to express a feeling, in which I am sure you will join with me, of my delight and satisfaction in seeing our illustrious host in such excellent health and spirits on the present occasion.' Loud cheering greeted these words, as the band struck up 'See the Conquering Hero Come.' At the end of the evening, despite having been on his feet with an endless roll-call of toasts, headed by 'the memory of those who fell at the battle of Waterloo', when the Prince left Apsley House at eleven o'clock the Duke called for his carriage and went off to two receptions.

The time was approaching for the Duke to leave the uncomfortable heat of London for the cooling sea-breezes of Walmer. The Douros had planned a trip to the Continent but evidently there were some problems. 'Lady Douro goes on the 2nd or 3rd of August,' he wrote to Lady Salisbury. 'Between ourselves, she did not appear so comfortable about going when I spoke to her about it as she had before. It appears to me she is going with one object in view. Her companion will go with a different one. This is not a comfortable prospect for fellow travellers even on a short excursion!'[54] Not for the first time, the Duke seems to be suggesting that all was not well with the Douro marriage. When at the end of the month he bade farewell to his cherished daughter-in-law, neither of them could know that they would never see each other again.

On his way to Walmer the Duke met an old acquaintance who was suffering from gout. 'I never saw such a wreck! . . . I do not think that in ten years I shall be as bad as he is now.'[55] He attributed his well-being to his strict regime – 'My only remedy is temperance, and keeping the skin in order by ablution and friction.' In the same letter to Lady Salisbury he boasted, 'I have none of the infirmities of old age! excepting *Vanity* perhaps! . . . ! If I was not deaf, I really believe there is not a youth in London who could enjoy the world more than myself.'[56]

When the Duke arrived at Walmer, he heard that his old friend John Wilson Croker was in the area, and decided to pay him a visit. He rode into Dover, caught the train to Folkestone and set off to walk what he believed was the last half-mile. Not only did it turn out to be three miles, but the house sat on a hill, and when the Duke got there he discovered that Croker had gone on an expedition to see him. Two days later, they managed a reunion, and Croker teased the Duke for not following his own mantra: always trying to guess what was on 'the other side of the hill'.[57] They chatted for three hours, with the Duke doing most of the talking. Their subjects ranged over topics as diverse as the Duke's horse Copenhagen, and his old adversary – 'Yes, Buonaparte was certainly the best of them all, and with his prestige worth 40,000 men.' On his way back to the castle he was waylaid at the station by an intoxicated Irishman who sported a Peninsular medal. The man's want of sobriety did not disqualify him from receiving a sovereign from the store the Duke always carried with him.

In early September Sophia and the grandchildren arrived at the castle, followed a week later by Charles. On the Saturday, Charles rode with his father to Dover, where the Duke inspected the works that were going on in the harbour, plying the men with questions. Charles later remembered that when his father looked out to sea, his sight was so good that he described what he could see on the French coast. The calm of these days was interrupted by a letter which arrived on Sunday 'from a Madman who announces that he is a messenger from the Lord, and will deliver his message to-morrow morning Monday at Walmer Castle. We shall see!'[58]

On Monday morning the Duke rose at 5.30 a.m. and walked round the garden, no doubt pausing to look at the lime trees he prized so much, and inspecting the vegetables growing in the moat, a feature he had introduced to the castle grounds. The gardener, Townsend, a veteran of Waterloo who had taken part in the famous charge against the Imperial Guard, would have been in attendance. When he had applied for a job with the Duke and been offered the post of gardener, he had protested that he knew nothing of gardening. 'No more do I,' said the Duke, 'but you can learn.'[59] Chirping robins dominated the dawn chorus; knowing the Duke had a great fondness for the little birds, the castle staff had encouraged their colonisation of the grounds.[60] Later a small frown may have crossed his brow when he read an account in *The Times* of a military parade in Paris two days before when the troops, passing in front of President Louis Napoleon, had cried 'Vive Napoléon'.

When in the afternoon the Duke returned from another short walk, some thought he looked better than he had done for a while.[61] In the evening he played with his grandchildren; perhaps there was one last staging of the 'battle of Waterloo'. He ate a hearty dinner of mock turtle soup, turbot and venison. He was in such good spirits that instead of retiring at his usual hour of ten, he sat up chatting to his son and daughter-in-law. It was past midnight when he finally climbed into his narrow camp-bed and laid his head on the hard pillow which he took with him wherever he went.

At 6.30 the following morning the Duke was awoken by Kendall, his valet. Half an hour later a maid heard the Duke 'making a great noise' and when a concerned Kendall went into the room, his master asked him to send for the doctor – 'I wish to speak to him'. Dr Hulke was at his breakfast table in Deal when he got the message but rushed immediately to the castle. At first it was thought that there was no great cause for concern, but soon after the doctor left, Kendall asked the Duke if he would take some tea. 'Yes if you please' were the last words he spoke. Several fits gripped the old man and, when Hulke hurried back, the Duke had lost consciousness. Various remedies that had worked before were applied, but to no avail; so, to make him more comfortable, Kendall placed him gently in his straight-back chair near the window. Many years later Sophia remembered that he showed 'signs of annoyance at having people about him (as was usually the case), so that those that remained in the room took care not to pass between him and the window'. When Charles took her into the room to bid farewell to her father-in-law, 'he was then in the arm-chair, his legs and feet rolled in blankets, very pale, his eyes closed and breathing heavily, but there was no appearance of pain or suffering'. Slowly he sank, and at 3.25 in the afternoon, he breathed his last. The end was so quiet and peaceful that Charles doubted he had gone, and a mirror was held against his mouth. 'The polished surface, however, remained undimmed, and the great commander had departed without a struggle or even a sigh to mark the exact moment when the vital spark was extinguished.'[62]

The whole country went into mourning. The Queen was in Scotland on, in her own words, a 'beautiful expedition' to one of the 'severest, wildest spots imaginable' when she received the news in a letter from Charles Wellesley. She wrote back immediately. 'The Queen is so stunned by the awful suddenness of this sad Event, that she cannot believe in the reality of it – & cannot realize the possibility that the Duke of Wellington, the greatest Man this Country ever produced, is no more!'[63] She knew her trusted Lady-in-Waiting would miss the grand old man more than anyone else:

> My dearest Bessie, I really know hardly *how* to begin my letter to you or how to *express half* of what I feel on the *sad & awfully sudden* event which has plunged us & the whole Nation into sorrow & which must overwhelm *you* with grief. I know well how dearly the dear old *Duke loved you &* how devotedly attached *you* were to *him*, & therefore I can but too well imagine your distress – & your sorrow … Pray express our sincere sympathy to Lord Douro who must be so much distressed to have been absent on this melancholy occasion.[64]

The Douros had been in Frankfurt when the news reached them. Finally the dreaded day had arrived when the son must step into the father's shoes. For several years the 2nd Duke could not bear to sign the name 'Wellington' and continued to write 'Douro'.

With the castle flag flying at half-mast, while plans where made for the state funeral, the Duke's coffin lay there for eight weeks, watched over by a round-the-clock guard of honour. Mrs Allen, the cook at Walmer, was distraught. 'It will indeed be agony when we lose Him altogether.'[65] Before his body left the castle 9,000 of the local people, for whom the Duke had been such a familiar figure on his walks along the beach or galloping across the Downs, filed past the coffin as it lay in the small room by his 'platform'. On the evening of 10 November, lit by the flames of torches and escorted by the constant peal of gun salutes, the body was taken by train to London for the lying-in-state in the Great Hall at the Chelsea Hospital.

The ceilings of the huge hall were draped to resemble a tent, the walls hung in black cloth covered in the Duke's armorial bearings; there were candelabras, spears swathed in black velvet and a plethora of personal escutcheons, batons and heraldic paraphernalia. Veterans of the Duke's campaigns sat round the coffin – old Generals in a last act of obeisance to their chief. The crowds outside the hall were desperate to get inside – to pass by the body of the most famous man in the land. Privately, the family were appalled by the vulgarity, an exhibition 'devoid of taste and feeling', wrote Douro to Miss Coutts. When, two days later, three people were killed in the crush, the lying-in-state had become 'a really disgusting affair'. But the Duke's sons also admitted that 'we have never regretted that we place ourselves at the disposition of the country'. The Queen's visit to the hall restored some dignity, but the Sovereign was unable to control her emotions; she reached the centre of the room but could go no further and, crying bitterly, returned to her carriage.

Bad weather often preceded the victories of the Duke – most notably at Salamanca and Waterloo. Perhaps, therefore, it was appropriate that there was a storm the night before the funeral. People had been gathering on the route since the early hours of the morning; for days before, prime viewpoints had been put up for sale in the advertisement sections of the newspaper – 'trading in death', as Dickens called it. Outside the Duke's office at Horse Guards, the troops were massed, spilling over into St James's Park. The funeral car, designed under the supervision of Prince Albert, was finished only minutes before the procession began. It weighed eighteen tons and the coffin, at six feet nine a foot longer than the Duke, seemed quite small perched on the top of it. The suggestion from one onlooker, that its shape recalled a railway truck, would have appalled the

Duke.[66] It was estimated that a million and a half people were on the streets of London. When the gun was fired to start the procession, the sun finally managed to filter through the clouds.

*

I have a slender connection to the funeral of the First Duke. Like all my siblings, when I was small I planted a tree in the Pleasure Grounds at Stratfield Saye: a tradition started by my grandfather and an echo of the planting of the First Duke's tree in 1817. The tiny tree grew to be a strong, tall cypress, and I was always told that it was a cutting from a cutting off a wreath at the First Duke's funeral. This was an evocative provenance, but I never knew how it had come about until I read an account of the day of the funeral in Lord Redesdale's memoirs. He had come to London with a group of other young Etonians and had an excellent vantage-point on the first floor of a hotel at the corner of Arlington Street and Piccadilly:

> As the great funeral car passed opposite the window where I was, one of the wreaths of cypress and bay leaves fell off. So soon as the last soldier closing the procession had disappeared, a poor old woman dashed forward and picked up the wreath. I ran down and tried to buy it off her, but she would not part with her precious relic. At last I persuaded her to sell me one cypress cone for a shilling. The cone was full of seed which I sent down to Exbury in Hampshire, at that time belonging to my father.[67]

I feel sure this solves a personal mystery. My cutting must have come from the cypress at Exbury. Happily for me, I was the next in line in the family to plant a tree. I trust that in future years, when the cypress is nearing its end, a future Duke of Wellington will take a cutting for another small Wellesley to plant nearby.

The three-year-old Prince Arthur, who ever since the Duke's death had been constantly intoning 'The Duke of Wellikon, little Arta's Godpapa', was inconsolable at not being allowed to go to the funeral. The Queen had asked the family for a lock of hair 'that she may keep it as a relic for his little godson', but had turned it into a bracelet which she wore herself on the day of the funeral. The cortège wound its way up the Mall and past Buckingham Palace, where the Queen was standing on the balcony. Once again she wept openly.

Opposite the Duke of York's statue in Pall Mall the huge funeral car sank in the mud, and sixty strong men were employed to move it. Punctuality, so prized by the Duke himself, was not a feature of his own funeral. The crowds stood hushed and reverential; every spectator had contrived to carry a token of mourning – a scrap of crape, or a strip of black cloth worn as an armlet.[68] Even the buildings were draped in black. Eighty-three Chelsea Pensioners – one for each year of the Duke's life – joined the procession at Charing Cross and, to the muffled roll of drums and wailing of bagpipes, the cortège proceeded on its route down the Strand, up Fleet Street and through Ludgate Circus to St Paul's. The funeral car itself was drawn by twelve huge dray horses from a London brewery; on the coffin lay the Duke's hat and sword. The 2nd Duke followed the car in an immensely long mourning cloak, and at the very end of the procession came the Duke's horse carrying, as was traditional at a soldier's funeral, his boots – reversed and empty. For many this symbolic detail brought tears to the eyes.

By the time the cortège reached Ludgate Hill the horses were worn out and sailors stepped in to help pull the coffin. Finally, the coffin was carried into St Paul's by eight pall-bearers, all veterans of the Duke's campaigns. As the bier entered the nave, a cool breeze swept down the aisle and 'waved the plume of the hat placed on the coffin. It seemed to flutter just as one might suppose the spirit did and then gently sank to rest – and it moved no more.' Two compositions by the Duke's father, Lord Mornington, were amongst the music that filled the cathedral. An old comrade-at-arms, Lord Anglesey, who had been present at so many different stages of the Duke's life, carried the Field Marshal's baton. When the time came for the coffin to be lowered into its final resting-place in the crypt, he stepped forward 'and, with tears streaming down his cheeks, placed his hand upon it, in a moving gesture of farewell'.[69] The choir burst forth with Handel's 'His body is buried in peace; but his name liveth evermore'. Garter King of Arms read out the long roll-call of titles and orders. As the booming of the guns of the Tower died away, the nation's farewell ended. Their hero could finally rest in peace.

As my father and I stand by the tomb of our great ancestor, I think of the shy boy in Ireland, 'abused' and 'vilified', who went on to achieve something close to immortality. But it is hard to feel a connection to the man whose bones lie here. The crypt of St Paul's is grand, solemn and impersonal; the black marble of the tomb itself, icily cold. The Duke believed that a soldier should lie where he fell. Would he have chosen to be buried in the village church at Walmer? Or might he have gone home, to the vault in the small church in the park of Stratfield Saye, where Kitty, separated from him for much of their married life, could have the consolation of his eternal companionship? For a man who was so organised in every department of his existence, it is strange that he failed to leave instructions for the management of his death. Perhaps he knew that a private burial would never be his right, and that any instructions he left would likely clash with the Queen's desire for a very public manifestation of national regard for 'the greatest man that ever lived'.

The Wellington of St Paul's crypt is the same remote character of his portraits and statues: the quintessential hero, who combined gallantry with duty and loyalty to Crown and Country. But the Wellington in my mind now is a great-great-great-grandfather to whom I reach out, through Valerian my father, Gerry my grandfather, and two more generations; still hero, but with faults and failings that make him more like one of us. In the way that one member of a family can criticise another, without permitting those outside the fold to follow suit, I wish he had been a kinder husband, and a better father. But he loved his grandchildren. And he might have loved me too.

Epilogue

In 2001 my parents moved out of Stratfield Saye House, back to Park Corner, where the family had lived for much of the time that my brothers and I were growing up. In 2004 they celebrated their diamond wedding anniversary; in 2005 my father entered his tenth decade; in January 2007, as the first snowdrops appeared, we marked my mother's eighty-fifth birthday.

Both my parents continue to ignore the normal boundaries of their age, and are active in both their public and private lives. An important focus of my mother's life has been her involvement with SSAFA, the Forces charity. She joined the organisation in 1944, as soon as she became a soldier's wife, and when my father succeeded to the title in 1972, she was invited onto the Council. Her participation has not been confined merely to the duties of patronage: awarded an honorary life membership in 2007, she continues to provide, in the words of SSAFA themselves, 'wise counsel, and a steely determination in pursuit of those causes she believes in'.

For my father, being appointed the only non-royal Colonel-in-Chief of a regiment was a great accolade, and for thirty-two years he took a keen and committed interest in the welfare and activities of The Duke of Wellington's Regiment (the 33rd), particularly when they were deployed in a war zone. It was a huge blow to him when, in 2006, as part of the reorganisation of the army, the regiment was abolished. He fought bitterly to have the decision overturned, but when the time came for the farewell, urged the soldiers, one and all, to turn the page and continue to 'vanquish those before them'. He ended his speech with the words, 'Long live The Dukes!', and as I watched him walk slowly, leaning on his forked stick, back to where my mother and I were sitting, the emotion of the moment was evident on his face. The spirit of the regiment may live on in its new incarnation as the 3rd Battalion The Yorkshire Regiment

(Duke of Wellington's), but his were not the only tears that were shed that day.

Undoubtedly my father had regrets that none of his own children went into the army. It therefore gave him immense pleasure to be present at Sandhurst in 2007 for the passing-out parade of his younger grandson, Gerald, who secured a commission into The Blues. After the ceremony, they were photographed standing in front of a cannon that was last fired at Waterloo. When Gerald was fighting in Afghanistan, his calls from the front line were eagerly awaited by my parents, who drifted back into old habits, sending him 'food parcels' with tins of tuna and sardines.

The view from Park Corner's side of the park is very different to that from the 'big house', but equally beautiful; on a clear day you can just see the reflection from the water of the River Loddon, and the landscape stretches as far as Beacon Hill. On a fine summer evening my parents can be found sitting in their canvas chairs on the lawn, drinking a 'copita' of ice-cold sherry, field glasses at the ready to catch a rare sighting of a red kite, or to follow the progress of a roe deer as it emerges from the nearby wood, and dares to stray close to the fence that borders the garden. As my father's gaze takes in features that would have been familiar to his great-great-grandfather, I hope he occasionally indulges himself by reflecting back on his long and honourable tenure of the Wellington title and legacy. I trust, too, that both my parents derive satisfaction from their enduring union. And with twelve grandchildren, and two great-grandchildren, the future is secure. With my brother Charles, and nephew Arthur, new chapters will begin.

ACKNOWLEDGEMENTS

The greatest debt of gratitude goes to my father and mother, who have been both gracious in their support, and generous with their time. Over the last few years, my father has spent hours and hours with me trawling through his memories and both my parents have tolerated my persistent questions and 'burrowing' with great patience and good humour. Rare is the occasion when I have not found myself pressing them to remember a detail of some far-off event. Without their blessing this book could never have happened.

I am most grateful to Her Majesty the Queen, for allowing me to include among my illustrations a photograph of the private ceremony of the presentation of the Stratfield Saye rental flag. The Hon. Mary Morrison, Lady-in-Waiting, kindly took the photograph.

My aunt Eliza has unearthed memories, letters and photographs; her enthusiasm and interest, for which I thank her warmly, have played an important part in the project. I have also appreciated talking to her son Jeremy Clyde about our common ancestors, near and far, and to my other first cousin Jonathan.

I am conscious that in writing this book I tread on territory common to all my siblings, so I thank them – Charles, Richard, John and Christopher – for tolerating my intrusion, and for their help, in different ways. And a warm mention goes to my sisters-in-law, Antonia, Joanna, Emma, and to Corinne, who kindly did a couple of translations for me.

My cousin Antony Grant has provided wise and helpful counsel, and I was pleased to visit with him Mary Wellesley, my father's one remaining first cousin, who, like him, was born in 1915. Ursula – Lady Westbury – daughter of 'Mitey' (Lady Serena James), and cousin to my father, has allowed me to pore over fascinating scrap books, and given permission for me to quote from letters to her mother.

On my mother's side of the family, Teddy – Edward Burn – who was married to my mother's first cousin Helen (née McConnel) passed to my mother and me a suitcase full of family letters and documents. Teddy was very close to my maternal grandparents, and amongst the pleasures of writing this book has been the opportunity to get to know him and his wife Marilyn. Roger (half-brother to Douglas) and Susan McConnel were extremely helpful and produced several interesting McConnel records. And Cecilia Irvine, my mother's cousin and my godmother, who has known Diana longer than anyone else, was always ready with another nugget of family reminiscence.

Several of my parents' longtime friends have spared the time to cast their minds far back to the lives of their younger selves, and to tell me stories and anecdotes about Valerian's and Diana's early years. I am grateful to them for doing so, and am sorry that I have been able to include only a tiny proportion of this material. Lord Bruntisfield – John – who talked to me for several hours when I visited him in Edinburgh, died in July 2007 and I am sad that he will not have the opportunity to read this, but I thank his widow Jan, Lady Bruntisfield for her hospitality. I am indebted too to: Lady Aldington (Minta); Colonel and Mrs Gerard Leigh – G and Jean; Colonel and Mrs Smiley – David and Moy; Lord Wigram – Neville; Malcolm Fraser; David and Mary Parsons; and Margery and Guy Routledge, who sadly died in the spring of 2008.

Penns-in-the-Rocks is now owned by Lady Gibson, who kindly allowed me to wander round her house and grounds. For the trip to Italy with my parents the Italian Ambassador in London, Giancarlo Aragona, was invaluable in helping us arrange our visit to Palena, where we were given such a warm welcome, for which I thank the Mayor and people of the town. I am grateful, too, to the Duke of Beaufort for allowing me access to the archives at Badminton, and to Margaret Richards and Elaine Milsom for being so helpful on my visits there.

In the last few years, while I have been researching and writing this book, the British Library has provided both an unlimited supply of source material, and a wonderful place to work, and my gratitude goes to the staff there.

I am fortunate to be published by Weidenfeld & Nicolson, not least because they were the publishers of the late Elizabeth Longford's two volumes, *Wellington: The Years of the Sword*, and *Pillar of State*. And though, of course, it is the spirit of the First Duke who has hovered over me while I have been writing this book, it is Elizabeth's insights into my ancestor which have been an inspiration throughout.

I will always be grateful to Alan Samson, my editor at Weidenfeld and Nicolson, for showing faith in me when he commissioned the book. His enthusiasm, support and patience have never flagged. There are many of his colleagues to whom I am indebted, including Bea Hemming, Lisa Shakespeare and Carole Green. In the final stages of editing, it was reassuring to work with Linden Lawson. And my thanks go to all those at Weidenfeld who have been involved in the design and production of this book.

Gillon Aitken has been the consummate agent: attentive, encouraging and always there with a guiding hand or firm steer. As a first timer, I have been extremely fortunate to be able to count on his wisdom and experience.

Through the long period that I have been working on this book, I have had help from many others – associates, acquaintances and friends. Numbered among this last group are my close friends, who all know how important they are to me, and how much I rely on them. They have propped me up in numerous different ways, and their encouragement and moral support has meant a great deal to me. I hope they will forgive me for including them in the following list, where varying degrees of thanks go to every person.

Melanie Aspey; Jane Bonham Carter; Kate Borland of Manchester City Council; Rosie Boycott; Melvyn Bragg; Robert Brodrick; Patrick Buckley; Bridget Calderwood; Stephanie Calman; Meriona Campion; Anne-Marie Casey; Belou Charlaff; Marie Colvin; Malcolm Dean; Falco Di Biase; Camilla Eadie; Helen Fielding; Scott Flaving of 'The Dukes'; Roy Foster; Kathleen Gallimore; Helen Gatley; Victoria Glendinning; Maria Gatti de Monréal; Christopher Golding; Warwick Gould; Loyd Grossman; Robert Halliday; Sandra Hanley of Royal Mills in Manchester; Shelley Harman; Richard Harvey; Max Hastings; Richard Hewitt; Anthony Holden; David Jenkins; Kate Jenkins, Curator of Stratfield Saye House; Jonathan Marsden, Deputy Surveyor of The Queen's Works of Art; Pauline and Lindsay Macdonald; Giani Manoj and other staff at the UN in Jerusalem; Jimmy McLachlan; Maren Meinhardt; Annabel Merullo; Comte Serge de Meeûs; Dr John Moses, former Dean of St Paul's; Mustapha Nabulsi; Juliet Nicolson; Mr Olearchick, the King David Hotel, Jerusalem; Colonel Shamus Olivier; Richard Phillips; Herbert du Plessis; Nicholas Pronay; Keith Raffan; Barone and Baronessa Bettino Ricasoli; Katherine Robertson; Helen Roche, the Merrion Hotel in Dublin; Sir Robin Ross; Salman Rushdie; John Severn; Patricia Sheppard; Alexandra Shulman; Emma Soames; Julia Somay, the Commonwealth War Graves Commission; Colonel Paddy Tabor; Penny Thomas; Christopher and Kristi Thorne; Griselda Ure; Hugo Vickers; Dorothy Viljoen; Philippa Walker; Ian Watson; Celia and Evelyn Webb-Carter; Gordon Welch; Rowena Willard-Wright, Curator Walmer Castle; Chris Woolgar, Southampton University; Aviram Zino.

Finally, Mick Imlah's friendship, wit and unerring judgement have sustained me throughout; without him I doubt the book would have been finished. I thank him, with all my heart.

NOTES

Unless otherwise stated quotations from letters are drawn from
private family correspondence.

Prologue

1 Brett James, Antony, *The Hundred Days, Napoleon's Last Campaign from Eyewitness Accounts* (London: Macmillan, 1964), p.39

2 Longford, *The Years of the Sword*, p.389

3 Stuart-Wortley, Violet, *Highcliffe and the Stuarts* (London: John Murray, 1927), p.236

4 Maxwell, Sir Herbert, *The Life of Wellington: The Restoration of the Martial Power of Great Britain*, Vol. 2 (London: Sampson Low, Marston, 1907), p.13

5 Longford, *The Years of the Sword*, p.418

6 Malmesbury, Earl of, *Letters of the First Earl of Malmesbury: His Family and Friends from 1745–1820*, Vol. 2 (London: Richard Bentley, 1870), p.446

7 Foulkes, p.38

8 Malmesbury, op. cit., p.447

9 O'Neil, Charles, *The Military Adventures of Charles O'Neil* (Worcester: Edward Livermore, 1851), pp.228–9

10 Wellington, ed. Lt-Col Gurwood, *The Despatches of Field Marshall the Duke of Wellington during his various campaigns*, Vol. 12 (London: 1834), pp.476–7

11 *The Times*, 17 June 1815

12 Haydon, B.R., *Correspondence & Table-Talk*, Vol. 2 (London: 1876), p.358

13 Cotton, Edward, Sergeant-Major, *Waterloo: Being Selections from Wellington's Despatches along with A Voice From Waterloo* (London: Blackie & Son, 1913), p.40

14 Longford, *The Years of the Sword*, p.409

15 Thornton, James, *Your Most Obedient Servant: Cook to the Duke of Wellington* (Exeter: Webb & Bower, 1985), p.74

16 Gronow, R.H., ed. Christopher Hibbert, *Captain Gronow: His Reminiscences of Regency and Victorian Life 1810–60* (London: Kyle Cathie, 1991), p.134

17 Holmes, p.239

18 Creevey, Thomas, ed. Herbert Maxwell, *The Creevey Papers: A Selection from the Correspondence & Diaries of the Late Thomas Creevey, M.P.* (London: John Murray, 1906), p.228

19 Low, Edward Bruce, *With Napoleon at Waterloo, and Other Unpublished Documents of the Waterloo and Peninsular Campaigns* (London: Francis Griffiths, 1911), p.124

20 Longford, *The Years of the Sword*, p.463

21 Ibid.

22 Pitt-Lennox, Sir William, *Three Years with the Duke of Wellington in Private Life by an Ex-Aid-De-Camp* (London: Saunders & Otley, 1853), pp.114–15

23 Gronow, op.cit., p.129

24 Kincaid, p.342

25 Pitt-Lennox, op. cit., p.117

26 Kennedy, James Shaw, *Notes on the Battle of Waterloo* (Staplehurst: Spellmount, 2003), pp.128–9

27 Gronow, Captain, *The Reminiscences and Recollections of Captain Gronow: Being Anecdotes of the Camp, Court, Clubs and Society 1810–1860*, Vol. 1 (London: John C. Nimmo, 1892), p.73

28 Kincaid, p.343

29 Sabine, Major-General Edward, *Letters of Colonel Sir Augustus Simon Frazer, K.C.B.* (London: Spottiswoode, 1859), p.553

30 Holmes, p.249

31 Gronow, *The Reminiscences and Recollections of Captain Gronow*, p.193

32 Longford, *The Years of the Sword*, p.481

33 Gronow, *The Reminiscences and Recollections of Captain Gronow*, p.204

34 Ibid.

35 Jackson, Basil, *Notes and Reminiscences of a Staff Officer: Chiefly Relating to the Waterloo Campaign and to St Helena Matters During the Captivity of Napoleon* (London: John Murray, 1903), p.60

36 Pitt-Lennox, op. cit., p.218

37 O'Neil, op. cit., pp.253–4

38 Colby, Reginald, *The Waterloo Despatch: The Story of The Duke of Wellington's Official Despatch on the Battle of Waterloo and its Journey to London* (London, 1965), p.28

39 *The Times*, 18 June 1915, quoting a letter from the Duke written on 19 June 1815

40 Shelley, Frances, ed. E. Edgecombe, *The Diary of Frances Lady Shelley*, Vol. 1. (London: John Murray, 1913), p.102

CHAPTER 1:
Born to Serve

1 Delany, Mary, *Letters from Georgian Ireland* (Belfast: Friar's Bush Press, 1991), p.134

2 Torrens, W.M., *The Marquess Wellesley: Architect of Empire. An Historic Portrait* (London: Chatto & Windus, 1880), p.8

3 Torrens, op. cit., p.12

4 Lynch, William, *A View of the Legal Institutions, Honorary Hereditary Offices, & Feudal Baronies, Established in Ireland during the Reign of Henry II* (London: Longman, Green, Longman & Roberts, 1830), p.102

5 Ibid., p.99

6 Granville, Mary, ed. Lady Llanover, *The Autobiography and Correspondence of Mary Granville, Mrs Delany: With Interesting Reminiscences of King George the Third and Queen Charlotte*, Vol. 3 (London: Richard Bentley, 1861), p.540

7 Guedalla, p.12

8 Gleig, p.3

9 Hamilton, John, *Sixty Years of Experience as an Irish Landlord* (London: Digby, Long 1894), p.12

10 Longford, *The Years of the Sword*, p.129

11 Butler, p.565

12 Ibid., p.35

13 Guedalla, p.18

14 Longford, *The Years of the Sword*, p.19

15 *The Times*, 8 January 1972

16 *The Collected Works of Gerald 7th Duke of Wellington*, p.29

17 D. Wellesley, *Far Have I Travelled*, p.119

18 *The Times*, 1 May 1914

19 Ibid.

20 D. Wellesley, *Far Have I Travelled*, p.120

21 Lister, Charles, *Charles Lister: Letters and Recollections with a Memoir by his Father Lord Ribblesdale* (London: Fisher Unwin, 1917), p.105

22 D. Wellesley, *Far Have I Travelled*, p.131

23 *The Times*, 18 and 19 June 1915

24 Rodd, James Rennell, *Social and Diplomatic Memories (Third Series) 1902–1919* (London: Edward Arnold, 1925), p.312

25 D. Wellesley, *Far Have I Travelled*, p.147

26 Lees-Milne, Vol. 1, p.179

27 Hibbert, p.6

28 *The Times*, 14 September 1944

29 *Bentley's Miscellany*, Vol. 16 (1844), p.434, 'Eton Scenes and Eton Men'

30 Gleig, p.5

31 Ibid., p.7

32 Ibid., p.6

33 Shelley, Frances, ed. E. Edgecombe, *The Diary of Frances Lady Shelley*, Vol 1 (London: John Murray, 1913), p.119

34 Timbs, John, *Wellingtoniana: Anecdotes, Maxims, and Characteristics, of the Duke of Wellington* (London: Ingram, Cooke, 1852), p.7

35 Longford, *The Years of the Sword*, p.21

36 Hamilton, op. cit., pp.19–20

CHAPTER 2:
The Cut of a Soldier

1 Longford, *Pillar of State*, p.142

2 Croker, John Wilson, *The Croker Papers: The Correspondence and Diaries of the Late Right Honourable John Wilson Croker 1809–1830*, Vol. 1 (London: John Murray, 1885), p.337

3 *Belgravia: A London Magazine* (July 1890), p.248, 'Fragmentary Recollections of Lady Eleanor Butler and Miss Ponsonby, the Ladies of Llangollen'

4 *The Hamwood Papers of the Ladies of Llangollen and Caroline Hamilton*, ed. G.H. Bell (London: Macmillan, 1930), p.72

5 *The Times*, 2 August 1791

6 Stratfield Saye MS

7 Longford, *The Years of the Sword*, p.34

8 McKibbin, Ross, *Classes and Cultures: England 1918–1951* (Oxford: Oxford University Press, 1998), p.33

9 Freeman, Charles, *Living Through History: Britain in the 1930s* (London: Batsford, 1985), p.9

10 Lambert, p.91

11 Graves, Robert and Hodge, Alan, *The Long Week-end: A Social History of Great Britain 1918–1939* (London: Cardinal, 1991), p.317

12 Channon, Henry, ed. Robert Rhodes James, '*Chips': The Diaries of Sir Henry Channon* (London: Weidenfeld & Nicolson, 1993), p.56

13 Brendon, Piers, *The Dark Valley: A Panorama of the 1930s* (London: Jonathan Cape, 2000), p.365

14 *The Times*, 16 June 1936

15 Graves and Hodge, op. cit., p.366

16 *The Bystander*, 5 May 1937

17 Yeats, p.125

18 Ibid., p.131

19 Graves and Hodge, op. cit., p.367

20 *Daily Telegraph*, 5 November 2005

21 *Tatler*, 12 July 1939

22 *The Speeches of The Duke of Wellington in Parliament.* Collected and Arranged by the Late Colonel Gurwood (London: John Murray, 1854), p.52

23 Wellington, *Private Correspondence*, pp.1–2

24 Stanhope, p.136

25 Ellesmere, p.161

26 Longford, *The Years of the Sword*, p.40

27 Ibid., p.41

28 Ibid., p.42

CHAPTER 3:
Gallantries of Dreams

1 Smiley, David, *Irregular Regular* (Norwich: Michael Russell, 1994), p.12

2 Smiley, op. cit., p.52

3 *The Sunday Times*, 23 February 2003

4 Wyndham, p.39

5 Ibid., p.40

6 D. Wellesley, *Beyond the Grave*, p.16

7 Astor, Michael, *Tribal Feeling* (London: John Murray, 1963), p.154

CHAPTER 4:
Beyond the Still Valley

1 D.C. McConnel, *Facts and Traditions*, p.131

2 Jardine, Ernest Whigham, *James McConnel of Carsriggan: His Forbears and Descendants* (privately published, 1931), p.27

3 Kennedy, John, *Miscellaneous Papers: Early Recollections* (private distribution, Manchester, 1849), p.6

4 J.W. McConnel, *Fine Cotton Spinning*, p.9

5 Trotter, Alexander, *East Galloway Sketches: Biographical, Historical, and Descriptive Notices of Kircudbrightshire, Chiefly in the Nineteenth Century* (Castle Douglas: James Maxwell, 1901), p.339

6 *The Lives of Frederic and John Anne McConnel*, (privately printed, 1963), p.130 (British Library)

7 D.C. McConnel, *Facts and Traditions*, pp. 145–6

8 Lee, C.H., *A Cotton Enterprise 1795–1840: A History of M'Connel & Kennedy Fine Cotton Spinners* (Manchester: Manchester University Press, 1972), p.52

9 D.C. McConnel, *Facts and Traditions*, p.146

10 Ibid., p.149

11 Holt, G.O., *A Short History of the Liverpool and Manchester Railway* (Railway & Canal Historical Society, 1965), p.9

12 Scottish Great Seal Register, letter no. 622 to Marquis of Lorne

CHAPTER 5:
A Soldier's Wife

1 *Royal Horticultural Society Journal*, Vol. 53 (1928), p.269, S.K. Garnett-

Botfield, 'The Garden at Beamish, Albrighton'

2 Ranfurly, *To War with Whitaker:* (London: Heinemann, 1994), p.103

3 Cooper, Artemis, *Cairo in the War 1939–1945* (London: Hamish Hamilton, 1989), p.123

4 Nevill, Dorothy, *Under Five Reigns* (London: Methuen, 1910), p.195

5 Wellington, *Private Corresondence*, pp.2–3

6 Ibid., p.3

7 Cole, Lowry, ed. Maud Lowry Cole and Stephen Gwynn, *Memoirs of Sir Lowry Cole* (London: Macmillan, 1934), p.27

8 Wellington, *Private Correspondence*, p.3

9 Elers, George, ed. Monson and Leveson-Gower, *Memoirs of George Elers, 1777–1842* (London: Heinemann, 1903), p.126

10 Wellington, *Private Correspondence*, p.4

11 Ibid., p.6

12 Ibid., p.56

13 Ibid., p.51

14 Cole, op. cit., p.30

15 Wilson, p.58

16 Ibid., p.61

17 Guedalla, p.117

18 Bryant, Arthur, *The Great Duke or the Invincible General* (London: Collins, 1971), p.85

19 Longford, *The Years of the Sword*, p.110

20 Wellington, *Private Correspondence*, p.7

21 Ibid., p.8

22 Ibid., p.9

23 Wilson, p.77

24 Shelley, Frances, ed. E. Edgecombe, *The Diary of Frances Lady Shelley*, Vol. 2 (London: John Murray, 1913), p.407

25 Wilson, p.81

26 Edgeworth, Maria, ed. Augustus J. C. Hare, *The Life and Letters of Maria Edgeworth* (London: Edward Arnold, 1894), p.151

CHAPTER 6:
Return to Palena

1 *London Magazine*, 14 June 1947

2 Hickey and Smith, p.69

3 Saunders, Hilary St George, *The Green Beret: The Story of the Commandos 1940–1945* (London: The New English Library, 1968), p.186

4 Hickey and Smith, p.235

5 Ibid., p.273

6 *The Iron Duke*, 2000, 'Salute to the Duke', p.71

7 *The Iron Duke*, 1944, p.6

8 Holmes, p.149

CHAPTER 7:
Heirs and Graces

1 Griffiths, *Patriotism Perverted: Captain Ramsay, the Right Club and English Anti-semitism* (London: Constable, 1998), p.115

2 Ramsay, A.H.M., *The Nameless War* (London: The Britons Publishing Society, 1952), p.103

3 Griffiths, op. cit. p.300

4 Ibid., p.301

5 Ibid., p.302

6 *The Times*, 4 May 1946

7 Hammick, Horacio H., *The Duke of Wellington's Spanish Estate: A Personal Narrative*, Vol. 1 [no second volume] (London: Spottiswoode, 1885), p.174

8 Reid, T. Wemyss. *The Life, Letters, and Friendships of Richard Monckton Milnes, First Lord Houghton*, Vol. 2 (London: Cassell, 1890), p.196

9 *The Times*, 28 May, 1901

10 Shelley, Frances, ed. E. Edgecombe, *The Diary of Frances Lady Shelley*, Vol. 2 (London: John Murray, 1913), p.321

11 Hare, Augustus J.C., *The Story of my Life*, Vol. 5 (London: George Allen, 1900), pp.11–12

12 Reid, op. cit., Vol 1, p.389

13 Gleig, G.R., 'The Second Duke of Wellington', *Fortnightly Review* (October 1884), p.433.

14 Ibid., p.434

15 Hare, op. cit., p.277

16 Longford, *The Years of the Sword*, p.486

17 Ford, Richard, *Apsley House and Walmer Castle, illustrated by plates and description* (London: 1853), p.1

18 Nevill, Dorothy, ed. Ralph Nevill, *The Reminiscences of Lady Dorothy Nevill* (London: Nelson & Sons, 1920), p.190

19 Fraser, p.95

20 Nevill, *The Life and Letters of Lady Dorothy Nevill*, p.227

21 Reid, op. cit., Vol. 1, p.497

22 Hare, op. cit., Vol. 4, p.344

23 Nevill, *The Reminiscences of Lady Dorothy Nevill*, p.200

24 *The Times*, 15 December 1881

25 *Survey of London*, Vol. 45, Knightsbridge (The Athlone Press for English Heritiage, 2000), p.61

26 Ibid.

27 Gleig, op. cit., p.442

28 Pickering, Anna Maria, ed. Spencer Pickering, *Memoirs of Anna Wilhelmina Pickering* (London: Hodder & Stoughton, 1904), p.28

29 Nevill, *The Life and Letters of Lady Dorothy Nevill*, p.229

30 Ibid., p.230

31 Wilson, p.90

CHAPTER 8:
Alone and Sad

Quotes from Kitty's journals come from a Stratfield Saye MS but often appear in *A Soldier's Wife* by Joan Wilson.

1 M. Wellesley, *The Man Wellington*, p.127

2 Wellington, ed. 2nd Duke, *Supplementary Despatches, Correspondence & Memoranda of Field Marshal Arthur Duke of Wellington*, Vol. 7 (London: 1858–64), p.5

3 *Childe Harold's Pilgrimage*, Canto the First, XXVI

4 Wilson, p.111

5 Calvert, Frances, *An Irish Beauty of the Regency: Compiled from the Unpublished Journals of The Hon. Mrs Calvert 1789–1822* (London and New York: John Lane, 1911), p.136

6 Thomas Pakenham, *Pakenham Letters 1800–1815* (London: John & Edward Bumpus, 1914), p.57

7 Longford, *The Years of the Sword*, p.228–9

8 Ibid., p.247

9 Kincaid, pp.72–3

10 Longford, *The Years of the Sword*, p.254

11 Haythornthwaite, Philip J., *The Armies of Wellington* (London: Arms and Armour, 1994), p.245

12 Holmes, p.153

13 Cooper, John Spencer, *Rough Notes of Seven Campaigns in Portugal, Spain, France and America* (Carlisle: G&T Coward, 1914), p.68

14 Tomkinson, William, ed. James Tomkinson, *The Diary of a Cavalry Officer in the Peninsular and Waterloo Campaigns 1809–1815* (London: Swan Sonnenschein, 1894), p.108

15 Wilson, p.144

16 Mills, John, ed. Ian Fletcher, *For King and Country: The Letters and Diaries of John Mills, Coldstream Guards, 1811–1814* (Staplehurst: Spellmount, 1995), p.99

17 Longford, *The Years of the Sword*, p.266

18 Ibid., p.267

19 Holmes, p.160

20 Severn, p.362

21 Stanhope, p.38

22 Holmes, p.168

23 *Pakenham Letters*, p.174

24 Cole, Lowry, ed. Maud Lowry Cole and Stephen Gwynn, *Memoirs of Sir Lowry Cole* (London: Macmillan, 1934), p.87

25 Mills, op. cit., p.211

26 Berry, Mary, ed. Theresa Lewis, *Extracts from the Journals and Correspondence of Miss Berry from the Year 1783 to 1852*, Vol. 2 (London: Longmans, Green, 1866), p.506

27 *Wellington Anecdotes: A Collection of Sayings and Doings of the Great Duke* (London: Addey, 1852), p.16

28 Wilson, p.148

29 Ibid., p.152

30 Edgeworth, Maria, ed. Augustus J.C. Hare, *The Life and Letters of Maria Edgeworth*, Vol. 1 (London: Edward Arnold, 1894), p.208

31 Edgeworth, *Letters from England*, p.61

32 Ibid., p.153

33 Longford, *The Years of the Sword*, p.330

34 Smith, Harry, ed. G.C. Moore Smith, *The Autobiography of Lieutenant-General Sir Harry Smith*, Vol. 1 (London: John Murray, 1901), p.126

35 Longford, *The Years of the Sword*, p.334

36 Cooper, op. cit., pp.114–15

37 Swinton, J.R., *A Sketch of the Life of Georgiana, Lady De Ros: With Some Reminiscences of her Family and Friends, Including the Duke of Wellington* (London: John Murray, 1893), p.143

38 Rogers, Samuel, ed. William Sharpe, *Recollections* (London, 1859), p.241

39 Wilson, p.155

40 Larpent, F.S., *The Private Journal of Judge-Advocate Larpent, Attached to the Head-Quarters of Lord Wellington During the Peninsular War, from 1812 to its Close* (Staplehurst: Spellmount, 2000), p.487

41 Rose, John Holland, *The Life of Napoleon I: Including New Materials from the British Official Records* (London: G. Bell & Sons, 1922), p.432

42 Ellesmere, p.94

43 Longford, *The Years of the Sword*, p.362

CHAPTER 9:
Prince of Waterloo

1 Views expressed, respectively, by Peel, Frances Leveson-Gower and Lady Wharncliffe.

2 Von Neumann, Philip, ed. E. Beresford Chancellor, *The Diary of Philip Von Neumann 1819 to 1850*, Vol. 2 (London: Philip Allen, 1928), p.200

3 Longford, *Pillar of State*, p.44

4 Neville-Sington, Pamela, *Fanny Trollope: The Life and Adventures of a Clever Woman* (London: Viking, 1997), pp. 20–21

5 Edgeworth, p.103

6 Ibid.

7 Von Neumann, op. cit., p.13

8 Longford, *Pillar of State*, p.75

9 Arbuthnot, Vol. 1, pp.168 and 169

10 Shelley, Frances, ed. E. Edgecombe, *The Diary of Frances Lady Shelley*, Vol. 2 (London: John Murray, 1913), pp. 312–13

11 Lieven, Dorothea, ed. Peter Quennell, *The Private Letters of Princess Lieven to Prince Metternich 1820–1826* (London: John Murray, 1937), p.19

12 Wellington, *Wellington and His Friends*, p.50

13 Lieven, op. cit., p.102

14 Arbuthnot, Vol. 1, p.105

15 Longford, *Pillar of State*, pp. 70–71

16 Shelley, op. cit., Vol. 2, p.109

17 Longford, *Pillar of State*, p.82

18 Shelley, op. cit., Vol. 2, p.312

19 *Bentley's Miscellany*, Vol. 16 (1844), p.434, 'Eton Scenes and Eton Men'

20 Wellington, *Private Correspondence*, p.20

21 Ibid., p.23

22 Ibid., p.25

23 Longford, *Pillar of State*, p.83

24 Wellington, *Wellington and His Friends*, pp.37–8

25 Arbuthnot, Vol. 1, p.422

26 Wellington, *Private Correspondence*, p.30

27 Arbuthnot, Charles, ed. A. Aspinall, *The Correspondence of Charles Arbuthnot, Camden Third Series Volume LXV* (London: Offices of the Royal Historical Society, 1941), p.87

28 Wellington, *Private Correspondence*, p.155

29 Parker, *Sir Robert Peel: In Early Life, 1788–1812*, Vol. 1 (London: John Murray, 1891), p.484

30 Shelley, op. cit., Vol. 2, p.172

31 21 June, 1950

32 Longford, *Pillar of State*, p.199

33 Ibid., p.147

34 *The Speeches of The Duke of Wellington in Parliament*. Collected and Arranged by the Late Colonel Gurwood (London: John Murray, 1854), p.260

35 Lees-Milne, James, *Prophesying Peace* (London: Chatto & Windus, 1977), p.48

36 Lees-Milne, James, *Midway on the Waves* (London: Faber & Faber, 1985), p.200

37 *The Spectator*, 12 December 1925

38 *New York Times*, 18 December 1902

39 *Chambers' Edinburgh Journal* (January 1837), p.393, 'The Lost Dahlia' by Miss Mitford

40 Edwin Sidney, curate of Acle in Norfolk, 1838, see www.lambethpalace library.org/news/Annualreport2002

41 Johnson, Bradley T., *General Washington* (New York: D. Appleton, 1894)

42 M. Wellesley, *Wellington in Civil Life*, pp. 327–8

CHAPTER 10:
'That Damned Infernal Family'

1 Shelley, Frances, ed. E. Edgecombe, *The Diary of Frances Lady Shelley*, Vol. 2 (London: John Murray, 1913), p.264

2 Lawrence, Thomas, ed. George Somes Layard, *Sir Thomas Lawrence's Letter-bag* (London: George Allen, 1906), p.262

3 *The Hamwood Papers of the Ladies of Llangollen and Caroline Hamilton*, ed. G. H. Bell (London: Macmillan, 1930), pp. 226–7

4 *The Hamwood Papers*, p.246

5 Ibid., p.152

6 M. Wellesley, *The Man Wellington*, p.3

7 Torrens, W.M., *The Marquess Wellesley: Architect of Empire: An Historic Portrait* (London: Chatto & Windus, 1880), p.108

8 Wellesley, Richard Colley, *The Wellesley Papers*, Vol. 2 (London: Herbert Jenkins, 1914), p.367

9 Butler, p.103

10 Ibid., p.214

11 Ibid., p.154

12 Ibid., p.230

13 Ibid., p.225

14 Ibid., p.255

15 Ibid., p.345

16 Wellesley, Henry, ed. Colonel Wellesley, F.A., *The Diary and Correspondence of Henry Wellesley First Lord Cowley 1790–1846* (London: Hutchinson, 1930), p.14

17 Severn, p.198

18 Butler, p.346

19 Torrens, op. cit., p.300

20 Calvert, Frances, *An Irish Beauty of the Regency: Compiled from the Unpublished Journals of the Hon. Mrs Calvert 1789–1822* (London and New York: John Lane, 1911), p.126

21 Marquess of Anglesey, *One Leg: The Life and Letters of Henry William Paget* (London: Jonathan Cape, 1961), p.99

22 Brett James, Antony, *Wellington at War, 1794–1815* (London: Macmillan, 1961), p.189

23 Torrens, op. cit., p.512

24 Butler, p.185

25 Ibid., p.506

26 Severn, p.507

27 Butler, p.448

28 Ibid., p.486

29 Ibid., p.532

30 Blakiston, Georgina, *Lord William Russell and his Wife, 1815–1846* (London: John Murray, 1972), p.41

31 Lieven, Dorothea, ed. Peter Quennell, *The Private Letters of Princess Lieven to Prince Metternich 1820–1826* (London: John Murray, 1937), pp.48–9

32 Ibid., p.26

33 *Harper's New Monthly Magazine*, September 1880

34 Arbuthnot, Vol. 1, p.421

35 Somerset Trust Archive

CHAPTER II:
No. 1 London

1 Arbuthnot, P., *Memories of the Arbuthnots of Kincardineshire and Aberdeenshire* (London: George Allen & Unwin, 1920), p.224

2 Pakenham, pp.200, 202

3 Wellington, *Wellington and His Friends*, p.94

4 Grosvenor, Caroline and Beilby, Charles, *The First Lady Wharncliffe and her Family 1779–1856*, Vol. 2 (London: William Heinemann, 1927), pp. 74–5

5 *The Times*, 28 April 1831

6 Brialmont, M. and Gleig, G.R., *History of the Life of Arthur Duke of Wellington*, Vol. 4 (London: Longman, Green, Longman & Roberts, 1860), p.86

7 Cole, Lowry, ed. Maud Lowry Cole and Stephen Gwynn, *Memoirs of Sir Lowry Cole* (London: Macmillan, 1934), p.60

8 Longford, *The Years of the Sword*, p.78

9 Delaforce, Patrick, *Wellington the Beau: The Life and Loves of the Duke of Wellington* (Adlestrop: Windrush Press, 1990), p.210

10 Grosvenor and Beilby, op. cit., p.138

11 Thornton, James, *Your Most Obedient Servant: Cook to the Duke of Wellington* (Exeter: Webb & Bower, 1985), p.32–34

12 Edgeworth, p.186

13 Longford, *Pillar of State*, p.52

14 Wellington, *Wellington and His Friends*, p.95

15 Ellesmere, p.74

16 *The Times*, 19 September 1831

17 *The Times*, 8 February 1831

18 Wellington, *Wellington and His Friends*, p.99

19 *Saturday Magazine*, April 1842

20 Wellington, *Wellington and His Friends*, p.96

21 M. Wellesley, *Wellington in Civil Life*, p.183

22 Ibid., p.189

23 Shelley, Frances, ed. E. Edgecombe, *The Diary of Frances Lady Shelley*, Vol. 2 (London: John Murray, 1913), p.219

24 Brialmont and Gleig, op. cit., p.66

25 Fraser, p.12

26 Hatherton, Lord, ed. A. Aspinall, *Extracts from Lord Hatherton's Diary* (London, 1952), p.141

27 Ellesmere, p.46

28 Croker, John Wilson, *The Croker Papers: The Correspondence and Diaries of the Late Right Honourable John Wilson Croker 1809–1830*, Vol. 2 (London: John Murray, 1885), p.228

29 Oman, Carola, *The Gascoyne Heiress: The Life and Diaries of Frances Mary Gascoyne-Cecil 1802–39* (London: Hodder & Stoughton, 1968), pp.132–3

30 Wellington, *The Letters of The Duke of Wellington to Miss J.*, p.44

31 Wellington, *A Great Man's Friendship*, p.84

32 Longford, *Pillar of State*, p.303

33 M. Wellesley, *Wellington in Civil Life*, p.239

34 Oman, op. cit., p.162

35 Ibid., pp.203–4

36 Ibid., p.163

37 Granville, Harriet, ed. F. Leveson-Gower, *Letters of Harriet Countess Granville 1810–1845*, Vol. 2 (London: Longmans, Green, 1894), p.225

38 Croker, op. cit., p.251

39 Oman, op. cit., p.146

40 Swinton, J.R., *A Sketch of the Life of Georgiana, Lady De Ros: With Some Reminiscences of her Family and Friends, Including The Duke of Wellington* (London: John Murray, 1893), p.181

41 Greville, Charles, ed. Lytton Strachey and Roger Fulford, *The Greville Memoirs 1814–1860*, Vol. 3 (London: Macmillan, 1938), p.374

42 Oman, op. cit., p.288

43 Bagot, Charles, *Links with the Past* (London: Edward Arnold, 1901), p.11

44 Napier, William, ed. H.A. Bruce, *Life of General Sir William Napier*, Vol. 1 (London: John Murray, 1864), p.485

45 Greville, op. cit., Vol. 4, p.66

46 Croker, op. cit., Vol. 2, p.330

47 Hibbert, p.343

48 *The Corsair (A Gazette of Literature, Art, Dramatic Criticism, Fashion and Novelty)*, New York, 20 April 1839

49 Wellington, *Private Correspondence*, p.53

50 Stanhope, p.102

51 *Quarterly Review*, March 1853

52 *The Times*, 11 March 1863

53 *The Times*, 26 July 1864

54 Hare, Augustus J.C., *The Story of my Life*, Vol. 5 (London: George Allen, 1900), p.30

55 *The Times* of 23 October 1928, from *The Times of 1828*
56 Hickey and Smith, p.70
57 Lees-Milne, James, *Ancestral Voices* (London: Chatto & Windus, 1975), p.151
58 *The Times*, 29 April, 1953
59 Ibid.
60 *The Times*, 24 March, 1926

CHAPTER 12:
Thistles and Thistledown

1 *The Complete Peerage*, ed. Geoffrey H. White (London: The St Catherine Press, 1953) p.812
2 D. Wellesley, *Far Have I Travelled*, p.93
3 Ibid., p.98
4 Wellesley, Dorothy, *Sir George Goldie: Founder of Nigeria* (London: Macmillan, 1934), p.92
5 D. Wellesley, *Far Have I Travelled*, p.56
6 Wellesley, *Sir George Goldie*, pp. 103–4
7 Glendinning, p.51
8 Lees-Milne, Vol. 1, p.62
9 Wellesley, *Sir George Goldie*, p.128
10 *Oxford Dictionary of National Biography*, Vol. 58 (2004), p.29
11 Glendinning, p.121
12 Lees-Milne, Vol. 1, p.179
13 Ibid., p.196
14 Glendinning, p.129
15 Lees-Milne, Vol. 1, p.194
16 Ibid., p.238
17 *The Spectator*, 22 March 1924
18 Glendinning, p.133
19 Ibid., p.137
20 Ibid., p.154
21 Sackville-West, Vita, ed. Louise DeSalvo and Mitchell Leaska, *The Letters of Vita Sackville-West to Virginia Woolf* (London: Hutchinson, 1984), p.110
22 D. Wellesley, *Far Have I Travelled*, p.189
23 Glendinning, p.161
24 Sackville-West, Vita, *The Land and the Garden* (Exeter: Webb & Bower, 1989), p.7
25 Sackville-West, Vita, *The Land* (London: William Heinemann, 1926), p.45
26 Sackville-West, *The Letters of Vita Sackville-West to Virginia Woolf*, p.181
27 Ibid., p.196
28 Ibid., p.247
29 Glendinning, Victoria, *Leonard Woolf: A Life* (London: Simon & Schuster, 2006), p.270
30 Woolf, Virginia, ed. Anne Olivier Bell, *The Diary of Virginia Woolf: Vol. 3, 1925–30* (London: Penguin, 1982), p.162
31 Glendinning, *Vita*, p.185
32 Ibid., p.187
33 Ibid., p.246
34 Letter from Vita to Harold in the possession of Lady Gibson
35 D. Wellesley, *Beyond the Grave*, p.11
36 Carney, Michael, *Stoker: The Life of Hilda Matheson OBE 1888–1940* (privately published, 1999), p.54
37 Glendinning, *Vita*, p.213
38 Carney, op. cit., p.54
39 Woolf, *The Diary of Virginia Woolf: Vol. 3*, p.267
40 Lees-Milne, James, *Fourteen Friends* (London: John Murray, 1996), p.211
41 Powell, Anthony, *To Keep the Ball Rolling: The Memoirs of Anthony Powell*, Vol. 3: *Faces in my Time* (London: Heinemann, 1980), p.123
42 D. Wellesley, *Far Have I Travelled*, p.178

43 G. Wellesley, *The Diary of a Desert Journey*, p.28

44 Ibid., p.15

45 Yeats, p.39

46 Wellesley, Dorothy, *Selections from the Poems of Dorothy Wellesley with an Introduction by W.B. Yeats* (London: Macmillan, 1936), p.xii

47 Yeats, p.84

48 Glendinning, *Vita*, p.279

49 Foster, p.545

50 Woolf, Virginia, ed. Nigel Nicolson, *Leave The Letters Till We Are Dead: The Letters of Virginia Woolf*, Vol. 6, 1936–1941 (London: Hogarth Press, 1980), p.110

51 Woolf, *The Letters of Virginia Woolf*, Vol. 6, p.96

52 Foster, p.562

53 Yeats, p.10

54 Ibid., p.118

55 Ibid., p.119

56 Ibid., p.46

57 Foster, p.546

58 *Journal of Contemporary History*, Vol. 19, No. 3 (July 1984), p.36

59 Chamberlain Papers, Birmingham University NCLAdd/14

60 Email from Nicholas Pronay, 7 June 2007

61 *Journal of Contemporary History*, op. cit., p.376

62 Foster, p.642

63 Yeats, p.190

64 Ibid., p.195

65 D. Wellesley, *Beyond the Grave*, p.42

66 Ibid., p.46

67 Cooper, Artemis, *Cairo in the War 1939–1945* (London: Hamish Hamilton, 1989), pp.246–7

68 D. Wellesley, *Beyond the Grave*, p.21

69 Ibid., p.63

70 Ibid., p.52

71 Ibid., p.63

72 Powell, Violet, *The Departure Platform* (London: William Heinemann, 1998), p.137

73 D. Wellesley, *Far Have I Travelled*, pp.238–9

74 Yeats, *Letters on Poetry*, p.xiii

75 Oman, Carola, *The Gascoyne Heiress: The Life and Diaries of Frances Mary Gascoyne-Cecil 1802–39* (London: Hodder & Stoughton, 1968), p.91

76 Glendinning, *Vita*, p.384

77 *The English Review*, December 1922

78 Lees-Milne, James, *Midway on the Waves* (London: Faber & Faber, 1985), p.166

79 Ibid., p.200

80 Gladwyn, Cynthia, ed. Miles Jebb, *The Diaries of Cynthia Gladwyn* (London: Constable, 1995), p.221

81 Ibid., p.337

82 Glendinning, *Vita*, p.356

CHAPTER 13:
Arthurolatry

1 Maxwell, Sir Herbert, *The Life of Wellington: The Restoration of the Martial Power of Great Britain*, Vol. 2 (London: Sampson Low, Marston, 1907), p.325

2 Ellesmere, *Personal Reminiscences*, p.171

3 Wellington, *A Great Man's Friendship*, p.105

4 Gleig, p.423

5 Raikes, Thomas, *A Portion of the Journal Kept by Thomas Raikes, Esq. from 1831 to 1847: Comprising Reminiscences of Social and Political Life in London and Paris During that Period*, Vol. 4 of 4 (London: Longman, Brown, Green,

Longmans & Roberts, 1857), pp.317–18

6 Stanhope, p.105

7 Greville, Charles, ed. Lytton Strachey and Roger Fulford, *The Greville Memoirs 1814–1860*, Vol. 4 (London: Macmillan, 1938), p.243

8 Maxwell, Sir Herbert, *The Life and Letters of George William Frederick, Fourth Earl of Clarendon, K.G., G.C.B.*, Vol. 1 (London: Edward Arnold, 1913), p.204

9 Broughton, Lord (John Cam Hobhouse), ed. Lady Dorchester, *Recollections of a Long Life*, Vol. 6 (London: John Murray, 1911), p.6

10 Wellington, *Wellington and His Friends*, p.174

11 Lyttelton, Sarah Spencer, ed. Hugh Wyndham, *Correspondence of Sarah Spencer Lady Lyttelton 1787–1870* (London: John Murray, 1912), p.334

12 Stanhope, p.199

13 Severn, *Architects of Empire*, p.517

14 Ibid., p.524

15 Ibid., p.526

16 Wellington, *Wellington and His Friends*, p.170

17 *The Times*, 25 May 1844

18 Gronow, Captain, *The Reminiscences and Recollections of Captain Gronow: Being Anecdotes of the Camp, Court, Clubs and Society 1810–1860*, Vol. 2 (London: John C. Nimmo, 1892), p.289

19 Delaforce, Patrick, *Wellington the Beau: The Life and Loves of the Duke of Wellington* (Gloucestershire: The Windrush Press, 1990), p. 244

20 Ellesmere, p.179

21 Burghersh, pp.175–6

22 Wellington, *The Letters of The Duke of Wellington To Miss J.*, p.161

23 Healey, pp.87–8, 90, 95, 96, 97, 109

24 Swinton, J.R., *A Sketch of the Life of Georgiana, Lady De Ros: With Some Reminiscences of her Family and Friends, Including The Duke of Wellington* (London: John Murray, 1893), pp.152–3

25 Curzon, George Nathaniel (Marquess), ed. Stephen Gwynn, *Personal History of Walmer Castle and its Lords Warden* (London: Macmillan, 1927), p.176

26 Ibid., p.174

27 Kerr, Mark, *Land, Sea and Air: Reminiscences of Mark Kerr* (London: Longmans, Green, 1927), p.345

28 Haydon, B.R., *Correspondence & Table-Talk*, Vol. 2 (London, 1876), p.661

29 Swinton, op. cit., p.158

30 Haydon, op. cit., p.654

31 Wellington, *Wellington and His Friends*, p.163

32 Ibid., p.201

33 Ibid., pp.197–8

34 *Quarterly Review*, March 1853

35 Ramsay, Balcarres D. Wardlaw, *Rough Recollections of Military Service and Society* (Edinburgh and London: William Blackwood & Sons, 1882), p.166

36 Hibbert, p.363

37 Lyttelton, op. cit., p.320

38 Froude, James Anthony, *Thomas Carlyle: A History of his Life in London, 1834–1881*, Vol. 2 (London: Longmans, 1884), p.46

39 Fitzmaurice, Edmond, *The Life of Granville George Leveson-Gower Second Earl Granville 1815–1891*, Vol. 1 (London: Longmans, Green, 1905), p.10

40 Taylor, Henry, *Autobiography of Henry Taylor, 1800–1875*, Vol. 2 (London: Longmans, Green, 1885), p.35

41 Longford, *Pillar of State*, p.387
42 Arbuthnot, P., *Memories of the Arbuthnots of Kincardineshire and Aberdeenshire* (London: George Allen & Unwin, 1920), p.229
43 Wellington, *A Great Man's Friendship*, p.102
44 Ibid., p.83
45 Timbs, John, *Wellingtoniana: Anecdotes, Maxims, and Characteristics, of the Duke of Wellington* (London: Ingram, Cooke, 1852), p.143
46 Wellington, *My Dear Mrs Jones: The Letters of the First Duke of Wellington to Mrs Jones of Pantglas* (London: Rodale Press, 1954), p.11
47 Ibid., p.7
48 Ibid., p.40
49 Wellington, *A Great Man's Friendship*, p.219
50 *The Times*, 26 January 1852
51 Wellington, *A Great Man's Friendship*, p.269
52 Ibid., p.280
53 Ibid., p.272–3
54 Ibid., p.291
55 Ibid., p.311
56 Ibid., p.314
57 Croker, John Wilson, *The Croker Papers: The Correspondence and Diaries of the Late Right Honourable John Wilson Croker 1809–1830*, Vol. 3 (London: John Murray, 1885), p.275
58 Wellington, *A Great Man's Friendship*, p.330
59 Burghersh, p.200
60 Timbs, op. cit., p.111
61 Ibid., p.108
62 Wellington, '*The Iron Duke*': *Memoirs of the Duke of Wellington from Authentic Sources* (York: J. Sampson, 1852), p.123
63 Wellington, *Private Correspondence*, p.220
64 Ibid., p.221
65 Ibid., p.223
66 Guedalla, p.473
67 Redesdale, Lord, *Memories* (London: Hutchinson, 1915), p.75
68 Redesdale, op. cit., p.87
69 Marquess of Anglesey, *One Leg: The Life and Letters of Henry William Paget* (London: Jonathan Cape, 1961), p.333

SELECT BIBLIOGRAPHY

Arbuthnot, Harriet, ed. Francis Bamford and the 7th Duke of Wellington, *The Journal of Mrs Arbuthnot*, 2 vols (London: Macmillan, 1950)

Burghersh, *Correspondence of Lady Burghersh with the Duke of Wellington*, ed. Lady Rose Weigall (London: John Murray, 1903)

Butler, Iris, *The Eldest Brother: The Marquess Wellesley 1760–1842* (London: Hodder & Stoughton, 1973)

Edgeworth, Maria, ed. Christina Colvin, *Maria Edgeworth: Letters from England 1813–1844* (Oxford: Clarendon Press, 1971)

Ellesmere, *Personal Reminiscences of the Duke of Wellington by Francis, the First Earl of Ellesmere*, ed. Alice, Countess of Strafford (London: John Murray, 1904)

Foster, R.F., *W.B. Yeats: A Life, Vol. 2: The Arch-Poet 1915–1939* (Oxford: Oxford University Press, 2003)

Foulkes, Nick, *Dancing Into Battle: A Social History of the Battle of Waterloo* (London: Weidenfeld & Nicolson, 2006)

Fraser, Sir William, *Words on Wellington: The Duke, Waterloo, The Ball* (London: Nimmo, 1889)

Gleig, George Robert, *The Life of Arthur Duke of Wellington* (London: John Childs & Son, 1864)

Glendinning, Victoria, *Vita: The Life of V. Sackville-West* (London: Weidenfeld & Nicolson, 1984)

Griffiths, Richard, *Patriotism Perverted: Captain Ramsay, the Right Club and English Anti-Semitism, 1939–40* (London: Constable, 1998)

Guedalla, Philip, *The Duke* (Ware: Wordsworth Editions, 1997)

Healey, Edna, *Lady Unknown: The Life of Angela Burdett-Coutts* (London: Sidgwick & Jackson, 1978)

Hibbert, Christopher, *Wellington: A Personal History* (London: HarperCollins, 1997)

Hickey, Des and Smith, Gus, *Operation Avalanche: The Salerno Landings, 1943* (London: Heinemann, 1983)

Holmes, Richard, *Wellington: The Iron Duke* (London: HarperCollins, 2003)

Kincaid, John, Captain, *Adventures in the Rifle Brigade: In the Peninsula, France and the Netherlands from 1809 to 1815* (Staplehurst: Spellmount, 1998)

Lambert, Angela, *1939, The Last Season of Peace* (London: Weidenfeld & Nicolson, 1989)

Lee, C.H., *A Cotton Enterprise 1795–1840: A History of M'Connel and Kennedy, Fine Cotton Spinners* (Manchester: Manchester University Press, 1972)

Lees-Milne, James, *Harold Nicolson: A Biography*, 2 vols (London: Chatto & Windus, 1981)

Longford, Elizabeth, *Wellington: The Years of the Sword* (London: Weidenfeld & Nicolson, 1969)

Longford, Elizabeth, *Wellington: Pillar of State* (London: Weidenfeld Nicolson, 1972)

McConnel, David Connor, *Facts and Traditions: Collected, for a Family Record* (Edinburgh: Ballantyne, 1861)

McConnel, John Wanklyn, *A Century of Fine Cotton Spinning: McConnel & Co.* (Manchester: George Falkner & Sons, 1913)

Nevill, *The Life and Letters of Lady Dorothy Nevill*, ed. Ralph Nevill (London: Methuen, 1919)

Pakenham, Eliza, *Soldier Sailor: An Intimate Portrait of an Irish Family* (London: Weidenfeld & Nicolson, 2007)

Ranfurly, Countess, *To War with Whitaker: The Wartime Diaries of the Countess of Ranfurly, 1939–45* (London: Heinemann, 1994)

Roberts, Andrew, *Waterloo: Napoleon's Last Gamble*, Making History Series, ed. Amanda Foreman and Lisa Jardine (London: HarperCollins, 2005)

Severn, John, *Architects of Empire: The Duke of Wellington and His Brothers* (Oklahoma: University of Oklahoma Press, 2007)

Stanhope, Philip Henry, 5th Earl, *Notes of Conversations with the Duke of Wellington, 1831–1851* (London: Prion, 1998)

Wellesley, Dorothy, *Beyond the Grave: Letters on Poetry, to W. B. Yeats from Dorothy Wellesley* (Tunbridge Wells: C. Baldwin, 1952)

Wellesley, Dorothy, *Far Have I Travelled* (London: James Barrie, 1952)

Wellesley, Gerald, *The Diary of a Desert Journey* (London: Putnam, 1938)

Wellington, Gerald 7th Duke, *The Collected Works of Gerald 7th Duke of Wellington* (privately published, 1970)

Wellesley, Muriel, *The Man Wellington: Through the Eyes of Those Who Knew Him* (London: Constable, 1937)

Wellesley, Muriel, *Wellington in Civil Life: Through the Eyes of Those Who Knew Him* (London: Constable, 1939)

Wellington, ed. Lady Burghclere, *A Great Man's Friendship: Letters of The Duke of Wellington to Mary, Marchioness of Salisbury 1850–1852* (London: John Murray, 1927)

Wellington, ed. Christine Terhune Herrick, *The Letters of The Duke of Wellington to Miss J. 1834–1851* (London: T. Fisher Unwin, 1924)

Wellington, ed. 7th Duke, *Wellington and His Friends: Letters of The First Duke of Wellington to The Rt. Hon. Charles and Mrs Arbuthnot, The Earl and Countess of Wilton, Princess Lieven, and Miss Burdett-Coutts* (London: Macmillan, 1965)

Wellington, ed. 7th Duke, *A Selection from the Private Correspondence of the First Duke of Wellington* (London: The Roxburghe Club, 1952)

Wilson, Joan, *A Soldier's Wife: Wellington's Marriage* (London: Weidenfeld & Nicolson, 1987)

Wyndham, Humphrey, *The Household Cavalry at War: First Household Cavalry Regiment* (Aldershot: Gale & Polden, 1952)

Yeats, W.B., *Letters on Poetry from W.B. Yeats to Dorothy Wellesley* (London: Oxford University Press, 1964)

INDEX

The abbreviation AW stands for Arthur Wellesley, 1st Duke of Wellington

Abel Smith, Henry, 63
Adam, Robert, 248
Adams, Mrs (*née* Coats; Maud Wellington's sister), 160
Adams, Samuel, 16
Adelaide, Queen of William IV, 258
Alamein, El: battle of (1942), 82, 84
Alava, General Miguel de, 195, 313
Albert, Prince Consort, 263, 313, 326, 330
Albuera, battle of (1811), 187
Aldington, Araminta, Lady (*née* MacMichael; 'Minta'), 111–12, 114, 116–17, 121
Alexander I, Tsar of Russia, 1
Alexandra, Queen of Edward VII, 264
Alfieri, Vittorio, 200
Alfonso XII, King of Spain, 162
Allen, Mrs (Walmer Castle cook), 330
Angers, France, 32
Anglesey, Charles Paget, 6th Marquess of, 51
Anglesey, Henry William Paget, 1st Marquess of (*earlier* 2nd Earl of Uxbridge): at Waterloo, 3, 8; runs away with Charlotte Wellesley, 234–5; at AW's funeral, 332
Apostles, Mrs (Stratfield Saye housekeeper), 218, 320–1
Apsley House, London: as Wellington home, 11; given to nation, 85, 162, 268; catalogue of pictures, 167; Richard buys, 237, 248; AW acquires and renovates, 248–9; designed and built, 248; art collection, 249–50, 262; stoned by mob, 251–2; iron shutters installed, 251–2, 262;

opened to public after AW's death, 262; Second Duke at, 262–3; entertaining and functions at, 263–5, 269, 326; royal papers kept at, 265; staff and organisation, 266; damaged in World War II, 267; private apartments, 270–1
Arbuthnot, Charles ('Gosh'), 259, 322–3
Arbuthnot, Harriet, 203, 207–8, 214, 240, 249, 251–6, 258, 311
Arkwright, Richard, 16
Armytage, John, 31–2
Arthur, Prince *see* Connaught, Duke of
Ashton, James (Dorothy's grandfather), 275
Ashton, Robert (Dorothy's brother; 'Scamp'), 20–1, 273, 277–9, 282, 291
Ashton, Robert (Dorothy's father), 273, 275, 278
Assaye, battle of (1803), 128
Astor, Gavin (*later* 2nd Baron Astor of Hever), 146, 148
Astor, Michael, 84
Astor, Nancy, Viscountess, 289
Atrash, Amal al-, 78, 119
Austerlitz, battle of (1805), 132

Badajoz, Spain, 186, 189
Bag of Nails (club), London, 49
Ball, Sir Joseph, 296–7
Bathurst, Henry, 2nd Earl (*earlier* Baron Apsley), 248
Beamish (house), 107
Beaufort, Emily, Duchess of (*née* Culling Smith; *earlier* Marchioness of Worcester), 241
Belle Alliance, La, Belgium, 7, 9

Bentinck, Lord Charles, 238
Bentinck, Lady Charles (*née* Anne Wellesley; Hyacinthe's daughter), 238
Beresford, Colonel Marcus, 124–5
Berners, Gerald Tyrwhitt-Wilson, 14th Baron, 280, 292
Birley, Maxine, 61
Bischoffsheim, Henri Louis, 158
Blenheim Palace, Oxfordshire, 216
Bligh, Helena, 2
Blücher, Marshal Gebhard Leberecht von, 2, 5, 9
Boer War (1899–1902), 164
Bonaparte, Betsy (*née* Paterson), 238
Bonaparte, Jerome, King of Westphalia, 238
Bonaparte, Joseph, King of Spain, 194, 196, 249
Bond, Billy, 119
Bowles, E.A., 107
Boxtel, Netherlands, 56
Bramshill, Hampshire, 199
Britain: war with France, 56, 228; war with USA (1812), 190; social unrest, 201–2
Broadstairs, Kent: Kitty in, 178–81, 188
Brodrick, George, 49
Brougham, Henry, 1st Baron, 220, 274, 314
Brown's Seminary, London (school), 18, 29
Bruntisfield, John Warrender, 2nd Baron: wartime service with Valerian, 59–64; tattoo, 61–2
Brussels: AW's youth in, 31–2
Bullingdon Club, Oxford, 43
Burdett-Coutts, Angela, Baroness, 317–19, 330
Burghersh, Priscilla (*née* Wellesley-Pole; AW's niece), 241, 314, 317, 319
Burgos, siege of (1812), 192
Bussaco, battle of (1810), 182–3
Butler, Lady Eleanor, 38, 227
Butler, Iris, 236
Byron, George Gordon, 6th Baron, 177, 305

Cairo: Valerian in during World War II, 78, 80, 85, 118, 299; Three-power conference (1943), 85, 117
Calvert, Frances, 234
Cambridge, Augusta, Duchess of, 326
Camden, John Jeffreys Pratt, 2nd Earl and 1st Marquess of, 56

Cannan, David (James McConnel's uncle), 90
Canova, Antonio: statue of Napoleon, 250, 268
Carlyle, Thomas, 322
Caroline, Queen of George IV, 204
Cassino, Monte (Italy), 141
Castlereagh, Robert Stewart, Viscount, 129
Catholic Emancipation: AW supports, 18, 54–5, 214
Cato Street Conspiracy (1820), 201–2
Chamberlain, Neville, 53, 109, 295–7
Charlotte Sophia, Queen of George III, 134
Chartists, 322–3
Chartley, George Ferrers de Chartley, Baron (*later* 3rd Marquess Townshend), 273–4
Chaworth, Mary (*later* Musters), 93
Chester Terrace, Regent's Park, 290–1, 304
Chiang Kai-shek, 85
Chowbent, Lancashire, 90
Churchill, John (Jack), 137–40, 155
Churchill, (Sir) Winston: wartime speeches, 59; and Middle East campaign, 65; attends Cairo summit (1943), 85; Douglas McConnel meets, 101
Cintra, Convention of (1808), 177, 235
Ciudad Rodrigo, Spain, 182, 189
Clyde, Lady Elizabeth (*née* Wellesley; Gerald/Dorothy's daughter): birth, 25; visits Valerian at Eton, 36; as debutante, 47–9; Klosters holiday with Valerian and Rose Paget, 51; at outbreak of war, 53; marriage, 53; wartime letters from Valerian in Middle East, 67, 75, 80–1; letter from newly married Diana, 122; attitude to 5th Duke and Duchess, 159; stays at Apsley House, 265–6; visits Mitey, 292; dislikes Yeats, 293; and care of mother in old age, 304; and mother's death, 305; in America, 308
Clyde, Jeremy (Elizabeth's son), 303–4
Clyde, Robin (Elizabeth's son), 303
Clyde, Thomas, 51, 53–4, 67, 75, 80–1, 155, 303
Cobbett, William, 236
Cole, Lady Frances (*née* Harris), 247
Cole, General Lowry, 125–7, 176, 178, 190, 193, 247

Connaught, Prince Arthur, Duke of, 264, 331

Cook, Captain James, 17

Cooper (Stratfield Saye gardener), 217

Cooper, Alfred Duff (*later* 1st Viscount Norwich), 46

Cope, Sir John, 258

Copenhagen (AW's horse), 4, 11, 23, 208, 218, 327

Corn Laws: repealed, 320

Cowley, Georgiana, Lady (*née* Cecil; Henry's second wife), 235

Cowley, Henry Wellesley, 1st Baron (AW's brother): birth, 17; at Eton, 31; captured and imprisoned by French, 228–30; escapes, 229–30; accompanies brother Richard to India, 230; marriage, 232–3; and wife's absconding with Paget, 234–5; divorce and remarriage, 235; as Envoy to Spain, 235, 249; liver complaint, 235; at 2nd Duke's wedding, 262; death, 263, 315; on AW's indifference towards money, 322

Cradock, General John (*later* 1st Baron Howden), 39

Croker, John Wilson, 252–3, 255, 260, 327

Crosbie, Richard, 17

Crystal Palace: burnt (1936), 47

Culling Smith, Lady Anne (*née* Wellesley; *then* Fitzroy; AW's sister): birth, 16; Hyacinthe's view of, 226; marriage, 226–7; captured and imprisoned by French, 228–9, 241; and husband's death, 228; second marriage, 240; letter to son Frederick, 241; pension, 242; death, 315

Culling Smith, Charles, 240, 242

Culling Smith, Emily, 240

Culling Smith, Major Frederick (Anne's son), 241

Cyprus, 81, 211–12

Daily Telegraph, The: Valerian writes to on Iraq, 72

Dangan Castle, Co. Meath, 13–14, 18, 39, 55

de Forest, Baroness, 278

Delany, Mary (*née* Granville), 13–14, 16, 18

d'Erlon, Marshal Jean-Baptiste Drouet, Comte, 5

Descamps, Mlle, 232

de Valera, Eamon, 85

Dickens, Charles, 330

Dilke, Sir Charles, 171

Donovan (Apsley House nightwatchman), 266

Douro, Arthur Charles Valerian Wellesley, Marquess of (8th Duke's eldest son): 155–6, 210–11, 270, 302

Douro, Bessy, Marchioness of *see* Wellington, Elizabeth, Duchess of

Dowe, Mrs (Apsley House housekeeper), 26

Dublin, 39–40, 174

Dubourg, Matthew, 14

Dungannon, Anne, Viscountess (*née* Stafford; AW's maternal grandmother), 31, 39, 227

Dunkirk evacuation (1940), 59

Dunn-Gardner, Cecil (Dorothy's grandfather), 273, 274

Dunn-Gardner, Emma (Cecil's wife), 274

Edgeworth, Maria, 193–5, 201, 245, 250

Edward VII, King, 264; birth, 314

Elizabeth II, Queen (*earlier* Princess), 269–70

Elizabeth, Queen of George VI (Queen Mother), 267, 306

Empress of Britain (ship), 60–3, 302

EOKA (Greek insurgent movement), 211

Eritrea, 300

Eton College, 29–31, 33–6, 165, 205–6, 315

Eva, 'Aunt' (Daisy Garnett-Botfield's companion), 107–8

Ewhurst, Hampshire, 163, 279

Farrer, Reginald, 107

Ferdinand VII, King of Spain, 194, 249

FitzGerald, Amelie Catherine (*née* Bischoffsheim), 158

Fitzherbert, Maria Anne, 265

Fitzroy, Lady Anne *see* Culling Smith, Lady Anne

Fitzroy, Anne Caroline (AW's niece), 241

Fitzroy, Henry, 227–8

Florence, Italy, 148–50, 152

Forbes, Admiral John, 232

Ford, Richard, 170, 262

Foster, Kate, 41

Foster, Roy, 295

Fowler, Corporal, 75

Foy, General Maximilien, 190

France: war with England (1793), 56, 228; in Syria in World War II, 73; wartime activities in Middle East, 74–8; AW enters from Spain, 195

Franco, General Francisco, 47, 52

Franz Ferdinand, Archduke of Austria-Hungary, 22

Fraser, Malcolm, 152

Fuentes de Oñoro, battle of (1811), 187

Garland, Sergeant-Major Lindsay, 138–40

Garnett-Botfield, Susan (née McConnel; Ruth's mother; 'Daisy'), 104, 106–7, 119

Garnett-Botfield, Walter, 106

Gaulle, Charles de, 60, 74

George II, King, 14

George III, King, 16; awards Order of Bath to AW, 129; approves AW's appointment to command in Peninsula, 177; Golden Jubilee (1810), 181; illness, 226

George IV, King (earlier Prince Regent): receives news of Waterloo victory, 10; coronation, 204; asks AW to form government, 209; visits Hyacinthe Wellesley, 232; admires Marianne Paterson (Wellesley), 239; anger at Marianne Wellesley's Catholicism, 240; and death of AW's mother, 251; papers stored at Apsley House, 265

George V, King, 45

George VI, King (earlier Duke of York): accession and coronation, 47–8; invites Valerian to remain in army, 210; funeral, 269

Gerard, Rupert, 49

Gerard Leigh, W.H.G. ('G'), 49, 63

Germany: as threat (1930s), 47, 52; Valerian serves in (1962–4), 212–13

Gladwyn, Cynthia, Lady, 307

Gladwyn, Gladwyn Jebb, 1st Baron, 307

Gleig, George Robert: and AW's childhood, 18, 30; on AW's marriage relations, 246; on AW's devotion to Walmer Castle, 312

Glendinning, Victoria, 287–8

Glentanar, George Coats, 1st Baron, 159

Glubb (Sir) John (Glubb Pasha), 66

Goldie, Sir George, 48, 277, 279, 303

Gooch, Colonel Eric, 77

Gordon, Alexander, 9

Gordon, Max, 63

Gosh see Arbuthnot, Charles

Goubert, Louis, 31

Goya y Lucientes, Francisco de, 190

Grattan, Henry, 39

Great Exhibition (London, 1851), 324

Greville, Algernon, 255, 322

Greville, Charles, 241, 260, 318

Greville, Lady Charlotte, 239, 241, 244

Grey, Charles, 2nd Earl, 257

Hall, Radclyffe: The Well of Loneliness, 290

Hamilton, Emma, Lady, 199

Hamilton, Helen (née Pakenham), 127

Handel, George Frederick, 14

Hannastoun (farm), near Dalry, Scotland, 87–9

Harding, Field Marshal Sir John (later 1st Baron) and Mary, Lady (née Rooke), 211

Hardinge, Sir Henry, 214

Hare, Augustus, 170

Hatherton, Edward Littleton, 1st Baron, 255

Haydon, Benjamin Robert, 319–20

Haye Sainte, La (farm), Belgium, 4, 6

Hayter, John, 262

Headlam, A.W. ('Tuppy'), 33–4

Healey, Edna, Lady, 317

Henley, Frank, 27–8

Henry II, King, 15

Hervey, Colonel Felton, 239

Hervey, Louisa, Lady (née Caton; later Duchess of Leeds), 239

Hill, Arthur (AW's maternal granfather), 16

Hitler, Adolf, 42, 52–3, 60, 85, 109, 157, 295

Hoey, Millie, 49

Hollway, Robin, 24–5, 280

Hoppner, John, 225–6, 241

Hougoumont (farm), Belgium, 4–6, 8

Houldsworth, Thomas, 93

Hulke, Dr, 328–9

Hume, Elizabeth, 207

Hume, Dr Thomas, 9, 186, 207

Huskisson, William, 96

India: AW sails for, 57; AW's military career in, 124–8; Richard's Governor-Generalship, 230; Dorothy Wellesley visits, 285

Ings, James, 202

Iraq: in World War II, 65–74; invaded (2003), 72

Ireland: AW's attitude to, 18; Richard's Lord Lieutenancy, 18, 238, 254; AW serves in, 39–40; and Act of Union (1801), 124–5; AW appointed Chief Secretary for, 174, 177; famine threat, 320

Irvine, Cecilia (*née* Banister), 109–10, 115, 117, 119

Irvine, Nigel, 117

Italy: in First World War, 23; declares war on Germany, 85; surrenders (1943), 85; Valerian serves in, 123, 135, 141–4, 148, 152; Valerian revisits with author, 135–6, 141–50, 152–3

James, Arthur, 267

James, Lady Evelyn (*née* Wellesley; 7th Duke's sister), 164–5, 306

James, Fay, 269

James, Robert ('Bobbie'), 165, 292, 306

James, Lady Serena (*née* Lumley; Dorothy Wellesley's half-sister; 'Mitey'): letters from Dorothy, 22, 281, 285–7, 291; marriage, 166; and daughter's coming-out dance, 269; birth, 276; letter from Gerald (7th Duke), 282; mentioned in mother's obituary, 292; and Gerald's military service in World War II, 299, 301; Dorothy thanks for Christmas present, 303; death of husband, 306; declines Gerald's proposal of marriage, 306–7; and theft of Dorothy's watch from Gerald, 308

James, Ursula (Mitey's daughter) *see* Westbury, Ursula, Lady

Jenkins, Anna Maria, 256–8

Jerusalem, 85, 105–6, 110–17, 123; King David Hotel bombed (1946), 112

John Bull (magazine), 156

Johnson, 'Snake Hips', 115

Joint Broadcasting Committee, 298

Jones, Mrs (of Pantglas), 325

Jones, Paul, 90

Josephine (de Beauharnais), Empress of Napoleon I, 57

Journal of the Scottish Rock Garden Club, 309

Joyce, William ('Lord Haw-Haw'), 157

Kawukji, Fawzi al, 66, 73–4, 76–7

Kendall (AW's valet), 313, 328–9

Kennedy, John, 89, 91–65

Kennedy, Shaw, 7

Kent, Tyler, 157–8

Kent, Victoria Mary Louisa, Duchess of, 259

Keppel, Alice, 20

Keppel, Violet, 20, 280

Knockdolion (estate), Ayrshire, 99–100, 108–9, 220, 308–9

Langtry, Lillie, 159

Lees-Milne, James, 161, 215, 267, 302, 307

Lennox, Lady Georgiana ('Georgie'), 2

Lennox, Lady Louisa, 155

Lieven, Princess Dorothea, 204, 239

Ligny, battle of (1815), 2, 5

Ligonier, Penelope, Lady (*née* Pitt), 200

Liverpool, Robert Banks Jenkinson, 2nd Earl of, 181, 189, 201, 238

Liverpool, Theodosia Louisa, Countess of (*née* Hervey), 181, 185–6

Llangollen, Ladies of (Lady Eleanor Butler and Sarah Ponsonby), 38–9, 226

Locke, John: *Essay Concerning Human Understanding*, 40

London: inter-war social life, 43–5, 49; Cafe de Paris bombed, 115; *see also* Apsley House

Long family, 243

Longford, Catherine, Lady (*née* Rowley; Kitty's mother), 184

Longford, Elizabeth, Countess of (Kitty's grandmother), 41

Longford, Elizabeth, Countess of (*née* Harman): on AW's giving up violin, 42; on Wellesley family, 227

Longford, Thomas Pakenham, 2nd Earl of (Kitty's brother): attitude to AW's courtship of Kitty, 42, 55, 131, 247; finds Broadstairs house for Kitty, 178; letter from brothers in Peninsula, 188–9; visits dying Kitty, 246

Louis XVI, King of France, 54–5, 228

Louis Napoleon (*later* Emperor Napoleon III), 328
Ludgrove (prep school), Barnet, 27–9
Lusitania (ship), 99

McConnel family, 87–8, 98–9
McConnel & Co., Manchester, 96, 98
McConnel, Diana *see* Wellington, Diana, Duchess of
McConnel, Major-General Douglas (author's grandfather): Palestine and Trans-Jordan command in World War II, 78, 110–11, 117; birth, 100; First World War service, 100–3; marriage, 103–4; military career, 106, 108, 308; at Knockdolion, 109, 308; and Diana's engagement and marriage, 118, 121; retirement and death, 308–9; garden writing, 309
McConnel, Edie (John's wife), 99
McConnel, Eryl (William Houldsworth/Florence's daughter), 100
McConnel, Florence (*née* Banister; William Houldsworth's wife), 100, 121
McConnel, Helen (Merrick/May's daughter), 103, 140, 309
McConnel, Henry (James's son), 94
McConnel, James (b.1762; author's great-great-great grandfather): life and career, 87–97; death, 97; grave, 97–8
McConnel, James, Jr, 94, 96
McConnel, John (William's son), 99
McConnel, Malcolm (William Houldsworth/Florence's son), 100
McConnel, Margaret (*née* Bradshaw; William's wife), 98–9
McConnel, Margaret (*née* Houldsworth; James' wife; 'Peggy'), 93, 95, 97
McConnel, Mary (*née* Cannan), 88
McConnel, May (Merrick's wife), 103
McConnel, Merrick (William Houldsworth /Florence's son), 100, 102–3, 140
McConnel, Muriel (William Houldsworth /Florence's daughter), 100
McConnel, Ruth (*née* Garnett-Botfield; author's grandmother), 103–4, 106–7, 110, 113, 117, 119–21, 123, 147, 309–10
McConnel, Samuel (James's grandfather), 88–9

McConnel, William (author's great-great grandfather), 98–9
McConnel, William Houldsworth (author's great-grandfather), 99, 117, 121
McLaren, Lady Rose (*née* Paget), 51
McLaren, Squadron Leader John, 51
MacMichael, Sir Harold, 111, 114
McNeill, Barbara (*later* Astor), 53, 61–2, 84
Mahratta War, Second (1803), 127
Manchester: James McConnel in, 91–6; AW's unpopularity in, 97; *see also* Peterloo Massacre
Manchester Guardian, The, 209
Margetts, John, 274
Maria 'La Penceija' (of Palena), 144–5, 153
Marie Antoinette, Queen of Louis XVI: executed, 228
Marie-Louise, Empress of Napoleon I, 186
Marochetti, Carlo, Baron, 218
Mary, Princess (Duchess of Cambridge's daughter), 326
Mary, Queen, 80
Maryborough, 1st Baron, William Wellesley-Pole (AW's brother; *later* 3rd Earl of Mornington): birth, 16; letter from AW in Peninsula, 190; Kitty visits, 191; chides AW for recklessness in Spain, 194; and AW's country house, 199; and brothers' absence in India, 230; adopts name Wellesley-Pole and marries, 232; as Chief Secretary for Ireland, 235; character and career, 237; at Second Duke's wedding, 262; and AW's stroke, 313; death, 315
Maryborough, Katherine, Lady (William's wife), 232
Masséna, Marshal André, 182, 184
Matheson, Hilda, 53, 289–90, 293, 298, 305
Maxted, Corporal-of-Horse, 68–70, 73, 76, 80
Mayo, Dr John, 183, 185–6, 192
Melbourne, William Lamb, 2nd Viscount, 259–60, 313–14
Mérimée, Prosper, 313–14
Metternich, Prince Clemens von, 204
MI5: Gerald Wellington and, 297
Mitey *see* James, Lady Serena
Mitford, Mary Russell, 217
Monarch of Bermuda (ship), 151
Moore, General Sir John, 247

Mornington (manor; originally Marinerstown), 1

Mornington, Anne, Countess of (*née* Hill; AW's mother): character, 13; marriage and children, 15–17; disparages son AW, 17, 19, 33, 225–6; widowhood, 19; in Brussels, 31–2; on AW's joining army, 38; Kitty's relations with, 178; and AW's relations with brother Richard, 225; relations with Hyacinthe, 226, 230; and mother's confinement for debt, 227; disapproves of Gerald's and Henry's wives, 232–3, 238; pension from state, 242, 251–2; death, 251–2

Mornington, Garret Wesley, 1st Earl of (AW's father): musical interests and compositions, 13–14, 18–19, 332; marriage and children, 15–17; moves to London, 17–18; financial difficulties, 18–19; death, 19

Mornington, Henry Valerian Wellesley, Earl of ('Morny') *see* Wellington, 6th Duke of

Mornington, Richard Colley Wesley, 1st Baron (AW's grandfather), 13–16

Mornington, William Wellesley-Pole, 3rd Earl of *see* Maryborough, 1st Baron

Morrell, Lady Ottoline, 293

Motley, John Lothrop, 172

Mussolini, Benito, 42, 47

Mysore, 124

Napier, General William, 260

Napoleon I (Bonaparte), Emperor of the French: Waterloo defeat, 1, 3, 5–7, 10, 197; suffers from haemorrhoids, 5; birth, 17; commands in Italy, 57; victories in Austria and Prussia, 133; and Peninsular War, 177, 236; abdicates, 195–6; attempts suicide, 196; death, 204; Canova statue at Apsley House, 250, 266, 268; reinterred in France, 313

Napoleon II, François Charles Bonaparte, King of Rome, 186

Nash, John, 284, 290

Nelson, Admiral Horatio, Viscount, 129–32, 233–4

Nevill, Lady Dorothy, 172

New Galloway, 89–90

New York Times, The, 159, 165, 216, 265

Ney, Marshal Michel, 6–7, 182

Nicolson, Sir Harold, 25, 27–8, 279–83, 287, 300, 305, 308; *see also* Sackville-West, Vita

Nicolson, Nigel, 285

Orde, Cuthbert ('Turps'), 165

Orde, Lady Eileen (*née* Wellesley; 7th Duke's sister), 164–5, 280

Oxford University: author's father attends (New College), 37, 42–3, 46, 210; AW's sons attend, 207; AW elected Chancellor, 255–6

Paget, Lady Elizabeth, 36

Pakenham, Bess (Kitty's sister), 193

Pakenham, Major-General Sir Edward, 182, 184, 188–90

Pakenham, Henry (Kitty's brother), 176

Pakenham, Sir Hercules (Kitty's brother), 188, 191–2

Pakenham, Thomas (Kitty's uncle), 41

Pakenham, William (Kitty's brother), 182, 188

Pakenham Hall, Ireland, 40–1

Palena, Italy, 135, 142–7, 152–3

Palestine *see* Jerusalem

Palmyra, 75–6, 80

Paterson, Robert, 238

Pearson, Trooper, 69–70, 84

Peel, Sir Robert, 209, 257–8, 320; death, 323

Pembroke, Reginald Herbert, 15th Earl of, 51

Peninsular War (1807–13): AW commands in, 177, 179–80, 182–6, 188–93; strategic importance, 236

Penn, Sir Eric, 49

Penns-in-the-Rocks, Withyham, Sussex, 34–5, 48, 53, 61, 287–8, 290, 295

Perceval, Spencer: assassinated, 189

Percy, Henry, 2, 10

Persia (Iran), 286

Pescetti, Mario, 153

Peterloo Massacre (1819), 201

Philip, Prince, Duke of Edinburgh, 269

Picton, General Sir Thomas, 247

Pierrepont, Henry, 316, 320

Pierrepont, Lady Sophia (*née* Cecil), 164

Pitt, William, the Younger, 133

Pollitt, Harry, 46

Ponsonby, Sarah, 38
Ponsonby, Major-General Sir William, 6
Portugal: AW campaigns in, 177, 182, 184, 186, 193; AW leaves, 194
Powell, Anthony, 304
Powell, Lady Violet, 304
Prince of Wales, HMS, 779
Profumo, John, 46
Pronay, Nicholas, 297
Puttenham, George, 26

Quatre Bras, 2
Quetta, India, 108

Raikes, Thomas, 312
Ramsay, Archibald, 156–8, 160
Ranfurly, Hermione, Countess of, 116–17
Redesdale, Algernon, 1st Baron, 331
Reeve, Corporal, 75
Reform Act (1832), 17, 253
Regiments (British): 1st Household Cavalry (1HCR), 64–6, 68, 75, 77, 81, 83, 85, 117, 123, 141, 151; 12th Lancers, 81–3; 33rd Foot (Duke of Wellington's), 55, 133, 334; 41st Foot, 39; 73rd (Highland) Foot, 38; 76th (Hindoostan) Foot, 38
Reith, John, Baron, 289
Repulse, HMS, 79
Rhys, Lady Anne (*née* Wellesley; 5th Duke's daughter; *later* Duchess of Ciudad Rodrigo), 47, 160
Rhys, Reginald David (*later* Duke of Ciudad Rodrigo), 161
Richmond, Charles Lennox, 4th Duke of, 2
Richmond, Charlotte, Duchess of: pre-Waterloo ball, 1, 10
Right Cub, 156–8, 160, 297
Rimini, Italy, 149
Rivers, George Pitt, 1st Baron, 199, 218
Rivers, George Pitt, 2nd Baron, 200
Roberts, Mrs Marshall, 265
Robespierre, Maximilien, 229
Rolande, Hyacinthe (*later* Marchioness Wellesley), 226
Roosevelt, Franklin Delano, 85

Sackville-West, Vita, 25, 27–8, 279–82, 284–9, 294, 298, 300, 305–6, 308; *The Land*, 285

St André, Jean Bon, 229
St Helena: AW visits, 129; Napoleon's death on, 204
St Jean de Luz, 195
St Paul's Cathedral: AW's tomb in, 332–3
Salamanca, battle of (1812), 190
Salerno, Italy, 137–8, 140–2, 154
Salisbury, Frances, Marchioness of (*née* Gascoyne), 256, 258–60, 313, 316, 322
Salisbury, Mary, Marchioness of (*née* Sackville), 323–7
San Sebastian: falls to Wellington, 195
Scarbrough, Alfred Lumley, 10th Earl of ('Dandy'), 20–1, 166, 275–6, 279, 291
Scarbrough, Lucy Cecilia, Countess of (*earlier* Ashton; *née* Dunn-Gardner; Dorothy's mother; 'Cissie'), 273, 275–9; death and will, 291–2
Schnabel, Artur, 298
Scott, Geoffrey, 284
Scott, Lady Mary (*née* Wellesley; 3rd and 4th Dukes' sister), 166
Sedgwick mill, Manchester, 92–3
Séran, Duchesse de, 32
Seringapatam, 127
Shelley, Frances, Lady, 203–5, 209, 221, 253, 261
Shelley, Percy Bysshe: 'Song to the Men of England', 201
Sherfield Court, Hampshire, 25–6, 34, 280–1, 285, 288
Shone, Corporal, 68–9
Sicily, 301
Slater, Josiah, 183
Smiley, Colonel David, 51, 63–4, 67, 74–5
Smith, 'Bobus', 30
Smith, Charles (watchman at Apsley House), 266
Somers-Cocks, Edward, 192
Somerset, Lady Emily (AW's niece), 2, 8, 202
Somerset, Lord Fitzroy (*later* 1st Baron Raglan; Emily's husband), 2, 8, 194, 202, 322
Spain: Wellington family properties in, 161–2; AW's campaign and victories in, 189–90, 194–5
Spanish Civil War (1936–9), 47, 52
Sparrow, Bernard, 125

Sparrow, Olivia (*née* Acheson), 124–8, 130–2, 134, 186, 246

Staël, Anne Louise Germaine, Baroness: *Corinne*, 185

Stanhope, Philip Henry, 5th Earl, 261, 312

Steegman, John, 293

Stern Gang, 105

Stratfield Saye (estate), Hampshire: AW's statue at, 11, 218; and death duties, 85; 5th Duke ('Uncle Charlie') moves into, 159; 5th Duchess (Maudie) moves from, 160; restoration, 162; animals at, 170; lacks smoking room, 170; given to AW, 198–200; improved and opened to public, 198–9, 215; Victoria visits, 198, 320–1; guests and social life at, 203–4; AW installs double-glazing, 208; Gerald (7th Duke) inherits and restores, 214–16, 301; swimming pool, 215; annual flag 'rental', 216; disparaged, 217–18; park and trees, 217–18, 331; portraits and pictures, 225, 244; 8th Duke and Duchess move to, 334–5

Strathnaver, SS, 110, 123, 141

Summerhill, Ireland, 40–1

Sunday Times, The: interviews 8th Duke about Iraq, 72

Swettenham, Ann Maria, 40

Syria: in World War II, 64, 73, 83–5; 8th Duke visits with wife, 77

Talavera, battle of (1809), 179–80

Taylor, Philip, 297

Tehran: 1943 conference, 85, 117

Tennyson, Alfred, 1st Baron: 'The Lord of Burleigh' (poem), 164

Thorburn, Robert, 166

Times, The: on Waterloo, 3; on 'the season', 44; announces engagement of Valerian and Diana, 120; on death of Frederick Culling-Smith, 241; announces Kitty's death, 246; criticises AW's mother's pension, 251; on social entertaining at Apsley House, 263–4; on death of Dorothy's mother, 292; obituary on AW's brother William, 315; on Charles Wellesley/Sophia Pierrepont's engagement, 316

Tone, Wolfe, 40

Torrens, McCullagh, 234

Torres Vedras, lines of (Portugal), 180–2, 184, 186

Toulouse, 195

Townsend (Walmer gardener), 328

Townshend, Sarah, Marchioness, 273–5

Trafalgar, battle of (1805), 132, 233

Trident, HMS, 129

Trim, Ireland, 39, 56

Tunbridge Wells, 182, 190

Turner, W.J., 298

Turnham (AW's coachman), 251

Tweeddale, Field Marshal George Hay, 8th Marquess of, 260–1

United States of America: war with Britain (1812), 190

Uppark, Sussex, 199

Uxbridge, 2nd Earl of *see* Anglesey, 1st Marquess of

Victoria, Queen: funeral, 165; visits Stratfield Saye, 198, 320–1; accession and coronation, 259–60; relations with AW, 259–60; Lady Douro serves, 262, 315–16; visits Apsley House, 263; betrothal to Albert, 313; children, 314; stays at Walmer, 315; and AW's death, 329–31

Vienna, Congress of (1815), 1

Villiers, Nicholas, 49

Vitoria, battle of (1813), 194

Wagner, Revd Henry, 205–6, 207–8

Wallscourt, 2nd Baron, 238

Walmer Castle, 258, 311–12, 315, 323–4, 327–30

Waterloo, battle of (1815): preparations, 1–2; conduct and victory, 2–9; casualties, 8–11; and AW's reputation, 197

Watt, James, 16

Wedderburn-Webster, Lady Frances, 3

Wellesley family: background, 14–15; disagreements, 235–6

Wellesley, Lady Anne (5th Duke's daughter) *see* Rhys, Lady Anne

Wellesley, Lady Anne (AW's sister) *see* Culling-Smith, Lady Anne

Wellesley, Arthur (Charles/Sophia's son): birth and death, 317

Wellesley, Lord Charles (AW's son): boyhood, 10, 192; death, 171–2; birth, 174;

education, 205, 207–8, 210, 255; relations with mother, 205; as father's Private Secretary, 254; relations with father, 255; marriage prospects, 258–9; at Apsley House, 271; marriage and children, 316; at Walmer Castle, 328; at father's death, 329

Wellesley, Lady Charles (*née* Augusta Sophia Pierrepont), 164, 271, 316–17, 328–9

Wellesley, Lady Charlotte (*née* Cadogan): marriage, 232–3; runs away with Lord Paget, 234–5, 238

Wellesley, Lord Christopher (8th Duke's youngest son), 302

Wellesley, Dorothy *see* Wellesley, Lady Gerald

Wellesley, Elizabeth (Gerald/Dorothy's daughter) *see* Clyde, Lady Elizabeth

Wellesley, Colonel Frederick, 167

Wellesley, Lady George (*née* Louise Nesta Fitzgerald; *then* Lady Richard Wellesley), 140, 158–9, 165

Wellesley, Lord George, 159, 164–5

Wellesley, Gerald (AW's brother): birth, 17; at Eton, 31; and AW's marriage to Kitty, 133–4; as Chaplain at Hampton Court, 230, 251; marriage and children, 232–3, 235; promiscuity, 233; denied bishopric, 238; wife leaves, 238; officiates at nephew Douro's wedding, 262; death, 315

Wellesley, Lord Gerald *see* Wellington, 7th Duke of

Wellesley, Lady Gerald (*née* Dorothy Ashton, 'Dottie'): marriage to Gerald, 19–22, 165, 273, 279–80; poetry and writings, 20, 27, 48, 277, 279, 292, 294, 304–5; in Rome during First World War, 22–4; returns to Britain, 25–6; marriage breakdown, 27–9, 166, 265, 272, 281–4; life at Penns-in-the-Rocks, 34–5, 61, 288, 290, 298, 302; sells Sherfield, 34; drinking and depressions, 36, 290, 298–9; and Valerian's coming-of-age, 46; and coronation season (1937), 48–9; at daughter Elizabeth's wedding, 53; on Valerian going to war, 61; on Valerian's MC, 80; birth, background and upbringing, 273, 275–8; appearance, 280; relations with Vita Sackville-West, 280,

282, 284–7; death and funeral, 283, 305–6; travels with Vita Sackville-West, 284–7; co-edits poetry for Woolfs, 287; lesbianism, 289–90; relations with Hilda Matheson, 289–90, 298; and mother's death, 291–2; friendship with Yeats, 293–5, 300, 302; and Munich Crisis (1938), 295; and deaths of Yeats and Hilda Matheson, 298; loneliness in war, 300, 302; restrained at wartime poetry reading, 300; first meeting with Diana, 302; and Valerian's absence in war, 302; and grandson Jeremy Clyde, 303–4; decline in later years, 304; watercolour painting, 310; *Beyond the Grave*, 80, 300, 302; *Early Light*, 304; *Early Poems*, 20; 'Exiled' (poem), 305–6; *Far Have I Travelled*, 20, 305; *Letters on Poetry, from W.B. Yeats to Dorothy Wellesley*, 298, 305

Wellesley, Lady Emily (*née* Cadogan), 232–3, 235, 238

Wellesley, Revd Gerald Valerian (Henry/Charlotte's son), 235

Wellesley, Gerald (8th Duke's grandson), 335

Wellesley, Henry (AW's brother) *see* Cowley, 1st Baron

Wellesley, Hyacinthe, Marchioness (*née* Roland; Richard's wife): marriage and children, 226, 230; remains in England during Richard's absence in India, 230–1; and Prince Regent, 232–3; and Richard's infidelities, 232; breach with Richard, 234; marriage ends, 237; daughter Anne absconds with Lord Charles Bentinck, 238; death, 238

Wellesley, Lord John (8th Duke's son), 211, 302

Wellesley, Marianne, Marchioness (*earlier* Paterson; *née* Caton; Richard's second wife), 238–40, 244, 315, 316

Wellesley, Lady Mary (AW's sister): birth, 17; accompanies Lady Dungannon to convent in France, 227; death, 228

Wellesley, Mary (Lord Richard/Nesta's daughter), 140

Wellesley, Nesta *see* Wellesley, Lady George

Wellesley, Pamela (*later* Berry), 140

Wellesley, Captain Lord Richard: killed at Ypres (1914), 140

Wellesley, Richard (15th century), 15
Wellesley, Lord Richard 'Dick' (7th Duke's brother; Nesta's first husband), 140, 159, 164–5
Wellesley, Richard Colley Wellesley, Marquess: birth, 16; education and scholarship, 17–18, 29; as Lord Lieutenant of Ireland, 18, 238, 254; and father's death, 19; and AW's attendance at Eton, 29; as MP, 39; sells Dangan, 55; renounces Ireland, 57; resigns as Governor-General of India, 129, 253; and death of Pitt, 133; letter from Kitty on marriage relations, 177; as Foreign Secretary, 181, 236; supports Kitty, 188; unpopularity, 189, 236; career and achievements, 225; relations with AW, 225, 235–7, 240; vanity, 225, 230, 233–4, 236; affair, marriage and children with Hyacinthe, 226, 230–1; and sister's Anne's marriage, 227; denounces French Revolution, 229; as Governor-General of India, 230; illness in India, 231–2; marquessate, 231; infidelities, 232; returns to England from India, 233; breach with Hyacinthe, 234; buys and sells Apsley House, 237, 248; marriage ends, 237; meets and marries Marianne Paterson, 238–40; resentment at AW's premiership, 240; and mother's death, 251; and AW's election to Chancellorship of Oxford University, 255; at Second Duke's wedding, 262; death and burial, 315
Wellesley, Lord Richard (8th Duke's son), 270, 302
Wellesley, Lady Richard (née Louise Nesta Fitzgerald) see Wellesley, Lady George
Wellesley, Sophia (née Pierrepont) see Wellesley, Lady Charles
Wellesley, Valerian (17th century), 15
Wellesley-Pole, Catherine Tylney (née Long; William's wife), 242
Wellesley-Pole, James (William/Catherine's son), 243
Wellesley-Pole, William (Maryborough's son; 'Wicked William'), 242–3
Wellesley-Pole, William Jr (William/Catherine's son), 243
Wellington, Arthur Wellesley, 1st Duke of: appearance and dress, 1, 39, 129, 190, 312;

Waterloo victory, 1–10, 197; reputation, 10–11; statues, 11, 23, 218–19; death, 12, 169, 311, 329; violin playing, 13, 32; birth, 16; childhood and education, 17–19; shyness as boy, 17–18, 29–30; favours Catholic Emancipation, 18, 54–5, 214; and father's death, 19; at Eton, 29–31; in Brussels with mother and Armytage, 31–2; attends Equitation School in Angers, 32–3; joins army (1787), 38; serves in Ireland, 39; serves in Irish Parliament, 39–40, 56; betting, 40; courtship and marriage to Kitty, 40–2, 54, 124–8, 130–4; reading, 40, 57, 128; burns violin, 42; speaks in Irish Parliament, 54; army promotions, 55; first active service (Netherlands 1794), 56; ill health, 56–7; sails for India (1796), 57; attends opening of Liverpool and Manchester Railway, 96; service in India, 124–8; meets Nelson, 129–30; returns to England from India, 129; unhappy marriage relations, 131, 176, 179–80, 183, 200–3; marriage settlement, 133; stands as MP for Westminster, 133–4; as Prime Minister, 160–70, 209, 213, 250; Thorburn portrait, 166; treatment of children, 169–70; will, 172; as Chief Secretary for Ireland, 174, 177–80; campaign in Peninsula, 176–7, 179–80, 182–93; hunting, 180, 195, 254, 259, 313; viscountcy, 180; gives ball in Lisbon, 184; earldom and Spanish dukedom, 189; sketched by Goya, 190; marquessate, 191; awarded Garter, 193; made Colonel of Royal Horse Guards, 193; welcomes news of Napoleon's abdication, 195–6; wounded in thigh, 195; dukedom, 196; returns to England from Peninsula campaign, 196; acquires and improves Stratfield Saye, 198–200, 220; as Master-General of Ordnance, 201; mistrust of mob and social unrest, 201–2; relations with Harriet Arbuthnot, 203; at George IV's coronation, 204; social activities and entertaining, 204, 258; relations with sons, 205–8, 254–5; deafness in one ear, 207, 322; resigns as C.in C. of Army (1828), 213; duel with Winchilsea, 214; poor shooting, 221; Hoppner portrait, 225; relations with brother Richard, 225,

235–7, 240; adopts nephew Gerald Valerian, 235; temperament, 236–7, 247–8; as Lord Lieutenant of Ireland, 238; infatuation with Marianne Paterson, 239; acts as guardian to William/Catherine Wellesley-Pole's three children, 242; family concerns, 242–3; and Kitty's decline and death, 245–6, 252; romantic liaisons, 247, 257; buys and occupies Apsley House, 248; collection of paintings and art objects, 249–50; public unpopularity, 250–3; resists reform, 250, 253; and mother's death, 251–2; 'iron duke' sobriquet, 252; disparages reformed Parliament, 254; elected Chancellor of Oxford University, 255–6; entanglement with Anna Maria Jenkins, 256–8; heads caretaker government during Peel's absence abroad, 257; at Walmer Castle, 258, 311–12, 315, 327–8; and sons' marriage prospects, 258–9; ageing, 260; and son Douro's marriage, 260–2, 311; funeral, 269, 330–2; disparages poets, 305; daily routine in later years, 312; suffers strokes, 313–14; and deaths of sister and brothers, 315; and death of first grandson, 317; relations with Angela Burdett–Coutts, 317–19; fondness for grandchildren, 319–20; pestered by portraitists, 320; supports repeal of Corn Laws, 320; church attendance, 321; fame and public adulation, 321, 324, 326; generosity and charitable giving, 322, 327; takes measures against Chartists, 322–3; temper, 322; friendship with Mary Salisbury, 323–4; grief at Gosh Arbuthnot's death, 323; attends Victoria's fancy-dress ball, 324–5; final entertaining at Apsley House, 326–7

Wellington, Arthur Charles Wellesley, 4th Duke of: and birth of Gerald, 20; plants acorn at Wellington College, 23; at Ewhurst, 25, 163, 279; on Eton shooting team, 34; death (1934), 47; inherits Stratfield Saye, 162–3; visits Spanish estate, 162; career, 166; and wife's death, 166; at Apsley House, 264–6

Wellington, Arthur Charles Wellesley, 5th Duke of ('Uncle Charlie'): succeeds to

dukedom (1934), 47; membership of Right Club, 156–60, 297; marriage, 165

Wellington, Arthur Richard Wellesley, 2nd Duke of (earlier Marquess of Douro), 161, 167–74; boyhood, 10; longs for father's nose, 197; relations with father, 204–7, 254; achieves majority, 209; career, 209–10, 254; in Parliament, 254; makes advances to Fanny Salisbury, 258; marriage prospects, 258; engagement and marriage, 260–2, 311; occupies Apsley House, 262–3; decline and death, 263; succeeds to dukedom on father's death, 329; at AW's funeral, 332

Wellington, Arthur Valerian Wellesley, 8th Duke of: birth, 10, 19–20, 23; career, 11–12; marriage, 11, 105, 121–2; infancy in Italy, 23–4; at prep school, 27–9; childhood, 27; parents' separation, 27, 29; at Eton, 29, 31, 33–6; shooting, 31, 34, 67, 220; pet dogs, 35; at New College, Oxford, 37, 42–3, 46, 210; dancing and social life, 43–5, 53; appearance, 46, 119; celebrates 21st birthday, 46; political views, 47; romantic affairs, 49–50; fails finals but achieves degree, 50; joins army (Royal Horse Guards; 'The Blues'), 50–2; courts Rose Paget, 51, 53; leaves letters unanswered, 51; and outbreak of war (1939), 53, 299; in military camp at Liverpool, 59–61; sails for Middle East, 61–3; with cavalry horses in war, 64–5; active service in Middle East (World War II), 65–76, 115, 299; awarded Military Cross, 80; serves in Cyprus, 81, 211–12; service in Western Desert, 82–3; burnt in accident, 84; in wartime Syria, 84–5; assumes title of Marquess of Douro, 85; courts Diana McConnel, 86, 117–18; wartime wedding bomb threat, 105, 121; engagement, 118–20; service in Italy in war, 123, 135, 141–5, 152; post-war revisit to Italy with author, 136, 141–50, 152–3; returns to England from Italy in war, 151, 302; children, 156; post-war career, 210; in post-war Germany, 212–13; as Military Attaché to Spain, 213; lives at Stratfield Saye, 216; made Knight of Garter, 217; fishing, 220; stays at Apsley House as boy, 265; ceremonial duties,

Wellington, Arthur Valerian Wellesley, 8th Duke of—*contd*
269–70; riding, 270–1; relations with mother, 279; dislikes Hilda Matheson, 290, 293; postcard from father in Egypt, 293; on Yeats, 293–4; relations with father, 299; attends mother's funeral, 305; as Colonel-in-Chief of Duke of Wellington's Regiment, 334; diamond wedding, 334; occupies Stratfield Saye, 334–5

Wellington, Catherine Dorothea Sarah, Duchess of (*née* Pakenham; 'Kitty'): and news of Waterloo, 3–4; character, 11; AW courts and marries, 40–2, 54, 124–8, 130–4; background and upbringing, 41; changed appearance, 124–5; romance with Lowry Cole, 125–7, 176, 247; religious faith, 126–7; unhappy marriage relations, 131, 176, 179–80, 183, 200–3, 247; marriage settlement, 133; birth of children, 174–5; and AW's absence in Peninsula, 176–9, 183, 187, 191; lends money to brother Henry, 176; devotion to sons, 178–9, 181, 192, 204–5, 209; keeps journal, 178–9, 181–2, 191–2, 270; stays in Broadstairs, 178–81; reading, 179, 181, 185; and AW's viscountcy, 180; in Tunbridge Wells, 182, 190; portrait by Slater, 183; depressions, 184–6, 208; nurses brother Edward, 188–9; dress, 194, 203, 213; life in London, 194–5; and AW's return from campaign, 196–7; fondness for Stratfield Saye, 200, 204; contemplates suicide, 203; social ineptness, 203; at George IV's coronation, 204; creates garden at Stratfield Saye, 217; adopts nephew Gerald Valerian, 235; as guardian to William/Catherine Wellesley-Pole children, 243; illness and death, 243–4, 245–6, 248, 250; portrait absent from Stratfield Saye dining room, 244; son Arthur Richard offers money to, 254; watercolour painting, 310

Wellington, Diana Ruth, Duchess of (*née* McConnel): marriage, 11, 105, 121–2; works in Jerusalem during World War II, 66, 86, 105–6, 111–13, 116–17, 122; Valerian courts, 86; birth, 104; bomb threat against, 105, 121; birth and

upbringing, 106–8; devotion to Knockdolion, 108–9; ill health, 108; in India, 108; education, 109–11; revisits Jerusalem with author, 112–15, 123; engagement, 118–20; appearance, 119; and Valerian's wartime absence in Italy, 135, 142, 147–8, 150, 178; returns to England from Palestine, 151, 302; in Cyprus, 211; gardening at Stratfield Saye, 217; first meets mother-in-law, 302; attends mother-in-law's funeral service, 305; on council of SSAFA, 334; diamond wedding, 334

Wellington, Dorothy, Duchess of *see* Wellesley, Lady Gerald

Wellington, Elizabeth, Duchess of (*née* Hay; 2nd Duke's wife; 'Bessy'): at husband's funeral, 168; character, 172–3; engagement and marriage, 260–2, 311; crayon drawings of, 262; serves at Queen Victoria's court, 262, 315; entertains at Apsley House, 263; childlessness, 311, 323; musical interests, 311, 315–16; relations with AW, 311–12, 322; AW pays off debts, 314; health worries, 314, 323, 325; visits Great Exhibition with AW, 324; attends Victoria's fancy-dress ball, 325; and AW's death, 329–30

Wellington, Evelyn Katrine Gwenfra, Duchess of (*née* Williams; 3rd Duke's wife; *later* wife of Colonel Frederick Wellesley), 163, 167, 264

Wellington, Gerald Wellesley, 7th Duke of ('Gerry'): marriage to Dorothy, 19–22, 165, 273, 279; and Valerian's christening, 19; diplomatic career and postings, 20–4; engagement to Violet Keppel, 20, 280; returns to Britain, 25; architectural career, 26–7, 284, 292; marriage breakdown, 27–9, 166, 265, 272, 281–4; writes to Valerian at prep school, 29; and Valerian's time at Eton, 35; as Surveyor of King's Works, 48, 293; at daughter Elizabeth's wedding, 53; in wartime Cairo, 80, 85, 299; succeeds to dukedom, 85, 301; writes to Diana on marriage, 122; life at Stratfield Saye, 123, 156, 198; gives Apsley House to nation, 162, 268; and Queen Victoria's funeral, 165; on father's death, 166; inherits and restores Stratfield

Saye, 214–16, 301; at Apsley House party, 264–5; and disposal of royal papers at Apsley House, 265; friendship with Harold Nicolson, 279, 283; attends Dorothy's funeral, 283, 305; writings, 284; house in Chester Terrace (Regent's Park), 290–1; interest in First Duke, 291, 301, 308; stays with Mitey, 292; and Munich Crisis (1938), 296–7; suspected work for MI5, 297; enlists in World War II, 299; relations with son Valerian, 299; wartime activities, 300–1; haughtiness, 304; public duties and offices, 304; proposes to Mitey, 306; cruises, 307; in later years, 307–8; death and cremation, 308; *The Diary of a Desert Journey*, 293; *The Iconography of the First Duke of Wellington* (with John Steegman), 293

Wellington, Henry Valerian Wellesley, 6th Duke of ('Morny'): killed and buried at Salerno, 85, 136, 138–40, 142, 150, 154–5, 160, 301; background and career, 136–7; memorial at Stratfield Saye, 156; will, 161; visits Spanish property, 162; at Apsley House, 267

Wellington, Henry Wellesley, 3rd Duke of, 162–3, 164, 166–7, 176, 264

Wellington, Kathleen Emily Bulkeley, Duchess of (née Williams; 4th Duke's wife), 29, 162–3, 165–6, 264

Wellington, Lilian Maud, Duchess of (née Coats; 5th Duke's wife; 'Maudie'), 139, 159–60, 165, 301–2

Wellington College, 23

Wellington Museum Bill (1947), 268

Wesley, Charles, 19

Wesley, Garret (Baron Mornington's uncle), 13

Westbury, Ursula, Lady (née James), 269, 307

Wharncliffe, Georgiana Elizabeth, Lady (née Ryder), 246

Whistler, Rex, 35–6, 49, 53

White, Field Marshal Sir George Stuart, 26

Wigan, Alfred and Leonora, 263

Wigram, Neville, 2nd Baron, 46

Wilkes, John, 17

Wilkie, Sir David, 320

William IV, King, 257, 259

Wills, Trenwith (architect), 27, 284, 292

Wilson, General Henry Maitland (*later* Baron; 'Jumbo'), 118

Wilson, Dr Gordon, 212

Wilson, Harriet, 247

Wilton, Mary Margaret, Countess of (née Stanley), 314, 320

Winchilsea, George William Finch-Hatton, 9th Earl of, 214

Windsor, Edward, Duke of (*formerly* Prince and Wales and King Edward VIII): and Mrs Simpson, 45–6; abdicates throne, 47

Windsor, Wallis, Duchess of (*earlier* Mrs Edward Simpson), 45–6

Winterhalter, Franz Xavier, 264

Wireless Publicity Ltd, 296–7

Wong, Anna May, 33–4

Woolf, Virginia, 281, 284–5, 287, 290, 294

Worcester, Emily, Marchioness of *see* Beaufort, Duchess of

Worcester, Georgiana, Marchioness of (née Fitzroy; AW's niece): death, 240

World War I (1914–18): outbreak, 22; Wellesley brothers serve in, 165

World War II (1939–45): outbreak, 53, 110, 299; conduct of, 85; ends, 155

Wyatt, Benjamin Dean, 198–200, 248–9

Wyndham, Captain, 249

Yeats, Georgie, 298

Yeats, William Butler, 46, 53, 293–5, 298, 300, 302–3, 305

York, Frederick Augustus, Duke of, 56